On Voluntary Servitude

On Voluntary Servitude

False Consciousness and the Theory of Ideology

MICHAEL ROSEN

Polity Press

First published in 1996 by Polity Press
in association with Blackwell Publishers Ltd.

Editorial office:
Polity Press
65 Bridge Street
Cambridge CB2 1UR, UK

Marketing and production:
Blackwell Publishers Ltd
108 Cowley Road
Oxford OX4 1JF, UK

ISBN 0–7456–0595–8
ISBN 0–7456–1596–1 (pbk)

A CIP catalogue record for this book is available from the British Library.

Typeset in 10½ on 12 pt Ehrhardt
by CentraCet Limited, Cambridge
Printed in Great Britain by TJ Press Ltd, Padstow, Cornwall

This book is printed on acid-free paper.

Contents

The truthful presentation of error is indirect
presentation of truth.
Novalis

Preface

This is a book that is written against a certain position, a position that, it also claims, has been taken for granted by many of the most influential social theorists of the nineteenth and twentieth centuries. As such, I am aware that it will invite a certain kind of response. Even if its arguments are successful (perhaps, particularly if its arguments are successful) it is likely that many of those whom it addresses will dispute the ascription: deny that they (or those famous names whose authority they follow) ever thought any such thing. Attributions of this kind are, of course, difficult to establish. It is one thing to argue against a position held and stated explicitly, it is another to show that that position is one to which an author is implicitly committed. In the end, perhaps, the most that one can hope for is to reverse the burden of proof. I think that those who believe they can draw the kind of conclusions that are characteristic of the theory of ideology without making the assumptions I attribute to them at least owe us a more explicit account of what different assumptions they make and why these are more defensible.

However that may be, I know of one undeniably appropriate target for my arguments: my own earlier self. I started to think about social theory in the early 1970s, a time when such thinkers as Lukács, Althusser, Sartre, Habermas, Foucault, Lévi-Strauss, Gramsci and Godelier were first becoming known in Great Britain. It seemed to me then that what these otherwise very disparate writers had in common was their conviction that the determination of ideas in society was something that needed to be explained systematically, as a result of social structure or historical forces prior to the individual. The chief line of cleavage, as I saw it, was between those who believed that the source of this determination lay in some kind of a collective, social subject and those who took the social process to be generative but agentless – between, to put it crudely, neo-Hegelians and structuralists. The questions that interested me were: Which of these two was right? and, What would follow philosophically from that fact?

What I did not consider at that time was the possibility that neither of the two positions was correct. Yet, as I continued to think about the issues, it became increasingly clear to me that the claims made on behalf of the social determination of ideas were both excessively sweeping and alarmingly imprecise, while such empirical evidence as I could find to support them was either thin or, to say the least, questionable. Thus another question more and more forced itself upon me: If claims made about the social determination of ideas were, in fact, not true, why should they nevertheless have seemed to be so obvious to so many? The task, then, was to look at the intellectual weaknesses of the position, while, at the same time, looking for the reasons for its appeal.

Having reached this point at the end of the 1970s, I might have set out to write a book whose conclusions would not have been very dissimilar to the ones presented here had it not been for the appearance of G. A. Cohen's *Karl Marx's Theory of History: a Defence*. In that justly celebrated book Cohen advances a position that I had not, until then, considered seriously: that it might be possible to make claims regarding the determination of one element of social life by another very similar in content to those advanced by the Continental theorists but without making any assumptions about 'collective agency' or 'generative structures' – indeed, without giving any ontological commitments that the most parsimonious natural scientist should find shocking. I find that position no more persuasive now than I did when I first encountered it, but the imagination and rigour with which its author has defended it set me a serious challenge, one which at once delayed my project and forced me to raise the level of its discussion.

As I have worked my way towards my present views I have incurred many debts that I must acknowledge, even if I cannot repay them. Alex Callinicos and Charles Taylor listened to my stuttering first attempts to articulate my sense of the problems with patience and sympathy. G. E. M. de Ste Croix very kindly gave me the benefit of his extensive knowledge regarding the development of Marx's thought. It was at an early stage, too – longer ago than I think either of us would care to remember – that John Thompson persuaded me to offer my project to Polity Press. Since then he has been an exemplary editor, fully equal to the heavy demands I have placed on his tolerance. I am deeply grateful for his engagement and support.

Later, I learned a great deal from a seminar at University College London, among whose participants I must single out Matt Brandi, Mark Hannam, Bill Hart and Andrzej Szahaj for special thanks. Martin Jay read a paper of mine that was later to be incorporated into Chapter 7 as well as discussing many other issues with me at, alas, all too infrequent intervals over the years, and I have benefited from his great knowledge of Continental social thought. I am grateful to the Rector and Fellows of Lincoln College, Oxford, for granting me two terms of sabbatical leave, and thank especially my colleague David Goldey for cheerfully taking on the burdens caused by my absence. That I managed to write a first version of the book during that precious time is due to my good fortune in being allowed to concentrate on my work while being able to take advantage of those around me. In particular, I would like to thank Rosamund Diamond and David Ish-Horowicz for their many acts of generosity.

That first version has now been transformed thanks to the enormously detailed comments of three friends: Jerry Cohen, Raymond Geuss and Jonathan Wolff. I cannot overstate how much I owe to their thoroughness, acuity and erudition. It would be impossible to acknowledge individually all the points I have taken from them; suffice it to say that any gross errors of fact or reasoning that still remain have in all likelihood been newly introduced by me or are the result of stubbornness on my part in the teeth of their good advice. In addition, I have received very valuable comments on all or part of the book from Stefan McGrath, Brian O'Connor, Alan Patten, Bob Stern, John Thompson, Gavin Williams and Hannes Wittig. I am most grateful to them all.

Thanks are due to Caroline Richmond for her skilful copy-editing and to Tom Runnacles for his work on the index.

I have left until last the debt that I owe Charlotte Klonk, for it is at once my greatest and least easy to express. Throughout, it has been her sympathetic criticism that has set me the standards at which to aim and her unwavering support that has given me the encouragement to do so.

I

Introduction

I Reich's Question

'What has to be explained', wrote Wilhelm Reich, 'is not the fact that the man who is hungry steals or the fact that the man who is exploited strikes, but why the majority of those who are hungry *don't* steal and why the majority of those who are exploited *don't* strike.'[1] That, as a simple first formulation, is the question which lies behind this book. Why do the many accept the rule of the few, even when it seems to be plainly against their interests to do so? The theory of ideology gives one very distinctive kind of answer to Reich's question. The reason, it claims, is that societies are systems that produce the kind of consciousness that prevents the members of a society from behaving as their interests would otherwise dictate. Ideology, in Theodor Adorno's phrase, is 'necessary false consciousness'.[2] But to assess this theory will turn out to be a complicated matter. In the first place, the nature of the answer that the theory of ideology is offering requires clarification. In what sense is ideological consciousness 'necessary'? In what sense 'false'? What is behind those terms? What assumptions must we make about the nature of society and the kinds of explanation

---

[1] Wilhelm Reich, *The Mass Psychology of Fascism*, p. 53.This quotation is the first illustration of an issue that will strike some readers very forcefully. It has been conventional, where reference to an indefinite subject has called for a third-person singular pronoun, for writers to use the masculine. In recent years, many – myself included – have tried to offer at least a gentle corrective to any biases that may be carried by this practice by reversing the convention. This book, however, inevitably contains a great deal of quotation, paraphrase and exposition of authors who uniformly adopted the traditional practice, and not to conform to it would entail not just a small and salutary jolt to expectations, but a serious sacrifice in readability.
[2] T. W. Adorno, 'Ideologie', pp. 162–81, p. 169.

that can be appropriately applied to it if a theory of ideology is to be possible? All of these issues will be addressed in more detail below, but, for now, it is important to pre-empt some misunderstandings.

First, I must make it clear that when I speak, as I shall throughout the book, of *the* theory of ideology, I am talking of a genus with a variety of species. It is no part of my case that all the theorists of ideology share exactly the same commitments – far from it. A browse through the Bodleian Library catalogue reveals more than 800 entries with the word 'ideology' in their title. Anyone hoping for some system in this profusion will be disappointed. They will find instead that the term has become part of a vast semantic delta through which shallow and muddy channels meander without apparent purpose. My object in this book is not to survey this delta but to guide the reader through it by locating what I take to be the main channel. To do so, I shall take a step back and identify the stream (or, as I shall argue, streams) of thought which originally fed it. Reich's question will be our guide, and it will turn out that many current uses of the term 'ideology' will be only distantly related to what I take to be the central issues.[3]

A second point to be made at the outset is that my use of the phrase 'false consciousness' is not meant to foreclose the issue of whether ideology is a matter of false *beliefs*. On the contrary, as I shall argue in the second chapter, that is only one form that the theory of ideology can take. For the moment, I hope that the reader will allow me to take the phrase 'false consciousness' informally, in its broadest possible sense, meaning simply consciousness that is, in some way or other, deficient or inadequate.

Nor should it be assumed that the theory of ideology is committed to the view that unequal societies are reproduced by means of some positive set of shared beliefs, values or cultural practices – a 'dominant ideology', as it is sometimes called. False consciousness can, in principle, just as well be something negative: the *failure* to form an adequate, shared system of beliefs, values or practices. So the mere absence of a dominant ideology does not contradict the theory of ideology in the sense at issue here; that very absence could itself be ideological.

Finally, let me clarify the sense in which the theory of ideology is committed to the view that unequal or otherwise illegitimate societies reproduce themselves *by means of* false consciousness. The claim here is merely that this is a necessary condition for such societies' preservation, not that it is always the sole means that they employ. As far as Marx is concerned, I believe that he thought ideology was indispensable to the survival of capitalist class society. But, of course, it would be absurd to say that Marx thought coercion played no part in the survival of capitalism; he simply believed that coercion was not enough.

[3] A consequence is that many of the well-known names of contemporary writing on ideology are not discussed in this book. My interest is in looking at the underlying structure of the theory of ideology and its presuppositions; to the extent that contemporary authors simply take those presuppositions for granted (for instance, by assuming some form of the Marxist theory of society) I take it that their theories are, by implication, condemned by my criticism.

The approach that I shall employ in this book is both historical and critical. At its centre is a historical account of the intellectual background from which the theory of ideology emerged. The point of this account is to help to identify the original scope and purpose of the theory and to articulate those conceptions of human nature and society that made it seem acceptable (or even self-evident) to social theorists. But I shall argue that we ought not to take for granted (that, indeed, there are good reasons for rejecting) the assumptions on which the theory of ideology has been based. The position I am presenting is thus critical not just of those theories of ideology that have actually been proposed but, more broadly, of any theory of ideology that proceeds from such assumptions.

Nevertheless, even if I succeed in unconvincing the reader about the theory of ideology, some fundamental issues remain. There is, first, Reich's problem itself: what other kinds of account might there be of the maintenance of order in society – in unequal societies in particular? Moreover, to reject the theory of ideology is not to eliminate the question of 'false consciousness'. While we may not be justified in supposing that unequal societies maintain themselves because societies in general have the power to produce 'false consciousness' in their citizens, there may still be a sense in which false consciousness is a pervasive feature of certain social orders (ours included). If so, then it is plainly a task of the very greatest importance to see what that sense might be. Finally, there is a question about the theory of ideology itself. Why did it seem so plausible? And what does it tell us about Western social thought that it should have been so?

II Method

For many, philosophers especially, such an attempt to marry criticism and history may seem to represent a confusion between distinct, even antithetical, enterprises. Put crudely, they see a division something like this. The philosopher clarifies and articulates a theory. The social scientist assesses it by confronting it with historical data. Finally, the historian of ideas retraces the development of theories and identifies the factors, rational or otherwise, that led to their adoption and abandonment.

It is a guiding supposition behind this book that such a division is oversimplified. On the contrary, to the extent that questions regarding the scope and structure of the theories themselves are intertwined with controversial questions of methodology and questions regarding the nature of the phenomena to be explained – and this is especially (although not exclusively) the case in the social sciences[4] – a historical approach can play a valuable role in the evaluation of theories.

[4] I am using this phrase without commitment to the assumption that the 'social sciences' are scientific *in the same way as* the natural sciences. It is simply too cumbersome to talk of 'human studies' or *Geisteswissenschaften* just to avoid this apparent implication.

Any kind of explanation (or presumed explanation) can be divided into three. There is, first, what is supposed to be explained, what philosophers call the *explanandum*. Secondly, there is whatever it is – theory or something different[5] – that we think is going to do the explaining, the *explanans*. Finally, there are the *standards* with regard to which we assess how well the explanation works: the structure and content of the *explanans* and the kind of relationship in which it stands to the *explanandum*. Now, what it is that theories attempt to explain and how they go about explaining them are not pure and presuppositionless starting points but will have their own history (which may, indeed, be the result of the development of theory elsewhere). To give an example, Darwinism explained something – why animals have characteristics that favour their survival in the environments they find themselves in – that other, pre-Darwinian biologies also explained. At the same time, it explained something else – why animals may also have characteristics that *don't* favour their survival – that predecessor theories did not.[6] After Darwin, Mendelian genetics then went on to explain one of the central parts of the Darwinian theory – how breeding could lead to the development of new species – and in this way amplified (and reinforced) Darwinism. Here, then, we have an explanation that vindicates itself by explaining both what its predecessors had explained and something further that those explanations had not. And it is itself explained (and thereby justified) by a successor theory.

But the development of the scientific view of the world is not simply a matter of accumulating and expanding explanations in this way. It also consists in deciding that certain things are *not* susceptible to explanation. Astrology, for example, starts from the idea that what has to be explained is that events, fortunate and unfortunate, happen to human beings at different times. What has led to the rejection of astrology among reasonable people is not that science has offered us a better explanation than the conjunction of the stars for this fact, but that we are now persuaded that it is not the kind of fact that can be explained at all.

Finally, then, there is the question of *how* to explain: what *counts* as a good explanation. This is the most controversial aspect, and, from the philosopher's point of view, the most interesting. One way of looking at it is to see it as a second-order transformation of the first two aspects. That is, by explaining an explanation – showing how its explanation works, as Mendelian genetics does for Darwinism – we help to justify it. This usefully brings out the reflexive aspect of the enterprise – and its potential

---

[5] I think that the tri-partite division is just as relevant if the *explanans* in question is not a *theory* in the strict sense of the term. For example, a mythical explanation also has something to explain, something that does the explaining and some characteristic standards by which it claims to be doing the explaining.

[6] That, as Stephen Jay Gould has emphasized, is a significant part of the case for the theory of evolution: '... the proof that evolution, and not the fiat of a rational agent, has built organisms lies in the imperfections that record a *history* of descent' (S. J. Gould, *Hen's Teeth and Horses' Toes*, p. 160).

for iteration: if we think that an explanation requires explaining, might that second explanation not require a further explanation and so on?

The dilemma posed by the attempt to find standards by which to measure theories is an example of a problem that is central to and ineliminable from philosophy: what I will call 'rational indeterminacy'.[7] The problem is this. Let us say that some subject-matter (a belief, a procedure, a theory) is assessed by a certain set of standards or criteria that it fails to meet. What should fall in consequence? The subject-matter or the standards? In most areas of intellectual life the answer is easy: the standards are stable and should take priority. But this is not the case everywhere and at all times. The problem is particularly acute in philosophy for the following reason. The subject-matter of philosophy includes the nature of reasoning itself. So philosophy is inevitably reflexive: it attempts to argue philosophically for a certain conception of reason. The method it employs is something that it is its own proper business to justify.[8]

Natural scientific theories, for the most part, can draw upon agreement both about the subject-matter to be dealt with by the theory and about the standards by which theories are to be assessed. But in the social sciences things are, in general, not so simple.[9] Ontology (what sorts of entities theories postulate), epistemology (what kind of access we have to those entities) and explanatory structure (the kinds of connection that we should look for between them) are all controversial. Those familiar with the literature on the philosophy of social science – in particular, the disputes surrounding 'methodological individualism' – will realize that we have reached a point at which dispute most often degenerates into a depressing sterility.

There are those philosophers and scientists whom we may call (I am afraid that not all of them will welcome the term) *positivists*. Positivists think that there are sufficient common features of good explanations to make it plausible, at least, to believe that there is a single set of standards against which all explanations can be measured. These standards are unchanging, although the appreciation of them may be greater or smaller at one time than another. For those who take this view the critical question is: does a particular explanation meet the standards that *any* explanation at any time must meet?

Then there are those who believe that different standards apply in different regions of human enquiry. For them the fact that an explanation

---

[7] John Rawls has identified a parallel phenomenon in moral theory as 'reflective equilibrium'.

[8] Hegel, of course, is the philosopher who most acutely embodies (and responds to) this dilemma. In Hegel's view, all of the subordinate conceptions of philosophical reason can be shown, in the end, to lead to his own. (See my *Hegel's Dialectic and its Criticism*, Chapter 2.)

[9] I am not saying that the natural sciences are *never* controversial (one need only think about the debates surrounding Newton's 'action at a distance' or those associated with the theory of evolution) or that the social sciences always are (some parts of economics, it seems to me, fit the model of 'normal science' perfectly well).

should fail to meet standards 'imported' from elsewhere is, in principle, wholly unsurprising. Yet if we are not to fall into the worst kind of relativism, the standards we apply cannot be solely those that a theory itself proposes: in that case we should be simply allowing every theory to write its own warrant. But then from where, if not from timeless standards, might rational criticism come?

A leading example of the attempt to reconstruct social scientific theories according to methodological standards that are justified by their acceptance elsewhere, to which I shall make reference a good deal in what follows, is G. A. Cohen's *Karl Marx's Theory of History: a Defence*. Cohen aims to show that 'functional explanation', which he takes to be characteristic of Marx's historical materialism, does not require commitment to anything that a physical scientist need find methodologically or metaphysically offensive, but corresponds to the kind of explanation to be found quite unproblematically in Darwinian biology.

It has been said in response to Cohen that his reconstruction represents only one aspect of Marx's enterprise and that Marx himself took himself to be operating according to different standards. As it stands, this is hardly a forceful objection. If it is the case that Marx's theory can be reconstructed satisfactorily, but at the cost of elements of his method that he may have thought to be of vital importance – the 'dialectic', for example – then this will only be doing to Marx's theory what he himself claims to have done to Hegel's: extracting the 'rational kernel from its mystical shell'.[10]

However, Cohen does not succeed, I will argue. I will try to show that his methodologically austere reconstruction fails to provide a sufficient defence for Marx's claims with respect to that part of his account that is most relevant to the theory of ideology – the functional interpretation of the relationship of correspondence between 'base' and 'superstructure'. The very great value of Cohen's reconstruction, in my view, is just the opposite of what its author claims. Rather than providing a convincing defence of Marx, it enables us to measure more precisely than ever before the great distance that exists between the methodological assumptions and standards of evidence that rule in the physical sciences and in evolutionary biology and what would be required to vindicate Marx's claims.

This throws important light upon Marx's theory. It is widely appreciated that there are apparently distinct methodological strands in Marx's work. This is unmissable in any comparison between the 'Hegelian' early writings and the later 'scientific' works on political economy. Marx's interpreters have generally argued for one or the other of these as the basis for an understanding of the 'true' or 'essential' Marx.[11] The interpretation of Marx to be presented in this book, however, will show that deep tensions

---

[10] *Das Kapital* 1, p. 27 [Eng. trans., p. 25].
[11] The line of division is between those who believe that there is an important discontinuity between the early and the later writings and those for whom the two periods form a single, basically consistent whole.

remain even in Marx's later (supposedly 'mature') works. These tensions do not simply amount to prevarication or vacillation on Marx's part but result from the strain of attempting to construct a theory that will do justice to two deep *background beliefs* about the ways in which societies change and, what is most fundamental to the theory of ideology, the reasons why they fail to do so.

A preliminary formulation of the two background beliefs informing the theory of ideology is, first, that societies are *systems*, in the sense that they maintain themselves (or change, as the case may be) in ways that cannot be understood simply from a common-sense individualistic perspective, and, second, that unequal societies are preserved not, or not simply, by coercion but by a form of 'false consciousness' on the part of those in whose interests it would be to change those societies. These beliefs are extremely important for the assessment of Marx's methodology, for they provide his theory with an important part of its *explanandum*. On the one hand, if they cannot be accounted for within the standard explanatory framework of the natural sciences, then commitment to them would provide a reason to accept that the methodology of the social sciences should be different from that of the natural sciences. On the other hand, to the extent that we were committed to the precepts of methodological positivism, we should have a reason to question the apparent self-evidence of the background beliefs themselves.

One purpose in making background beliefs explicit is to make them open to assessment and history is one way to gain such a perspective. To realize that a belief that was once (or, indeed, is now) taken for granted is not universal but arose at some particular place and time is to invite certain questions: was it simply a discovery, a rational product of intellectual progress, or did other factors play a role? Were there, perhaps, not fully rational reasons why it was found to be inspiring or consoling? Are those reasons to which we ourselves now would continue to adhere?

Marx always insisted that his approach to the study of society was 'scientific' and 'materialist' and he consciously tried to purge himself of assumptions that were incompatible with these two commitments. But this did not mean that he simply applied to society a method of which he had a clear and fixed conception in advance. On the contrary, the eclecticism of Marx's method suggests that it was in fact much more of a response: a willingness to make those assumptions he felt were necessary in order to make sense of things that he, unwaveringly and unchangingly, felt had to be accounted for.

III Background Beliefs

The test of having background beliefs in the sense that I am using the concept is that attributing them makes the best sense of the structures – the concepts and patterns of inference – that we find in texts. It is not necessary that the beliefs should have been given clear and explicit formulation. When an interpreter talks about establishing an author's 'beliefs' the aim is to identify not only those propositions that an author consciously and explicitly maintained but also the systematic ways of using words that are implicit in his texts. So, for example, when philosophers talk about 'causes' they may believe that these are the kind of things that have 'necessary connections' to their effects. They may express this explicitly, but, then again, they may not; they may, for example, simply have taken it for granted that causes and effects are necessarily connected (who, before Hume, even thought that it was something that had to be argued for?).[12] It is here that 'background beliefs' come in.

There is no reason to suppose that background beliefs would, or even could, have been expressed independently of the actual theories that were produced in response to them. On the contrary, when an old set of background beliefs is displaced by new ones, the latter typically manifest themselves first as a powerful image, a metaphor or an analogy. Only later do they become objects of clarification and analysis.[13] When we meet background beliefs initially, they may seem to be confused or incoherent and, for that reason, the philosopher might assume that they do not represent a proper object of study. He would be wrong. When models and assumptions of this kind inform philosophy, they penetrate its structure and give sense to that level of explicit inference on which philosophers commonly concentrate.[14] That a background belief is not expressed explicitly does not mean that it is a mere artefact of interpretation. The fact that background beliefs are implicit is a potential source of ambiguity, certainly, but they are no less real or powerful for that.

The sharp line between 'observation' (open, receptive, particular) and 'theory' (empirically well-defined universal propositions within a coherent logical structure) presented in the logical positivists' account of science is, at best, an ideal. Our conception of reality typically incorporates models or images ('folk theories') regarding the nature of the subject-matter rather

---

[12] For a somewhat more detailed examination of this point, see *Hegel's Dialectic and its Criticism*, Chapter 1.

[13] To say that a belief is not articulated is not, however, to say that it is unconscious in the psychoanalytic sense of being hidden from the awareness of the person who holds it by some kind of concealment or distortion.

[14] I am not saying that inferential validity is of no importance, but it is rare indeed for a serious philosophical position to be defeated by inconsistency alone. Theories that appear to us to be fundamentally inconsistent often turn out to be consistent, but consistent with respect to background beliefs and unstated assumptions that we do not share. (In *Hegel's Dialectic and its Criticism* I tried to show that Hegel's philosophy could be understood as remarkably consistent – but consistent with respect to a set of neo-Platonist assumptions that most philosophers would now find wholly unacceptable.)

In recent years a number of imaginative attempts have been made to interpret aspects of the history of philosophy from the point of view of the unacknowledged hold exercised over philosophers by such background beliefs and assumptions. See, for example, I. Hacking, *Why Does Language Matter to Philosophy?*, E. Tugendhat, *Vorlesungen zur Einführung in die sprachanalytische Philosophie*, A. MacIntyre, *After Virtue*, R. Rorty, *Philosophy and the Mirror of Nature*, E. Craig, *The Mind of God and the Works of Man*, C. Taylor, *Sources of the Self*.

than well worked out hypotheses whose predictive scope (and hence testability) is clear. It is here that we find background beliefs.[15]

One way that models can be justified is by being associated with a well-attested empirical theory of which they are, as it were, an informal representation (most educated non-physicists, I suppose, have an image of the earth swinging round the sun like a ball on the end of a piece of string). But the absence of such a theory is not a sufficient reason to abandon the model. No one would give up the view of human beings as having beliefs and desires, and as being capable, to some extent, of bringing the former to bear on the way that they go about realizing the latter, just because of the poverty of the theorizing of empirical psychology. They are too important a part of our background beliefs. The fact that they are not accompanied by a well-attested empirical theory represents a challenge for the construction of such a theory rather than a deficiency that should lead automatically to their rejection.

IV Society as a System and 'Political False Consciousness'

Two background beliefs provide the core of Marx's answer to Reich's question: the belief that societies are self-maintaining entities, and the belief that, in the case of *prima facie* illegitimate societies, the way in which they do this is by means of false consciousness on the part of those who live in them.

The idea that societies operate in ways which, though systematic, cannot be taken to be just the immediate results of the conscious intentions of the individuals who compose them has been called the 'law of unintended consequences' by Ronald Meek.[16] But this risks underplaying an important aspect of the idea, namely, that such consequences represent something different in kind from mere unforeseen causal chains (like the stone that starts an avalanche when someone kicks it on a mountain path).

The notion of 'consequences' at issue is analytically complex. A 'consequence' in this context, it is important to note, is not necessarily a separately identifiable succeeding event. For an example let us consider briefly a market in equilibrium under perfect competition. Such a system of exchanges will be what economists call 'Pareto-optimal' (that is, it is not possible to increase welfare for any individual without loss of welfare to at least one other individual). But Pareto-optimality is not a consequence of the system in the sense of being a further state that follows from some previous state. Pareto-optimality is a (desirable but not intended) feature

---

[15] Typically, background beliefs are not direct empirical beliefs with a clear factual content (nor, for that matter, are they *a priori* in the way that the axioms of logic and mathematics are). What they seem most to resemble are those propositions that Kant called 'transcendental' or 'metaphysical' – propositions that are foundational for empirical science but that are not themselves established observationally.

[16] R. Meek, *Social Science and the Ignoble Savage*, p. 1.

of the system. The point of equilibrium itself is a consequence to the extent that it is a state that was reached in virtue of previous states of the system (the initial endowments of the participants of the market and their preferences). But the fact that it is an *equilibrium* (i.e., that there is no endogenous tendency for the market to move away from that point) is, once again, a feature of the system rather than a consequence of a previous state.

For the theory of ideology, two further features of the idea of unintended consequences are important. First, actions are taken to have consequences that are not apparent to those that engage in them. Secondly, this fact itself is not adventitious: there is held to be a significant reason *why* actions which have unintended consequences have the consequences that they do (if that reason is not apparent to the agents themselves, then the absence of understanding is a form of false consciousness on their part).

False consciousness also requires some preliminary explanation (Chapter 2 will continue this analysis in more detail). The distinctive background belief whose course we will trace is the idea of *political false consciousness*. We may distinguish three forms of this idea.

(1) The first is a commonplace. Since ancient times, writers have pointed out that false consciousness – deception and irrationality, for example – may have political consequences. For the Greeks, political false consciousness was an instance, a central and extremely painful one, to be sure, of a general problem: the failure of human beings to live up to standards of rationality. The classic presentation of this comes in Plato's *Republic*. In Plato's view, the irrationality of the soul necessarily leads to the injustice of the state. What makes false consciousness political in this case is the character of its *effects*.

(2) A second form of the idea of political false consciousness is the idea that consciousness that is directed towards particular kinds of subject-matter (politics among them) is especially prone to false consciousness. In other words, political false consciousness is false consciousness because of its *content*. We shall see an example of this in Hume's account of the illusions of enthusiasm and superstition. It is Hume's view that subjects which are both emotionally important to human beings and also matters of uncertainty (religion and politics are the chief examples) are areas where we may expect people to show excessive credulity – in other words, they are especially liable to false consciousness.

(3) Finally, there is the idea that false consciousness is political not just because of its subject-matter or its consequences but because of the way that it is *determined*. One form of this view that will take a good deal of space in what follows will be the idea of *sociable consciousness*. False consciousness is sociable to the extent that it involves wanting to be seen in a certain way. Individuals want, in Rousseau's phrase, not to be but to seem. In the Christian moralists, Pascal and La Rochefoucauld, *sociable desire* is implicit in Man's willingness to turn away from the problem of

his salvation and to lose himself in the vanity of the world. Thus politics itself, as the sphere of vanity or *amour-propre*, constitutes a general realm of false consciousness. Rousseau takes up this idea in a way that is at once more secular and historical. According to Rousseau, *amour-propre* is a specific feature of those modern, urban, commercial societies, in which the virtues of individuals and the ties of mutual *pitié* that would keep them spontaneously in harmony with one another have been corrupted. The idea that false consciousness might be political in this sense is distinctively modern. *Amour-propre* is a form of false consciousness to the extent that it leads people to pursue not what is really good for them but whatever will make them appear enviable. It is political, to the extent that these objects are determined externally, by society, not by the individual.

In Chapters 3 and 4 I shall examine these background beliefs at some length. Chapter 3 will show the way in which the second and third conceptions of political false consciousness emerged to supplement the first conception in the seventeenth and eighteenth centuries. Chapter 4 will show the emergence of the idea of society as a system from earlier, providential ideas of history. The theory of ideology, the argument is, is the product of the confluence of these two streams.

V Ideas and Historical Narrative

Described in this way, it may seem that what I have in mind for this book is objectionably circular or self-undermining. The object of the book is to assess a theory about society according to which beliefs, including theories about society, are the result of non-rational determinants and I appear to be suggesting that one of the ways in which we should do that is by considering whether those theories themselves may not to some extent be the product of non-rational determinants. Am I assuming the truth of the theory of ideology to explain the theory of ideology itself? The circularity is certainly present but it is inevitable and, I believe, not vicious. To claim that the factors affecting some of our most fundamental beliefs – about nature, history and society – are not purely rational is not to commit oneself to a theory of ideology in the Marxist or neo-Marxist sense. The conclusions that I draw regarding the best way of understanding non-rational beliefs will be consonant, I hope, with the methods that I apply in reaching them: to that extent, the argument is indeed intended to be self-supporting.

This is not to deny the difficulties involved in constructing and presenting an argument along these lines. Anyone who approaches the history of ideas with anything more than the most limited ambitions must pick their way through a veritable elephants' graveyard of grand theories. This book is aimed at one of the oldest and grandest of them all: the theory of ideology. And yet, how does one deal with this subject without subscribing (implicitly, if not explicitly) to some such theory? How is it possible to write, as I have done, of depicting the 'emergence' of background beliefs without inviting the reader to reify them into healthy, Hegelian seedlings, forcing their way vigorously towards the sunlight? All that I can do at this stage is to put my cards on the table. The narrative of this book is written from the perspective of ideas. That is, it assumes that such a perspective has explanatory power: that it matters whether ideas are cogent and powerful; whether the assumptions on which they rest are plausible; that this is a part of what makes ideas persuasive to individual thinkers; and that their persuasiveness is the major part of the explanation of why they come to be accepted. But that does not mean that ideas are to be explained ultimately in terms of ideas alone: that they are self-sufficient and self-generating. Moreover, the terms that I have just used – 'persuasiveness', 'plausibility', 'explanatory power' – are not as neutral as philosophers who would insulate philosophy from history like to suppose. What makes an idea 'plausible' is not something that can be derived from the nature of rationality alone; ideas may be plausible because they incorporate background beliefs that are quite local and specific. Thus the sociological or historical understanding of the history of ideas need not come at the expense of the cognitive perspective, properly understood. Ideas of what is persuasive or plausible contain both culturally variable as well as invariant elements. Both elements must be part of a comprehensive explanation. Unlike the vulgar-Marxist version of the theory of ideology, this approach does not make ideas into puppets on the end of its strings. But how do these different elements come together?

In *The Birth of Tragedy*, Nietzsche suggests that there are three ways in which human beings make the world acceptable to themselves. Tragedy, he argues famously, is a mixture of two of them: Dionysian intoxication and the Apollonian realm of beauty. The self either attempts to escape from suffering in self-abandonment or it imagines a perfect realm. Yet both of these strategies have been displaced in the modern world, Nietzsche argues, by a third, which he calls *Socratism*: the idea that there is a reason for everything – suffering included. Much later, in *On the Genealogy of Morals*, he writes:

> Man, the bravest of animals and the one most accustomed to suffering, does not *repudiate* suffering as such; he *desires* it, he even seeks it out, provided he is shown a *meaning* for it, a *purpose* of suffering.[17]

Socratism is part of the attempt to make the world acceptable by making it intelligible. At a certain point, as Nietzsche describes it, the Socratic ideal comes into conflict with itself: the explanations offered to make the world intelligible come up against the spirit of criticism (itself a consequence of Socratism) that requires that ideas should be justified.

Broadly speaking, I (like Max Weber) think that Nietzsche is right. The

---

[17] *On the Genealogy of Morals*, p. 162.

drive for justification that is characteristic of philosophical reasoning and the non-rational beliefs about the nature of reality that the drive for justification criticizes are both a part of the search for understanding. If we want an overall perspective from which to comprehend the rise and fall of background beliefs in Western thought then the best one is to see them as having their place within this dialectic. This is not the whole of the story, to be sure, but it is an important part of it, and it is from this point of view that the narrative of this book is constructed.

In essence, the book presents a picture of discontinuity and continuity. The new background beliefs that came on the scene in the eighteenth and early nineteenth centuries, the changed conception of political false consciousness and the idea of society as a system, from which the theory of ideology arose, made their appearance in the context of certain broad continuities in the understanding of human nature and of the character of society and the natural world. These continuities, *rationalism* and *providentialism* as I shall call them, are themselves capable of being understood, I suggest, from a quasi-Nietzschean perspective. Both are, in Nietzschean terms, a way of giving meaning to the world and accommodating oneself to it intellectually.

No historical narrative can be comprehensive, of course. Deterministic theories accommodate this uncomfortable fact by turning it into a virtue: focusing on what they take to be essential structures and pivotal episodes. If one does not believe in such sharp boundaries, however, any account must involve a painful degree of simplification and schematization. In my case, this selection involves a focus on the structure of ideas themselves and their changing pattern from thinker to thinker at the expense of a broader account of their intellectual and social context. Yet this concentration on ideas inevitably carries with it the suggestion that ideas are self-developing quasi-agents.

One way of countering this tendency is to make it clear that when the ideas in question appeared they did so as part of the project of some particular thinker. Thus in presenting those figures whom I take to be most significant for the background to the theory of ideology – chiefly, Hume, Smith, Rousseau, Herder and Hegel – I shall try to give the reader a sense of what was at stake in their wider enterprise (at the cost, perhaps, of seeming at times to digress from my main point). This carries its own dangers, however. To give one's attention to only a few figures appears to suggest that the history of ideas is a matter of a small number of 'great thinkers', sitting isolated on their mountain peaks and yodelling to one another across the empty valleys.

Unfortunately, it is very difficult to oppose any simplistic historical account without seeming to be proposing an alternative oversimplification of one's own. Rather than irritating the reader by describing further what I am *not* going to be able to do, let me simply make it clear that I am aware of how much would have to be done to turn this partial explanation into a complete one.

VI The Rise of 'Social Science'

One consequence of my account of the emergence of the theory of ideology as motivated by the confluence of background beliefs is that it calls
into question a picture of the development of social science that is to be
found in the standard histories. The received view represents the rise of
social science in the eighteenth and nineteenth centuries as part of the
Enlightenment enterprise: an attempt to bring to bear on society the
methods and standards that were proving so successful in the natural
sciences.[18]

Of course, it is generally accepted by the advocates of the received view
that the history of social science cannot be represented as so smoothly
triumphal as the positivist picture of the development of physical science,
so the received view also includes a place for the opponents of Enlightenment, stout defenders of human meaning or reactionary know-nothings
according to which side of the debate one is on, whose central commitment
is to the distinctiveness of the study of society from the natural sciences.
Nevertheless, the received image remains misleading.

First of all, it presents the initial impulse for the development of social
science as if it were methodological, originating outside the study of society
itself: a group of would-be scientists are inspired to extend a successful
method to a new domain of objects, while others resist them in the name
of the distinctiveness of the human realm and the kind of understanding
appropriate to it. This understates the extent to which development
resulted from a change in the perception of society itself.

The received view represents those who rejected the idea of a science of
society on the model of physics as advocating the subjective understanding
of particular events as the goal of social theory instead. Here too it is
misleading. While that might be a fair picture of some of the debate that
took place in Germany at the end of the nineteenth century, it is
particularly unhelpful for the understanding of those social theorists whose
ideas form the background to the theory of ideology.

Although there was, of course, some conscious comparison between the
study of society and the natural sciences (one thinks of Dugald Stewart's
famous description of Adam Smith as the 'Newton' of the social realm[19])
methodological commitments were secondary factors.[20] Behind the disa-

---

[18] For example: 'Sociology is part of that great revolution of thought in Western Civilization
which passes from religion through philosophy to science' (D. Martindale, *The Nature and Types
of Sociological Theory*, p. 4). See also: H. Becker and H. Barnes, *Social Thought from Lore to
Science*, and R. Brown, *The Nature of Social Laws*.
[19] The phrase seems to have become a *topos*: Kant is supposed to have said exactly the same
things about Condorcet.
[20] Having objected to the oversimplification of the received view, I do not want to replace it with
a monocausal view of my own. An adequate history of the development of social science would

greement as to the extent to which the proper method for the study of society resembled or differed from physics was a more widespread commitment to the idea that society acted as a system. Yet, paradoxically from the standpoint of the received image, the first consequence of this idea was actually to put the analogy between social science and physics into doubt. For, if it is true that society maintains itself as a system by acting in ways that transcend the actions of the individuals that compose it, then this, it seems, shows that it is radically *unlike* the corpuscularian picture of matter in motion. Hobbes in the middle of the seventeenth century was actually far closer to the idea of a social physics than were the leading social theorists of the eighteenth and nineteenth centuries. So far from being driven by the extension of a successful method from physics, the view of society as a system was methodologically and ontologically equivocal in its implications. If there was a natural science that appeared to provide a parallel to the study of society it was biology, not physics.

In its classic form, the organic analogy committed those who held it to two theses about the nature of social theory, the acceptance of which would place them on both sides of the received view's assumed cleavage between objective explanation and subjective understanding. To see society as an organism was to see it as an 'organized whole' – that there was a special relation of internal interdependence between its parts and that it was self-maintaining in ways that contrast specifically with what were presumed to be the characteristic features of those systems that formed the subject-matter of physics. On the other hand, this was supposed to be a general fact about societies, the basis for a form of social explanation that was no less valid or objective than the explanations of physics.[21] For Hegel, it is only because we ourselves are vehicles for the unfolding of *Geist* that we are able to grasp the (wholly objective) way in which *Geist*'s structures

---

give some weight to each of the following factors:

1 the debate among natural lawyers regarding the relationship between *jus naturale* and the *jus gentium*
2 the impact of contact with 'primitive' cultures as narrated in the various *Histoires de Voyages*
3 the 'quarrel' between the 'Ancients' and the 'Moderns'
4 an attempt to come to terms theoretically with *de facto* religious diversity
5 the perceived loss of community consequent upon the development of commercial society
6 the theological debate regarding the 'particular' or 'general' role of Providence (whether there is divine intervention in particular cases or whether it is only the general framework of laws that is providential) and the attempt to provide a 'general' providential interpretation of history
7 the perception of the economy as an autonomous region of social life, not requiring constant direct intervention from the political realm
8 the successful development of scientific methods in the natural sciences.

The interaction between these factors is immensely complicated and I do not want to commit myself to any definite view regarding the balance between them. It is important, however, to recognize that no single factor can give the whole explanation.

[21] No less valid – but not necessarily in just the same way. In particular, it may be the case that social explanation requires some special connection between observer and observed.

determine and its striving for self-realization motivates the development of history.

The received view does not appear to recognize the possibility of such a position – social theorists are either advocates of social science on the analogy with the natural sciences or they deny that objective explanations of the realm of 'understanding' are possible at all. According to G. A. Cohen, Hegel, unlike Marx, offers no more than a 'reading' of the nature of history:

> ... we may attribute to Marx, as we cannot to Hegel, not only a philosophy of history, but also what deserves to be called a *theory* of history, which is not a reflective construal, from a distance, of what happens, but a contribution to understanding its inner dynamic. Hegel's reading of history as a whole and of particular societies is just that, a *reading*, an interpretation which we may find more or less attractive. But Marx offers not only a reading but also the beginnings of something more rigorous.[22]

This is plainly wrong. Whatever one thinks of its success, Hegel's intention was to offer an explanation of historical development every bit as objective, just as much of a contribution to 'understanding its inner dynamic', as the explanations of the natural scientists. To assume that an approach that does not employ those methods that Cohen finds (in their 'beginnings', at least) in Marx is therefore no more than a 'philosophy' (*quelle horreur*!) rather than a 'theory', is to beg the question that should, I suggest, be at issue.[23]

VII Rationalism

The first part of this book explores the emergence of the two background beliefs – a political conception of false consciousness and the idea of society as a system – behind the theory of ideology. My argument is that these ideas did not belong to an unchanging stock of thought about politics but started to emerge in the forms with which we are now familiar only in the eighteenth and early nineteenth centuries. Insofar as this is a change that can be explained (rather than simply a brute fact to be recorded), it must be understood, I suggest, in the context of changes in the dominant conceptions of human nature and of society and history, respectively.

---

[22] *Karl Marx's Theory of History*, p. 27
[23] Another example comes from the anthropologist Evans-Pritchard. According to Evans-Pritchard, anthropology 'studies societies as moral systems and not as natural systems ..., it is interested in design rather than in process, and ... it therefore seeks patterns and not scientific laws, and interprets rather than explains' (E. Evans-Pritchard, *Essays in Social Anthropology*, p. 26, quoted in D. Sperber, *On Anthropological Knowledge*, p. 9). The contrast between 'moral' and 'natural' systems may be dubious (what is more natural to human beings than morality?) but much more so is the assumption that the first terms in each of the contrasting pairs necessarily go together and imply the exclusion of each of the second terms. Could there not, for example, be an *explanation* in terms of design? What entitles Evans-Pritchard to assume the contrary?

But although the conception of the political role of false consciousness can be seen as changing, the dominant Western view of human nature (and thus its conception of what it is for consciousness to *be* 'false') has remained broadly constant. That conception has been in almost all cases a *rationalist* one.

According to the main stream of philosophers, theologians and political theorists from the time of the Greeks onwards, to be fulfilled, mature and happy, the rational aspect of the self must be in control of its sensuous nature and desires. The rationalist sees the self from a dual perspective. On the one hand, there are the desires that the individual has; on the other, the power of choice and decision, the ability to select actions which are consonant with the pursuit and satisfaction of those desires. Now the desires we have are not all of a piece. Some are simple, some more complex. Nor are they simply brute, unalterable facts about our nature. On the contrary, we certainly have many desires and impulses which do not (or, at least, do not in the long-term) bring us satisfaction. To be rational, then, is to be able to select our actions so that they further our long term interests, to choose the course of greatest advantage instead of following the line of least resistance.

In general, rationalism takes the view that the good for human beings consists in exercising and, if possible, increasing the individual's discretionary powers of conscious choice and voluntary action and using them to select between those desires that are, and those that are not, truly desirable. However, rationalists do divide quite radically in regard to three other important questions:

1 *Are ends objective?* Some rationalists believe that ends are objectively rational or irrational, while others believe that the adoption of ends is ultimately a matter of contingent, subjective choice.

2 *Are desires bad?* The characterization of rationalism that I have given straddles what is often taken to be the central point of disagreement in the theory of the self: between those for whom self-fulfilment lies in suppressing or otherwise transcending one's physical being – the ascetic ideal – and those whose ideal is an integration of the rational and physical aspects of human nature. Nevertheless, whether self-fulfilment is seen as a matter of rising above our physical desires or of bringing the latter into rational harmony, it is, in each case, reason which sets the standard, which tells us what desires (if any) we *should* have.

3 *Is reason independent?* Finally, most rationalists believe that reflection – argument and discursive activity – is an effective means to increase the individual's powers of conscious choice and voluntary action (although, of course, not limitlessly so). Nevertheless, there is a sharp division between those rationalists who consider that reason is an irreducibly autonomous faculty of the mind and those for whom the capacity for reflection is in some way derivative from or dependent upon the emotions.

Taken in these broad terms, rationalism has set the framework within which Western philosophy and social thought has conceived the nature of the self from the time of Plato and Aristotle to our own day. Yet there has also been a significant history of dissent from rationalism. Such dissent is to be found for the most part outside the borders of what is officially counted as philosophy – one thinks, for example, of William Blake's celebration of impulse and desire over repression and constraint, or of the mystical tradition of self-abandonment – yet it does not deserve to be ignored just for that reason, for it amounts to an implicit critique of the dominant philosophical view.

The rationalist view of the self sets up an opposition in human beings between the desires which they have and their capacity to deal with them – either by modifying those desires or by acting in ways which are unaffected by them. In a sense, then, the rational man[24] is the one who succeeds in maximizing the 'discretionary power' of the self. But there is a price to be paid for this, the critic of rationalism believes. To the extent that we succeed in establishing control over our desires, the rationalist view of the self places a distance between our emotional life and our selves. What we gain in freedom we lose in affective richness and authenticity: we become spectators to rather than genuine participants in our own lives.

In the nineteenth century – which on one level, of course, was the high tide of the rationalist ideal of the self – this unease came to be a pervasive theme in literature and culture. It helps to explain, for example, the romantic attraction to the figure of the outsider and the motif of the 'double', that dark 'other self' which is depicted so as to suggest that it is the repressed side of rational man.[25] Nietzsche's rebellion against the

---

[24] 'Man' is certainly the word here!

[25] A recent article in the *TLS* discusses the theme:

'In 1852, Mathew Arnold published a poem entitled "The Buried Life". He laments that all men are now out of touch with their real selves:

> I knew they lived and moved
> Trick'd in disguises, alien to the rest
> Of men and alien to themselves . . .
> And long we try in vain to speak and act
> Our hidden self, and what we say and do
> Is eloquent and well – but 'tis not true.

In similar vein, his friend Arthur Hugh Clough wrote:

> Excitements come, and act and speech
> Flow freely forth; – but no,
> Nor they, nor ought beside can reach
> The buried world below.

This is from 'Blank misgivings of a Creature moving around in Worlds not realised' – inconceivable as the title of a poem before the Victorian period. James Thompson voices a similar distress in 'The City of Dreadful Night' – 'I was twain / Two selves distinct that cannot join again'. Charles Dickens became increasingly interested in people containing 'two states of consciousness which never clash, but each of which pursues his separate way as though it were continuous instead of broken' (*Edwin Drood*). Just such an idea generates the first great English detective novel, *The Moonstone* by Wilkie Collins. And, of course, we have *Dr Jekyll and Mr Hyde*, not to mention Tweedledum and Tweedledee. Double, divided,

tradition – the substitution of will-to-power for the rational, controlling ego – is well known, but there were others too. In Ibsen's plays, even apparently 'bourgeois' characters – the Master Builder, Solness, for example – are depicted as *daemonic*, motivated by forces within themselves which are stronger than their powers of conscious decision-making, while those who are deprived of contact with those inner sources, like Mrs Solness, are condemned to a life of impoverished feeling and dry, unrewarding 'duty'.[26]

There are three quite different ways in which rationalism might be opposed and it is important to be clear as to the distinction between them.

1 *Irrationalism.* One view – one might call it *irrationalism* – in effect accepts the rationalist depiction of human nature but argues that what for the rationalist is good – conscious deliberation and control – is not good at all, while what rationalism rejects – passion and impulse – are good in themselves. There have, perhaps, been no pure irrationalists; at least, irrationalism seems to me to be of rather small potential interest and significance unless it goes beyond simply inverting the values of rationalism to call into question the picture of human nature on which the latter draws.

2 *Pessimism.* A second form of anti-rationalism – we might call it *pessimism* – is, in a sense, the exact opposite of irrationalism, inasmuch as it accepts the value of the ideals of rationalism but disputes whether the facts of human nature (at least, unaided) are such as to make it possible for them to be realized. This strand of thought is represented most strongly within the tradition of religious thought, and we shall encounter two of its greatest protagonists, Augustine and Pascal, below. Freud, too, in his more conservative moments could be counted as a pessimistic anti-rationalist in this sense.[27]

---

hidden selves; buried life, secret life, hidden life, private life – two 'self-systems' – these phrases, themes, problems, obsessions pervade Victorian literature' (Tony Tanner, 'In Two Voices', p. 12).

[26] Mrs Solness is often taken to be a kind of moral automaton – the epitome (and the *reductio ad absurdum*) of the Kantian ideal of duty. But this (quite apart from the injustice that it does to Kant) is to ignore the *pathos* that lies behind her suffering – whose source Ibsen clearly depicts. Mrs Solness describes (in perhaps the most personal speech she is given) how a fire in her home destroyed her collection of dolls. As we listen to the speech, we realize that, for Mrs Solness, the dolls were, in some way, the focus for her inner capacity to love and experience. As they were destroyed, so was that aspect of herself, leaving the fearsome monster we see in the play. To put it in Benjaminian terms, the dolls were the focus for the *mémoire involontaire* without which Mrs Solness cannot form her life into an integrated *Erfahrung*.

[27] Freud is adamant in refusing to see the 'higher' faculties of human nature as having any effective power other than the affective basis that they have in common with the (supposedly) lower drives. For Freud, 'logical arguments are impotent against affective interests' ('Thoughts for the Times on War and Death', p. 75). To this extent, Freud is clearly, in my terms, a pessimistic anti-rationalist.

On the other hand, there is, just as clearly, a rationalist element in Freud, focused on the idea of the 'talking cure' – the idea that 'Through talking about sexuality, we can control it, so that the healthy man can choose to express his sexual appetite and yet not be irrationally driven by it. Self-mastery being a function of self-consciousness, by making sexual desires conscious, says

3 *Anti-rationalism.* Finally, however, there are those who question in some degree *both* the values of rationalism *and* its account of human nature. Central to this point of view is the question whether the rationalist ideal of the increase of our discretionary power of action (the ideal of 'self-mastery' said to be characteristic of 'positive liberty' by Berlin – 'self-tyranny', as Nietzsche calls it) does not come at an excessive price. In general, two themes underlie this criticism: first, there is the idea that, although we may increase our capacity for acting in ways that we choose, in doing so we cut ourselves off from the proper perception of what is outside us so that we do not respond to it adequately. We become, to our own ultimate disadvantage, spectators rather than engaged agents. If so, we may fail to recognize values and authorities (either external or internal) that have genuine claims on us; or, if we do respond to them, then we come to do so only in a way that does not afford us any genuine satisfaction. Secondly, there is the idea that rationalism exacts its price in terms of the experience of the individual: to the extent that everything is sacrificed to the individual's drive for rational self-control, the individual loses the capacity to integrate his experience into a meaningful unity: in this case, he becomes cut off from himself as well as from others. To raise such possibilities does not mean that we have to endorse irrationality. On the contrary, if rationalism has deformed the notion of rationality by its commitment to the idea of maximizing the consciously applied discretionary power of the self, then the critique of rationalism would be not a rejection of rationality but an attempt to rescue it. Rationalism, in restricting the rational to the *voluntary*, the argument would be, misses how far questions of rationality arise in relation to what is not voluntary at all: our attitudes, dispositions, experiences and memories.

Rationalism, according to its critics, is not simply a false theory about an unchanging subject-matter, human nature, but corresponds to something about the way that human beings in society actually do live – to the repression which is characteristic of life in a 'rationalized' (if not, for that reason, 'rational') society. In this way the critique of rationalism is potentially a powerful ingredient in a radical social critique.

In fact, however, with only marginal exceptions,[28] Marxism has

---

Freud, we gain mastery over them to a degree no system of repression can possibly equal. Talk – language – is the essential medium of consciousness, and therefore the essential means of liberation' (Philip Rieff, *Freud: the Mind of a Moralist*, p. 335).

Not just the values presented here – choice, self-mastery – but the means to their attainment – talk, language, consciousness – are quintessentially rationalistic. Freud is, in my terms, a *pessimist* rather than an *irrationalist*, for, unlike many of those whom he has influenced, Freud attributes no value *per se* to the expression of primitive feeling, whose destructive potential he plainly fears. Rieff's classic study gives a superb account of the tensions that arise in Freud's work as a result of these opposed but equally fundamental aspects of his thought.

[28] Apart from Benjamin and Adorno, the most significant contribution was made by the 'Situationists' – in particular, their theoretician, Guy Debord, whose 'Society of the Spectacle' represents one of modern Marxism's very few original developments beyond Marx.

remained untouched by this current of thought: the dominant conceptions of human nature to be found in it are rationalist through and through.[29] According to Marxism, society based upon the production of commodities is both exploitative and impersonal: it makes human beings the 'playthings of alien forces':

> As long as there exists a cleavage between the particular and the common interest, as long therefore as activity is divided not freely but naturally, man's own deed becomes an alien power standing over him, subjugating him instead of being dominated by him.[30]

The moral superiority of socialism and communism thus consists not merely in the abolition of injustice but in allowing the producers to establish control over the process of production. One reason for the catastrophic consequences of attempts to realize Marxism in practice has been its failure to provide a decent account of how this collective control might be exercised, thus leaving the field open for the Bolshevik vanguard party to impose its appalling mixture of bureaucracy and *jacquerie*. But criticism must go deeper and call into question the ideal of control itself.[31]

In the *Critique of the Gotha Programme* Marx remarks that, under communism, labour will become 'not only a means of life but life's prime want'[32] – an apparently extraordinary idea, which seems to go way beyond anything justified by his critique of capitalism: if to labour under conditions outside one's own control is bad, it certainly does not follow from this that to labour for its own sake is good (that it is, indeed, the *prime* good). In fact, the idea of production as an end in itself seems to embody precisely

---

[29] There has recently been some debate as to whether Marxism has a conception of human nature at all. Paul Tillich wrote on this question in 1933:

> Without some notion of human nature, of its powers and tensions, one cannot make any statements about the foundations of political existence and thought.

And this is no less true of Marxism:

> The distrust of anthropology shown by many Marxist theoreticians has its historical basis in Marx's turn away from Feuerbach. Against the Feuerbachian picture of 'humanity in general' Marx places actual human beings, determined by class and society. But even these class determined human beings are still human, that is, beings that can have a history, that can live in society, that can be split into classes, that fall into 'dehumanization' and 'reification', and that can struggle for a social order in which their destiny, a 'real humanism' is fulfilled. (P. Tillich, *The Socialist Decision*, p. 2 and p. 2n).

Tillich seems to me to say here everything that needs to be said – the real issue is what that conception of human nature is and whether it is defensible.

[30] K. Marx, *The German Ideology*, quoted in A. Wood, *Karl Marx*, p. 50.

[31] An insight for which Adorno deserves credit. 'The ideal of the uninhibited, creative man, radiant with power, is saturated with that fetishism of commodities, which, in bourgeois society, carries with itself inhibition, impotence and the sterility of the immutable ... The image of unbound activity, uninterrupted production, freedom as flat-out activity, lives off that bourgeois conception of nature whose sole function was to proclaim social power as unalterable, a piece of healthy permanence' (T. W. Adorno, *Minima Moralia*, pp. 206–7.)

[32] K. Marx, *Critique of the Gotha Programme*, p. 569.

the kind of spurious transformation of means into ends that Marxists themselves criticize when they talk about capitalism as engaged in production 'for profit not for use'. In order to justify such passages, commentators sympathetic to Marx have interpreted the good in question not intrinsically (the idea that to transform reality limitlessly would be good in itself) but indirectly: such transforming activity is good to the extent that it leads to the greatest possible realization of human powers. As Allen Wood points out, the ideal of the maximal realization of human powers is very much part of the Western philosophical tradition:

> ... Marx's emphasis on "self-activity" or "self-exercise" involves an affirmation of the value of human freedom, and belongs to a definite tradition of thinking about what this value consists in. Freedom for Marx is self-determination, the subjection of one's self and its essential functions to one's own conscious rational choice.[33]

Yet for Wood this is a point in defence of Marx: he fails to ask whether Marxism's rationalist Prometheanism – 'the subjection of one's self and its essential functions to one's own conscious rational choice' – represents a satisfactory ideal. Does beating the drums for the continual expansion of human powers not evade the question of how a mortal being, susceptible to suffering, can find meaning in a world that – however much he and his kind may have transformed it – ultimately, he has not made? The point of criticism of Marxism would be not that it represents an eccentric departure from the solid, traditional framework of Western values but that in its rationalism it conforms to – and exposes – them all too much.

VIII Providentialism

When it comes to the background belief in society as a system, however, the contrast between the ancient and the modern world is more drastic: this idea is a modern (that is to say, late eighteenth- and early nineteenth-century) transformation of a providentialist view of history and society that is itself not so much older. With the revival in the seventeenth and eighteenth centuries of a view of reality as an expression of divine benevolence (as opposed to the Augustinian view of this world as cut off from the direct realization of divine goodness by the Fall of Man) it became possible to see history and society as incorporating (as A. O. Lovejoy has termed it) a temporalization of the Great Chain of Being. As history develops, so it manifests the plenitude of possibilities that, taken together, constitute the perfection of creation. Furthermore, each individual society, like an organism, shows a benevolent adjustment of parts for the benefit of the whole. The organic metaphor for society is, as those who

[33] A. Wood, *Karl Marx*, p. 51.

write about it usually point out, almost as old as systematic thought about political life itself. Yet few accounts do justice to the way that this idea changed and developed in the eighteenth and early nineteenth centuries. Thus it is one of the subsidiary tasks of Chapter 4 to fill in the necessary background.

For the eighteenth century, providentialism and naturalism fit together easily. There is no contradiction in an explanation of history or society that situates them in relation to natural processes and an explanation of them in terms of transcendent purpose: on the contrary, the two are complementary, to the extent that nature itself has been divinely ordered.

Hegel's account of history as the process of *Geist*'s self-realization epitomizes this providentialist view as well as bringing together the idea of false consciousness and that of unintended consequences for the first time. History, for Hegel, progresses through a series of changes, brought about by the conscious actions of individuals, but whose true significance is apparent only from the higher standpoint of philosophical knowledge: it is the 'cunning of reason' that the passions of individuals should be set to work to realize the higher purpose of *Geist*. At each stage before its final achievement of self-knowledge, consciousness is limited by the intellectual framework of its own period. It is unable to recognize forms of its own manifestation as being what they really are, aspects of its own self. In the end, consciousness learns to recognize itself in its supra-individual (that is, cultural) forms and as 'outside itself' in nature – as an aspect of the self-unfolding Idea that gives all of reality its essential unity.[34] In this way we can see the idea of society as a system emerging from, in some cases still very much intertwined with, earlier notions of 'fate' and 'Providence'.

The perspective of the quest for meaning is illuminating in relation to both rationalism and providentialism. They are both, in Nietzsche's terms, forms of Socratism; that is, both make the human situation intelligible in ways that also make it more acceptable.

At the core of rationalism is the idea of coming to terms with the world (and its potential for suffering) by means of *self-control*. Rationalist self-command enables the self to rise above the desires and impulses that threaten it from outside, either by cutting itself off so far as possible from desires and impulses altogether (the ascetic strategy) or by following only those that can be shown to meet the test of reason (the idea that dominates the tradition of German Idealism from Kant to Habermas).

Providentialism is based on the idea of the fundamental goodness of the

---

[34] Although Hegel is surely the great founder-figure of relativist theories of culture, it is important to note that his own theory is neither – ultimately – relativist (apparent relativism is superseded by and subsumed within *Geist*'s embracing final standpoint) nor does it rest on the 'neo-Kantian' or 'perspectivist' epistemological assumption that our encounter with the world is always conceptually mediated. On the contrary, the Introduction to Hegel's *Phenomenology of Spirit* provides one of the earliest and most forceful critiques of perspectivist epistemology; for Hegel, concepts are not simply an *intermediary* between reality and ourselves – this is a form of consciousness that must itself be transcended on the way to the truth that, ultimately, reality *is* conceptual.

world – whether because the world is simply good in itself or because it is the result of action by a Creator who intends it to be good for his creatures (in the eighteenth century this line was notoriously thin and easily crossed). Providentialism, too, is a response to the problem of suffering. In its classic form, it says that apparent evil is part of the necessary price to be paid for the achievement of a state that is good.

Hegel brought rationalism and providentialism together as part of an objective '*Wissenschaft*' which would, he believed, find a place within itself for the claims of modern science. For later authors, however, the idea of a scientific attitude towards reality and the providentialist idea of the intrinsic goodness of the world are clearly incompatible. Yet one should not assume for this reason that the problem of reconciling oneself with the world does not arise for the 'disenchanted' scientist. It does, but in a different form. If the world is not intrinsically good, the question still arises of its goodness for human beings and, to the extent that it is not good, of how to come to terms with it. Rationalism, as a conception of what is good for human beings, persists (indeed, is even reinforced) in the face of an indifferent world; if the world is not such as human beings can identify themselves with rationally, then, at least, they should make themselves as independent of it as possible.

IX Marx and the Frankfurt School

With Marx, the first and still the most thorough-going attempt was made to accommodate the two background beliefs within an account of history and society from which all providentialist beliefs in the intrinsic goodness of the world have been purged. What is unprecedented is the way in which Marx brings the two background beliefs together and places them at the centre of an account of society that is explicitly scientific and secular in intention. It is this that – whatever may be the fate of the political projects undertaken in his name – guarantees Marx's position at the centre of the development of modern social theory. The question, however, is: does Marx succeed? Or does he, his own intentions to the contrary, still remain subject to metaphysical commitments of whose full scope he stands unaware?

So far I have followed convention and referred to the emergence of the *theory* of ideology. In fact, however, Marx does not have a theory of ideology, in the sense of a single, mutually coherent set of concepts and well-defined empirical claims. On the contrary, we can find in Marx's writing traces of no fewer than five conceptually distinct models, all of which have some claim to be the basis for a theory of ideology but none of which amounts to one. (A brief example of the contrast between model and theory: the claim that the sun stands at the centre of the solar system is part of a *model*; Kepler's laws of planetary motion are a *theory*. The distinction is not absolute, however. Darwin's theory of evolution is properly so-called, despite not being quantified and despite lacking an account of the genetic basis of inheritance.)

The first two models are to be found in *The German Ideology*: the model of reflection (the suggestion that ideology reflects material life 'as in a *camera obscura*') and the model of interests (that ideas are conditioned pragmatically, by the practical interests which they serve). The weaknesses of these two models have often been noted: how, for example, is the reflection model supposed to account for the falsehood of ideology – if all consciousness is an 'inverted reflection' of real circumstances, what room is there for the distinction between true and false forms of it? The interests model, on the other hand, leaves unclear how it is that people come to adhere to ideas which go against their interests (as when subordinate classes are in the grip of the dominant ideology).[35]

But there are alternatives in Marx to these relatively early conceptions. A third possibility lies in developing an account of ideology that draws on the idea of a functional 'correspondence' between base and superstructure, as presented by Marx in the Preface to *A Contribution to the Critique of Political Economy*. Beyond this, Marx makes repeated use in *Das Kapital* of a contrast between the immediate, surface appearance of social reality and its deep, essential structure, and a number of defenders of Marx have seen this as his definitive solution to the problem of ideology, while yet a fifth possibility (also based upon *Das Kapital*) would be to read Marx's theory in neo-Hegelian terms, as imperfect stages in the self-discovery of a historical 'collective subject'. It will be my argument that there is some degree of support in the text for all these approaches (although no one of them is sufficiently fully worked-out to count as Marx's final view of the issue) but that there are fundamental criticisms to be made of each. Either, as I will argue, the evidence is too thin for the kind of explanatory model that would put Marx in line with the natural scientists or else he is committed to ontological assumptions that go far beyond what an avowed materialist ought to make use of. I conclude that the problem of ideology remains essentially unresolved for Marx.

Finally, I shall discuss the neo-Marxist theory of ideology as it developed among the authors of the 'Frankfurt School', concentrating in particular on the debate between Theodor Adorno and Walter Benjamin on the notion of the 'fetishism of commodities'. Benjamin and Adorno were friends and, after Benjamin's death in 1940, Adorno was the chief protagonist of Benjamin's writing on social theory. Nevertheless, there is, I suggest, a deep and significant difference of principle in their approaches. One of Adorno's most celebrated doctrines is that 'The Whole is the untrue' ('*Das Ganze ist das Unwahre*') – apparently a direct contradiction of Hegel.[36] Yet Adorno's approach to social theory, I shall argue, is deeply

---

[35] '. . . the chief weakness of the interest theory of ideology lies perhaps less in its crude psychological portrayal of its beneficiaries than in its inability to account for the *acceptance* of ideological beliefs by non-benefiting groups' (J. G. Merquior, *The Veil and the Mask*, p. 9).

[36] *Minima Moralia*, p. 57.

Hegelian. He accepts Hegel's understanding of society as a single, self-differentiating totality at the same time as rejecting Hegel's positive evaluation of this picture. To this extent, Adorno is the most significant example of what a full-scale Marxist-Hegelianism looks like. The methodological standards to which it appeals would, of course, seem vastly overindulgent to interpreters such as Cohen or Elster, but, within those standards, Adorno's theory is remarkably consistent – and it does, as I shall argue, have strong claims to be a legitimate continuation of Marx's mature thought.

Benjamin, on the other hand, was wholly immune to the influence of Hegel, a fact which Adorno seems to have disregarded as no more than a sign of Benjamin's general lack of interest in abstract conceptual issues. In my view, this seriously underestimates the force and distinctiveness of Benjamin's position. Implicitly, at least, Benjamin's work presents highly original answers to two of the outstanding questions for any theory of ideology. First, Benjamin presents a novel answer to the question of the *mechanism* of ideology. If it is the case that consciousness responds in some way to the exigencies of society, what are the connections that make it do so – where are the 'invisible threads' holding them together? Benjamin's conception of a 'mimetic capacity' suggests how there might be unconscious relations of representation between one region of social life and another and so make the connection between economic life and the wider culture less mysterious. This issue is especially important because, as we shall see, it is in relation to the mechanism of ideology that readings such as Cohen's most conspicuously fail to provide a satisfactory defence of Marx's theory.

By *mechanism* I mean the explanatory connection that underlies the relation between *explanans* and *explanandum*. It is, of course, a deep question whether, at the ultimate metaphysical level, there are such connections (and, if there are, whether we could ever know what they were). However, it seems indisputable that, as a matter of practical explanation, the provision of such a connection is an important desideratum for any theory. What is much more open to question is whether all such connections have a single form. In this sense, Hegel's theory of *Geist* might be said to provide a *mechanism* underlying his account of the nature of historical change, just as the theory of natural selection provides a mechanism for the evolution of species.

As Rom Harré has put it:

Science follows the generative rather than the successionist theory of causality. The discovery of the mechanism of chemical reactions, of the mechanism of inheritance, and so many more, are examples of the fulfilment of this search. But a word of caution is needed here as to the meaning of "mechanism". In ordinary English this word has two distinct meanings. Sometimes it means mechanical connection, a device that works with rigid connections, like levers, the intermeshing teeth of gears, axles, and strings.

Sometimes it means something much more general, namely any kind of connection through which causes are effective. . . . It is in the latter sense that the word is used in science generally, in such diverse expressions as the mechanism of the distribution of seeds and the mechanism of star formation. In hardly any of these cases is any mechanical contrivance being referred to. So we must firmly grasp the idea that not all mechanisms are mechanical.[37]

A second reason why both Benjamin and Adorno should command our attention is that their writings contain an important alternative to the rationalist tradition's dominant conception of the self and its experience. In *The Dialectic of Enlightenment* in particular, Adorno continues and refines the Nietzschean account of the search for meaning. Nietzsche understood the Socratic spirit as consisting essentially in the attempt to make the world intelligible by a comprehensive system of reasons. Adorno adds his own interpretation of Enlightenment as an attempt by the self to come to terms with what is different from itself by taking *control* of it. These two elements, in Adorno's view, are in permanent conflict with one another. Benjamin's writings are important because they attempt to work out an alternative to the rationalist conception of the self. According to Benjamin, a truly non-alienated self would not be one that had established rational control over its emotions but one which could integrate its memories without the need for repression.[38]

Is such an engagement with the Marxist tradition and its social theory at all urgent? This book is being written at a time when the political collapse in Eastern Europe has almost certainly brought with it the end of Marxism as a serious political force. That the sinking of the Eastern European ship appears to have taken down those in the water around it might seem somewhat surprising. The opponents of Marxism, of course, tried their best to identify Marxian socialism with the regimes in Eastern Europe, but, by the time of the collapse, very few avowed Marxists in the West (and, as it now turns out, even fewer in the East) still had any confidence that those societies provided any model of social progress. So one might think that the end of 'really existing socialism' would have proved, if anything, a liberation for Marxists.

What the collapse in Eastern Europe robbed Western Marxists of was not, in the end, an ideal with which they could identify but, far more significantly, a villain whom they could blame. How better to rationalize the failure of their projects than through the usurpation of Marxism by this sinister and powerful enemy? For the Trotskyists who dominated the

---

[37] R. Harré, *The Philosophies of Science*, p. 118. What counts as an acceptable mechanism? That is the philosophically fundamental and profoundly troubling question which – if we are not to commit ourselves dogmatically to some form of materialism – there would appear to be no *a priori* way to answer. As Whitehead warns: 'What is the sense of talking about a mechanical explanation when you do not know what you mean by mechanics?' (A. N. Whitehead, *Science and the Modern World*, p. 24.)

[38] 'Glücklich sein heisst, ohne Schrecken sich selbst innewerden' (W. Benjamin, *Einbahnstrasse*, p. 113).

Far Left in the West, the fall of the Soviet monolith occupied an eschatological position akin to Armageddon: only with the defeat of Stalinism would the small band of the Elect come into their own and the socialist destiny of mankind be fulfilled. But, in fact, things have developed quite differently. People at all levels of society in Eastern Europe turned to capitalism rather than socialism as a solution to their immense problems. Such uncomfortable facts do not, of course, constitute a *refutation* of Marxism, and there will undoubtedly be some Marxists – so well practised at maintaining belief in the face of contrary evidence – who will not avoid the challenge of finding new excuses for failure. But these are hardly partners with whom it is likely to prove productive to open discussion. So why discuss Marxism now, if not to dance on its grave? Two reasons seem to me important.

There is, first, the question of the sources of Marxism's appeal. Those who have at some time or other felt their force will know better than to dismiss Marxism as simply a fantasy for fanatics. I shall try to show that, whatever we might think about the success of its proposed solutions, the preconceptions from which Marxism starts are not absurd and the questions that motivate it are not closed. Another reason concerns the consequences of the collapse. Fortunately, the fall of Marxism does not mean the end of egalitarian values or of projects of human emancipation, perhaps not even of socialist ones. There is no question, however, but that the latter have, in practice, become so interwoven with Marxism that, if there is to be any prospect of their surviving and developing independently, there will have to be a great deal of disambiguation beforehand. We must first determine where Marxism ends – its intellectual and moral limits, not just its historical ones – if we are to have any hope of finding where progressive values can begin.

X Preview

The next chapter will attempt to clear the ground for the historical and interpretative argument that follows by examining the notion of 'false consciousness' and asking what conditions must be met for a form of false consciousness to count as 'ideological'. It is the most 'analytical' part of the book. Chapters 3 and 4, on the other hand, are historical surveys with some detailed textual interpretations. They trace the idea that false consciousness has a specifically political character and the idea of society as a self-reproducing organism respectively. Chapter 5 shows how those two ideas are brought together in the context of Hegel's Idealist theory of history and society. Chapter 6 looks at Marx. Marx, too, tries to do justice to both elements while maintaining a materialist, scientific approach to the study of society. My argument is that the strains of doing so pull Marx's theory apart. One of the strands – the commitment to scientific materialism – is captured by the methodological individualism defended by such authors as Cohen and Elster. I shall argue that this approach is incapable of giving a satisfactory defence of the theory of ideology. The other strand, a neo-Hegelian one, saves the claims of the theory of ideology at the price of a collectivist ontology. This strand was taken up by the authors of the Frankfurt School, most notably Theodor Adorno. Chapter 7 compares Adorno's thoroughgoing Marxist-Hegelianism with Walter Benjamin's very different approach to Marxism, an approach that I call, in contrast, 'Marxist Kantianism'. Finally, Chapter 8 brings the discussion together and asks how, if not by means of the theory of ideology, Reich's question should be answered.

2

The Forms of False Consciousness

I Analysis

In its post-war heyday, the attitude of 'conceptual analysis' towards ordinary language oscillated between passive pluralism and stipulative monism. Authors were either content to review the range of usage to which a term was subject (a practice for which 'dictionary-philosophy' is one of the milder descriptions) or else they would claim (generally, quite implausibly) to have identified the single, core 'concept' beneath the multiplicity of 'conceptions' to which less perceptive users of ordinary language were subject. If the analysis of ideology is neither to capitulate to the diversity of usage (and few terms have been used more diversely) nor to try to wish it away, some better principle of organization ought to be found.

The aim of analysis, in my view, should be to look at what a term or complex of terms has been used for – its point. In the case of ideology, the point is explanatory: to explain the persistence of unequal (and unjust) societies. Adorno's definition of ideology as 'necessary false consciousness' forms a useful guide. It registers the central idea that societies have a systematic character and that they are maintained, apparently irrationally in many cases, by virtue of the attitudes and beliefs of those who live in them.It is with the idea of 'false consciousness' that this chapter is concerned.

'False consciousness' may be differentiated in two ways. The first is by the question of its scope (the 'extension'): what sorts of things may be included as cases of false consciousness? The second is by 'intension': what is it that makes such forms of consciousness 'ideologically false', and in what sense are we to understand them as being so? The next section will address the first question and present a sub-division of the ways that consciousness might be held to be 'false'. The third and fourth sections will take up the second question. I will ask, first, if there is a specific kind of irrationality that would enable us to identify a form of consciousness as 'ideologically irrational'. Secondly, I shall argue that, the assumption of many commentators to the contrary, not all ideological false consciousness can be understood as being *irrational*.

II The Scope of 'False Consciousness'

What are false in the normal understanding of the word are attempts to depict or describe reality and its structure – assertions and beliefs. But, from the point of view of the theory of ideology, to restrict false consciousness in this way would be to narrow the matter too much: there is no reason to suppose that the aspects of mental life most relevant to the reproduction of social orders are the specifically cognitive ones. One of the most significant themes running through theories of false consciousness has been sensitivity to the ways in which consciousness goes beyond simply attempting to depict the state of the world or to satisfy the greatest possible number of a given set of desires. An adequate account of false consciousness should leave open a place for those aspects.

Thus I shall divide the possible modes of false consciousness into three main regions:

1 *cognitive false consciousness* – disorders of the system by which we perceive, judge and reflect upon nature, society and ourselves. Cognitive false consciousness, in turn, may be divided into disorders of (a) *belief*, (b) *attitude*, and (c) *perception*.

2 *practical false consciousness* – disorders in the way in which we respond to and act within the world. These latter may be disorders of (a) *desire and the will*, (b) *values, ends* or *norms*, (c) *disorders of emotion*.

3 what I shall call *distortions of identity*. Distortions of identity involve the deformation of a subject and may be divided initially according to whether the subject in question is (a) *individual*, (b) *collective*, or (c) *metaphysical* or *cosmic*.

A warning is in order at this point. The sub-divisions are presented here for the sake of clarity and completeness. But not all of them will feature in the discussion that is to follow, which is organized along historical lines. Examples of all these conceptions of false consciousness can be found somewhere in the history of Western social thought, but not all of them are in places relevant to the necessarily selective examples of the theory of ideology with which I shall be dealing in this book.

1 *Cognitive false consciousness*

a *Beliefs* The kind of empirical false beliefs – errors of perception and memory, refuted scientific theories – that are central to philosophical questions of truth and falsehood are likely to be peripheral to a theory of ideology. One reason for this is easily seen. Ideological beliefs must be related to society in two ways. First, it must be the case that such a belief has the consequence of preserving a particular structure in the society in question. Secondly, the false consciousness of which the belief is an expression must be social in origin (in a sense that will be explored in more detail below). The thought behind the need for this second criterion is this. A belief – for example, a particular myth regarding a society's origins – might very well have extremely important social consequences, but, if the reason why it is held is arbitrary from the point of view of society, then the existence of the belief is simply a single, contingent, if interesting and important, fact about a particular case, not part of any general explanation of the way in which unequal and unjust societies preserve themselves.

Beliefs in the natural sciences are simply less likely to meet these two criteria. If they play a role in preserving social structures, they will, in general, do so less directly than beliefs about human beings and their social relations or beliefs about a transcendent order. However, it would be stipulative to assume that ideological beliefs are restricted by definition to beliefs about a certain subject-matter.[1] Beliefs in the natural sciences are not isolated from social consequences altogether. Some natural scientific beliefs relate immediately to social concerns (beliefs about the biological basis of personality and intelligence; beliefs about health and heredity; also, in earlier societies particularly, beliefs about meteorology or agriculture). Other scientific beliefs act causally upon society, but less directly – notably, when they are combined with further beliefs and attitudes. So, for example, many Marxists would argue that the corpuscularian physics of the seventeenth and eighteenth centuries played an ideological role, inasmuch as it was incorporated into a world-view that promoted an individualistic, atomistic form of society.[2]

[1] Cohen may seem to be doing just this when he writes: ' . . . science is not ideology, since it is a defining property of ideology that it is unscientific'. However, he goes on to claim that: 'Science may contain unscientific ideological elements, but it is despite them that it is science' (*Karl Marx's Theory of History*, p. 46). Thus he would appear to be using the term 'scientific' in a way that entails that whatever is scientific is rational, rather than, as one might have expected, to identify a particular field of enquiry.

[2] The fact that a certain scientific belief has conservative social consequences, however, is not *sufficient* to qualify the belief as ideological unless it also meets the second criterion of being social in origin. This (we might suppose) is less plausible for the scientific revolution of the early modern world. There are, of course, radical sceptics about the objectivity of science who would argue just that, however. If they are right, then there is no sufficient reason in the nature of the reality dealt with or in the independent logic of the development of science to explain why corpuscularian physics was adopted at the time it was, so it would not be implausible to suppose that it was purely 'social in origin'. However, the theory of ideology does not *have* to be taken in this extreme form.

There is a further reason why false beliefs about the world are less central to the theory of ideology than one might expect. This is because of the way in which ideological beliefs are located in a wider picture of belief and action. Put most generally, the theory of ideology is a theory of how forms of consciousness *stabilize, promote,* or *maintain* a particular society or structure. In other words, the theory of ideology is an account of how agents act in a sense *successfully* – successfully, that is, but in relation to interests that are not their own. From which it follows that a large proportion of their beliefs must be at least adequate for practical purposes. Beliefs, beliefs about society included, must be sufficiently accurate to allow the society to continue.[3]

In consequence, the subject-matter of ideological beliefs has typically been taken to be beliefs that are (overtly) not directly about the empirical world or society at all – most obviously, religious beliefs. Many of the beliefs on which theories of false consciousness focus have the character of 'category mistakes': treating the inanimate as animate or even divine (the 'pathetic fallacy' of the fetishist) or treating what is historical and contingent as if it were something fixed and inevitable. Alternatively, the domain of ideological beliefs has been taken to be second-order beliefs or second-order aspects of otherwise accurate empirical beliefs.

Marx himself clearly recognized this problem. Thus, in the famous analogy in *The German Ideology*, in which he compares ideology to a '*camera obscura*', the suggestion is that ideological beliefs are both accurate (reproducing the structure of reality) and misleading (inverted) at the same time. Later in the same book Marx alleges that it is characteristic of ideology that ideas are taken to arise in a sphere of mental life that is independent of interests. It is this latter belief *about* ideas, rather than the particular content of the ideas themselves, that is the source of their ideological character: we ascribe to them a false autonomy and disinterestedness.

One particularly significant way in which a single phenomenon might unite first- and second-order beliefs, the first of which is correct and the second false, is when an action invites interpretation on more than one level. On this view, the immediate account given by an agent of his or her action is not false in its own terms, but must be 'completed' by a further, higher explanation that, on the one hand, does not 'compete' with the lower-level explanation and, on the other, cannot be reduced to it. It is the lack of this higher perspective that condemns an individual to 'false consciousness', in the sense of failing to understand the full significance of his own actions. This idea, which had its origins in theological attempts to marry providential with empirical causal accounts of history and nature, was, we shall see, taken up by Hegel as part of what he called the 'cunning

---

[3] Marxist theorists have frequently expressed the idea that a belief may be adequate up to a point but, beyond that, misleading or even false, in unnecessarily paradoxical language (for example, by saying that ideology is 'both true and false'). There is, however, nothing intrinsically paradoxical or mysterious in the idea.

of reason' – his account of how it was that the spontaneous actions of individuals could realize wider, systematic purposes.

I have explained that the falsehood of a belief (in the plain sense of its failing to correspond to the facts) is not a sufficient condition for the belief being ideological. Less obviously, it is not a necessary one either. An example will illustrate why. Imagine that a society believes that the earth goes round the sun. But imagine that it believes this fact not because it has developed anything like a good scientific theory of the universe but because the members of the society conceive the universe as a macrocosmic version of their own society: the sun is taken to represent their emperor and the earth to correspond to his subjects, who move in accordance with his wishes. Would it not be reasonable to count this belief as 'ideological'? The point is that a belief can be true without being justified or rationally held. So, if it has consequences in serving to maintain the social order, and if it is held for reasons that are social in origin but not rational, then it could meet the two criteria for being ideological identified above *despite* being true.

One reason to refer to 'beliefs' (rather than asserted sentences or propositions) is that it is an important possibility that such beliefs may not be conscious – that they may, indeed, be *concealed* from those who hold them (and the concealed beliefs may be part of the explanation of the ideological character of those beliefs that are explicitly acknowledged). If one reason why some explicit beliefs are ideological is that they are characteristically *irrational*, then one of the most likely ingredients in that irrationality would be that the person who holds the belief is not aware of the reasons – the real reasons – for holding it. In that case, as well as the original explicit belief, they may have a second, conscious false belief – a belief about the first belief – which is the account that they would give to themselves of their reason for holding it. In potential conflict with this second belief (which the agent, furthermore, believes to be the reason for the first belief) may be a third belief, one that is not recognized or acknowledged but that is in fact the real reason for the first belief. So, for example, a discriminatory employer may believe:

1 that blacks make less good employees;

and believe:

2 that this belief is based on experience and observation (both beliefs (1) and (2) being false).

In fact, however, the true basis of the first false belief may be:

3 the unstated belief (which the employer would fail to acknowledge himself as believing) that blacks are innately inferior.[4]

---

[4] The idea of implicit (or repressed) beliefs is, of course, particularly characteristic of psychoanalytic approaches to false consciousness.

It seems appropriate to say that in this example there are *three* ideological beliefs, although only the first two are *consciously held* beliefs.

b *Attitudes*   Such tacit beliefs shade across into what are commonly called 'attitudes'. Someone may be said to be suffering from 'false consciousness' if there is a discrepancy between their attitudes and their avowed beliefs. The philosophers who have done most to draw attention to failures of attitude as a form of false consciousness have been Sartre and, above all, Heidegger. Both authors make a kind of 'ontological false consciousness' – practical versions of the 'category mistakes' identified above – central to their philosophical accounts of human beings' self-misunderstandings. For Sartre, the central such attitude is *mauvaise foi* ('bad faith'): the failure (or, rather, refusal) of human beings to recognize the fact of their own radical freedom leads to a reification of reality. For Heidegger, the 'fall' into inauthentic being represents a clear analogy to the Marxist account of the alienated self. In 'everydayness' the attitude towards the world that regards it as standing independent of the perceiving subject and its activities is taken to be absolute, thus turning the individual away from concern with its own particularity and, ultimately, avoiding confrontation with its ineliminable finitude. In each of these cases, the failure of attitude is primarily *philosophical*; the 'false consciousness' consists in a failure to acknowledge and express a fundamental truth about the human condition.

   For the theory of ideology, the most important mistaken attitude is that complex of failures of *recognition* expressed in Marx's early writings as 'alienation'. Alienation is, in the first instance, a mode of life. The alienated worker's failure to recognize himself in the product of his labour and the failure of isolated individuals to recognize each other fully as fellow human beings are expressions of false consciousness that are lived and experienced before they are theorized about or reflected upon.[5]

c *Perceptions*   It may be thought that to call a perception 'false' is epistemologically misguided: judgements may be false, and perceptual content is a source of evidence for judgements, but how could that content itself be 'false'? From the point of view of the theory of ideology, however, the idea that there is a distinctively perceptual kind of false consciousness is important. The idea has its roots in an epistemology which we may call in the broadest sense 'Kantian'. This view maintains that perception is a kind of tacit judgement by which a given material is organized by a concept

---

[5] In counting alienation as a cognitive failure, I do not mean to exclude the possibility that it also involves a loss of identity. See Section 3 below.
   One disappointing feature of recent discussions of Marx in English has been the tendency to treat 'alienation' and 'ideology' as two unrelated issues. The theory of alienation, to put it briefly, offers a critical account of forms of life in a bad society. The theory of ideology, on the other hand, seeks to answer the question why such societies are able to maintain themselves without recourse to violence. Thus, while there is no *necessary* connection between the solution to the first problem and the solution to the second, the problems overlap very largely.

or concepts into a perceptual object. From which it follows that perception may be 'false' in two ways. First, it may be false inasmuch as the concepts applied to a given material are misleading, inadequate or partial. We shall see an example of this in the adaptation of instrumentalist epistemology for the purposes of the theory of ideology in the writings of Jürgen Habermas. Second, the entire process of perception and judgement may be, in a sense, false: the very operation of conceptual judgement interposes a barrier between self and world, it is said, that cuts the self off from reality.

For a tradition of philosophical and cultural criticism that goes back to Nietzsche and Schopenhauer, the alienating separation of self and world is an inescapable consequence of the cognitive enterprise. Not to be *overcome*, this separation can, on this view, at best be temporarily escaped by the subject's engagement in non-conceptual realms – above all, in art.

However, the idea of change in the *forms* of perception creates the possibility of a more historical critique. The idea is that the alienated understanding of the world as inert and atomistic is associated with the domination exercised over perception by one particular form of it: vision. For Schopenhauer and Nietzsche, the sense of hearing (and the art particularly associated with it, music) is especially connected with the overcoming of the '*principium individuationis*' (the cognitive division of the world into neutral and independent items) characteristic of vision. Subsequently, this contrast between vision and hearing became the basis for a rejection of the 'primacy of vision' as a form of consciousness particularly characteristic of modernity.[6]

A similar idea is to be found in Adorno and Horkheimer's *The Dialectic of Enlightenment*. As they present it, the Enlightenment self tries to establish control over a reality that seems to it alien and threatening by imposing universal concepts on the material of perception. In consequence, earlier, mimetic ways of relating to the world are destroyed or repressed, content is lost and a disjunction is introduced between perception and emotion. In Adorno's later writings, this critique of the role of concepts in perception was developed into an attack on the connection between '*Identitätsdenken*' ('identity-thinking') and the development of modern 'exchange society' in a way that brings sociology and epistemology together.

d *Cognitive procedures*   As well as beliefs and attitudes taken individually, there may be ideological false consciousness in the way that beliefs and attitudes are formed and the structures of explanation into which they are fitted. In general, deficient cognitive procedures may be identified either positively or negatively. Positively, it may be thought that ideology is

---

[6] The critique of 'ocularcentrism' has two possible forms (not always especially clearly distinguished by the critics). First, there is the argument that vision has displaced the other senses; second, the claim that vision itself has become, in some way, neutralized or detached. See M. Jay, *Force Fields*, especially chs 8 and 9, and *Downcast Eyes: the Denigration of Vision in Twentieth-Century French Thought*.

characterized by the adherence to certain misguided aspirations or erroneous explanatory patterns (the search for totalizing explanation, for example, or the tendency to explain the unfamiliar as a form of the familiar); negatively, ideology is identified by a failure to stick to established canons (not weighing up evidence objectively or not exposing a questionable belief to testing). On this view, ideology is a failure of explanation – a pseudo-explanation that does not meet the standards of rational explanation but that is, in a sense, parasitic on it, exploiting its prestige.

One example of this is particularly important to Marx. According to Marx, the characteristic of a truly scientific procedure is that it should go behind the appearance of reality to come into contact with its 'essence'. It is a mark of the ideological form of economic theory which he calls 'vulgar economy', on the other hand, that it should rest content with 'the alienated outward appearances of economic relations'.[7]

2 Practical false consciousness

a *Desires and the will* The desires to be criticized in a theory of false consciousness can be divided in two ways. First, desires might be either of the first or of a higher order. In other words, they may be desires directed at particular things, states of affairs or experiences, or they may be desires that relate to other desires. Second-order desires can act as a standard of criticism for first-order desires (so the fact that I desire not to desire to smoke may be taken as an indication that the desire to smoke is – for me at least – undesirable). But they can themselves also be open to criticism. Thus the guilt someone feels at their sexual desire (their desire not to feel sexual desire) may be regarded as something bad, not good. This illustrates the way in which there may be desires of a higher order than the second; the critical standpoint can be represented as a third-order desire: if I want to free myself from sexual guilt then I could be said to desire not to desire not to desire what I do, in fact, desire. And there are, perhaps, even more complex combinations!

A second way in which desires may be sub-divided is according to whether they include essential reference to subjective states other than those of the individual who has the desire or not. Recently, several moral philosophers have objected to the assumption prevalent in (Anglo-American) moral philosophy that desires for an individual to experience a particular state are, in the end, the only rational desires. They have pointed out that there is no good reason to deny that a desire whose satisfaction I do not – indeed, could not – myself experience may be perfectly rational. For example, I may rationally desire that the planet's eco-system survive into the distant future without supposing that I will be around to witness it. From the point of view of the theory of ideology, however, the relevant

[7] *Das Kapital*, 3, p. 825 [Eng. trans., p. 817].

dividing line is whether the desires in question involve the subjective states – judgements, attitudes or desires – of others.

Once admitted, desires that involve others' states open up a great range of complex possibilities. We may simply desire others' subjective states with no reference to ourselves – we might endow an art gallery because we desire the aesthetic gratification of human beings in a hundred years time, for example. But we may also desire subjective states on others' part that do make reference back to us: that they love us, or fear us, or esteem us. And our desires may then make reference to their desires in turn: we may desire to be what others desire us to be (or, indeed, in adolescence in particular, the reverse) and we may desire that they desire to do what we desire them to do. We may desire attitudes towards us on their part in conjunction: for example, we may desire that we be desired by others *and* that we be seen by them as unattainable; and we may desire that people hold attitudes towards us in a certain way and for certain reasons: for example, we may desire to be respected by others not just in general but because they judge that we possess those qualities that we ourselves value.

Evidently, such a range of possible types and levels of desire and of relationships between them creates a correspondingly complex range of possible forms of false consciousness. This theme – the *sociability of desire* – came to take on a central position in eighteenth-century social theory. For the present, it is worth pointing out that apparently the same phenomenon can be interpreted in more than one way. The fact that we form our desires on the basis of what we believe that others desire us to desire may be, on the one hand, interpreted as a loss of authority on our part, an abandonment of the individual to external power. From another point of view, however, it may just as easily be seen as a source of harmony and stability: that people want others' approval is the condition for a non-coercive reconciliation of private self-seeking with collective order. Thus it can form part both of a theory of false consciousness and of a theory of benevolent adaptation.

For rationalism, however, the principal form of false consciousness involving desires is the inability of individuals to overcome their dependence upon desires. The falsehood of consciousness in this case lies in the limitation of individuals' powers to shape and choose the course of their lives in the way that they want. This is what we might call (following the Aristotelian term that has become standard for 'weakness of will') *akratic* false consciousness. Akratic false consciousness may take two forms. First, people may have desires that are stubborn or recalcitrant to their wills – they cannot adjust their desires as they would wish to. Secondly, they may be incapable of translating their desires (or, at least, a significant proportion of them) into action. These two features have been the principal ingredients in rationalists' conceptions of false consiousness. For the rationalist, the rational man is capable of 'the subjection of one's self and its essential functions to one's own conscious rational choice',[8] and it is the failure to

---

[8] See quote from A. Wood, p. 22 above.

achieve this that constitutes the primary failure of rational agency. As will be apparent, I think that this ideal is a misguided one, and that the rationalists' neglect of other possible forms of false consciousness has led to a regrettable narrowing of their account of human nature. However, it should not be assumed that anti-rationalists must be correspondingly indifferent to discrepancies between desires and the will; while critics of rationalism might be less inclined than rationalists to presume in favour of higher-order desires over 'lower' ones, they will have their own criticisms of the way that desires are formed and the detachment of the individual from active engagement. What separates rationalist and anti-rationalist is not what sorts of things they think can be false so much as the reasons why they consider them to be so and, above all, the remedies that they propose.

b *Values, ends and norms* The inclusion of this category as a potential form of false consciousness is controversial. The point in question is whether values *could* be 'false' at all – whether they fall within the domain of what is potentially open to objective evaluation or not. Each position has been argued within the Marxist tradition and the claim made that the contrary position represents 'ideology'. On the one hand, Marxists who have followed a 'Hegelian' line of interpretation have maintained that to deny the objectivity of questions of value would be to capitulate to the 'instrumental', Enlightenment conception of reason (itself, allegedly, a product of the quantifying, market relationships characteristic of commodity production). In other words, the *loss* of the sense of the objectivity of values is itself a form of false value (as they would argue, an unjustified absolutization of the value of subjectivity). On the other hand, many Marxists (Lenin and Trotsky, for example) have argued that it is precisely the belief in the existence of 'values' as objective and independent features of reality that has helped to obscure the truth of the matter: that values are simply the expression of social interests and forces.[9]

c *Emotions* As well as getting to know the world and acting upon it we react to it – by feeling pleasure and pain and by other, more complicated, emotions. What might make an emotion 'false'? In the first place, our emotional life has a value in itself. Thus, if we should be deprived of emotions altogether (or if our emotions were to lose their intensity) then that in itself would be a kind of impoverishment. Another kind of loss is when the dominant emotions in an individual's life are negative, not positive. It has been a common criticism made by Marxists of capitalism

---

[9] Although this latter position denies the objectivity of value, that is not incompatible with the thought that values may be a part of 'false consciousness'. It may be argued that, while values themselves are neither true nor false, the attitude that treats values *as if* they were true (or false) *is* something that is open to criticism (and is, in fact, false). In other words, we have here an instance of the first-order/second-order phenomenon that I suggested was typical of ideological beliefs: while the values are neither true nor false, the beliefs held about them are.

(and by many non-Marxist critics of industrial civilization) that individuals lead lives dominated by punitive and unpleasant emotions – fear, anxiety, guilt – rather than being able to enjoy true happiness. There are also accounts of emotion that hold up for criticism the quality of the emotion (the idea that certain sophisticated and complex emotions are more valuable than other, more basic, ones is a familiar ingredient in rationalist high-mindedness).[10] Finally, there is the view that certain emotions are in a sense 'true' (or false) by being the *appropriate* emotions in particular circumstances. Certain emotions may be necessary in order to provide a foundation for moral responses, while other emotions, even unpleasant ones, may have their proper place in a well-ordered mental life (for example, people may suffer from the inability to feel the emotion of grief).[11] On the other hand, emotion out of place – emotion for emotion's sake – may be thought to reflect an inappropriate detachment.[12]

Rousseau provides a very clear example of a theory of this kind. In Rousseau's view, the emotion of *pitié* is at the root of morality. Thus it is fundamental to his criticism of modern society that its self-seeking nature cuts individuals off from this immediate form of engagement with one another and substitutes instead the spurious and self-indulgent emotions of the imagination (such as we experience in the theatre, for example).

3 Disorders of identity

a *Individual identity*   Hegel, in a famous phrase, describes freedom as remaining '*in seinem Anderen bei sich selbst*' (roughly, 'with oneself in otherness').[13] On this view, the autonomous self is one that neither witholds from nor loses itself in its actions: its expressions remain truly its own. Correspondingly, the unfree self, in becoming separated from otherness, can be said to have suffered a 'loss of identity'. What is meant by the phrase?

On one level, the idea of a 'loss of identity' might amount simply to the failure by an agent to recognize an activity or the product of an activity as having the origin that it does. In that case, one might think, the phrase 'loss of identity' is just a somewhat colourful way of putting something philosophically unproblematic: it represents a cognitive failure, a failure of recognition, of a familiar kind. However, more may be involved. Hegelianism and Marxism, especially in Marx's early writings, inherit the Romantic view of the essential importance of expression to the self.[14]

---

[10] John Stuart Mill's contrast between the 'higher' and the 'lower' pleasures is the classic presentation of this contrast.
[11] The 'inability to mourn' has been explored by many psychoanalytically influenced authors.
[12] Hence the suspicion of the emotions evoked through fiction.
[13] *Enzyklopädie der philosophischen Wissenschaften* I, *Werke*, VIII, para. 24, *Zusatz* 2, p. 84.
[14] The nature of this view and its roots in German thought are explored magisterially in Part I of Charles Taylor's *Hegel*.

Expression is connected with a variety of other values, cognitive and emotional. In the first place, expression is *revelation*: to express oneself is to make oneself open to understanding – by others and, not least, by oneself. Expression is also *release*: it allows the discharge of emotions that, otherwise, would become sour and destructive. But, beyond this, it is also held to be connected with a distinct value. Expression allows for the articulation of the particularity of each individual – their *Eigentümlichkeit*.[15] An expression can be thought of as part of the individual (of the individual's life). Hence a failure to express oneself adequately can be seen as a loss of identity: the individual does not become what they potentially (and desirably) might be. An expression may be inadequate because the expression is not truly an expression *of* the self – this is what is lacking, for the Marxist, in alienated labour.[16]

Such a loss of identity is not to be confused with what philosophers standardly think of as the problem of 'personal identity': the problem of the conditions under which the self constitutes a numerically identical individual through time. An individual may suffer a 'loss of identity' through a failure of expression without losing their personal identity altogether. In fact, the condition mentioned earlier – that ideological thought must, in general, be *adequate* – makes it implausible to think that there will be any case of false consciousness relevant to the theory of ideology that involves a loss of identity of this radical nature. Nevertheless, conceptions of false consciousness that are important for the theory of ideology, dissociation of personality and the failure to integrate memories into a single whole involve damage to features, the unity and continuity of experience, that may be thought to be essential for personal identity. In this sense, identity may be *weakened* by false consciousness, if not actually destroyed.[17]

But, if the self can be thought of as suffering from false consciousness to the degree that it lacks the conditions for establishing the unity and continuity of its experience, there is another point of view that would situate false consciousness in exactly those conditions. On this view, it is the unified subject that is the source of false consciousness. Personal identity is a fiction (an artificially constructed reality, that is to say) that is

---

[15] The idea is not just that different things – different ways of life, for example – are good for different individuals (although that may well be true) but that this very difference is itself something good. Taken over by John Stuart Mill from Humboldt, the idea of *Eigentümlichkeit* was to become an important part of the foundations of liberal political theory. (One of the few treatments of this important connection between Romantic individualism and liberalism – fortunately, a reliable and perceptive one – is N. Rosenblum's *Another Liberalism*.)

[16] '[Alienated labour is the relationship of the worker to his own activity as something which is alien and does not belong to him, activity as suffering, power as impotence, procreation as emasculation, the worker's *own* physical and mental energy, his personal life – for what is life but activity? – as an activity directed against himself, which is independent of him and does not belong to him' (*Early Writings*, p. 327).

[17] Those who take the view that identity (as a logical relation) is not something that *could* be weakened might prefer to say that what are undermined are the *conditions for identity*.

basic to ideology.[18] The 'death of the subject' is, at the same time, the condition for its liberation.

b *Collective identity* The idea that individuals may have their identities damaged does not call into question ontological 'common sense'. But an important strand of thinking about false consciousness and ideology which we may call, loosely, *organicism* represents a direct challenge to the assumptions of individualism. Organicism maintains that social groups are collective entities, with their own irreducible conditions of identity, properties and powers. The apparent common sense that leads to ontological individualism itself incorporates an ideological distortion. Modern society is a collective entity whose collective character has become lost to itself, a mere 'piecing together' out of 'lifeless parts', as Schiller puts it in his *Letters on the Aesthetic Education of Man*. Marx has a similar point to make in *Das Kapital*. Under capitalism, he claims, the social relationship of the producers to their collective labour has been transformed into 'material relationships between persons and social relationships between things'.[19] To this extent, for the organicist, individualism is an adequate immediate reflection of how society is. Yet individualism does not represent the final truth about society in general. But for collective identity to be recovered more must happen than that there should be a change of attitude towards society on the part of observers and theorists: society itself must be transformed.

c *Metaphysical identity* The claim that individuals, taken collectively, form supra-individual entities is one alternative to methodological individualism. Another, even stronger, claim is associated with one author in particular, Hegel. For Hegel, the collective subject that loses and recovers itself in history is, ultimately, the source of order and meaning in non-human nature as well. Indeed, it is only by realizing the unity of its self-conscious and unconscious aspects that *Geist*, the subject of history, comes to be restored to itself. To this extent, the individual that recognizes its oneness with *Geist* must recognize not just the products of human activity but the non-human aspect of reality with which it is confronted as something that is not alien to it. Although Absolute Idealism does not play a significant role in the theory of ideology itself, it does play a crucial role, a negative one, in the background to it. As we shall see, several important themes – the relationship between individual agents and historical pro-

---

[18] According to Althusser, it is the function of ideology to 'interpellate individuals as subjects'. He writes: 'I say: the category of the subject is constitutive of all ideology, but at the same time and immediately I add that *the category of the subject is only constitutive of all ideology insofar as all ideology has the function (which defines it) of "constituting" concrete individuals as subjects*' (L. Althusser, 'Ideology and Ideological State Apparatuses', p. 45). A more interesting (although even more obscure) version of this kind of view informs Deleuze and Guattari's eclectic *L'Anti-Oedipe: capitalisme et schizophrénie*.

[19] *Das Kapital*, 1, p. 87 [Eng. trans., p. 84].

cesses and the apparently independent life taken on by certain material objects, for example – are brought out in Hegel's work. The challenge for the theory of ideology, as it was understood by Marx and by later Marxists, was to give an account of such phenomena *without* commitment to the idealist assumptions with which they are surrounded in Hegel's system.

III Ideological Irrationality

The label 'false consciousness' is, if taken too literally, misleading, both because the scope of the theory of ideology can extend to areas of mental life (attitudes, actions and emotions) that are not true or false in virtue of corresponding to mind-independent reality, and also because beliefs that *are* actually true might still be ideological. It might seem, then, that it would be better to identify ideology not with *false* consciousness but with consciousness that is *irrational*. However, there are difficulties.

Very many different kinds of phenomenon – inconsistency, lack of self-knowledge, disregard of relevant information, failure to meet standards of efficiency in reasoning – are included in our ordinary thought about rationality and irrationality and this suggests that, if rationality is not to be restricted to some formal set of decision-rules (which, clearly, would exclude much that is relevant to the theory of ideology), it will not be possible to give a single, tight and inclusive definition of it. Nevertheless, irrationality might at least provide a starting point. One plausible notion of rationality, one that is 'thin' (in the philosopher's sense of committing itself to little specific content) but nonetheless general, is that of consciousness that is formed (beliefs or values held, action taken) *for good reasons*. Correspondingly, irrationality would involve consciousness formed for bad reasons. The question is: is there a particular kind of irrationality that is characteristically ideological?

It seems as though the theory of ideology does give an account of a particular kind of bad reason that could be supposed to be characteristic of ideological thought. In the previous section I argued that it was part of ideological consciousness that it should be social in origin. Could the notion of irrationality not be interpreted with this as its criterion so as to yield a definition of ideological false consciousness as follows?

1 *Ideological consciousness is consciousness that is formed for reasons that are social in origin.*

But this is not a satisfactory solution. It is clear that some beliefs that are social in origin are not in any way irrational, let alone ideological. To be caused socially to believe something may be a good reason to hold it – that we have been taught it by competent and benevolently motivated teachers, for example. Thus my belief that I should brush my teeth after meals is a belief that was inculcated in me (with some difficulty) by my parents.

The term 'origin' also carries an apparent difficulty with it. In explaining phenomena it is often important to draw a distinction between why something came about and why it persists. Now a phenomenon might fail to be social in the way that it came about while still being ideological in the way that it persists (a religion, say, could come about by chance but be preserved by some social selection mechanism). Would it not then be ideological without being social in origin? This is, I think, merely a terminological difficulty. Let me make it clear that I intend the term 'origin' here in a broader sense, such that we should say that something was social in origin *either* if it came about *or* if it were to persist for social reasons.

But there is a further, more substantive objection. Much of our consciousness – many of our beliefs and perhaps most of our values – is not formed for reasons (in the sense of being the outcome of some kind of reflective process) at all. Yet, so far from being a defect of our mental life, the fact that we come to many appropriate and desirable beliefs unreflectively has obvious advantages. It is, as Hume puts it, 'conformable to the ordinary wisdom of nature to secure so necessary an act of the mind, by some instinct or mechanical tendency, which may be infallible in its operations, may discover itself at the first appearance of life and thought, and may be independent of all the laboured deductions of the understanding.'[20] Is it then wrong to use any test of origin as a criterion of rationality?

The alternative would seem to be to define the rationality of a form of consciousness as consisting in its having good reasons in its favour, irrespective of its origin. Thus:

2 *Ideological consciousness is consciousness that lacks good reasons in its favour.*

But what would be 'bad' reasons? Again, it seems that the theory of ideology offers an obvious answer: ideological consciousness promotes or preserves a certain social order. Thus we might give a version of (2) as follows:

2a *Ideological consciousness is consciousness that benefits some social entity or structure.*

Yet this is still not satisfactory. Two contrasting examples of consciousness that benefits a social order might be the following: (1) the belief among members of a community that it is good to help other members of the group when they are in difficulty; and (2) the belief among slaves that

---

[20] 'As nature has taught us the use of our limbs, without giving us knowledge of the muscles and nerves, by which they are actuated; so she has implanted in us an instinct, which carries forward the thought in a correspondent course to that which she has established among external objects; though we are ignorant of those powers and forces, on which this regular course and succession of objects totally depends' (*Enquiry Concerning Human Understanding* [1748], Sect.V, Part 2, p. 55).

a divine ordinance entitles the slave-owners to exercise authority over them. Each is a belief that benefits a social order but, intuitively, while the second example is potentially ideological, the first is not. The belief that individuals should help each other is a perfectly reasonable belief to hold, while the belief in the divine ordination of slavery, in contrast, is implausible, to say the least (even if there is a benevolent Deity, it is hard to suppose that slavery is part of his plan). What divides the two examples is that in the case of mutual aid the belief is in the interests both of the individual who holds it and of the social order of which they are a member; slavery, however, is in the interests of a social group within the social order (the slaveholders) and, perhaps, of the social order as a whole but it is not in the interests of the individual.

It might seem, then, that the notion of 'interests' provides the relevant further criterion:

2b *Ideological consciousness is consciousness that benefits some social entity or structure and goes against the interests of the individual who holds them.*

But it is not true that all beliefs that go against our interests are irrational. Many factual beliefs that are rationally held will go against our interests. What is more, there are many attitudes that we hold and principles upon which we act that appear to be perfectly appropriate, despite going against our interests – on one view, that is just what moral values in general call upon us to do. If a Roman hero sacrifices himself for his country, is he not, quite rationally, going against his interests? To say that an agent like this is acting in (what they have shown by their action to be) his true interests is simply to trivialize the notion of interests. If interests are identified merely by 'revealed preference' the notion is deprived of critical purchase, for false consciousness is excluded at the outset.

For the idea of interests to play a critical role we must, it seems, distinguish between what we desire and what is ('really') in our interests. To show that a form of consciousness is in our real interests, then, is one way of showing that there is a good reason to hold it. But how are we to bridge the gap between what we do want and what we ought to want (that is, what is truly in our interests)? The idea (associated particularly with the Frankfurt School writer Jürgen Habermas) that those desires are rational which we would continue to hold *even if* the limitations of knowledge and preference-formation under which we currently labour were removed involves, at the least, a counterfactual of truly heroic proportions.[21]

In any case, the weight of the definition has now shifted from the idea

---

[21] See R. Geuss, *The Idea of a Critical Theory*, pp. 45–54, for an admirable discussion of the difficulties.

of interests to the idea of justification. Thus we might, it seems, reformulate the criterion of ideological irrationality as follows:

2c *Ideological consciousness is consciousness that benefits some social entity or structure and is not capable of being justified.*

This formulation overcomes the problem of the Roman hero (for it seems that there are good reasons in favour of his sacrifice). But, just as a belief may be true but not rationally held, so, too, it may be *capable* of being justified while still being ideological (in the example discussed above, the belief that the earth goes around the sun is capable of being justified, even though the reasons why it is in fact held have nothing to do with that justification).

It seems, then, that both of the approaches so far canvassed are unsatisfactory. The definition of ideological consciousness as being of directly social origin or as promoting some form of social order counts as 'ideological' consciousness that we would think of as anything but 'false', while if forms of consciousness are assessed solely in terms of their justifiability, then their ideological character may be missed. Is there an alternative? I believe that there is.

The solution, I suggest, is to try to combine both elements. A form of consciousness is *prima facie* reasonable if we can point to its having been formed by a good mechanism or procedure; potentially a form of false consciousness if it results from a defective one. Our ordinary mechanisms of belief formation – sense-perception and inference – are (it may be thought) reasonable ones, and so a belief may be counted as reasonable, even if it is false and unreflectively formed, in virtue of having been obtained as a result of such a process. Thus we would have a definition of ideological false consciousness as follows:

3 *Ideological consciousness is consciousness that benefits some social entity or structure and has been formed according to a poor mechanism.*

Although this definition deals with the problem of unreflective beliefs and cases such as the belief that is true-but-ideological, it is not comprehensive. In the first place, there is a (deliberate) element of circularity: a mechanism or procedure for the formation of consciousness is poor *because* it leads to 'false' consciousness. The definition does not specify independently what makes that form of consciousness poor or deficient.

Secondly, it includes within the definition of ideological false consciousness beliefs that benefit a particular social order but that are formed for what one might call reasons of general irrationality – that is, they are *not* 'produced' by special features of the social order that they benefit or (which is a stronger form of this requirement) *because* they benefit that order. Thus, as Jon Elster has pointed out in many writings, 'adaptive preference formation' (the idea that human beings adapt their desires to what they perceive to be available to them) is a mechanism which will, in general, produce compliance with existing social orders. But, rather than being an instance of the ideological formation of consciousness, such mechanisms provide a competing explanation to the theory of ideology, Elster argues. We shall discuss a number of theories involving such mechanisms in the next chapter.

One way of drawing the line between such cases would be to strengthen the requirement that ideological consciousness must be social in origin even further so that, in order to be ideological, a form of consciousness must not only benefit a social order but must have come about or persist because it benefits the social order in question.[22] Thus:

4 *Ideological consciousness is (i) consciousness that benefits some social entity or structure and has been formed according to a poor mechanism and (ii) comes about or persists because of the fact that it benefits the entity or structure in question.*

In that case, the form of consciousness would not only be *functional for* the social order but it would (in G. A. Cohen's terms) be *functionally explained by* its relation to that social order.

Adapted and strengthened in this way, this account has a good deal to recommend it. The vulgar economist, for example, would be someone who formed beliefs by looking only at the surface of things. At the same time, there would have to be some social explanation for this deficiency of method, some reason other than a sheer failure of rationality. However, while the definition is clearly a sufficient condition for ideological consciousness, it excludes a class of cases that seem to fall within, rather than outside, the scope of a theory of ideology. Such cases would have the following structure:

i A form of consciousness results from a poor mechanism.

ii It benefits a particular social order.

iii It is *specific to* that social order (it may be taken to result from features that are specific to that social order).[23]

But:

iv It does not exist *because* it benefits that social order.

In other words, the form of consciousness is explained in relation to the social order but not by the benefit that it brings to that order.

---

[22] This is to reiterate the point made earlier about origins: a phenomenon may be social in origin if it has come about randomly but is selected for reasons that are social.

[23] It is not just *contingently* restricted to that particular social order, as a matter of historical accident (in the way that the Ragusan Republic was destroyed by an earthquake), but in a way that is explanatorily related to its specific features. There is something about (say) capitalism that leads to this particular form of consciousness.

Nor is this simply a philosopher's counterexample. In fact, a great deal of thought about false consciousness can be interpreted in this way. Rousseau, for example, sees the domination of human beings by *amour-propre* as characteristic of life in modern society – and as a fundamental cause of the deplorable fact that modern men have lost their desire for freedom. But there is in Rousseau no trace of the 'fully functionalist' idea that the reason why this form of false consciousness obtains is *in order that* modern society should be able to maintain itself. It just so happens to be the case that modern society produces that kind of consciousness – although the fact that it does helps to explain why it survives.

IV Is All Ideological Consciousness Irrational?

So far, the assumption has been made that ideological false consciousness is in all cases a form of *irrationality*. While this assumption has the advantage of making it clear that ideological consciousness is not necessarily false, the identification of false consciousness with irrationality – even on the thin definition of the latter – is too narrow. Irrationality in general represents a failure of competence on the part of the individual: to say of someone that they formed a belief for bad reasons is to suggest that it was – or ought to have been – within their power to form it for better reasons. But there are defects in consciousness that do not consist in failures of rationality in this sense. For example, if someone is *deceived* then the fact that they believe something that is untrue (and, quite possibly, very much against their interests) is nevertheless not a failure of rationality on their part. Although some forms of ideological false consciousness are irrational, it should not be assumed that all will be.[24] Thus the characteristic defect of ideological false consciousness may be that it is formed according to a (remediably) poor mechanism, but it may also lie in the circumstances under which the consciousness is formed, for example, or in the nature of the subject-matter that is being dealt with.[25]

[24] An alternative might seem to be to extend the notion of rationality to include values and norms. Thus, for Jürgen Habermas, deception would be a violation of rationality to the extent that deception violates the implicit norm of truthfulness in communication. However, what is irrational in this case is not the individual who is deceived but the institution that is the source of the deception, and this distinction ought to be kept clear. It seems artificial to describe as *irrational* forms of consciousness that have been formed for what are, by the standards of what is available to the agent in the circumstances, perfectly good reasons.

[25] This distinction seems more helpful than the one proposed by Jon Elster. Elster suggests a distinction between 'cold' and 'hot' forms of deception, depending on whether we refer belief formation back to 'failures in the cognitive processing system' or to 'some motivational or affective drive' (*Making Sense of Marx*, p. 466).

In very many cases, the distinction between the cognitive and the affective is not a clear one. Consider the following example. On Elster's view, is the fact that I drive badly because I am worried about my mother's health a 'hot' or a 'cold' disorder? Since it involves a failure in what Elster calls the 'cognitive processing system', it should be cold. On the other hand, worry is clearly affective.

We can easily take this further. Imagine that I drive badly because my mother is in the

From the point of view of the theory of ideology, three forms of not-irrational false consciousness are particularly significant.

1 *Perspectival consciousness*

If it is true, as some of the authors of the Frankfurt School have maintained, that all our judgements are formed through a matrix or veil of concepts, then it follows that such consciousness may be said to be false consciousness without being *irrational*. It is not open to the individual to change their concepts, so perspectival consciousness is not in any sense a remediable deficiency on the part of the individual. What makes such consciousness *false* is its partiality.

2 *Deceptive objects*

Just as we would not say that someone who failed to recognize figures in the distance or to pick out voices in a crowded room was *irrational* in failing to perceive accurately, so it may be that the person under the sway of ideology is someone who finds themselves trying to judge rationally under unfavourable circumstances. This idea is not, however, so far as I know, an idea of any consequence for the theory of ideology. To the extent that the idea that those in the grip of ideology judge reasonably under unfavourable circumstances appears it does so in conjunction with a more radical idea: that ideology comes about because the object to be known is itself deceptive.

To say of something that is independent of a subject that it has, objectively, a property (deceptiveness) that makes essential reference to the quality of the subject's experience may seem to be metaphysically problematic – and the fact that the idea of society as a characteristically deceptive object makes its appearance in the theory of ideology under the auspices of Hegelian thought will do little to counteract that impression. But, in fact, the notion is in no way peculiar or questionable. The natural world abounds with examples of 'Batesian mimicry' – fish that look poisonous, insects that look like leaves, plants that look like insects, and so on. Of course, in each case, the deceptiveness is deceptiveness directed at a particular group of perceivers (in general, potential predators or prey), but deceptiveness is part of the repertoire of objective properties that must

---

passenger seat, telling me about her visit to the doctor. Is that 'hot' or 'cold'? We might think that it is 'hot' if the reason is that I lose concentration because I am upset. But what if I am *distracted* rather than *upset* by her talking to me? Does it become 'cold' again?

To avoid losing ourselves in such trivialities a better general distinction is that between misjudgements whose origins lie in remediable deficiencies (whether 'affective' or 'cognitive') on the part of the judging subject and misjudgements that are, in some way, objectively rooted outside the subject.

be referred to in order to give explanations of the phenomena in question (the orchid flourishes *because* it has evolved to look like an insect, or whatever). If the object that it perceives is inherently deceptive, the perceiver may be short-sighted (the butterfly should have been more cautious about that innocent-looking twig) but is not to be counted as cognitively deficient or irrational.[26]

3 *Defective objects*

A *deceptive* object is one that seems to be what it is not. A *defective* object, on the other hand, is one that is not as it ought to be. Again, the idea of defectiveness need not be in any way metaphysically problematic. Examples abound: sick animals, broken watches, leaking roofs, etc., etc. Defectiveness and deceptiveness may be subtly intertwined: one aspect of the defectiveness of the object may be just that it (deceptively) appears *not* to be defective. Consider, for example, a political party that consistently fails to get its message across. But the party, let us say, is so structured that its members listen primarily to each other: it is they alone who read the party newspaper, applaud each other's speeches, etc. In other words, there is no mechanism by which the members of the party can come to perceive their lack of success and this is a reason why it remains so unsuccessful. Here it is a consequence of the defectiveness of the organization – its inward-lookingness – that it hides its defects from its members.[27]

For Marxism, the conjunction of defectiveness and deceptiveness is of overwhelming importance. The alienated individual, living a fragmented and inadequately expressed life, may think of himself as an isolated, passive subject – quite accurately. But that does not mean that there is not also false consciousness. Passive, isolated subjectivity may be said to be false because individuals who live that way are leading lives that are false – lacking in identity, perhaps. Furthermore, it is also false to the extent that it goes together with the thought that this way of being is *not* deficient, that it is a normal, acceptable way of being. The language in which Marxists have chosen to express these ideas – talk of consciousness as

---

[26] There may be border-line cases where opinions divide as to whether it is a matter of the deceptiveness of the object or a deficiency on the part of the judge. There is a famous story told about Wittgenstein. 'Why', he asked his interlocutor (Norman Malcolm), 'did people think that the sun went round the earth?' 'I suppose', replied Malcolm, 'because it looked that way.' To which Wittgenstein countered: 'But how would it have looked if it were different?' The remark, brilliant though it is, ignores the fact that it is reasonable to judge things on the basis of an extension of experience elsewhere. Our experience of relative motion suggests that a single object changing its spatial relations to all other perceptible objects when all other objects maintain their relations to one another is in motion. That this is *wrong* in the case of the sun doesn't mean that it is wrong to say that it looked that way.

[27] The importance of 'perverse' phenomena of this kind in politics and society has been brilliantly explored by Albert O. Hirschman in *Exit, Voice and Loyalty*.

being 'true and false', and so on – may seem wilfully confusing. But the claim that society is both defective and deceptive is not in any way paradoxical (although whether it is true is, of course, another question again). Marx returns to this idea, as we shall see, in his treatment of the fetishism of commodities. Fetishism, on Marx's account, is both an objectively rooted illusion – a response to the deceptive nature of capitalist reality – and an accurate registration of the fact that, under capitalism, the 'collective labourer' has become divided and individualized. Fetishism is a *false perception* of a *false reality*.

V Is All Ideological Consciousness 'False'?

So far, then, following Adorno's description of ideology as 'necessary false consciousness', we have an order of sub-division as follows. Ideological false consciousness is divided between false consciousness that is and false consciousness that is not irrational (in the sense of being part of a remediable deficiency on the part of the individual). Within those divisions we have further divisions between those forms of false consciousness that are cognitive (and so can be, in the narrowest sense, true or false) and those that are not. This division is appropriate, for the central intuition behind the theory of ideology is that of society maintaining itself through false consciousness. Nevertheless, one very prominent idea regarding the mechanism of ideology does not embody the idea of ideological consciousness as something false. This is the idea (as in the famous analogy in *The German Ideology*) that ideological consciousness *reflects*, *echoes* or is in some other way *expressive* of a particular society or aspect of society.

The fact that societies express themselves in a characteristic form of consciousness may be a characteristic that is beneficial to the societies in question without itself being a form of false consciousness. But it may also be *part* of an account of false consciousness. This may be because the representation in question is in some way distorted or misleading (Marx's famous metaphor of ideology as a representation of the world 'upside-down') or because of the way in which the representation – though accurate in itself – is understood. Thus, if it is not appreciated that the representation *is* a reflection of existing society, then the qualities it has in virtue of being a reflection may be falsely believed to be intrinsic to it.

The thought that men's gods resemble them (that, as Montesquieu reports it, 'if triangles were to worship a God, it would have three sides')[28] might serve as an example. Let us say that it is intrinsically arbitrary how men conceive their gods, but that religion becomes more acceptable to human beings to the extent that the gods depicted in it resemble themselves. In that case, the fact that a religion expresses social reality

---

[28] The *topos* goes back to Xenophanes.

would be a feature that was functional for it, on the condition that the adherents of the religion should believe that the resemblance is a fact about the intrinsic nature of the gods (and not a product of the fact that the religion is an expression of social reality). It is this belief about the expression rather than the expression itself that makes the phenomenon as a whole one of false consciousness.[29]

It is worth mentioning at this point an approach to the theory of ideology that is quite widespread in contemporary writing: the idea that there is a close connection between the theory of ideology and what is known as *discourse analysis*. Discourse analysis is perhaps best understood as the successor to what was once called 'rhetoric'; roughly, it is the study of those wider aspects of communication that go beyond truth, falsehood and valid inference. Evidently, such a broad enterprise, if successful, could hardly fail to be of interest for the theory of ideology. Nevertheless, there are reasons to be cautious. Discourse analysis is primarily a matter of description – for instance, it identifies the type of narrative structure that we find in a work of literature. To be part of a theory of ideology, however, it would be necessary to show two further things, neither of which are part of discourse analysis as such. First, it would have to make plausible the claim that the presence of such a structure has particular, politically significant, effects. If, for instance, it can be shown that certain narratives typically show men as active agents and women as passive then this has effects in maintaining established structures of inequality only if such structures are treated by readers as normative, thus promoting a certain pattern of behaviour between men and women. Secondly, granting the first point, a connection must be established between those effects and the society that they help to maintain. The theory of ideology requires more than that effects that maintain the social system are simply accidental by-products of a particular form of discourse or the product of conscious intentions to deceive on the part of interested parties (in that case it would be *propaganda*, not ideology). This again is something that discourse analysis by itself cannot show.[30]

In conclusion, ideological 'false consciousness' may or may not be irrational, may or may not be cognitive and may or may not be false. What

---

[29] In the case of religion, knowledge that the resemblance is social in origin would undermine its force. But other cultural expressions might have the functional feature without false consciousness. Thus a particular style of music may appeal to a certain group *because* it is expressive of their home region (country music and Southern American whites, for instance) without knowledge of that connection undermining the force of the appeal – on the contrary, it reinforces it.

[30] For example, John B. Thompson writes in *Ideology and Modern Culture*: 'To interpret ideology is *to explicate the connection between the meaning mobilized by symbolic forms and the relations of domination which that meaning serves to establish and sustain*' (*Ideology and Modern Culture*, p. 293). Whatever this 'explication' (the outcome of discourse analysis, as I take it) might amount to, it presupposes (1) that we have established that the meaning explicated does, in fact, 'establish and sustain' relations of domination, and (2) that this fact is not merely coincidental or adventitious but is a response in some unconscious way to the 'needs' of the system. If 'explication' is all that a theory of ideology has to offer then it begs the question.

it must be is socially related, either because it is functionally explained by social circumstances or because it is causally related to them in some other way. It will be the task of the subsequent chapters to show how these formal possibilities were realized in the context of particular theories.

3

Rationalism and False Consciousness

This chapter deals with the history of false consciousness – not with all of it, of course, for false consciousness is a vast (although important and too little explored) subject. The material that I shall present has been selected with two aspects in mind: (1) to show, in general terms, how conceptions of false consciousness have changed, and (2) to present some of the different ways in which the connection between false consciousness and politics has been conceived.

Platonist rationalism and Augustinian pessimism, the theories with which I shall start, see human beings as caught in a conflict between two faculties, reason and desire. Both contain a fundamentally *akratic* conception of false consciousness: false consciousness consists in the failure of human beings to act in a self-directed way. Akratic false consciousness results from the fact that unreasonable or inappropriate desires exercise power over the self and this, in Plato's view, is itself the result of a cognitive deficiency: a failure of rationality. The connection between false consciousness and politics, in this case, comes as a consequence of the fact that the domination of human beings by sensuous appetites leads to tyrannous forms of society.

The treatise of the sixteenth-century humanist Étienne de la Boetie, *De la servitude volontaire*, raises Reich's question quite explicitly. Yet his answer to it is far from the modern theory of ideology. 'Voluntary servitude', for de la Boetie, is not something historically specific. It is either a result of conscious deception by the ruler or of a general failure of rationality on the part of those who are ruled.

In the seventeenth and eighteenth centuries we find the re-emergence of a view of reason as, fundamentally, 'passion's slave' – lacking on its own the power to initiate action. Nevertheless, the conception of false consciousness that is associated with this view is not importantly different from that of Platonic rationalism or Augustinian pessimism: false consciousness consists in the dominance of the stormy or destructive passions over the calm and reasonable ones – the 'interests'. Such undesirable desires and appetites make authoritarian political orders a necessity.

However, three genuinely new developments that took place in the seventeenth and eighteenth centuries are significant in representing moves towards a more political conception of false consciousness.

1 There is the thought that the fierce passions themselves may have unintended consequences: that they may be a necessary means by which humanity moves from a coercive to a cooperative political order. From this perspective, the passions are necessary and cannot be dismissed as forms of 'false consciousness' (although they may be undesirable, compared with the more civilized emotions that will replace them). What is significant about this new conception of the passions is that it brings together the idea that forms of consciousness change from one society to another with a conception of history as purposive (but not consciously intended) development.

2 The second important new element is the idea that a particular kind of desire – sociable desire – plays a central role in false consciousness. '*Amour-propre*', vanity, the desire for esteem are desires to be *seen* in a certain way. To the extent that such desires are judged to be deviant or reprehensible, they make the public realm central to false consciousness.

3 Finally, there is the belief that certain kinds of subject-matter (primarily, religion) are particularly prone to false consciousness and that they are a prime source of political disorder. As we shall see, Hume, in the eighteenth century, develops this idea and gives it a sophisticated epistemological underpinning. On Hume's analysis, forms of religious false consciousness both cause and *result from* political disorder.

Hume's theory is a paradigm of an *Enlightenment* critique of false consciousness. In his view, the misperceptions and false beliefs involved in 'enthusiasm', superstition or fetishism are simply illusions, without foundation in the objective order: the result of the intrusion of emotion into the formation of belief. They are not (as Romantics and Idealists would later come to believe) symbolic versions of higher truths or alienated forms of self-expression. Nevertheless, the emotions in question are themselves socially rooted. Thus rational criticism cannot be successful against such false consciousness unless it is also able to deal with the sources of the emotional disorders behind it.

I shall discuss both Rousseau and Adam Smith in detail, for their complex theories form an important link between such lines of thought and the theory of ideology itself.

Rousseau is important above all because of the explicit connection he makes between false consciousness and the maintenance of oppressive forms of political order. There are, moreover, three aspects of Rousseau's thought that make it distinctively modern and point the way to later developments.

1 Rousseau makes the idea of sociable desire specific to particular forms of society. His account of the pervasiveness of *amour-propre* sees it not simply as an eternal and irremediable characteristic of fallen humanity but as a result of the way in which in metropolitan, commercial society healthy *amour de soi* (natural self-interest) and the moral emotion of *pitié* (spontaneous fellow-feeling) have been suppressed in favour of private self-seeking.

2 Rousseau is the first author to raise the idea that in false consciousness the self itself may become 'lost' (that it suffers from a 'disorder of identity', as I termed it in the previous chapter).

3 Finally, Rousseau's account of false consciousness represents an early example of a critique of rationalism. Instead of seeing the remedy for false consciousness in an increase in the reflective power of the self, Rousseau looks for the roots of right action in the self's openness and responsiveness to the claims made upon it by others. Subjective reflection and the private use of the imagination isolate the individual, rather than emancipating it.

Adam Smith's ideas are in many ways the converse of Rousseau's. Like Rousseau, Smith gives sociable desire a central role in the understanding of the maintenance of political order, but he differs sharply from Rousseau in three important respects.

1 Smith does not regard sociable desire as a form of false consciousness. On the contrary. Although sociable desire is, from the point of view of the individual, non-rational, from the collective standpoint it is a thoroughly positive feature of society, one that mediates private self-seeking with the public good.

2 Similarly, although Smith, too, has an account of the psychological mechanisms by which the many consent to be ruled by the few, this is not, for him (as it is for Rousseau) just a matter of illegitimate authority being preserved by 'voluntary servitude'. For Smith, these mechanisms are, in general, beneficial, not oppressive.

3 Thirdly, Smith has a much more specific account of the connection between consciousness and society than Rousseau. Where Rousseau's treatment of history is speculative and at times fantastic, Smith (as we shall see in Chapter 4) integrates his account of consciousness within a historically detailed and economically sophisticated account of the operation of unintended consequences.

Putting these ideas together, the distance from these two authors to the theory of ideology is then very short indeed.

I Rationalism and Pessimism: Plato and Augustine

As we know from their literature and their religion, the Greeks were preoccupied with understanding those forces – 'fate' or 'destiny' – that permanently undermine and frustrate human rationality.[1] But, by the time of Socrates and Plato, a picture was emerging that emphasized the rational potential of human nature and it is this that has been the basis of the Greeks' legacy to our own thought about politics.[2]

Plato's *Republic*, of course, is the most resonant of all accounts of the connection between ignorance and political disorder. Plato gives his account of the role that ignorance plays in political life as part of a theory of human nature that has three central features. First, there is the connection between knowledge and the good. According to Plato, not only is the good knowable, but knowledge, not pleasure, is the highest good. It is the essential structure of reason that underlies the world. Second, there is the connection between knowledge and action. Knowledge of the good is not simply the registering of a fact towards which one can remain indifferent. To know the good is to be motivated by it and, although human beings differ considerably in their capacity for knowledge of the good (in effect, in their fundamental rationality), such knowledge is at least sufficiently possible for it to represent a serious ideal for human beings to aim at. Indeed, it should be made the fundamental object of education and politics. Finally, Plato draws a distinction between intellectual and sensual forms of pleasure. Indulgence in the lower pleasures – in particular the physical and erotic pleasures – he believes, is part of a spiral in which the need for them increases the more that they are met.

Plato describes vividly how false consciousness prevents men from even recognizing the kind of rule (and ruler) that they need. Present society, says Socrates, on Plato's behalf, is like the crew of a ship who not only do not know how to navigate themselves but are so ignorant that they cannot recognize the skills of a navigator for what they are when they come across them. That is why they denigrate the philosopher. For this reason, human beings are fated to live without proper government in one or another imperfect form of society. Plato identifies four kinds of imperfect society and character-type, linked to each other by a kind of logic of moral degeneration. Of these, the fourth, and worst, is *tyranny*.

Even in the best of us, Plato claims, our natures have a 'sleep' side of immoral desire, although this normally remains under control. The tyrannous character is the one who lives under the hegemony of such

---

[1] Described in E. R. Dodds, *The Greeks and the Irrational.*
[2] For all of its speculative elements (criticized with authority by Dodds) Nietzsche's *The Birth of Tragedy* remains the classic account of this process.

desires. His passions are set on a path of self-reinforcing excess, so that his personality comes to combine 'the characteristics of drunkenness, lust and madness' (573). Such characters are not able to sustain true friendship – the condition for a political society based on citizenship. They 'must always be either master or slave' (576).

This is Plato's answer to how it is that unjustly unequal societies come into being and maintain themselves: they do so because their members have become too corrupt to sustain any superior form of political life. What makes false consciousness political on this view are its *consequences*. Rather than a theory of ideology (for which false consciousness would be social in origin) it is irrationality that leads to tyranny. Irrationality perpetuates itself through the vicious circle of sensual self-indulgence.

The Republic thus embodies rationalism in the very fullest measure. It depicts a clear hierarchy between reason and desire and sees no virtue in indulgence in the latter – in fact, it is the prime source of evil. What is more, there *are* means available to promote the authority of reason over desire and those means are characteristically rational ones – the use of human beings' conscious powers of discursive reasoning themselves, not least.

Nietzsche's jibe that Christianity is Platonism for the people is at best one-sided. But it is certainly noteworthy how far the Christian debate develops within the framework of concepts and problems established by Plato. St Paul echoed Platonic language when he described the human condition in this life as one of looking 'through a glass darkly'. Like the Platonist, the Christian sees this world as just an echo or shadow of God's true reality. But what we must do to ascend to that reality is in this case quite different.

As monotheistic religions, neither Christianity nor Judaism need have any particular difficulty in finding common ground with that aspect of Greek philosophy that emphasizes the eternity and unity of the rational order. The Greek tradition – Platonism, Neo-Platonism, Aristotelianism, especially in the role of the last as a teleological philosophy of nature – incorporates the view of reality as embodied *logos*, as the differentiated expression of an overall rationality. Evil, on this view, can be understood as a necessary part of an order that is, ultimately, good. But the Judaeo-Christian deity is a personal deity who is held to be entirely benevolent. How, then, to account for evil? To say merely that there is an inevitable 'falling away' in the transition from the infinite to the finite, as neo-Platonism would have it, is not enough to do justice to the idea that creation is an expression of the benevolence of an all-powerful God.[3] For Augustinian Christianity, the answer lies in its central doctrine – man's

---

[3] This is the theme of Hans Blumenberg's magisterial *Die Legitimität der Neuzeit*. For Blumenberg, Western thought has been haunted by what he calls the 'threat of gnosticism' – the danger that evil will come to be seen as a principle in its own right and so undermine the avowed monotheism of our central religious tradition. For the Middle Ages, Boethius's *Consolations of Philosophy* provided an important way of mediating the Christian with the neo-Platonic tradition – the medievalist F. P. Pickering perceptively entitles one of his books *Augustinus oder Boethius*.

fall into sin and his redemption by the incarnation of the deity.[4] To be redeemed, however, is not to receive a deserved reward for one's efforts. On the contrary, in orthodox Christian doctrine, redemption is above all a matter of *grace*.

The way that this change of doctrine leads directly from Platonic rationalism to pessimistic anti-rationalism is apparent in the thought of St Augustine. Augustine accepted a great deal of Platonism (he concedes in the *City of God* that the Platonists 'approached the truth more nearly than other philosophers')[5] but in his account of knowledge and the will he consciously inverts the Platonic metaphor of the self-development of the individual by the light of reason. As he describes it in the *Confessions*: '. . . I did not know [before becoming a Christian] that the soul needs to be enlightened by light from outside itself, so that it can participate in truth, because it is not itself the nature of truth.'[6] Human beings, according to Augustine, cannot reach truth unaided. Nor are they able to control their passions, even to prevent themselves from acting in ways in which they do not want. In our fallen state, our bodies are motivated not by reason and the will, but by *lust*. So, fallen human beings are doubly removed from true goodness and suffer from 'false consciousness' in two ways. First, their desires are not those that a truly good being would have; but, secondly, there is an akratic gulf between desire and the capacity for action. In consequence, human beings are not even able to live their lives so as to realize those evil desires that they actually have:

> It was because man forsook God by pleasing himself that he was handed over to himself, and because he did not obey God he could not obey himself. Hence came the more obvious misery where man does not live as he wishes to live. If he lived as he wished, he would consider himself happy; yet even so he would not be really happy if he lived in degradation.[7]

Augustine recognizes how characteristically human it is to find oneself out of one's own control – gripped by an illicit passion we would much rather be rid of, or inhibited by fears and anxieties from doing what we know we could and should and desperately want to do, for example – and how feeble, in those circumstances, an appeal to our voluntary powers can be. The story of Augustine's friend Alypius, which Augustine relates at

---

[4] But the objections to both the idea of the Fall and the idea that evil is the price that must be paid for good are obvious. What should we think of a God who is held to be just and merciful who 'punishes' with natural evil (death and disease) not only the perpetrators of a crime – Adam and Eve – but their descendants? And what are we to make of the claim that God is omnipotent, if he is obliged to allow those evils into his creation with the justification that they are a necessary part of a greater good? As Hume remarks in the *Dialogues Concerning Natural Religion* (1776): 'Epicurus's old questions are yet unanswered. Is he willing to prevent evil, but not able? Then he is impotent. Is he able but not willing? Then he is malevolent. Is he both able and willing? Whence then is evil?' (p. 63).

[5] St Augustine, *City of God*, p. 580.
[6] St Augustine, *Confessions*, p. 68.
[7] St Augustine, *City of God*, p. 589.

one point in the *Confessions*, is one of the most vivid and poignant accounts of akratic false consciousness ever written:

[Alypius] arrived in Rome before I did to study law. There he had been seized by an incredible obsession for gladiatorial spectacles and to an unbelievable degree. He held such spectacles in aversion and detestation; but some of his friends and fellow-pupils on their way back from a dinner happened to meet him in the street and, despite his energetic refusal and resistance, used friendly violence to take him into the amphitheatre during the days of the cruel and murderous games. He said: "If you drag my body to that place and sit me down there, do not imagine that you can turn my mind and my eyes to those spectacles. I shall be as one not there, and so I shall overcome both you and the games." They heard him, but none the less took him with them, wanting perhaps to discover whether he could actually carry it off. When they arrived and had found seats where they could, the entire place seethed with monstrous delight in the cruelty. He kept his eyes shut and forbade his mind to think about such fearful evils. Would that he had blocked his ears as well! A man fell in combat. A great roar from the entire crowd struck him with such vehemence that he was overcome by curiosity. Supposing himself strong enough to despise whatever he saw and to conquer it, he opened his eyes. He was struck in the soul by a wound graver than the gladiator in his body, whose fall had caused the roar. The shouting entered by his ears and forced open his eyes. Thereby it was the means of wounding and striking to the ground a mind still more bold than strong, and the weaker for the reason that he presumed on himself when he ought to have relied on you. As soon as he saw the blood, he at once drank in savagery and did not turn away. His eyes were riveted. He imbibed madness. Without any awareness of what was happening to him, he found delight in the murderous contest and was inebriated by bloodthirsty pleasure. He was not now the person who had come in, but just one of the crowd which he had joined, and a true member of the group which had brought him. What should I add? He looked, he yelled, he was on fire, he took the madness home with him so that it urged him to return not only with those by whom he had originally been drawn there, but even more than them, taking others with him.[8]

Against this, the rationalism that has dominated Western moral philosophy seems shallow and unilluminating. It is not that rationalism fails to recognize the existence of a tension between human reason and what we actually do, but its assumptions about human nature – the idea that consciously guided rational action is itself the best remedy for the limitations of rationality – lead it to inadequate remedies. It emphasizes either (with Plato) argument and reflection, or else (with Aristotle) the role of habit and training – high-minded talks in the headmaster's study or cold showers and cross-country running.[9]

---

[8] St Augustine, *Confessions*, pp. 100–1.
[9] In this respect, the Aristotelian picture of human beings was not dramatically opposed to the Platonic: Aristotle, as much as Plato, depicts human beings as caught in a permanent struggle to overcome their affective side by means of their rational nature – a struggle to which they bring

The consequence to be drawn if we believe both that the good life is one lived in accordance with reason and that reason is not enough to control the passions is simple: the pessimistic view that human beings are not made for happiness, in this life at least. This is Augustine's position. He fully endorses the primacy of reason over the passions – his ideal individual is the one who has withdrawn so far as possible from sensible pleasures and holds those that he does indulge in firmly under the hegemony of the will. But, in contrast to rationalism, he does not make the assumption that what is higher in *value* is for that reason higher in *effective power* – that all we need to do is to counterpose calmly two rival claimants on our wills and the 'experienced observer' will inevitably gravitate towards the 'higher pleasures'.[10] In fact, the presumption is just to the contrary: the only thing that can save us from the perversity of our corporeal and appetitive nature in relation to our wills is the mysterious beneficence of divine grace.

From the point of view of politics, the consequences are clear. In the first place, no secular measures – education or civic order – will remedy the evils of human nature. So the best to be hoped for is a political regime that will, at least, hold destructiveness in check, by whatever means necessary. Politics is a distraction from what should be the Christian's true concern: the achievement of salvation. Thus, although false consciousness is pervasive in Augustine's theory, there is no specific problem of political false consciousness. If the many are ruled by the few, then this is not in any way especially deplorable but simply a manifestation of the inevitable corruption of life in this world.

II Political Humanism, Tyranny and Deception: De la Boetie and Machiavelli

Between them, the Platonic and the Augustinian conceptions of the relationship between reason and desire dominated thought about human nature in the West for more than a thousand years. Indeed, so far from being displaced by the upheavals of the Reformation and Counter-Reformation, the doctrine of Original Sin and the corresponding emphasis on the role of divine grace rather than the human will in redemption were actually revitalized in the ultra-Augustinian theology of early Protestantism.

The early modern picture of human cognition as perpetually prone to being 'blown off course' by passion – and the idea that reason must be

---

native endowments of varying amounts of discretionary power that they must try to increase. Aristotle, however, does give more emphasis to the role of custom and training in developing man's rational powers (although his conception of training is by no means behaviouristic and Plato, of course, did not wholly deny it any role) and he draws a distinction of principle (rather than merely one of degree) between practical reasoning and theoretical knowledge.

[10] The phrases are, of course, John Stuart Mill's.

provided with a sustaining foundation in 'affect' in order to become effective – is quite consonant with this kind of Augustinian pessimism. However, perhaps surprisingly, although the writings of authors such as Hobbes and Spinoza do indeed give a very bleak picture of the place of reason in the political domain, this idea of the dominance of the passions has little connection with the modern theory of ideology.[11] The reason lies in the very radicalism of the position. Since it is assumed that the susceptibility of human rational capacities to being nullified by the passions is a fixed fact about human nature, this is a form of false consciousness that is perennial, not historically variable, and, for that reason, not a possible object of political action. It was only with the growth of a more differentiated account of the passions that the way was opened to a view of consciousness as historically specific and, potentially, socially determined.

However, with the revival in Early Modern Europe of the study of pagan authors – particularly, the ancient historians – a new kind of political literature started to emerge, one whose roots lay more in the study of rhetoric than in theology and whose concerns were more practical and this-worldly than philosophical or edifying.[12] It was in this 'humanistic' context that a work was written that provides the first direct and extended treatment of the problem of false consciousness not as a failure of rationality with political consequences but from the point of view of its relationship to unjust and unequal political rule.

Étienne de la Boetie, the author of *De la servitude volontaire*, died young, in 1563, at the age of thirty-two. But, had he never written a word, his name would remain known to students of humanism as the friend of Montaigne, about whom Montaigne's great essay on friendship was written. *De la servitude volontaire* was apparently written in 1552 or 1553, during de la Boetie's time as a law student at the University of Orléans.

That the many are ruled by the few is, says de la Boetie, everywhere evident. The question that concerns him is why this should be so. Why, when the balance of force is so obviously on their side, do the mass of men submit even to the rule of tyrants?

> Shall we say that those who serve him are cowardly and faint-hearted? If two, if three, if four, do not defend themselves from the one, we might call

---

[11] A high proportion of the literature on ideology traces the idea to Bacon's doctrine of *idola*. This seems to me unjustified, however. It is true that Bacon is interested in questions having to do with deception and illusion, although he is by no means unique in this respect. He also asserts strongly that there is a connection between reason and affect: 'The human understanding resembles not a dry light, but admits a tincture of the will and passions which generate their own system accordingly, for man always believes more readily that which he prefers' (Bacon, *Novum Organon*, Sect. 49). Yet there is no suggestion in Bacon's writings that this is anything other than a permanent and invariable defect in human beings' formation of beliefs: it is not thought of as being specific to any particular kind of political order.

[12] Machiavelli is, of course, the name that springs to mind immediately. But, as Quentin Skinner, among others, has shown, Machiavelli, however original and distinctive a turn he may have given to certain themes, can best be seen as adopting and transforming motifs and concerns that were coming to the fore in Renaissance humanism much more widely.

that circumstance surprising but nevertheless conceivable. In such a case one might be justified in suspecting a lack of courage. But if a hundred, if a thousand endure the caprice of a single man, should we not rather say that they lack not the courage but the desire to rise against him, and that such an attitude indicates indifference rather than cowardice?[13]

In stating this question so plainly, de la Boetie articulates (for the first time to my knowledge) the central problem that was to motivate the theory of ideology that I have called Reich's question. But, although his problem is formally the same as that of later authors, the answers he provides come from a different world of thought about politics. In particular, there is no trace whatsoever in the essay of a dynamic conception of history and society, of forces other than the will of individuals or the inertial power of habit and custom that might determine the way men come to think and act in relation to the political order.

In the course of his essay, de la Boetie points to three kinds of factor that lead to the maintenance of unequal political orders. First, there is the force of custom and habituation. Unused to freedom, those who are born, as de la Boetie says, 'under the yoke' do not struggle for what they have never known. Enslaved people lose their energy and courage and they become 'degraded, submissive and incapable of any great deed'.[14]

Second, tyrants augment these effects by trading on the gullibility of their subjects. De la Boetie continues:

> It is indeed the nature of the populace, whose density is always greater in the cities, to be suspicious toward one who has their welfare at heart, and gullible toward one who fools them. Do not imagine that there is any bird more easily caught by decoy, nor any fish sooner fixed on the hook by wormy bait, than are all these poor fools neatly tricked into servitude by the slightest feather passed, so to speak, before their mouths. Truly it is a marvellous thing that they let themselves be caught so quickly at the slightest tickling of their fancy. Plays, farces, spectacles, gladiators, strange beasts, medals, pictures, and other such opiates, these were for ancient peoples the bait toward slavery, the price of their liberty, the instruments of tyranny.[15]

Thirdly, de la Boetie draws attention to the fact that tyrants surround themselves with close associates who become directly dependent upon them; that these associates in turn have their own dependents, and so on. Whereas the first two factors maintaining tyrannical rule relate to the limitations of human rationality – human beings' susceptibility to the inertial force of custom and their gullibility – this third factor alters the circumstances under which even rational prudential calculations are made.

There are in fact two possibilities here, although de la Boetie does not

[13] *De la servitude volontaire*, p. 48.
[14] Ibid., p. 68.
[15] Ibid., pp. 69–70.

distinguish between them. First, it may be that those closest to the tyrant benefit from his rule to such an extent that it is actually in their interests for it to continue. In this case, appearances to the contrary, the tyrant does not rule alone and the servitude of others is, to that extent, involuntary.

The other and more significant possibility, however, is that, even though it may be in the interests of those closest to the tyrant for him to be overthrown, the fact that they suffer and benefit to different degrees and in different ways makes it more difficult for them to coordinate the collective action necessary for his overthrow – in modern terms, that they face the 'prisoners' dilemma'.[16]

None of de la Boetie's three answers identifies any forms or sources of irrationality that were not fully available to earlier writers. The idea that we are habituated by custom to certain patterns of life and that, never having experienced something, we do not feel its lack, is the most trivial commonplace. Think, for example, of Plato's parable of the Cave – of how the majority of men, living in the world of shadows, could not recognize the true forms even were they to encounter them. Nor is the idea that tyrants seek to divert their subjects by 'bread and circuses' in any way a new idea. It might be argued that de la Boetie's analysis of the relationship between the tyrant and those who surround him is something novel – certainly, his treatment of it is original and perceptive – but ancient writers, especially those who wrote about the later Roman emperors, were well aware of its importance, even if they did not treat it in such detail. Furthermore, de la Boetie's predecessor, Machiavelli, had dealt repeatedly with this theme, both in *The Prince* and in the *Discourses*.

The whole of Machiavelli's enterprise is governed by the study of what men *believe* and its effects in the political world. 'Men in general', he writes, 'are as much affected by what a thing appears to be as by what it is, indeed they are frequently influenced more by appearances than by the reality.'[17] Machiavelli is concerned, too, with the particular way in which, in politics, things do not turn out as agents intend. He was clear that the kinds of causal interactions that take place in the political realm, mediated as they are through interlocking networks of expectation and belief, show different kinds of predictability (and, equally importantly, different kinds of unpredictability) from what we would expect in the physical realm.

Thus it is unsurprising that Machiavelli should be extremely interested in (and notoriously cold-eyed about) the use of deceit in politics and he has some illuminating remarks to make on the subject. For example, he notes in the *Discourses* that one of the things that makes men most susceptible to deception is the way in which their own passions lead them to neglect a wider for a narrower perspective:

---

[16] This aspect of the problem of resistance is expressed in a famous joke. Khrushchev is delivering his 'secret speech' cataloguing Stalin's crimes to the XXth Party Congress when a voice shouts from the hall 'So why did you do nothing?' Khrushchev stops, furious. 'Who said that?', he roars. There is dead silence. 'Well now you know', says Khrushchev and continues.

[17] Machiavelli, *Discourses*, I, 25.

For men, as King Ferdinand used to say, resemble certain small birds of prey in whom so strong is the desire to catch the prey which nature invites them to pursue that they do not notice another and a greater bird of prey which hovers over them ready to pounce and kill.[18]

Yet, vivid though this simile is, the thought behind it goes little beyond the commonplace and, overall, Machiavelli contributed little new to the understanding of the ways in which *de facto* authority is maintained. Nevertheless, the kind of 'civic humanist' discourse represented by Machiavelli or, in his own way, de la Boetie, does form an important background to the theory of ideology by opening up the idea that the political domain is something to be dealt with in its own right, not as an expression or application of theology or moral philosophy.

III The Changing Passions

In the course of the seventeenth and eighteenth centuries the Augustinian picture of human beings as cut off from God's goodness was more and more displaced by an understanding of the world as an expression of divine benevolence. One particularly significant aspect of this change was its extension to the passions themselves. The idea is that, although the passions may be bad – destructive and inimical to reason – when taken in isolation, it is possible that they can be seen to play a positive role when evaluated in a broader context. Increasingly, that context came to be thought of as being given from the perspective of the historical development of humanity: forms of consciousness change through history as part of a process in which apparent evil is the means by which a greater good is brought about.

The idea is of evident importance for the background to the theory of ideology. It informs eighteenth-century views regarding the contrast between rational and non-rational forms of religious belief (an issue which will be discussed later in this chapter) as well as providing a path of continuity connecting ideas about Providence with the emergence of those conceptions of society as an organism or developing system, which will be the subject of the next chapter.

This re-evaluation of the passions involves a distinction within the domain of the emotions themselves between those that are held to be basically destructive and those that, potentially at least, are conducive to civil order and happiness. In consequence, the picture of 'false consciousness' that emerges is more complex than the rationalist opposition between reason and desire – a triangle rather than a simple polarity. Turbulent emotions – the passions in the full modern sense – are opposed not just by reason, thought of as the cognitive faculty, but also by another kind of

[18] Ibid., I, 40

more desirable (or, at least, less undesirable) desire: the 'interests'.[19] As human beings move from one stage to another, so, it is hoped, the disruptive and primitive passions will come to be replaced by the more stable, orderly and predictable interests that are the characteristic motivating forces behind civilized human beings.

The transition from the fierce and primitive passions to a world of calm and stable emotions is a stage on the way towards an 'Age of Reason', in which human beings could properly be left to take charge of themselves – an example of God's benevolence expressing itself as a process of historical fulfilment. To follow Turgot, for instance, it is just in moving human beings from earlier to later stages that the turbulent, apparently destructive, passions have their vindication:

> Men who are taught by experience become more and more humane; and it would appear that in recent times generosity, the virtues, and the tender affections, which are continually spreading, at any rate in Europe, are diminishing the domination of vengeance and national hatreds. But before laws had framed manners, these odious passions were still necessary for the defence of individuals and peoples. They were, so to speak, the leading-strings with which nature and its Author guided the human race in its infancy.[20]

Fortunately, there are several excellent treatments of this theme in the literature,[21] but I should like to make three general points here.

1 It is clear that, if we view the passions as leading to some further, greater good, then what we are dealing with is in a sense just the opposite of the Marxist conception of ideology. Instead of agents engaging in (apparently) good or rational conduct that then leads to unwanted (and unforeseen) bad effects, apparently bad things are on this view held to produce a greater good. What is common to both cases, however, is that there is a discrepancy between what agents immediately perceive and what, from a more complete perspective, turns out to be the true significance of their actions. Thus there is good reason to describe each as a kind of 'false consciousness': what was thought (wrongly) to be good turns out to be bad in the one case, while what was thought (wrongly) to be bad is seen to be actually good in the other.

2 An important further issue concerns which desires and emotions are to

---

[19] To refer back to the classification introduced in the previous chapter, the primary kind of false consciousness at work here is a false consciousness regarding the relationship between desires. The passions, in setting their force against interests, undermine otherwise desirable desires. It is worth noting that just this argument – the idea that 'ideological' politics are passionate and disruptive while modern politics are secular, and interest-driven and safely apathetic – was taken up again by American political science in the 1950s.

[20] A. Turgot, 'On Universal History', pp. 70–1.

[21] See especially A. Hirschman, *The Passions and the Interests*, and A. O. Lovejoy, *Reflections on Human Nature*. R. Meek's *Social Science and the Ignoble Savage* is another invaluable source.

be counted as part of human beings' positive 'interests' and which are thought of as undesirable and destructive. It is notable that the seventeenth and eighteenth centuries saw a radical polarization between those for whom the public aspects of the self – its desire to be seen in a certain way by others – is the bond by which virtue and order in society can be peacefully maintained (the force that ensures that, in Pope's phrase, 'self-love and social be the same') and those for whom it is the epitome of alienation and inauthenticity.

3 Finally, this view of the self, although very different from the ancient ones, deserves to be called 'rationalist' just as much as they do – if not even more so. The feature celebrated by those who traced the rise of the 'calm passions' was their prudential quality: their availability to voluntary control and conscious direction, whether by the agents themselves or by others. There is no suggestion that anything valuable is lost by the transition from a world dominated by fierce, unpredictable and mutually incompatible appetites to one in which the desires are stable and can be fulfilled in ways that are, to a considerable degree, self-reinforcing.

IV *Amour-propre*

When, in the seventeenth century, we find the first beginnings of a conception of human desire that was to make a fundamental contribution to thought about political false consciousness, the context in which it appears is neither that of the 'civic humanist' discourse represented by Machiavelli and de la Boetie nor the optimistic and developmental view of the passions just discussed, but the classic Augustinian (in this case, Jansenist) view of the passions as a mark of the inevitable corruption of fallen mankind.

What this conception involved was the identification (and radical condemnation) of a specifically public set of desires, desires that relate to the perception of individuals by others and that are characteristically exercised in the public realm. Its basic ideas came to expression in a concept that plays a central role in the writings of the seventeenth-century writers, Pascal and La Rochefoucauld: *amour-propre*.[22] *Amour-propre* – it can be translated as 'vanity' or 'self-love' – is a distinctive kind of emotional attitude. First of all, it is not merely *selfishness*, the willingness to place one's own needs or desires above those of others. Although vanity is self-centred, one may be very selfish without being in any way vain. Part of the significance of *amour-propre* is that it is initially a social desire, a desire to be seen in a certain way by others, and to be seen in this way not for instrumental reasons (as one individual might want to be seen as honest by another if they wished to persuade them to engage in an economic

[22] Although they emphasize different aspects, Pascal and La Rochefoucauld are sufficiently agreed about the nature of *amour-propre* to make it reasonable to discuss their views together here.

transaction) but as something valued for its own sake. Pride and its complement shame – the pleasure we take (or the pain that we feel) in being seen as worthy or unworthy – are also non-instrumental desires involving others' approval or disapproval.[23] *Amour-propre* is more complicated, however. *Amour-propre* drives human beings because they want to be seen in a certain way without reference to any underlying reality, unlike pride, in which we need to believe as well that the judgement implicit in the way in which we are seen is justified (we could not take pride in something that we knew was not our own achievement, even if other people believed that it was and admired us for it). What is more, *amour-propre* extends from the way that others see us to the way that we see ourselves: 'We are so used to disguising ourselves from others that we end by disguising ourselves from ourselves.'[24] We may, as a result, act in certain ways out of the belief that we are acting disinterestedly, when, in fact, it is our *amour-propre* that we are really seeking to satisfy. According to La Rochefoucauld, *amour-propre* is best taken not as a first-order desire that can be seen in isolation but as a second-order one: a kind of Protean animating force that sets other desires in motion.[25] In particular, it gives rise to other desires that are apparently (perhaps even to those who have them) desires for their own sake.[26]

Nevertheless, although *amour-propre* engenders other desires, it is not itself completely unmotivated. Rather it results from (is a response to) the most fundamental features of the human condition: its misery and impotence in the face of death:

> Imagine a number of men in chains, all under sentence of death, some of whom are each day butchered in the sight of the others; those remaining see their own condition in that of their fellows, and looking at each other with grief and despair await their turn. That is an image of the human condition.[27]

In this situation, according to Pascal, the only truly rational response would be to turn to religion. But this is not what human beings do. On the contrary:

> Being unable to cure death, wretchedness and ignorance, men have decided, in order to be happy, not to think about such things.[28]

---

[23] Dodds takes the view that Greek culture is primarily a 'shame' culture (in which human beings' perceptions of their own worthiness and unworthiness are fundamentally a result of the way in which they are seen publicly) as opposed to a 'guilt' culture, in which worthiness and unworthiness are a private matter for the individual (or the individual and his God).

[24] *Maxims*, No. 119.

[25] 'The passions are merely the various whims of *amour-propre*.' *Maxims*, No. 531.

[26] 'Interest speaks all manner of tongues and plays all manner of parts, even that of disinterestedness.' *Maxims*, No. 39.

[27] *Pensées*, No. 434.

[28] *Pensées*, No. 133.

This is where *amour-propre* has its function: in providing us with an image of ourselves according to which we are as others see us, we can believe (falsely) that we are truly happy and, in seeking to correspond to that image, we gain an absorbing object of activity that in its turn distracts us from reflection on the inherent misery of our situation. Thus the search for distraction is not to be condemned entirely, however vain and foolish its apparent objects, since it does at least represent a partially adequate response to a genuine problem:

> Thus men who are conscious of what they are shun nothing so much as rest; they would do anything to be disturbed. It is wrong then to blame them; they are not wrong to want excitement – if they only wanted it for the sake of diversion. The trouble is that they want it as though, once they had the things they seek, they could not fail to be truly happy. That is what justifies calling their search a vain one. All this shows that neither the critics nor the criticized understand man's true nature.[29]

Amour-propre, then, is a response to human wretchedness (the point emphasized by Pascal) and itself a form of wretchedness (La Rochefoucauld's central point). It is a form of false consciousness in three ways.

1 Human beings mistake *amour-propre* for that which is truly good: religious redemption from sin, ignorance, misery and death.

2 Human beings fail to recognize that what motivates them is, in fact, *amour-propre*, believing, for example, that what they in fact pursue to satisfy *amour-propre* are things that they desire for their own sakes.

3 Finally, the kinds of desire that *amour-propre* leads to are, typically, insatiable (the desire for wealth, the desire for glory, and so on). Moreover, if those who are led by *amour-propre* to pursue a particular objective *do* happen to obtain it, then they discover that it does not satisfy them. That (according to Pascal) is precisely the point of the objects of *amour-propre*. We do not really want what we take it that we want for its own sake. What we want is the distraction – the absorption of our energies – that comes from *thinking* that we want it and pursuing it.

V Religious False Consciousness

It is well known that the 'Young Hegelian' critique of religion played a seminal role in the development of Marxism. What is less often appreciated is how far earlier criticism of religion had gone in preparing the ground for the theory of ideological false consciousness.

Initially, this critique was not the full-scale rejection of all religion that

---

[29] *Pensées*, No. 136.

we find, for example, in the writings of Feuerbach or David Friedrich Strauss, but attempts at a critical diagnosis of what were held to be deviant forms of it.[30] For enlightened authors in the Christian societies of the seventeenth and eighteenth centuries, these were of two main kinds. First, there were the non-Christian religions – polytheistic ones in particular. Christian writers had from the beginning been forced to engage with the dominant paganism of the classical world. In the early modern period, however, this was supplemented by the need to give accounts of the increasing number of polytheistic religions encountered in the course of the European expansion.[31]

In addition, many writers sought to identify and criticize deviant forms of the Christian religion itself. Protestant writers were, naturally enough, concerned to identify what they took to be the deformation of Christianity in Roman Catholicism. In general, Catholicism was rejected for its idolatry, superstition and the submission it required to priestly authority. To this (especially after the experiences of the English Civil War) was added a concern with those – Protestant sects for the most part – who claimed the authority of direct divine revelation for their religious beliefs and practices: the *enthusiasts*.[32]

What these endeavours had in common was that they represented the beginning of a *naturalistic* account of religious illusion. There were many such explanations in the ancient world. The gods were the products of emotions – fear (Democritus and Epicurus) or gratitude (Proclus); they were the conscious inventions of political cunning (Critias); they were exaggerations – apotheoses of past heroes and rulers (Euhemerus); or else they were allegories – of virtue and vice, in particular (Plato and the Stoics).[33] For the early Church, however, non-Christian religion was not merely an indifferent phenomenon, susceptible to natural explanation: it was blasphemy, to be explained in the context of the grand struggle

---

[30] Of course, there *were* explicit atheists in the eighteenth century, La Mettrie and Holbach, for example. But their thinking was, in general, less fruitful for the theory of ideology than those who attempted to develop a more differentiated view of religion.

[31] Unlike Judaism and Islam (which could be accounted for as deviant forms – rejections – of revealed religion) the paganism encountered outside Europe and the Mediterranean world appeared to represent the spontaneous religion of man cut off from the special redemptive grace of the Judaeo-Christian historical process.

[32] The name 'enthusiasm' was applied initially to those 'God-possessed' Protestants, the Anabaptists (known in German as *Schwärmer*). According to the *Oxford English Dictionary*, the word appears first in English in 1579, with no pejorative sense but meaning direct, divine possession. The *OED* illustration of the pejorative connection between *enthusiasm* and extreme Protestantism comes from Hickman's history of 1674 (surely too late). The enthusiasts were repressed by their fellow-Protestants with furious savagery. Although Martin Luther himself had justified his actions in rebelling against Rome and breaking his monastic vows on the ground that he had received a divine summons, by the seventeenth century, in the opinion of the sociologist, Kai Erikson, 'no item stood higher on the Puritan list of heresies than the claim that God revealed himself directly to men' (*Wayward Puritans*, p. 98).

[33] It is notable, however, that, while there were those who regarded religious phenomena as a form of spontaneous illusion and others who connected the gods to political life (as in Plato's 'Noble Myth'), the explanation of religion as a form of spontaneous political deception does not, so far as I know, play any part in ancient thought on the subject.

between God and Satan. Thus, for orthodox Christianity until the Renaissance, the pagan gods were embodiments of evil: demons or fallen angels. The emerging tendency in the seventeenth and eighteenth centuries to view enthusiasm, superstition, primitive religion and related phenomena from the point of view of what Frank Manuel has called 'psychopathology'[34] represented, then, a very considerable departure, one that fitted in particularly neatly, of course, with the idea of the course of civilization as a progress from turbulent to calm passions.[35]

The idea that deviant religion was principally a matter of medical, not theological or philosophical, concern can already be found in that source of so much that is characteristic of seventeenth-century English thought, Burton's *Anatomy of Melancholy* (1621).[36] Hobbes, too, mentions enthusiasm in Chapter 8 of the *Leviathan* ('Of Man') as a species of madness. Similarly, the Anglican theologian, Meric Casaubon published *A Treatise concerning Enthusiasm* (1655) with the subtitle: *As it is an effect of nature: but is mistaken by many for either Divine Inspiration, or Diabolical Possession.*

Casaubon's subtitle is significant. To represent enthusiasm as a medical or psychological problem is, of course, to disqualify it from a legitimate hearing in the sphere of reasonable debate, and, to that extent, constitutes an intolerant response. But, in the seventeenth-century context, this must be set against the kind of savage repression traditionally practised by Christians against those whom they considered to be heretics and blasphemers. That advocates of the medical approach to enthusiasm were well aware of the contrast between their attitude and the fiercer forms of clerical reaction is made clear in the 'Epistle to the Reader' of Henry More's *Enthusiasmus Triumphatus* (1656). More presents an ironic dialogue between a first-person interlocutor and the author:

> I asked him if it seemed not something maimed in the enumeration of the *Causes* of *Enthusiasme*, because there is nothing set down there concerning the Devil, nor the *wilfull wickednesse of the mind* of man; but all is resolved into *Complexion* or the present Temper or Distemper of the body, arising from natural causes that necessarily act thereupon. For thus this Discourse, said I, may seem as well an *Excuse for*, as *Discovery of* this disease of *Enthusiasme*. Why, said *Mastix*, I hope it is not your designe, I am sure it is not mine, to incense the mindes of any against *Enthusiasts* as to persecute them: all that I am at, is only this, that no man may follow them.[37]

Although Casaubon does undertake a typology of different forms of enthusiasm – divinatory, contemplative and philosophical, rhetorical, poetical and precatory – neither he nor any of his contemporaries goes far

---

[34] F. Manuel, *The Eighteenth Century Confronts the Gods*, Ch. 3, Section III, 'A Psychopathology of Enthusiasm'.
[35] See particularly R. Meek, *Social Science and the Ignoble Savage*.
[36] Part III, p. 341.
[37] Henry More, *Enthusiasmus Triumphatus* [Unpaginated].

towards offering a causal hypothesis regarding its origins. It is only at the beginning of the eighteenth century that writers on deviant religion begin to move towards a differentiated psychological account of the phenomenon.

A short work of this kind is Trenchard's *Natural History of Superstition* (1709), which, according to Frank Manuel, Hume himself probably perused (certainly the title is close enough to Hume's own *Natural History of Religion*). The *Natural History of Superstition* is an essay, as Manuel puts it, of 'Deism militant'.[38] Trenchard diagnoses enthusiasm as due to a blockage of communication with the real world,[39] when 'the Organs of Sense (which are the Avenues and Doors to let in external objects) are shut up'.[40] The natural connection between the mind and the world thus being dislocated, there is a compensatory stimulation of the imaginative faculties.

Trenchard's theory suggests that deviant mental phenomena result from the individual being deprived of the natural and necessary amount of sensory stimulation. A similarly structured but opposite view is to be found in Shaftesbury, who locates the origin of such phenomena in the need to vent 'certain humours':

> There are certain humours in mankind which of necessity must have vent. The human mind and body are both of them naturally subject to commotions: and as there are strange ferments in the blood, which in many bodies occasion of extraordinary discharge; so in reason, too, there are heterogeneous particles which must be thrown off by fermentation.[41]

Trenchard and Shaftesbury are examples of an account of pathology that sees it as the result of a kind of hydraulic imbalance – an excess of pressure requiring discharge or a vacuum to be filled. These are, however, more in the nature of speculative models implicit in their writing than anything by way of well-developed theory. Nevertheless, there is one eighteenth-century author who presents a comprehensive account of superstition, enthusiasm and primitive religion as part of a general theory of belief and action: Hume.[42]

It is often assumed that Hume's scepticism commits him to the view 'that belief is not only natural, but also essentially irrational.'[43] If this were so, then there would be no vantage point from which a theory of the role of belief in *false* consciousness could consistently be developed. But, in

---

[38] Manuel, *The Eighteenth Century Confronts the Gods*, p. 72.
[39] An idea, according to Manuel, that he takes from Bayle.
[40] Quoted, Manuel, *The Eighteenth Century Confronts the Gods*, p. 76.
[41] Shaftesbury, *Characteristics of Men and Manners*, I, 12, quoted in Manuel, *The Eighteenth Century Confronts the Gods*, p. 76.
[42] Hume's account is plainly indebted to Bayle, but its detail and sophistication are of a far higher order.
[43] Such, according to David Fate Norton, is the interpretation of 'Kemp Smith and his followers', *David Hume: Common-Sense Moralist, Sceptical Metaphysician*, p. 16, although this seems to me an ungenerous view of Kemp Smith (see N. Kemp Smith, *The Philosophy of David Hume*).

fact, Hume does have a theory of rational belief, both in the sense of an account of the kinds of belief which it is reasonable to hold and of the procedures and processes (that is to say, voluntary and involuntary factors) which favour the formation of such beliefs. Although Hume does not give an account which explains us as forming beliefs for rational reasons alone – that is what his naturalism denies – this does not mean that beliefs are arbitrary.[44]

That the subject of irrational belief does not simply fall by the wayside for Hume becomes apparent when *The Natural History of Religion* (1757) and the earlier essay, 'Of Enthusiasm and Superstition' are read in the light of the theory of association developed in the *Treatise of Human Nature*. The *Treatise*'s simple (some would say, simplistic) mechanism of association allows Hume to develop (1) a naturalistic account of error (2) an account of the interaction of belief and emotion in the genesis of false belief, and, finally, (3) in outline at least, an account of the connection between false belief and social circumstances.

The origin of enthusiasm and superstition, according to Hume, lies in the intrusion onto the formation of our beliefs of our hopes and fears (respectively). The beliefs which are formed in this way are not sheer hallucinations, however. The imaginative mechanism in operation corresponds rather to what would, in modern terms, be called a theory of *projection*.

'There is', writes Hume:

> an universal tendency among mankind to conceive all beings like themselves, and to transfer to every object, those qualities, with which they are familiarly acquainted, and of which they are intimately conscious. We find human faces in the moon, armies in the clouds; and by a natural propensity, if not corrected by experience and reflection, ascribe malice or good-will to every thing, that hurts or pleases us.[45]

Let us examine this passage from the point of view of the theory of association. According to Hume, although ideas are associated by resemblance, contiguity and causation, impressions are associated solely by the principle of resemblance, and so, presumably, it is resemblance that initially moves us to identify the impression of a certain 'figure' (say, the shape which corresponds to the shape of a human face) with what it commonly resembles, namely, the idea of a face.

The error in this is one of interpretation: to believe that whatever *looks like* a face *is* a face (in the sense of conforming to whatever empirical laws govern faces). A more refined judgement, based on causality, will enable us to amend our classification so that we judge that what we see is a face-

---

[44] An excellent discussion relevant to this topic with some very interesting material regarding Hume's views about pathological mental states (his own psychosomatic illnesses included) is to be found in Chapter 5 of John P. Wright, *The Sceptical Realism of David Hume*.
[45] *The Natural History of Religion*, p. 29.

shaped heavenly body, conforming to the laws governing heavenly bodies, not the face of some person in the sky. On this view, then, error lies in endorsing the immediate consequences of the principle of association, rationality in the revision of immediate generalizations in the light of more extensive and systematic data. Since this process is indefinite, the difference between truth and error becomes one of degree.

In this way, Hume provides his answer to the objection that, on his view, belief is not only natural but 'essentially irrational'. He considers a version of this objection in Book I of the *Treatise*. The objector, as Hume describes him, takes him to be committed, in consequence of his view that 'all reasonings are nothing but the effects of custom', to the belief that 'our judgement and imagination can never be contrary, and that custom cannot operate on the latter faculty after such a manner, as to render it opposite to the former' – in other words, that experience and habit can never be misleading because that, in the end, is all that knowledge itself amounts to.[46]

But we can, and *ought* (Hume's word) to regulate our judgements about cause and effect by means of 'general rules' – rules which enable us to separate 'accidental circumstances from the efficacious causes':

> The following of general rules is a very unphilosophical species of probability; and yet 'tis only by following them that we can correct this, and all other unphilosophical probabilities.[47]

So far, then, Hume's account of irrational belief forms practically a caricature of an Enlightenment theory of progress. Irrationality is a matter of jumping to hasty conclusions through ignorance. What dispels illusion is the steady accumulation (and organization) of evidence given to the senses. But why on this account, one might ask, should mankind be subject to the particular delusion that all beings are like themselves? And where do the emotions – hope and fear – come in? In answering these questions it becomes apparent that Hume's theory is a good deal more sophisticated than it at first sight appears.

The Natural History of Religion suggests two answers, one, as it were, negative and the other positive, to the question of why we personify nature. The first is, indeed, a consequence of ignorance: it comes from our attempt not simply to find causes for events, but to make those causes intelligible to ourselves. Hume's own account of the ultimate explanation of reality is a characteristically 'disenchanted' and materialist one:

> Could men anatomize nature, according to the most probable, at least the most intelligible philosophy, they would find, that these causes are nothing

---

[46] Ibid., p. 29.
[47] *Treatise*, p. 150. It seldom seems to have been noticed that the word 'philosophical' has an important technical meaning for Hume. It does not mean 'pertaining to philosophy' but something much more like 'rational' or 'sustainable by reason'.

but the particular fabric and structure of the minute parts of their own
bodies and of external objects; and that, by a regular and constant machinery,
all the events are produced about which they are so much concerned.[48]

But, lacking such a view of the world, the 'ignorant multitude' employ
their imaginations in forming some 'particular and distinct idea' of the
unknown causes which govern their lives – indeed, philosophers themselves are hardly exempt from such illusions.[49]

The positive answer complements this: men are led to form beliefs
about the causes governing the natural world not from purely speculative
motives but because of the effect – both fortunate and unfortunate – which
the natural world has on their lives. In that case, we can see the following
association: what is pleasurable has something benevolent as its source, what
is painful something ill-disposed. The resemblance lies not so much at the
purely perceptual level (the cloud is taken to be an army because it looks like
an army) as at the level of causal generalization (a man hurts me because
he wishes me harm; a stone hurts me so it must wish me harm too).

Primitive religion, says Hume, is for this reason naturally polytheistic.
Human beings are led to religion not from speculative investigation into
the order of nature but by the desire for immediate answers to the
questions that concern them, and these are likely to be unusual events.
Thus they look for the particular causes of exceptional phenomena rather
than asking themselves for comprehensive explanations of what is truly
remarkable: the 'beautiful connexion . . . and rigid observance of established rules'.[50]

But it is the account he gives of the interaction between emotion and
belief which takes Hume's account beyond the naive picture of the gradual
accumulation of enlightenment. In outline, the theory is exceptionally
simple:

1 For an idea to be believed is for it to have a 'force and vivacity' by which
it approaches that of an impression. That, as Hume always insisted (to
the despair of his commentators), is all that belief amounts to.[51]

2 When we are in the grip of a passion our feelings are thereby aroused.

3 This emotion transfers itself – leaches over, as it were – to any idea
which happens to be present, thus increasing its force and increasing
the propensity to belief beyond what it would otherwise be.

Hume illustrates what he has in mind in the *Treatise* with respect to the
emotion of fear (the source of superstition), but what he says could equally
apply to the overoptimistic emotions of the enthusiast:

[48] *The Natural History of Religion*, p. 29.
[49] Ibid.
[50] Ibid., p. 42.
[51] *Treatise*, p. 119.

... a person of sorrowful and melancholy disposition is very credulous of every thing that nourishes his prevailing passion. When any affecting object is presented, it gives the alarm, and excites immediately a degree of its proper passion; especially in persons who are naturally inclined to that passion. This emotion passes by an easy transition to the imagination; and diffusing itself over our idea of the affecting object, makes us form that idea with greater force and vivacity and consequently assent to it . . .[52]

On the face of it, this account appears to be viciously circular: the 'affecting object' excites its 'proper passion' in the fearful person and leads them to believe in its presence. But, presumably, the fearful person is one who mistakes as fear-inspiring things which need not be fear-inspiring at all. In which case, the passion is improper, not proper, as Hume supposes – it would hardly be a sign of timorousness to be frightened by the real existence of a charging lion.

But, if we allow that there is a kind of immediate supposition on the part of the perceiver, the circle does not have to be a vicious one. The process might be something like this: I hear a creaking on the stairs late at night. I think that it *might* be a burglar. If I am timorous, then this excites my fear and the fear itself reacts back on the idea to produce belief. Emotion converts ideas which we might *entertain* into ones we believe.

The relationship between belief and passions runs in both directions, Hume argues: belief, being more intense than a mere fancy, is better able to arouse the passions and, hence, to motivate us to action:

... the ideas of those objects, which we believe either are or will be existent, produce in a lesser degree the same effect with those impressions which are immediately present to the senses and perception.[53]

What is more (though Hume does not explain exactly how), belief can counteract the passions: 'despair has almost the same effect upon us as enjoyment, and . . . we are no sooner acquainted with the impossibility of satisfying any desire, than the desire itself vanishes'.[54]

Knowledge can thus, to some extent, counteract superstitious or enthusiastic irrationality. Writers on Hume's epistemology seldom fail to mention the role of everyday life in counteracting the corrosive force of philosophical scepticism, but the role of theoretical knowledge as a remedy for delusion is also important to Hume. Hume would not be Hume, however, if he were so sanguine as to believe that knowledge was enough to dispel all our irrational beliefs. He represents the limitations of the remedies open to us with typically Humean irony:

[52] Ibid., p. 120.
[53] Ibid., p. 119.
[54] Ibid., p. xxii.

To oppose the torrent of scholastic religion by such feeble means as these, that *it is impossible for the same thing to be and not to be*, that *the whole is greater than a part*, that *two and three make five*; is pretending to stop the ocean with a bullrush. Will you set up profane reason against sacred mystery? No punishment is great enough for your impiety. And the same fires which were kindled for heretics, will serve also for the destruction of philosophers.[55]

In counteracting irrational belief, though knowledge may be of some help, it is to its emotional origins that we should chiefly look. In principle, according to the theory of association, the source of irrational belief could be in any emotion: *all* passions make one credulous. But Hume has particular reasons to single out hope and fear as the sources of enthusiasm and superstition.

Hope and fear, Hume says, arise when circumstances which would give us joy or grief are only probable and uncertain. Uncertainty is a kind of oscillation between conflicting views, none of which we can settle on: we move *between* joy and sorrow as we momentarily judge the event true or false. In this way, the passions do not cancel each other out but (since they have the same object), Hume claims, synthesize to produce a third whose 'agitating' power is particularly intense. It is this oscillation which gives hope and fear their particular psychological power when it comes to upsetting the reasonable processes of judgement.

The connection between ignorance and irrational belief, then, is by no means as direct and simplistic as it appeared at first sight. Ignorance leads to uncertainty, uncertainty leads to hope and fear, hope and fear intensify the ideas produced by the imagination and so lead to credulity:

In proportion as any man's course of life is governed by accident, we always find, that he encreases in superstition; as may particularly be observed of gamesters and sailors, who, though, of all mankind least capable of serious reflection, abound in most frivolous and superstitious apprehensions ... All human life, especially before the institution of order and good government, being subject to fortuitous accidents; it is natural, that superstition should prevail every where in barbarous ages, and put men on the most earnest enquiry concerning those invisible powers, who dispose of their happiness or misery.[56]

So it is apparent that Hume's position is some way from the complacent picture of a steady 'march of mind' from error to reason. Knowledge, of course, will diminish uncertainty. But not all knowledge is equal in this respect: it is knowledge of those causes which affect our central concerns – our health or our happiness – not abstract knowledge of natural laws for their own sake, which will have most effect in diminishing the kinds of uncertainty that lead to superstition and enthusiasm.

[55] *The Natural History of Religion*, p. 54.
[56] Ibid., p. 30.

What is more, the sources of uncertainty are not purely intellectual: uncertainty can have objective origins in the lives people lead as well as subjective ones in their ignorance of the state of the world. It has often been noted how far stability and predictability are central political values for Hume (so much so that Hume's phrase in the passage quoted about the establishment of 'order and good government' is practically a tautology).[57] But if, as I have argued, Hume sees uncertainty as such a potent force in generating irrational belief, then the value of stability is underpinned by a kind of double argument: stability is good both in itself and as a way of avoiding unleashing the irrational side of human nature – which, of course, has as the consequence that stability is undermined, and so the whole process becomes self-amplifying.

In summary, circumstances, social ones in particular, lead to emotion, and emotion leads to excessive credulity in judgement – an unwillingness to amend immediate judgement in the light of reflection. The characteristic error of immediate judgement is to explain by resemblance and this leads to a kind of 'category mistake': the assumption that natural phenomena that are hurtful (or pleasurable) to us have malice or benevolence as their origin, as they would do if we encountered them in our dealings with other human beings. Hence the 'universal tendency among mankind to conceive all beings like themselves'.

From the point of view of the structure of its explanation, Hume's theory is exemplary. Hume does not draw a sharp line between rationality and irrationality but makes the difference one of the degree to which we subject our judgement to 'general rules'. That we judge without proper reflection may be the result of simple ignorance, the lack of the calm spirit of enquiry that would lead us to try to penetrate the surface appearance of phenomena to look for underlying causes, or else it may be because of the particular emotions, hope and fear, that lead to an increase in credulity. Thus 'false' consciousness can be understood as the result of deviant forms of the same processes that lead us to 'correct' or 'reasonable' beliefs, while at the same time they are shown to be distinct from the 'ordinary error' of everyday false beliefs.

Hume has considerable right to be seen as one of the progenitors of the modern theory of ideology: in particular, his account of projection can be seen as the earliest example of a theory of *fetishism*. There is also, if

---

[57] Duncan Forbes has dealt quite conclusively with this supposed 'conservatism' of Hume's thought:

> ... it is not "conservatism" but the sceptical Whiggism involved in the philosophical approach to politics which gives Hume's thought its unity and continuity. Scientific Whiggism was sceptical because it questioned the value and holiness of the holy cows of the Whigs: the justification of the Revolution ... the contrast between English liberty and French "slavery"; the "ancient constitution" of the common lawyers and Commons' apologists in the seventeenth century and later modifications; the wickedness of the Stuart kings ... It is hardly surprising that this sort of thing appeared in the eyes of a good Whig like Horace Walpole, as "Toryism", or worse. (*Hume's Philosophical Politics*, p. 139)

Manuel is correct, a historical connection. The general use of the term 'fetishism' to refer to animistic religious beliefs comes from Hume's French contemporary Charles de Brosses's *Du culte des dieux fétiches* (the source for Marx's famous concept of the 'fetishism of commodities'). De Brosses was directly inspired by Hume.[58] De Brosses, however, consciously offers no specific explanation of fetishism at all:

> These and similar facts prove with final clarity, that, as the religion of African negroes and other barbarians now appears, so once did that of the ancient peoples, and that at all times and in all places on earth this immediate cult ruled, dedicated formlessly to animal and vegetable creation. It is sufficient to have established this fact by a multitude of proofs. It is not necessary to give explanations of a subject where none exists: and I believe that it would be quite useless to seek for explanations other than the fear and insanity of which the human mind is capable, and the ease with which, from such pre-dispositions, it is capable of generating all forms of superstition. Fetishism belongs to those things so absurd that it can be said of them that they cannot be touched by the argument that would combat them. How much more difficult would it be to offer plausible grounds for so senseless a doctrine! Yet the impossibility of adorning it before reasonable eyes in no way diminishes the certainty of the fact itself, and it would be to carry historical Pyrrhonism beyond all limits were one to deny the reality of this simple and immediate cult in Egypt and among the Negroes.[59]

Both Hume and de Brosses can be seen as giving an *Enlightenment* account of fetishism. Fetishism is a false belief or attitude in which a non-physical property is attributed falsely to a natural thing. For Hume, unlike de Brosses, there are *reasons* for this false belief: a sophisticated account of the connection between social circumstances and emotion that places the (presumed) irrationality of primitive religions, enthusiasm and superstition in the context of a general account of the mechanisms of belief formation.[60] But the processes lying behind fetishism and similar religious illusions do not justify such beliefs; they serve simply to explain them. In contrast to the Idealist theory of *Schein* (to be discussed in chapters 5, 6 and 7) there is no suggestion that the perception of this property in the object is the result of a really existing agency or process whose true significance is not fully appreciated. For Hume and de Brosses, fetishism is simply an illusion, to be dispelled if at all possible.

Hume's theory is a clear example of the way in which in the eighteenth century conceptions of false consciousness were coming to be connected more closely to the problem of political order – not seen simply as invariant

---

[58] *The Eighteenth Century Confronts the Gods*, p. 187. In fact, the book includes a long direct quotation from *The Natural History of Religion* that de Brosses was too cautious to attribute to Hume by name.

[59] C. de Brosses, *Du culte des dieux fétiches*, pp. 182–3.

[60] Hume's argument, connecting as it does political instability with irrationality via a naturalist epistemology, seems to me to be an exceptionally important contribution to political theory – it is quite scandalous that it should have been explored so little by writers on Hume's politics.

features of human nature whose political consequences have to be taken into account. But Hume's is not a theory of ideology in the sense at issue in this book, for, although false consciousness is both a cause and an effect of political instability, there is no suggestion of any kind of functional or systematic relationship between consciousness and social order.

VI Rousseau: *Amour-propre* and False Consciousness

If Voltaire was (as Roland Barthes perceptively called him) the 'last happy writer', there is a sense in which Rousseau was the first of the unhappy ones.[61] Not, of course, that there had been no writers before him who had been miserable, or made unhappiness their subject (or, indeed, that Rousseau was always unhappy). But, for Rousseau, not only was unhappiness the most pervasive feature of contemporary political life, he was arguably the first author to deal with that political unhappiness in a personal way. Rousseau wrote about politics and society not – or not just – as a detached observer calmly surveying the panorama of history, but as an engaged participant. If he felt himself to be wretched and acted in ways that failed to measure up to his own best intentions, then this, he believed, was symptomatic of the way in which men in his society were in general deformed: 'Society must be studied in the individual and the individual in society'[62] was his maxim.

Although Rousseau believed that his own life had social significance, this was not for either of the two most obvious reasons. He did not take himself to represent a moral ideal or to be superior to the mass of mankind; nor did he think that he was simply the same as them. As he says at the beginning of the *Confessions*, ' . . . I am made unlike any one I have ever met; I will venture to say that I am like no one in the whole world. I may be no better, but at least I am different.' Rousseau regarded himself as unique – like everybody else. He is perhaps the first writer on politics who must be read in the characteristically modernist way: in whose writings – quite deliberately – what is *revealed* is as important as what is *stated*. His writing operates on the principle that, as Theodor Adorno put it, 'the splinter in your eye is the best magnifying glass'.[63] It is the phenomenon of false consciousness (to which he does not assume himself to be immune) that connects the self-absorbed autobiographer and the political philosopher.

In the *Social Contract*, Rousseau makes it clear how indispensable he regards the phenomenon of uncoerced compliance to the understanding of political order. 'The strongest is never strong enough always to be master, unless he transforms his force into right and obedience into duty', he

---

[61] *Critical Essays*, p. 83.
[62] *Émile*, p. 197.
[63] *Minima Moralia*, p. 57. The subtitle of *Minima Moralia* is 'from a damaged life'.

writes.[64] Rousseau sees that this compliance can be of two kinds: legitimate authority (to identify the conditions for which is the purpose of the *Social Contract*) and that kind of voluntary servitude that is preserved by the false consciousness of the citizens: 'Slaves lose everything in their chains, including the desire to quit them; they love their servitude as the companions of Ulysses loved their bestiality.'[65]

The concept of *amour-propre* is the central element in Rousseau's account of false consciousness. Compared to that of the *moralistes* of the seventeenth century, Rousseau's account of *amour-propre* is both more political and more historical. For Pascal, *amour-propre* is (to put it in Heideggerian language) a *fleeing* from the – to us – unacceptable consequences of Original Sin.[66] Rousseau, however, does not believe in the intrinsic evil of the natural world. On the contrary, it is man who is the source of evil – and this not because (as Augustine would have it) man shares in the corruption of fallen nature but because of the abuse of human freedom.[67] Both the origins of *amour-propre* and its consequences are, in Rousseau's view, social: it arises subsequent to (and it is not to be confused with) *amour de soi* (the simple desire for one's own welfare) which is characteristic of human beings in the state of nature. Moreover, *amour-propre* is – however pessimistic Rousseau is regarding the prospects of this in practice – remediable:

> *Amour-propre* is only a relative sentiment, factitious [*factice*] and social in origin, that leads every individual to give greater weight to himself than to any other, that inspires in men all the evils that they do to one another and which is the true source of *honour*.
>
> Having regard to this, I maintain that, in our primitive state, in the true state of nature, *amour-propre* does not exist. For, each particular man regarding himself as the only spectator observing him, as the only being in the universe who takes an interest in him, as the only judge of his own merit, it is not possible that a sentiment that has its source in comparisons that he is not capable of making could grow in his soul; for the same reason, this man could not have hate or the desire for vengeance, passions that can only be born from the idea of some received offence; and, as it is respectlessness or the intention to harm, and not the evil itself, that constitutes the offence, men who cannot value or compare themselves can do each other a great deal

[64] *Du contrat social*, Bk I, Ch. 3, p. 44.
[65] Ibid., Bk I, Ch. 2, p. 43.
[66] The parallel between Heidegger's account of 'ontological false consciousness' and Pascal is unmissable – and certainly more than accidental. Heidegger identifies *fleeing* as a 'turning-away' from the ontological anxiety (*Angst*) of Being-in-the-world in favour of a concern with worldly, 'ontical' concerns: 'Thus the turning away of falling is not a fleeing that is founded upon a fear of entities within-the-world. Fleeing that is so grounded is still less a character of this turning-away, when what this turning-away does is precisely to *turn thither* towards entities within-the-world by absorbing itself in them. *The turning-away of falling is grounded rather in anxiety, which in turn is what first makes fear possible*' (M. Heidegger, *Being and Time*, p. 230).
[67] 'I do not see where we can look for the source of moral evil except in man, a free, improved, yet corrupted creature.' 'Letter to Voltaire on Optimism, 18 August 1756', in *The Indispensable Rousseau*, ed. J. H. Mason, p. 113.

of mutual violence when some advantage comes to them from it, without ever offending one another.[68]

The picture of the human being in the state of nature left by this famous passage is of an innocent selfishness – a war of all against all, although one conducted without malice or rancour. But Rousseau goes beyond this. For there is also a natural virtue, *pitié* (sympathy), that moderates even primitive selfishness and brings human beings together spontaneously and unreflectively:

> But there is another principle [beyond private selfishness] that Hobbes did not notice at all and which, having been given to man to soften in certain circumstances his *amour-propre* (or the desire to preserve himself, prior to the birth of this form of love) tempers the ardour that he has for his own welfare with an innate repugnance for seeing those who are like him suffer. I do not think that I need fear contradiction in attributing to man the sole natural virtue that the most extreme detractor of human virtues would be forced to recognize. I am speaking of *pitié*, a disposition appropriate to creatures so feeble and subject to so many ills as ourselves; a virtue all the more universal and all the more useful to men for preceding in them the use of any reflection, and so natural that even the beasts at times show visible signs of it.[69]

Pitié is, then, the most fundamental moral emotion. It is more than just a passive reaction to the perception of suffering. *Pitié* is both a feeling and a motivation to action: individuals who feel *pitié* act morally, not because they *judge* that it is moral to act in that way, but out of regard for what are, in the end, their own feelings. *Amour de soi, amour-propre* and *pitié* thus form a triangle. As *amour-propre* develops, it has consequences both for the way in which the self views itself and for the way in which individuals treat each other.

Rousseau gives two accounts of the growth of *amour-propre*, the one in the context of the development of the species, the other in relation to the individual. In each case, he sees *amour-propre* as a phenomenon that, once initiated, comes to take over and dominate society and the individual, as a disease comes to dominate a body after the initial infection has taken hold.

In the case of society, *amour-propre* is released by the development of inequality. With the establishment of private property, Rousseau argues, individuals first come to have regard for themselves and so the first of the *sociable emotions*, pride, is born. As agriculture and metalwork are developed, so human beings' natural inequalities become the basis for (and are reinforced by) the social inequalities of industry and the division of labour. It is at this point that *amour-propre* truly comes to dominate and human beings are led into a fatal division between being and appearing:

---

[68] *Discours sur l'origine de l'inégalité*, p. 196n.
[69] Ibid., pp. 196–7.

To be and to appear became two entirely different things, and from this difference there emerged imposing splendour, deceptive trickery and all the vices that they carry in their train. On the other side, as free and independent as man was before, now we see him made subject, as one might say, to a multitude of novel needs – to all of nature and above all to his fellows, whose slave he becomes in one sense, even in becoming their master.[70]

As in Plato's view of sensible desires, the desires that come from *amour-propre* are insatiable, but in this case they are, above all, *sociable*: desires to be seen in a certain way. This is the true cause of the differences between human beings in their 'savage' and 'civilized' states. While the savage lives 'within himself', the 'sociable man, always outside himself, can only come to life in the opinion of others' and thus becomes dependent upon others: 'it is, as one might say, from their judgement alone that he draws the feeling of his own existence.'[71] In other words, lacking a true, independent identity, civilized man adopts a false identity that he draws from others.

The false desires of civilized man are thus social as well as physical. The social element is added to our basic appetites with the result that even that which would otherwise be good and natural comes to be corrupted. The increase of appetite, in turn, brings with it a pernicious stimulation of passion, so that the dominant characteristic of civilized man is restlessness and anxiety. For man in society, says Rousseau:

> ... the less natural and pressing his needs, the more his passions increase and, what is worse, the power to satisfy them; with the result that, after a long course of prosperity, having swallowed up quantities of treasure and ruined many men, my hero will end up slaughtering everyone until he is the sole master of the universe.[72]

Although such desires are redundant from the point of view of natural, uncorrupted man, once man lives in society, they are not something that can be adopted or discarded at will. The society that lives under the auspices of *amour-propre* is one in which each individual does not merely *desire* the opinion of others (and, hence, is led to strive for those goods – luxury and status – that bring opinion with them) but *needs* it. Thus Rousseau is contemptuous of the contemporary argument that society is in some way benevolently held together by a harmonious balance of interests.[73]

A society may indeed be 'held together' by *amour-propre* up to a certain point, but its cohesion is brittle and artificial. It is a cohesion based on inequality and corruption. Corrupt men who are motivated by *amour-propre* are more easily ruled than independent citizens; but it is their own

---

[70] Ibid., pp. 216–17.
[71] Ibid., p. 234.
[72] Ibid., p. 173n.
[73] Ibid., p. 173n.

volatile ambitions and desire for domination that make them susceptible to domination in their turn:

> Moreover, the citizens do not let themselves be oppressed except insofar as they are carried by a blind ambition and, looking more below than above themselves, domination becomes more dear to them than their independence, and they consent to wear chains in order to be able to impose them themselves.[74]

The social union based on interest in this way is precarious, but it is forced on contemporary society because it has undermined the proper source of mutual engagement and egalitarian solidarity: *pitié*:

> ... commiseration will be all the more powerful, the more intimately the observing animal identifies itself with the suffering animal. Now it is evident that this identification must have been infinitely more close in the state of nature than in the state of reasoning. It is reason that engenders *amour-propre*, and it is reflection that strengthens it; it is reason that turns man back upon himself; it is reason that separates him from everything that disturbs or afflicts him; it is philosophy that isolates him; through it he says, secretly, to the image of a suffering man: 'Perish if you will, I am secure.' Only the dangers that threaten society as a whole trouble the tranquil sleep of the philosopher and draw him from his bed.[75]

Rousseau believes that it is always in the interests (narrowly understood) of the unjust to break any kind of compact or covenant that is based on arguments of rational self-advancement. It is only when, through *pitié*, morality has a firm foundation in affect – the welfare of others has become part of our own interests – that we can claim that 'Self-love and Social' are 'the same'.[76]

Amour-propre, for Rousseau, has a double aspect: it is at one and the same time a *turning-outwards* – a socialization of desire that makes individuals become dependent for their sense of themselves and their own worth on how others see them – and a *turning-inwards* – a process involving the increasing isolation and privatization of the self and its ends and feelings; and this double aspect directly inverts the combination of individual self-preservation and spontaneous engagement for the well-

---

[74] Ibid., p. 229.
[75] Ibid., p. 198.
[76] The wicked man takes advantage both of the uprightness of the just and of his own injustice; he will gladly have everybody just but himself. This bargain, whatever you may say, is not greatly to the advantage of the just. But if the enthusiasm of an overflowing heart identifies me with my fellow-creature, if I feel, so to speak, that I will not let him suffer lest I should suffer too, I care for him because I care for myself, and the reason of the precept is found in nature herself, which inspires me with the desire for my own welfare wherever I may be. From this I conclude that it is false to say that the precepts of natural law are based on reason only; they have a firmer and more solid foundation. The love of others, springing from *amour de soi* is the source of human justice. (*Émile*, pp. 196–7n).

being of others that Rousseau takes to be characteristic of *amour de soi* and *pitié*.[77]

Rousseau, like Plato, does not believe that increasing our discretionary power to satisfy desires is good for that reason alone. On the contrary, he thinks that many – in civilized society, almost all – desires are bad. Unlike Plato, however, Rousseau believes that the insatiable desires that threaten human rationality, are social, rather than natural: the other-directed 'sociable' desires arising from *amour-propre* weaken the individual's sense of self and capacity for independent action.[78] Moreover, such desires are very frequently self-multiplying (as we indulge our appetite for luxury or for exercising domination, so that appetite increases) and incapable of mutually consistent satisfaction (while we can all *desire* to be master of others, it is not possible that we can all actually *be* master of others). Finally, the desires that flow from *amour-propre* have a fundamentally

---

[77] A recent book by N. J. Dent has presented a completely different view of the relationship between *amour de soi* and *amour-propre* from the one argued for here.

According to Dent, *amour-propre* expresses 'the need to come to be to yourself, and for others, a "human presence"'. Thus '*amour-propre* may be benign, creative, humanly essential, not to be censured or displaced' (*Rousseau*, p. 24).

Dent's interpretation is based on a number of passages in *Émile* in which, he argues, *amour-propre* is presented favourably.

I cannot review all of these texts, but it is worth quoting *in extenso* Dent's presentation of the central passage that he cites in support of his interpretation (Dent's references are to the Bloom translation of *Émile* and to the Pléiade edition of Rousseau's works):

> Not doubtful is the passage at E 4, 235 (IV, 523) where Rousseau is considering 'the point where *amour de soi* turns into *amour-propre* and where begin to arise all the passions that depend on this one'. (Which point this is, and why it is so significant will be explained.) Rousseau goes on:
>
>> But to decide whether among these passions [which are those that arise from and depend on *amour-propre*] the dominant ones in his [Émile's] character will be humane or gentle or cruel and malignant, whether they will be passions of beneficence and commiseration or of envy and covetousness, we must know what position he will feel he has among men, and what kinds of obstacles he may believe he has to overcome to reach the position he wants to occupy.
>
> If this is read with attention, we see that Rousseau is claiming that such passions as cruelty, malice, envy and covetousness are *not* inherent to or necessarily attendant upon *amour-propre*. According to Rousseau, the 'secondary' passions (which arise from and depend upon *amour-propre*) may *quite as well* be humanity, gentleness, benevolence and compassion instead. (*Rousseau*, p. 24)

This is a complete misinterpretation. Take the first sentence that Dent cites. The French reads as follows: 'Voilà le point où l'amour de soi se change en amour-propre, et où commencent à naître toutes les passions qui tiennent à celle-là.' Now *celle-là* means 'the former', so for Dent to render it as 'this one' is a mistranslation that completely inverts the sense: Rousseau is speaking about the passions that arise from *amour de soi*.

Thus the interpellation that Dent inserts into the next quoted sentence is spurious and misleading. The only way to read the passage is to see it as referring to the secondary passions which arise from *amour de soi*, not *amour-propre*. I am no more convinced by the rest of Dent's interpretation.

[78] In other words, what matters is not just *how much* we can do but *what* we can do. If the price of being able to do more things that we want to do is that those wants are formed not autonomously and naturally but as a result of what 'society' or 'public opinion' determines that we *ought* to want, then we are, in Rousseau's terms, less free.

deleterious effect on human welfare to the extent that they develop at the expense of the naturally beneficial sentiment of *pitié*. Nor, although this is one of the pervasive myths about him, is Rousseau an *irrationalist*. Reason is not redundant in the moral sphere, for: 'Reason alone teaches us to know good and evil'.[79] Rousseau endorses the ideal that human beings should be ruled by reason rather than appetite. (Indeed, in Book 5 of *Émile*, Rousseau explicitly endorses the rationalist value of mastery over the passions.)

As I have defined it, rationalism consists in the identification of the good for human beings with an increase in their discretionary power and the belief in the efficacy of rational means (the power of reasoning) in order to achieve that goal. Rousseau's opposition to rationalism lies in his rejection of this second element. Like Augustine, Rousseau challenges the idea that *reasoning* (the private and independent exercise of the power of reflection) is a suitable means to achieve moral rationality and self-command.[80] Yet, unlike Augustine, he does not believe that self-command is impossible, except by the miraculous means of divine grace.

Rousseau believes in the natural goodness of the world. There *is* an order to the world and it is both discernible by human beings and capable of being followed by them – although to be able do so their reason must be (as Rousseau expresses it in *Émile*) 'perfected by feeling'. Our failures are the result of lives lived wrongly in societies that are badly arranged, not inevitable consequences of Man's Fall. (Rousseau is no *pessimist*.) For reason and feeling to be brought into agreement with one another, reasoning alone is not sufficient. As Rousseau puts it:

> Whilst it might be possible for Socrates and minds of his calibre to acquire virtue by means of reason, the human race would long ago have ceased to be if its conservation had been dependent solely on the reasonings of its members.[81]

Reason must be supported by feelings of the right kind. Such morally appropriate feelings are threatened by the withdrawal of the self into the private realm of subjectivity. Not only does the self-centred use of reflection, motivated by *amour-propre*, fail as a means of moral self-improvement, but private subjectivity is pervaded by feelings that, unlike the moral emotion of *pitié*, are detached from practical engagement. The source of such feelings – the imagination – is examined by Rousseau at length.

Rousseau's *Letter to D'Alembert* is an extended response to one (as the

---

[79] J.-J. Rousseau, *Émile*, quoted in *The Indispensable Rousseau*, p. 185.
[80] It seems clear that, for Rousseau, 'reason' has more than one sense. Affirmatively, it is the capacity to judge rightly, to feel appropriately, and to match our actions to our feelings. Negatively, it is the exercise of reflection and speculation in abstraction from direct experience. It is all too easy, therefore, to suppose either (on the basis of his critical remarks) that Rousseau is an irrationalist, or, if the more positive statements are included, that he is simply confused.
[81] *Discours sur l'origine de l'inégalité*, p. 199.

author himself would have seen it, minor) aspect of D'Alembert's article for the *Encyclopédie* on Rousseau's home town, Geneva. In it, D'Alembert regrets the absence from Geneva of a theatre; in an open letter of two hundred pages, Rousseau takes issue with him. What concerns Rousseau – as it had Plato and St Augustine – is the theatre's moral effects and, in particular, its relationship to the conditions for civic virtue. Rousseau claims that in this respect the theatre is thoroughly corrupting, and the arguments that he presents to sustain this position are significant for the light they throw on his whole view of the passions.

One might, perhaps, have supposed that Rousseau, with his concern to bring reason and feeling into line with one another, could have seen in the theatre a suitable school for moral education. Rousseau believed, after all, that 'The heart of man is always right about what does not relate to himself personally. In the quarrels of which we are purely spectators, we immediately take the part of justice, and there is no act of wickedness that does not produce in us a lively indignation, although we draw no profit from it . . .'[82] How better to teach judgement than from the disinterested vantage-point of the 'impartial spectator' seated in front of an unfolding drama?[83] Yet this is far from Rousseau's view. He absolutely rejects 'those exclusive entertainments which dismally shut up a small number of people in a dark cavern; which keep them fearful and motionless in silence and inactivity; which only display prisons, swords, soldiers, and distressing images of servitude and inequality.'[84]

It is not just the subject-matter of the theatre that Rousseau rejects – that, after all, could be quite easily remedied – but its inevitable effects (as he sees them) on the feelings. As we have seen, it is feeling, not reason, that, in Rousseau's view, is the true condition for moral judgement, and the responses to situations affecting human well-being that ought to issue from feeling are quite unlike the detached and calm observations of the state of things that we call 'judgement' in relation to the realm of natural events. In the moral sphere, for Rousseau, to make an 'accurate' judgement really means to show the proper response: to make another's suffering a part of our own self-interest and to show ourselves willing to intervene unhesitatingly – as Rousseau says that primitive and uneducated people, the *'canaille'* and the *'femmes des halles'*, do[85] – on behalf of those who come under attack.

In the context of this view, the dangers of the theatre are clearly apparent. The whole situation of the theatre – the separation between the

[82] *Lettre à M. D'Alembert*, p. 77.
[83] This is the programme put forward by Bertolt Brecht in his *Messingkauf Dialogues* for what he calls *'thaëter'* – a non-Aristotelian theatre of investigation and contemplative judgement, in which the actors are not to be identified with their roles and which the audience can watch without having to become emotionally involved (they can even smoke in the auditorium!).
[84] *Lettre à M. D'Alembert*, p. 233.
[85] *Discours sur l'origine de l'inégalité*, p. 198. If one would like to encapsulate everything that Rousseau's view of morality is *not*, one might consider the title of Dame Iris Murdoch's recent work: *Metaphysics as a Guide to Morals*.

actor and the spectator, and the fact that the latter observes the action under the guiding premise that he is witnessing something artificial and unreal – breaks the link between feeling and action. Events are, indeed, presented with the object of producing emotion in the spectator: the spectator is supposed to be 'moved' – but where?

Even if the emotions produced in the theatre – pity, for example – correspond to the emotions that morality would require of us if we were to engage directly with our fellow human beings and their sufferings, the detachment with which those emotions are felt is corrupt:

> I hear it said that tragedy leads through terror to pity. Perhaps so, but what is this pity? . . . In giving our tears to these fictions we have satisfied all the rights of humanity without having to risk anything of our own – without the unfortunates personally requiring from us care, relief, consolations, deeds that might associate us with their suffering and for which we would at least pay a price in terms of our own indolence; an expenditure of which we are happy to be relieved.[86]

The theatre reduces virtue to a 'theatrical game, fit to amuse the public, but which it would be madness to wish to see seriously transferred into society.'[87] It can in no way contribute to the *correction* of morals, according to Rousseau, for it merely depicts them. The indulgence in emotions in the theatre leads the spectator away from commitment to others and to take pleasure in the experience of emotions for their own sakes. The healthy flow that should lead from the perception of a situation in the outside world, via a subjective reaction on the part of the observer, back to an active intervention in the world by that observer, is interrupted and dammed, and, instead, a hypertrophy of subjective feeling is produced: we become spectators of our own emotions and are led to the false pleasures of the imagination. This is why the theatre indulges our emotions and does nothing to favour those emotions that we ought to feel rather than those to which we are naturally inclined. Furthermore, we become, in general, Rousseau believes, 'more incapable of resisting our passions' and put feeling in place of virtuous action: 'the sterile interest that we take in virtue only serves to satisfy our *amour-propre*, without compelling us to practise it.'[88]

Unlike his romantic successors, who celebrate the freedom and spontaneity of the imagination and its ability to soften the conflict between form and content, universal and particular, Rousseau holds a view of imagination that is highly critical. For instance, he makes the imagination responsible for destroying the direct and natural relationship between the sexes:

[86] *Lettre à M. D'Alembert*, pp. 78–9.
[87] Ibid., p. 80.
[88] Ibid., p. 108.

Imagination, which causes such ravages among ourselves, does not speak to savage hearts; each waits peacefully for the impulse of nature, delivers himself over to it without choice, more with pleasure than with fury, and, once needs are satisfied, all desire is extinguished. It is thus incontestable that love itself, as with all the passions, only acquires in society that impulsive ardour that often makes it so disastrous for men.[89]

Rousseau does, however, recognize the dominating role of imagination in his own character and one of the recurring themes of the *Confessions* is his picture of its effects on his own life. He relates, for example, how he would withdraw even from the woman with whom he was in love, Mme de Warens, so that he might enjoy the thought of her in privacy, unconstrained by any unpleasant reality that might come from actual contact with her:

I only felt the full strength of my attachment to her when she was out of my sight. When I could see her I was merely happy. But my disquiet when she was away became almost painful.[90]

Rousseau makes no effort to conceal the parallel between his fantasies of disengaged sexual gratification and the use that he was later to make of the power of his imagination to give *La Nouvelle Héloïse* its – to contemporary readers – sensational emotional intensity.[91] As Rousseau describes it, the novel had its origin at a period of his life when he allowed himself to be taken over by his own self-pity and yearning for an absolute – unmediated and unconditional – love.[92]

To this state of self-absorbed unhappiness, Rousseau responded, to follow his own account, by escaping into a world of imaginary satisfaction:

What then did I do? My reader has already guessed, if he has paid the least attention to my progress so far. The impossibility of attaining the real persons precipitated me into the land of chimeras; and seeing that nothing existed worthy of my exalted feelings, I fostered them in an ideal world that my creative imagination soon peopled with beings after my own heart. Never was this resource more opportune, and never did it prove more fertile. In my continual ecstasies I intoxicated myself with draughts of the most exquisite sentiments that have ever entered the heart of a man. Altogether ignoring the human race, I created for myself societies of perfect creatures celestial in their virtue and in their beauty, and of reliable, tender, and faithful friends such as I had never found here below. I took such pleasure in thus soaring into the empyrean in the midst of all the charms that surrounded me, that I

---

[89] *Discours sur l'origine de l'inégalité*, p. 200.

[90] *Confessions*, p. 107.

[91] Hume, for example, considered *La Nouvelle Héloïse* to be Rousseau's 'masterpiece': 'I consider this work his masterpiece though he himself told me that he valued most his *Social Contract*; which is as preposterous a judgement as that of Milton, who preferred the *Paradise Regained* to all his other performances.' Quoted in *The Indispensable Rousseau*, p. 146.

[92] *Confessions*, pp. 396–7.

spent countless hours and days at it, losing all memory of anything else. No sooner had I eaten a hasty morsel than I was impatient to escape and run into my woods once more. When I was about to set out for my enchanted world and saw wretched mortals appearing to hold me down to earth, I could neither restrain nor conceal my annoyance.[93]

Rousseau's object, however, was not to develop his imaginings into a novel: on the contrary, he deplores the emotional indulgence of novels and sees his own disposition towards the kind of fantasy that is their raw material as evidence of weakness. The fact that these fantasies should issue in a novel was his way of freeing himself from them: *La Nouvelle Héloïse* was perhaps the first (although certainly not the last) novel to be written as a form of therapy for its author.[94]

The novel, he claims, was 'the best use I could have put my follies to', for in it he tries not simply to indulge the fantasies of author and reader but to advance the claims of virtue – of 'morality and marital fidelity . . . harmony and the public good'.[95] It was a work of the imagination that, at the same time, sought to depict the limits and dangers of the imagination, rather than indulging them. That the imagination must be restricted is something he argues for explicitly in the course of the novel itself:

> The real world has boundaries, the world of the imagination is infinite. Since we cannot enlarge the real one, we must restrict the imaginary one, since all the suffering that makes us really miserable arises from the disparity between them.[96]

Although Rousseau identifies the inflammatory power of the imagination in motivating his characters, he does not endorse it.[97] Nevertheless, his

---

[93] Ibid., p. 398.
[94] Ibid., pp. 404–5.
[95] Ibid., p. 405.
[96] *La Nouvelle Héloïse*, p. 45, quoted in M. Berman, *The Politics of Authenticity*, p. 268.
[97] Berman gives the following interpretation of the passage just quoted:

if (as Rousseau feared to be the case) we cannot enlarge the real world so that it will fulfill the ideals that we imagine, *then* we must contract the scope of our imagination so that we will not want more than the world is apt to give . . . This was the source of what I have called the politics of inauthenticity . . . If men could be protected from the dream of being themselves, they would not despair at the gulf between this dream and the reality of the world they lived in. If their ideals could be formed to fit existing realities, they might find a peace and equilibrium that Rousseau had never known. Wherever the imagination was freest and the self most fully developed, the politics of inauthenticity would have to be most relentlessly total. (*The Politics of Authenticity*, pp. 268–9)

Although Berman's book is otherwise sensitive and illuminating, this interpretation represents a misreading of Rousseau's views. The reason for Rousseau to limit the imagination is not pessimism about the possibility of the realization of freedom or a desire to protect his contemporaries 'from the dream of being themselves' (an idea of Rousseau's attitude towards his time which sits very oddly indeed with the philippics to be found in his writings) but his view of the nature of the imagination itself. Imagination, for Rousseau, is a form of inactive indulgence and a source of purely private gratification, not part of an ideal of freedom and self-development. Rousseau was not a Romantic and no slogan could be more inappropriate to him than '*L'imagination au pouvoir!*'.

Romantic successors (against Rousseau's own intentions) took up the figure of Saint-Preux from *La Nouvelle Héloïse*, just as they were to take up Goethe's Werther, as a symbol; of alienation and authenticity: the lover as outsider. There is no better illustration of this transformation in the perceived value of the imagination – or more interesting argument in its favour – than Stendhal's *De l'amour* (1822). *De l'amour* (which Stendhal, in admiration of Destutt de Tracy, calls a 'book of ideology')[98] was, like the *Nouvelle Héloïse*, written as an exercise in self-therapy – although not as a surrogate for the absence of an ideal love, but in order to come to terms with the existence of a real, unrequited one. Stendhal's key idea is love's release of the transformative power of the imagination: what he calls 'crystallization', based on an analogy that he repeats (rather irritatingly) several times in the book:

Leave a lover with his thoughts for twenty-four hours and this is what will happen:

> At the salt-mines of Salzburg, they throw a leafless wintry bough into one of the abandoned workings. Two or three months later they haul it out covered with a shining deposit of crystals. The smallest twig, no bigger than a tom-tit's claw, is studded with a galaxy of scintillating diamonds. The original branch is no longer recognizable.
> What I have called crystallization is a mental process which draws from everything that happens new proofs of the perfection of the loved one.[99]

The imagination, in other words, enriches and beautifies experience for us, at the same time as it can lead us to be deluded and enslaved. How necessary this is, Stendhal explores in arguing for the superiority of love in the manner of Werther over love in the manner of (Mozart's) Don Giovanni.[100] Don Juan (as Stendhal calls him) is a kind of *reductio ad absurdum* of rationalism: the price that he pays for his amorous success is that he reduces love to the level of mere business:

> Instead of losing himself in the bewitching reveries of crystallization his attitude is that of a general to the success of his tactics, and in brief he destroys love instead of enjoying it more than others, as is commonly believed.[101]

Don Juan's triumph is that of vanity and his motivation the need for *divertissement*. The echo of Pascal is unmistakable when Stendhal writes:

[98] Stendhal read Destutt de Tracy, he says, to 'de-Rousseauize' his thinking.
[99] *Love*, p. 45.
[100] It is clear that Stendhal has Rousseau consciously in mind in drawing this contrast. As he himself writes, 'The distinction would be more precise if I cited Saint-Preux, but he is such a dull character that I should be wronging the sensitive if I were to choose him as their champion' (*Love*, p. 204).
[101] *Love*, p. 206.

Love as understood by Don Juan is a feeling akin to a taste for hunting. It is a craving for an activity which needs an incessant diversity of stimuli to challenge skill.[102]

Don Juan is thus a man whose sexual appetites are sociable in the worst way ('publicity is essential for the triumphs of a Don Juan') and who, instead of truly taking pleasure in women, even comes 'to regard women as ... enemies'.[103] His conquests leave the Don Juan sated, but not satisfied. As Stendhal replies to his imaginary Don Juan:

Only imagination can escape once and for all from satiety ... Your relationship with women destroys all the other joys in life; that of Werther multiplies them a hundredfold.[104]

Thus Stendhal, just as much as Rousseau, is morally opposed to vanity and emotional disengagement. The difference is that, for Stendhal, the imagination itself can act as a source of engagement and genuine emotion, not simply as a substitute for and escape from them.

Overall then, Rousseau offers a genuinely *political* theory of false consciousness: an account, that is to say, of how oppressive social orders result from and are sustained by false consciousness. It is, in the terms of the previous chapter, an account of *practical false consciousness*. The man under the hegemony of *amour-propre* suffers from false consciousness in relation to action (he fails to respond properly to the situations with which he is faced); in relation to desire (his desires are fundamentally *sociable* – desires that depend on the opinion of others); and in relation to emotion (his emotions are excessive, futile and detached from action). Against this, Rousseau's response is not to seek to use reflection to increase the discretionary power of the self, but to try to develop 'reason' (by which he means the power of the self to act, feel and judge rightly) by bringing the self into balance with its environment. In fact, Rousseau claims to have had an extensive plan for a book on this very subject:

It has been observed that the majority of men are often in the course of their lives quite unlike themselves; they seem to be changed into quite different people. But it was not for the purpose of establishing such a well-known fact that I planned to write my book; I had a more original and important purpose, which was to trace the causes of these changes, isolating those that depend on us in order to show how we may ourselves control them, and so become better men and more certain of ourselves. For it is, indisputably, more difficult for a decent man to resist the desires he should subdue, once they are formed, than to prevent, change or modify these same desires at their source if he were in a position to go back so far. A man resists temptation once because he is strong, and succumbs on another occasion

---

[102] Ibid., p. 209.
[103] Ibid., p. 205.
[104] Ibid., p. 208.

because he is weak, though if he had been in his previous state he would not have succumbed.

Looking within myself and seeking in others for the cause upon which these different states depended, I discovered that they had a great deal to do with our previous impressions from external objects, and that, being continually a little changed through the agency of our senses and our organs, we were unconsciously affected in our thoughts, our feelings, and even our actions by the impact of these slight changes upon us. Numerous striking examples that I had collected put the matter beyond all dispute; and thanks to their physical basis they seemed to me capable of providing an external code which, varied according to circumstances, could put or keep the mind in the state most conducive to virtue. From what errors would reason be preserved, and what vices would be choked even before birth, if one knew how to compel the brute functions to support the moral order which they so often disturb? Climates, seasons, sounds, colours, darkness, light, the elements, food, noise, silence, movements, repose: they all act on our machines, and consequently upon our souls, and they all offer us innumerable and almost certain opportunities for controlling those feelings which we allow to dominate us from their very onset ... I made very little progress with this work, however, the title of which was *La Morale Sensitive ou le Matérialisme du sage*.[105]

The contrast between this unrealized project and the attitude towards the senses of Plato and Augustine (or, indeed, Pascal) is striking. Where Augustine, as the story of Alypius illustrates, considers the senses to be a permanent threat to the feeble defences of reason, for Rousseau, the world of the senses is not held to be inherently inimical to human rationality (or compatible with it only to the extent that the senses discern within the material world the traces of the buried *logos*); nor is the remedy for incontinence the development of discursive reasoning or the dull repetition of habit, but rather a healthy and balanced form of experience.[106]

Rousseau is significant for the argument of this book both for his political theory of false consciousness and for his anti-rationalism. But there is a further novel element in his thought that has, as yet, barely been touched: Rousseau was the first thinker to raise the idea of false consciousness as a form of *false identity*. The idea is embodied in the phrase quoted above that men do not 'resemble themselves' (*ne sont pas semblables à eux-mêmes*). The idea is not just that they do not appear as they really are (although this disjunction between seeming and being is characteristic of the world of *amour-propre*) or that they are untrue to their values and ideals, but that they have in some way lost themselves ('they seem to be changed into quite different people'). Unfortunately, Rousseau does not pursue this idea to the extent of giving any detailed account of what the loss of identity might mean for the individual, and one must assume that

---

[105] *Confessions*, pp. 380–1.
[106] The work that we may suppose stood in for *La morale sensitive* is *Émile*, Rousseau's description of an education and moral development that are, as he believes, truly in accord with nature.

he intended the phrase to refer to that general weakening of autonomy that comes as a necessary consequence of the socialization of desire.

There is, however, another way in which Rousseau pioneers the idea of lost identity. At several points in his writing, but, above all, in the first book of the *Social Contract*, Rousseau develops an account of the way in which individuals can come together to form a collective, social identity, and contrasts this with the way in which, in illegitimate societies (by which he means all contemporary ones), individuals are held together without forming a whole:

> ... it is, if you will, an *aggregation* but not an *association*; there is to be found there neither public good nor body politic.[107]

The most famous of the concepts that Rousseau uses to express this contrast is that of the *volonté générale* (the 'general will', to be contrasted with the *volonté de tous* – the 'will of all') but there are many others: the state is a *personne morale*, an organism, a body of which 'each member is an indivisible part of the whole':

> Immediately, in place of the particular person of each contracting party, this act of association produces a body that is moral and collective, composed of as many members as the assembly has votes, and which, from this very act, receives its unity, its collective *ego*, its life and its will. This public person which thus forms itself through the union of all other persons once took the name of *city*, and nowadays that of *Republic* or *body politic*.[108]

Thus individuals who remain isolated in a mere 'aggregation' lack this dimension of their identity: the collective entity simply does not exist and so they cannot participate in it. How literally did Rousseau suppose that the analogy between the state and an 'organism' should be taken? Is the isolated individual really as ontologically defective as a leg would be without a torso, or should we take it more as a typically extravagant metaphor for the ways in which the relations of individuals in groups generate effects that go beyond the intentions and awarenesses of the individuals that compose them? These questions are difficult – indeed, perhaps they are unanswerable. It seems quite possible that Rousseau did not see any clear contrast between 'realist' collectivism – the way that a particular connection of chemicals and cells makes a flower – and 'conventionalist' collectivism – the way that agreeing with others could make one a member of a club. Yet, however we answer them, it is significant to notice that, with Rousseau, we have reached the point at which the two 'background beliefs' which, I claim, provide the framework informing the theory of ideology, start to come together: Rousseau presents us both with a historical answer to the question of how it is that the many

---

[107] *Du Contrat Social*, Bk I, Ch. 2, p. 49.
[108] Ibid., Bk I, Ch. 2, p. 49.

come to be ruled by the few and the materials, at least, for a conception of society as an agent in its own right. What he does not do is make any explicit theoretical connection between the two.

VII Adam Smith: Sympathy and Authority

The works of Rousseau that we have been discussing were written in the 1750s and 1760s. At the same time, a quite different account of sociable desire and its role in the maintenance of political order was being advanced in Britain by Adam Smith.[109] While Rousseau is writing a jeremiad against the unnaturalness and corruption of contemporary society and morals, Smith is concerned to bring out the beauty that lies in the 'utility' of the great system of modern society, that adjusts means to ends as if (as Smith famously – but so rarely – says) by an 'Invisible Hand'.[110] Smith seeks to show how even good and benevolent – hence rational – social orders are sustained, not by conscious processes of reflection, but spontaneously and non-rationally. Authority is reasonable, but it is nature (or, rather, Nature) that supplies that disposition to submission that mere *reasoning* does not:[111]

> That kings are the servants of the people, to be obeyed, resisted, deposed, or punished, as the public conveniency may require, is the doctrine of reason and philosophy; but it is not the doctrine of Nature. Nature would teach us to submit to them for their own sake, to tremble and bow down before their exalted station, to regard their smile as a reward sufficient to compensate any services, and to dread their displeasure, though no other evil were to follow from it, as the severest of all mortifications . . .[112]

In the *Lectures on Jurisprudence*, Smith makes it clear that he regards it as absurd to imagine that obedience in general is founded on reason or a 'social contract':

[109] The *Theory of Moral Sentiments* was first published in 1759 and the *Lectures on Jurisprudence*, as we have them, is based on the form in which the lectures were delivered in the early 1760s. So different is Smith's account of society from Rousseau's, that one might be tempted to see in it a deliberate counter-argument to Rousseau. Smith was certainly one of the earliest British readers of the *Discours sur l'origine de l'inégalité*, as is shown by his 'Letter to the Editors of the *Edinburgh Review*' (1755), which urged the Scottish public to turn their attention to it.

[110] Once in the *Theory of Moral Sentiments* and once in the *Wealth of Nations*. It has been pointed out that Smith first uses the expression in his lectures on astronomy (sarcastically, in the phrase 'the invisible hand of Jupiter', as a description of the superstitious character of primitive cosmic beliefs) but it may well have been an eighteenth-century commonplace for Providence (Washington speaks of the 'invisible hand of Providence' in his Inaugural Address).

[111] It is too often assumed that the Enlightenment is characterized by a shared belief in the power and competence of individual reason. Thus thinkers such as Smith and, in particular, Hume, who question the scope and power of reason as an independent faculty, are assumed to be, in some way, *opposed* to the Enlightenment. This neglects, however, the extent to which the Enlightenment was concerned to vindicate the rationality of the natural and (at least, potentially) the social order as a whole – a view which is, as in this case, perfectly compatible with a picture of the scope of individual reason far less extensive than, for example, that to be found a century earlier in Descartes.

[112] *The Theory of Moral Sentiments*, p. 55.

Ask a common porter or day-labourer why he obeys the civil magistrate, he
will tell you that it is right to do so, that he sees others do it, or perhaps that
it is a sin against God not to do it. But you will never hear him mention a
contract as the foundation of his obedience.[113]

The true foundation of society lies in the 'principle of authority': the
way in which 'superior wealth . . . contributes to confer authority'. The
principle of authority is something which 'proceeds not from any dependence that the poor have upon the rich'; although 'in general the poor
are independent and support themselves by their labour, yet, tho' they
expect no benefit from them, they have a strong propensity to pay them
respect.' This propensity is anchored psychologically in the fact that
'our sympathy with our superiors [is] greater than that with our equals
or inferiors: we admire their happy situation, enter into it with pleasure,
and endeavour to promote it.'[114] The fact that we sympathize more easily
with those in a superior station is, Smith himself says, 'fully explained
in the *Theory of Moral Sentiments*'. The account that he gives there locates
it as part of a process in which individuals' original self-interest is
developed by and transformed into the disposition to identify ourselves
sympathetically with others and our own desire to be seen sympathetically
by them.

The *Theory of Moral Sentiments* opens with the reflection by Smith that
'How selfish soever man may be supposed, there are evidently some
principles in his nature, which interest him in the fortune of others, and
render their happiness necessary to him, though he derives nothing from
it except the pleasure of seeing it.'[115] In other words, Smith (like Rousseau
with his own concept of *pitié*) is concerned to find a foundation in affect
for morality and to show that the 'unselfishness' of the latter is motivated
by a source within the self. 'Of this kind', Smith says, 'is pity or
compassion, the emotion which we feel for the misery of others, when we
either see it, or are made to conceive it in a very lively manner'.[116]
Sympathy is not in the first instance a distinctive emotion, but the capacity
to feel that emotion – or an analogy of it – to which the person with whom
one is in sympathy is subject. As such, of course, it is not intrinsically
pleasurable: to feel the pain of another (or that one thinks that the other is
feeling) is itself painful. How, then, can sympathy act effectively as a
positive force to bring individuals together? Smith's answer is that what is
pleasurable is not the original sympathetic reaction itself, but a second-
order pleasure: the 'pleasure of mutual sympathy'. What pleases us is an
awareness of the harmony of our reactions with those of the person with
whom we sympathize:

---

[113] *Lectures on Jurisprudence*, pp. 402–3.
[114] Ibid., p. 401.
[115] *The Theory of Moral Sentiments*, p. 9.
[116] Ibid., p. 9.

When the original passions of the person principally concerned are in perfect concord with the sympathetic emotions of the spectator, they necessarily appear to this last just and proper, and suitable to their objects . . .[117]

But sympathy and the harmony of feelings requires more than just the disposition to feel the same thing as someone else in the same circumstances. With those things that affect us most closely, it is very often the case that what produces the emotion is an event that concerns us alone. We are separated by our personal good or bad fortune from those around us and from this it follows, Smith maintains, ' . . . the emotions of the spectator will still be very apt to fall short of the violence of what is felt by the sufferer. Mankind, though naturally sympathetic, never conceive, for what has befallen another, that degree of passion which naturally animates the person principally concerned.'[118] Since we are creatures of limited sympathies, we must – if we are to be able to induce the fellow-feeling of others – try to moderate our passions. In this way, we are led to become spectators to our own selves; to ask ourselves about our own feelings: What *could* others identify with? and to try to bridge the gap between what we feel and what they feel. The word that Smith uses to describe this is *propriety* – not in the anodyne modern sense of what fits inside the limits of social convention, but as what is *proper* and *appropriate* for someone to feel in the circumstances. Unlike Rousseau, for whom the desire to be seen by others in a particular light leads to weakness, dissimulation and the loss of identity, for Smith it is the source of morality. Self-command and unselfishness become cardinal virtues, for those who can moderate their feelings in response to misfortune and who act for ends that are not purely personal are the most easy to sympathize with.

Thus Smith gives a modern twist to an ancient rationalist conception of virtue: where the Stoics regarded self-command as a virtue that enabled the individual to make himself independent, to withdraw from the evil of the world, Smith presents it as the means to establish our connection with others. Rousseau traces the decline of fellow-feeling to the corrupting influence of *amour-propre*, but in Smith there is a continuous line connecting vanity with the desire for 'true glory'. The latter emotion – although not as noble as the 'love of virtue' for its own sake – is in no way reprehensible; what is wrong with vanity is not that it is motivated by the desire for the esteem of others but only that it aims to acquire this esteem illicitly, without properly deserving it:

There is an affinity between vanity and the love of true glory, as both these passions aim at acquiring esteem and approbation. But they are different in this, in that the one is a just, reasonable and equitable passion, while the other is unjust, absurd and ridiculous.[119]

---

[117] Ibid., p. 16.
[118] Ibid., p. 21.
[119] Ibid., p. 310.

Just as it is easier for others to identify with us if we do not appear to take too great an interest in our own welfare (and, in particular, to feel too keenly our own suffering) so it is easier for us to identify with those whose stations we judge to be 'fortunate':

> When we consider the condition of the great, in those delusive colours in which the imagination is apt to paint it, it seems to be almost the abstract idea of a perfect and happy state. It is the very state which, in all our waking dreams and idle reveries, we had sketched out to ourselves as the final object of our desires. We feel, therefore, a peculiar sympathy with the satisfaction of those who are in it.[120]

Thus it is imagination and sympathy – not reason and the will – that lie behind the 'principle of authority' and cement societies together:

> Upon this disposition of mankind, to go along with all the passions of the rich and powerful, is founded the distinction of ranks, and the order of society.[121]

The account that Smith gives of the 'principle of authority' refers it back to a form of consciousness which is the product of a distinctive, non-rational psychological mechanism – a mechanism that does indeed involve both the presence of false belief (we believe, falsely, that the great are happy and that we ourselves would be happy if only we could occupy their situation) and a distortion of the normal processes of moral assessment (we do not require that the great show the self-restraint that in other cases is the condition for our endorsement of the propriety of someone's actions). Nonetheless, it is not clear that this deviation from the normal processes of sympathy is a form of *false consciousness* in the sense of something to be

---

[120] Ibid., pp. 51–2. It is an established fact that Smith knew the *Discours sur l'origine de l'inégalité* (see note 109 above) but did Rousseau also know *The Theory of Moral Sentiments*? Although the editors of the Glasgow edition of Smith's works do not mention it in their discussion of *The Theory of Moral Sentiments*' influence on the Continent, one might think so from the direct contradiction of the idea that we sympathize with the happiness of the rich to be found in *Émile*:

> Man's weakness makes him sociable ... Hence it follows that we are drawn to our fellow-creatures less by our feeling for their joys than for their sorrows; for in them we discern more plainly a nature like our own, and a pledge of their affection for us. If our common needs create a bond of interest, our common sufferings create a bond of affection. The sight of a happy man arouses in others envy rather than love, we are ready to accuse him of usurping a right which is not his, of seeking happiness for himself alone, and our *amour-propre* suffers an additional pang in the thought that this man has no need of us ...
> It is not in human nature to put ourselves in the place of those who are happier than ourselves, but only in the place of those who can claim our *pitié*.
> If you find exceptions to this rule, they are more apparent than real. Thus we do not put ourselves in the place of the rich or great when we become fond of them; even when our affection is real, we only appropriate to ourselves a part of their welfare. Sometimes we love the rich man in the midst of misfortunes; but so long as he prospers he has no real friend, except the man who is not deceived by appearances, who pities rather than envies him in spite of his prosperity. (*Émile*, pp. 182, 184.)

[121] *The Theory of Moral Sentiments*, p. 52.

regarded as a deficiency – much less a remediable deficiency – in the way that human beings think and feel. Smith's question regarding political authority is not the same as Reich's: Smith does not ask specifically why men comply with an unjust social order when it is against their interests to do so, but why they comply with social order in general.[122] The tendency that we have to sympathize with our social superiors is a phenomenon that has extremely significant consequences for political order, but it is not itself a feature that results from any particular social order; it is a kind of generalized conservatism that works in favour of all kinds of social order, both good and bad.[123]

VIII Conclusion

In this chapter we have discussed the most significant accounts of false consciousness that formed the background for the theory of ideology. The tradition that comes to us from Plato and Augustine takes false consciousness as it affects politics to be simply one aspect of that general tendency to irrationality that lies at the core of human nature. With the early modern period, we see both the problem of 'voluntary servitude' – how it is that the many are ruled (unjustly) by the few – discussed explicitly (for instance, by de la Boetie) and the identification of a specifically *sociable* form of desire – *amour-propre* – as a symptom and cause of false consciousness. At the same time, as the Augustinian view of the world as cut off from God's goodness by original sin recedes, there comes the idea that the human passions themselves are refined and moderated with the development of society. Finally, in the eighteenth century, we have, with Hume, an account of false belief that shows it as both the cause and the effect of social disorder; Rousseau's account of *amour-propre* as a historically specific (and thus, in principle at least, remediable) deficiency in human nature; and, in Smith, a general account of the maintenance of social order through sociable desire.

On this basis, it seems justifiable to say that we have traced the beginnings of a *specifically political* account of false consciousness, meaning by this not simply that writers on politics were aware that false consciousness had political consequences and that these could favour tyranny, but that they adhered to either or both of two further propositions:

1 that false consciousness involves the desire to be seen (by others, but possibly also by oneself) in a certain way

---

[122] In general, Smith believes that society is benevolently ordered, but he is not so much of an optimist (perhaps one should say, he is too much of a Whig) to believe that there are *never* unjust or oppressive social orders against which rebellion would be justified.

[123] In other words, it meets one, but not both, of Cohen's requirements for a functional explanation: it is *functional for* the social order in question but it does not owe its existence to the fact that it is functional in this way.

2 that false consciousness is not an unchanging feature of human nature but varies with (perhaps as a result of) different forms of society

What we do not see in the authors considered so far, however, is an account of false consciousness that explains it functionally (as a result of the needs of a particular society) or in some other way systematically as a result of the structure of society. The authors lie on the other side of that divide after which it became possible for a writer on society to say, as if it were the merest commonplace: 'It is not correct to say that each society gets the men it deserves. Rather, each society produces the men it needs.'[124] What separates us, of course, is that, before Rousseau and Smith, none of the authors under discussion thought of society as the sort of entity that could 'produce' what it needed (and they, as we have seen, did not extend that view into a historically specific account of the origin of false consciousness in society). We can speak of a theory of ideology in the full sense, I suggest, only when the explanation of 'voluntary servitude' through a political conception of false consciousness is brought together with the belief in society as a self-maintaining system. It is to this latter belief that I shall turn in the next chapter.

---

[124] Peter Berger, *Invitation to Sociology*, p. 110.

4

Unintended Consequences and the Idea of a Social System

Both the belief that societies are entities that preserve themselves by shaping the individuals and institutions of which they are composed and the belief that history is a process in which 'nations stumble upon establishments, which are indeed the result of human action, but not the execution of any human design'[1] emerged in the eighteenth century. By the middle of the nineteenth century, however, they had become established commonplaces in social thought. The main purpose of this chapter is to trace that emergence and to provide the background to it.

The two beliefs are instances of the broader notion of 'unintended consequences'. The sense of this idea has two significant ingredients. In the first place, the actions of individuals in society are held to have consequences that go beyond what the individuals themselves intend or foresee. But, this commonplace apart, it also contains a more distinctive element: namely, that there is a superior perspective from which those consequences can be understood and explained. What gives that perspective? There are three possibilities.

1 that the actions of individuals should be seen providentially, as the realization of the Divine Will

2 that actions have a wider significance as part of a progressive process of historical development

---

[1] Adam Ferguson, *An Essay on the History of Civil Society*, p. 122. Ferguson continues: 'If Cromwell said, that a man never mounts higher, than when he knows not whither he is going; it may with more reason be affirmed of communities, that they admit of the greatest revolutions where no change is intended.'

3 finally, that action should be interpreted from the perspective of society, treated as a self-maintaining entity.

This chapter will show the emergence of the second and then the third of these conceptions from the first. But this process is more complicated than the simple substitution of a secular for a religious view of history. In the first place, the idea of history as the realization of Divine Will takes two radically different forms. Its earlier, Augustinian form is at odds with the view of history as a process of secular progress. God's purpose in history, on this view, is primarily didactic. In the seventeenth and eighteenth centuries, however, the bleak Augustinian view gave way to a view of the world as a manifestation of divine benevolence, and this brought with it the possibility of a more affirmative attitude towards history: history could be seen as a progressive process by which God enables the condition of mankind to improve.

Thus the three possibilities, although conceptually distinct, are not mutually exclusive. If God's Providence is exercised generally (in the purposive character of the world that he has created) rather than by particular interventions, then there is no necessary incompatibility between the view that history is providential and that, at the same time, it embodies an intelligible process of development – one that could be studied scientifically. Nor is there a conflict between the conception of history as a progressive development through stages and the idea that each of those stages is self-maintaining or -preserving. Indeed, as we shall see in the next chapter, all three ideas are explicitly present together in Hegel's account of history as the realization of *Geist*.

Historically, the idea of society as a self-maintaining system is intertwined with the idea of it as an *organism*, and a further task of this chapter is to put this idea into context. The organic analogy is one of the oldest elements in thought about politics. Yet it would be wrong to assume that it has had a fixed and clear significance. Both the force of the analogy (in what respects society was supposed to resemble an organism) and what it means to say of something that it *is* an organism have changed substantially in the course of history. A revolution took place in Germany in the late eighteenth century that was aimed at rethinking the nature of development in the organic realm. Only after this revolution do we find the familiar contrast between organic and mechanical models of organization and self-reproduction. It is this new conception of organism, applied to society, that forms the point of departure for the theory of ideology.

I Antecedents: Aristotle and Augustine

There is a conventional explanation for the fact that we do not find the idea of unintended consequences in the ancient world. The Greeks, it is said, lacked any conception of history as a unified process, developing in a certain direction. When Christianity, in the person of Augustine, turned its attention to secular history, it did so with the goal of showing the latter's compatibility with – indeed, its subordination to – biblical history. Thus, although history comes to be seen as unified in Christian orthodoxy, this unity is sacred, not profane: secular history is part of the history of salvation.[2] It was only in the eighteenth century, when the dominance of the Augustinian view of history was effectively replaced by conceptions of history that were progressive and secular, that the idea of unintended consequences could come into its own.[3]

There is something basically correct about this account. There were indeed profound differences between the Greek and the early Christian views of history, and, again, between these and the conception of history as progressive and secular.[4] But by itself it is not sufficient to explain the absence of the idea of unintended consequences. For while it is true that the appearance of the idea of unintended consequences in social thought was, as a matter of fact, intertwined with the idea of history as a developing process, it is not evident that the two themes are indissoluble. The idea that history is moving – continuously or discontinuously – in a progressive direction and the idea that society is such that it maintains itself other than by the rational and conscious choices of individuals (and that this fact itself is not accidental, but results in some way from the nature of society) are conceptually distinct: if they emerged at the same time, that does not establish that the former was a condition for the latter. One can easily imagine an account of societies as self-maintaining organisms without supposing that there is any line of development by which they are all linked and ordered.[5]

Indeed, there is good reason to suppose that this is precisely the case with Aristotle. As Kenneth Bock has pointed out, Aristotle's account of the *polis* as 'both natural and prior to the individual'[6] draws on a view of

---

[2] As Frank Manuel puts it:

> The great light is always focused on the men of the City of God. The history of the Gentiles is merely tributary to the history of Israel and the Church; it has import only insofar as it affects them either as a scourge of God for sin or as an agent helping in the attainment of necessary ends among the chosen people. If there is an 'ascendant trajectory' to the pilgrimage of man on earth, it is limited to the history of the City of God, and if there is a progression toward the better it is a purely spiritual one. (*Shapes of Philosophical History*, p. 30.)

[3] To say that history had become secularized does not mean that the purposes involved were themselves purely this-worldly. The point is, however, that the goal is fulfilled in the ordinary working out of the processes of history in this world: it does not have to wait for divine intervention or a world beyond.

[4] It is true that the idea that the Greeks had no idea of progress has been disputed. The evidence, so far as I am aware of it, however, seems to establish that the Greeks believed that there was progress *in some areas*, but not that they believed that history as a whole was progressive. Apart from Manuel, good and accessible treatments are to be found in K. Löwith, *Meaning in History*, and F. Heer, *The Intellectual History of Europe*.

[5] In other words, as in pre-Darwinian biology, there would be development at the level of individual organisms, but there would be no 'history of nature'.

[6] Aristotle, *The Politics*, Book I, Ch. 2.

nature as incorporating orderly and purposeful development. Natural things are defined by Aristotle as 'those which do move continuously, in virtue of a principle inherent in themselves, towards a determined goal'.[7] They will develop in a purposeful way, so long as they are not interfered with by artificial means and provided that they remain protected from the entropic forces of chance and spontaneity. In Bock's view:

> It is not difficult to read a doctrine of progress as improvement into this. Granted that Aristotle and his contemporaries saw all processes of coming to be in nature followed by processes of passing away, in picturing the upward phase of the cycle they were delineating a process of realization of an end, and in Aristotle's conception of final causes the 'end' of anything in nature was the achievement of what was 'best' in it, not the death of it . . . If such a state was also going to decay in time, well, that could be said of any lion or olive tree or horse or any other natural thing as well. The world was full of things perfecting themselves eternally.[8]

Bock's discussion is very much to the point, but it does not, I think, justify attributing a 'doctrine of progress' to Aristotle. Bock appears to be confusing the idea of history as a developing process with that of society as a self-maintaining organism. So far as it goes, all that it establishes is that individual states – as natural beings – have their processes of development and decay; there is no indication that they are all connected, through time, into a single, significant whole.[9] On the other hand, it does seem that Bock has identified the presence in Aristotle of the very ideas that would be the essential components of later, 'organic' theories of society. Aristotle believes: (1) that states are entities which are 'self-directing and independent';[10] and (2) that states are prior to the individuals that compose them. Furthermore, he is interested in the way that states are preserved. Thus he takes it to be one of his fundamental tasks to enquire 'what factors make for the preservation of constitutions, both in general and of each kind separately'.[11]

Nevertheless, Aristotle does not, so far as I know, present any instances of how states act to preserve themselves – automatically, as it were – that we would recognize as examples of the idea of unintended consequences.[12] Where one might have expected to find examples of this kind, in the discussion in the *Politics* of how tyrannies are preserved, Aristotle is

---

[7] Aristotle, *Physics*, Book 2, quoted, Bock, 'Theories of Progress, Development, Evolution', p. 43.

[8] K. Bock, 'Theories of Progress, Development, Evolution', p. 45.

[9] It seems to me that a doctrine of progress presupposes a picture of history as forming a unity: the various events that take place must be seen as part of a single history. It is just this that Augustine's vision of history *sub specie aeternitatis* provides.

[10] *The Politics*, Book IV, Ch. 4, p. 157.

[11] Ibid., Book V, Ch. 1, p. 189.

[12] It is worth noting that the passage just quoted ends with the question of the 'means' – presumably to be applied by individuals as a conscious policy – by which 'each of the types of constitution could best be preserved'.

content simply to present what even he appears to accept is a banal and obvious enumeration of the strategies available to tyrants:

> They might all be grouped under three heads, corresponding to tyranny's three aims in relation to its subjects, namely that they shall (a) have no minds of their own, (b) have no trust in each other, and (c) have no means of carrying out anything. Of the three points the first is obvious; resistance is not planned by puny minds. On the second, no tyranny is ever brought low until a certain degree of self-confidence is established; hence tyrants are always hostile to the men of merit as being hostile to them, not only because of their resistance to tyrannical rule but because they command confidence, both among themselves and others, and abstain from making accusations of each other or anybody. The third group is also clear; no one attempts what is quite beyond his powers, so nobody attempts to destroy a tyranny if the power to do so is not there.[13]

As an account of the operation of oppressive societies this seems – how shall one put it? – not especially helpful or informative. So how is this absence to be explained? Is there any particular reason why Aristotle should not be sensitive to the idea – which will be so important in later organic theories – that states (like other organisms) are composed of particular parts that are shaped by them to suit their needs? One might suppose that it had something to do with his metaphysical commitments.

For Aristotle, what is 'natural' is both self-directed and *good*. Thus what is bad – a tyrannical state, for instance – will, to some extent at least, lack the quality of self-direction (in other words, the ability to shape its parts in conformity with its needs). The good state, on the other hand, is one that is in harmony with reason and so it will not be necessary that the citizens of such a state should be ruled in any way deceptively. If this interpretation is sound, it could explain why we look in vain for an account of 'necessary false consciousness' in Aristotle: either the state will be bad, and so not fully 'self-maintaining', or it will be good – and false consciousness will not be needed. One might still suppose that Aristotle would have been struck, as the authors of later, providential, accounts of nature and society plainly were, by ways in which, even in good societies, phenomena that are apparently bad (or, at least, morally indifferent) serve good ends. But, for whatever reason, this idea appears to play no significant role in Aristotle's writing about politics, and so, although he is, obviously, the ancestor of organicism, his role as a pioneer of the modern idea of unintended consequences is surprisingly limited.

Aristotle's 'organicism' is characteristic of the metaphysics of the ancient world. In fact, what the ancient world appears to have lacked was the modern idea of 'machine' and, hence, of the contrast between the 'organic' and the 'mechanical'.[14]

---

[13] *The Politics*, Book V, Ch. 11, p. 227.
[14] See note 30 below.

The analogy with the body was very widespread in ancient and early modern political discourse. The political significance of the analogy was, initially, to show the interdependence of the parts of the 'body politic' (thus Menenius Agrippa, as described by Livy, ended a plebeian revolt against the Senate by comparing the parts of the state to parts of the body) and, in the Middle Ages, in particular, to show the propriety of the subordination of one part to another. In Hobbes, who describes the state as an 'artificial body', the object is to establish the legitimacy of the sovereign's actions as embodying in a collective form the identity of all the individual members of the community. What does *not* appear to be present in either case, however, is the idea of the state as automatically self-preserving or self-sustaining.[15]

The early Christian view of history, as articulated by St Augustine, is that history is the history of salvation. History's meaning lies in the history of the 'city of God', expressed visibly on earth in God's Church, its *corpus mysticum et sacrum*.[16] Life in this world is lived under the shadow cast by Original Sin and God's goodness is veiled from mankind, except as mankind turns towards him in his Church. Progress, if progress there is, is not to be understood in secular (much less, in material) terms.

Nevertheless, two points from Augustine's account of history are important in preparing the way for later authors. First, it is clear that, if history is the history of God's will for mankind, then history is unified both temporally and spatially: there is no (human) event that is not implicitly part of this single, great fabric. Even events that do not interact causally have a relation to one another – albeit indirectly – through the fact that they are all observed (and judged) by the one God.[17]

Second, the whole of the account of history in the *City of God* is written in the light of two doctrines: first, that God is omnipotent, omniscient and benevolent – that his intentions for mankind are good, and that he is able to carry them out, however improbable the events involved may seem to us – and, secondly, that man has cut himself off from God's goodness by

---

[15] See D. G. Hale, 'Analogy of the Body Politic'.

[16] 'For as the body is one, and hath many members ... so also is Christ ... And the eye cannot say unto the hand, I have no need of thee: nor again the head to the feet, I have no need of you ... Now ye are the body of Christ and members in particular...' (St. Paul, I Corinthians 12: 12–27). It is Christ's love that unifies these apparently diverse members.

[17] This idea of history as brought together and unified by the observer who judges it has had an immensely important secular residue. As the idea of God standing outside and judging history has been abandoned, so the broad process of history itself – but, in particular, the contemplation of it by posterity – has come to be regarded as giving significance to events: *die Weltgeschichte*, in Schiller's famous phrase, *ist das Weltgericht* (Schiller, *Resignation*). History is not simply the destiny that determines whether our projects are successful or not (and so establishes whether the sacrifices made by us or exacted from others had good consequences) but a judge whose gaze can unify and redeem the past. '*La postérité pour le philosophe*', writes Diderot, '*c'est l'autre monde pour l'homme réligieux*' (quoted in C. Becker, *The Heavenly City of the Eighteenth-Century Philosophers*, p. 119). This theme is most marked among those political radicals who apparently reject most vehemently a divine perspective on history: the Jacobins, the anarchists and the Bolsheviks (see Becker, Ch. 4, 'The Uses of Posterity', for a general discussion and, for a specific modern example, Fidel Castro's *History Will Absolve Me*, a speech made from the dock in 1959).

his own sin. Which sin (it follows from the first doctrine) God must have foreseen and been capable of preventing but counted to be not incompatible with his own benevolence. In other words, man's fall is itself to be counted as being in some way good and foreseen by God: man's redemption through Christ is an 'unintended consequence' of Adam's sin, his *felix culpa*:

> It follows that the actions of sinners, whether angels or men, cannot obstruct the 'great works of God, carefully designed to fulfill all his decisions', since in his providence and omnipotence he assigns to each his own gifts and knows how to turn to good account the good and the evil alike ... [Since] God was well aware that man would fall as he did, was there any reason why he should not have allowed him to be tempted by the malice of the jealous angel? God was perfectly certain that man would be defeated, but he foresaw with equal certainty that this same Devil was to be overcome by the man's seed, helped by God's own grace, to the greater glory of the saints ... Who would dare to believe or assert that it was not in God's power to ensure that neither angel nor man should fall? But God preferred not to withdraw this issue from their power, and thus to show the magnitude of their pride's power for evil and of God's grace for good.[18]

On Augustine's account, even a world in which man is cut off from God's goodness (or, to be more precise, in which he has cut himself off from God's goodness) is a providential expression of that goodness. But the role of providence is now essentially didactic: to show man that the apparent goodness of this world is not true goodness and so to turn him away from it to the world beyond. To bring this point home is the purpose of human history as a whole and of the greatest of all miracles: Christ's death and resurrection. Augustine does not discount the possibility of other miracles. Indeed, he describes miracles that he claims to have witnessed himself. That purpose will not be to alleviate pain and physical suffering, however. Since God is omnipotent, we must count the suffering that is part of the world as we know it to be part of his purpose. Miracles, even those that *do*, in fact, alleviate suffering, are there 'to win the world's belief'.[19]

Thus, although events in human history have a true significance that is not immediately apparent to the participants, their role is to lead the observer (including the agent, insofar as he reflects on events) to direct his hopes from this world to the next. Moreover, God works through history not simply by means of natural processes inevitably unfolding in the way that he had ordained that they should, but by particular interventions, not foreseeable by or comprehensible to human reason.

It seems plausible to suggest that these two ingredients in particular stood in the way of the development of a historical or social conception of

---

[18] *City of God*, Book XIV, Ch. 28, pp. 592–3.
[19] Ibid., Book XXII, Ch. 8, p. 1033.

unintended consequences. If God intervenes unpredictably from time to time in the historical process, history will not be just the inexorable working-out of a discoverable plan. Moreover, if worldly events and objectives are not themselves good, no inferences can be drawn about divine benevolence from the way in which society coordinates the fulfilment of human goals.

II Bossuet and Providentialism

In the sixteenth and seventeenth centuries the Augustinian world-view was challenged by a more optimistic picture of the natural world as both *knowable* and *good* – good not just when seen in relation to the next world (in the way that a punishment, though bad for the person punished, might be good because of its consequences) but good in its own right, an expression of God's love and care. The 'book of nature' came to be regarded as a source of revelation comparable to the Bible itself.[20] The development of a 'providentialist' view of history, as the realization of God's purposes and the expression of his goodness in this world, can be seen in part as a by-blow of the secularizing of the natural order that took place with the Copernican revolution and the emergence of modern science. If this world is good, then apparently bad things within it may nevertheless be justified because they are the means to other good things.[21]

The effects of this change on Christian views of history are beginning to become apparent in Bossuet's *Discourse on Universal History* of 1681. Bossuet, the Chaplain to Louis XIV, wrote with the consciously reactionary intention of upholding Augustinian orthodoxy. However, the way in which he does so itself reflects something of the new context in which he found himself writing. Like Augustine, Bossuet sees the providential nature of history as lying primarily in its *exemplary* character. The lessons that history has to teach are of two main kinds. Gentile history – the history of the classical world and of the barbarian empires – is essentially cyclical: a history of rise and fall. In this way, God reveals himself by fulfilling the prophecies of those whom he has inspired and points the contrast between

[20] This theme is always (and rightly) associated with Bacon. However, it is a pervasive trope among the early modern scientific thinkers. Thus Boyle writes: 'The world is an epistle written by God to mankind (as I believe Plato has said); he could have added, written in mathematical characters' (Robert Boyle, 'About the Excellency and Grounds of the Mechanical Hypothesis', p. 152). It is explored with characteristic brilliance in H. Blumenberg, *Die Lesbarkeit der Welt*.

[21] The contrast between the *didactic* justification of apparent evil – that it turns men's minds from this world to the next – and the 'providentialist' idea that bad things bring about something that is good in this world, is, it should be said, an oversimplification, for the didactic and the providentialist idea are not necessarily opposed to one another. Providentialism is also didactic – what more worthy object of contemplation and better lesson could there be, the providentialists argued, than the wonderful ways in which God works for man's benefit?

A. O. Lovejoy's celebrated 'principle of plenitude' is something different again. The idea here is that reality contains all possibilities. Thus bad things are seen as a logically necessary part of – but they are not themselves a causal means to – a whole that is perfect, hence good.

the transience of the empires of this world and the eternity and stability of his own order. In addition, the fate of empires shows the vanity of earthly things.[22] However, the history of the sacred peoples – the Jews and the Christians – has a more direct message: it shows that piety is rewarded (even in this world) and godlessness punished. This is the sense in which the Jews are a 'chosen people'.[23] After the life of Christ and St Paul's opening up of the Gospel to the Gentiles, the prosperity of the Church and the ill fortune of the Jews are each clear demonstrations of God's will:

> Thus, besides the advantage which the Church of Christ has of being the only one founded upon miraculous and divine events that were written about openly and without fear of being refuted, at the very time they happened, there is also in favour of those who did not live during these times an everlasting miracle which confirms the truth of all the rest, and that is the continuity of the religion which is always victorious over the errors that have striven to destroy it. To this you may likewise add another consequence, namely, the visible progression of a continual chastisement of the Jews who have not received the Christ promised to their fathers.[24]

For Bossuet, although the *meaning* of history is not itself temporal, its sacred purpose has manifest consequences in this world: the truth of the

---

[22] In this manner the empires of the world have served religion and the preservation of God's people; and for this reason the same God who inspired his prophets to predict the various situations of his people also inspired them to predict the succession of empires ... The successive fall of these famous empires is shown there, and the new empire which Jesus Christ was to establish is marked so specifically by its own characteristics that it is impossible not to recognize it. It is the empire of the saints of the Highest; it is the empire of the Son of Man: and this empire shall stand when all others fall, since it alone is promised eternal duration ... But even from a merely human point of view, it is extremely useful, especially for princes, to contemplate this passing of empires, since the arrogance which so often attends their eminent position is greatly dampened by this sight. For if men learn moderation when they see the death of kings, how much more will it strike them to see even the death of kingdoms! And what can teach us a more beautiful lesson of the vanity of human greatness? (*Discourse on Universal History*, pp. 301–3.)

[23] ... nothing can be conceived more worthy of God than to have, first of all, chosen to himself a people who should be an example of his eternal Providence; a people whose good or ill fortune should depend upon their piety or impiety and whose condition should testify to the wisdom and justice of him who governed them. (*Discourse on Universal History*, p. 113.)

Voltaire found this outrageous – and dared to say so:

> What I admire most in our modern compilers is the wisdom of good faith with which they prove that all that happened once in the greatest empires of the world happened only for the instruction of the inhabitants of Palestine. If the kings of Babylon in their conquests fall incidentally upon the Hebrews, it is only to chastise these people for their sins. If a king named Cyrus becomes the master of Babylon, it is in order to allow a few Jews to go home. If Alexander is victorious over Darius, it is in order to establish some Jewish second-hand dealers in Alexandria., When the Romans annex Syria and the small district of Judea to their vast empire, it is again for the instruction of the Jews. Arabs and Turks came in only to correct these fortunate people. We must admit that they have had an excellent education: nobody has ever had so many teachers. This shows how purposeful history is. (Voltaire, article 'Histoire', in *Dictionnaire Philosophique* (1765), p. 355.)

[24] *Discourse on Universal History*, p. 291.

Church's doctrine is the guarantor of its temporal success (hence, in the other direction, the Church's worldly success is the sign of its truth) while the fate of the Jews is a just punishment (and those who 'chastise' the Jews are plainly carrying out God's will). To this extent, Bossuet's account is thoroughly Augustinian. What is particularly interesting, however, is his explanation of how it is that Providence intervenes in history to ensure that what God intends actually does come about. This is not, by and large, by miraculous interventions against the order of nature (although Bossuet, of course, as an orthodox Catholic, does not deny their possibility) so much as by God acting on the 'hearts of men'. That is to say, men do indeed make their own history, but their motivations are not unaffected by divine intervention, and this is the particular channel by which God communicates his intentions for mankind through his chosen instruments, the princes and rulers of this world:

> You should recall, however, Monseigneur, that this long concatenation of particular causes which make and unmake empires depends on the secret decrees of Divine Providence. From the highest heavens God holds the reins of every kingdom and holds every heart in his hands. At times he bridles man's passions, at others he gives them free rein; and that is how he moves all of mankind. Should he wish to see a conqueror, he will spread terror before him and will inspire him and his armies with invincible boldness. Should he wish to see legislators he will send them his spirit of wisdom and foresight; he will cause them to forestall the evils that can befall a state and lay the foundations for public tranquility . . .
>
> Alexander did not think that he was working for his captains or for the fall of his house when he made his conquests. When Brutus inspired the Romans with a boundless love of liberty, it did not occur to him that he was planting the seeds of that unbridled license through which the very tyranny he wished to destroy was one day to be restored in a harsher form than under the Tarquins. When the Caesars flattered the soldiers they did not intend to make them masters over their successors and the empire. In a word, there is no power which does not unintentionally serve other ends than its own. God alone can subject everything to his will.[25]

Bossuet's account of providential intervention is tailored for philosophical dualism. God does not intervene visibly and publicly in order to put his purposes into effect. But there *is* specific Divine intervention in individual cases: consciousness – the 'hearts and minds of men' – is where the rise and fall of kingdoms is engineered. To the extent that Bossuet allows for specific divine intervention without calling for the alteration or suspension of the laws governing the material world, we can see his dualism as allowing him to make concessions to the advance of the physical

[25] Ibid., pp. 373–4.

sciences without falling into a full-scale naturalism.[26] Bossuet's overall view of history's purpose, however, remains impeccably Augustinian. The primary purpose of life in this world is to turn men's eyes to God: the goods of this world are illusory and its triumphs fleeting. Yet, at the same time as Bossuet was writing, the idea of the goodness of the world was being radically rehabilitated, nowhere more manifestly than in the writings of Locke, an approximate contemporary. Locke underpins his political theory with the idea of a 'Fundamental Law of Nature' – discoverable by man through the use of his own reason – that mankind is 'to be preserved, as much as possible'.[27] In such a world, apparently bad (or indifferent) events could be seen to be sources of a wider good.

The search for benevolent concatenations of causes and initial conditions appeared to be particularly fruitful in economic life. Jacob Viner, in his book *The Role of Providence in the Social Order*, notes two examples in particular: the idea that what is most necessary to human beings (water, for instance) is most abundant while luxuries, such as diamonds, are scarce (the ancestor of Adam Smith's 'water-diamonds paradox'); and the notion that the dispersal of resources over the globe is providential in encouraging trade. In neither case was the idea original to the seventeenth century. Viner traces both views to non-Christian authors (Philo of Alexandria and Libanius of Antioch, respectively) and from them to the Church Fathers. Nevertheless, as Viner makes clear, they remained a very minor current in Christian thought before the seventeenth and eighteenth centuries and were not shared 'by those in the Augustinian tradition, whether Protestant or Catholic', for whom 'the doctrines of the Fall of Man, the curse of Adam, the second Fall of Man and the Flood, were insurmountable barriers to acceptance of optimistic pictures of the destiny of man while on this earth'.[28]

Apart from many examples of particular interconnections, of which Viner notes some picturesque examples,[29] there is the emergence in the

---

[26] In Ronald Meek's view, Bossuet 'made a number of significant bows in the direction of the "modernist" trends which it was one of his main purposes to oppose, and his book in fact prepared the way for the new philosophy of history of the Enlightenment much more directly than he himself would have desired or indeed thought possible' (R. Meek, *Social Science and the Ignoble Savage*, p. 24).

[27] *Second Treatise of Government*, pp. 296–7.

[28] *The Role of Providence in the Social Order*, p. 25.

[29] 'Increase Mather in New England expounded the serviceability to mankind of the signs in the heavens. These gave man awareness of the passage of time and upon occasion acted as special warnings that important events were imminent. He interpreted the eclipse in Boston in August 1672 as evidence that nature shared with Harvard grief at the death of President Chauncey' (*The Role of Providence in the Social Order*, p. 24).

Apparently, Harvard's view of its place in the scheme of things goes back some way.

But Viner warns, too, that 'it was the practice of some anonymous wits of the period, especially in France, to invent fantastic examples of such fitness and attribute them falsely to particular providentialists.' Many of what have come down to us as the most eccentric cases of providentialist credulity – the way in which the colours of the landscape were supposed to have been formed to rest the human eye, or coastlines to permit the protection of ships – were not meant seriously, he

seventeenth and eighteenth century of the more general analogy between the self-sustaining character of economic life, the mutual adjustment of its elements to one another, and the operation of a machine, specifically a watch.[30] Again, the concept is by no means new. The idea that God is a 'watch-maker' (or, earlier, 'clock-maker') goes back a very long way (Viner claims to find it in Cicero, Epictetus and Epicurus). But, according to Hans Blumenberg, the implications that the 'machine' metaphor carried in the ancient and medieval worlds were quite different from its modern connotations:

> If, for example, we encounter in a historical text the expression '*machina*' . . . it is very difficult for the modern interpreter to step aside from his conception of 'machine' and to come to terms with the much less specific intuitive content of the ancient word . . . But *machina* is only as part of its extension a 'machine'; its overriding semantic content is of an entity that is complex, goal-directed, although not immediately transparent in that goal-directed-ness: a cunning manoeuvre, a deceptive trick, an amazing effect. Machines in the narrow sense (for lifting loads or siege-engines) belong in this genus because they achieve an effect that is astonishing to the uninitiated observer (which is why the expression has spent a great deal of its history in the world of the theatre, where the effect on the spectator is not extrinsic) . . . Above all it is important to keep the idea of the *machina mundi* separate from the notion that was only combined with it by modern deism: that of the automatic 'functioning' of the world – guaranteed by its immanent perfection – without the need for transcendent subvention. It was the metaphor of 'clockwork' that gave the thin and unspecific expression *machina mundi* such pregnant specification: the unwinding of a once tensioned spring, that is constrained to reliable uniformity.

The clock analogy in a recognizably modern sense became increasingly important for writing about economic life in the seventeenth and eighteenth centuries. As early as 1601, the English writer Gerald de Malynes (discussing the way in which the export of money forces discrepant price levels in different countries to adjust to one another) comments:

> We see how one thing driveth or enforceth another, like as in a clocke where there be many wheels, the first wheel being stirred, driveth the next, and

---

thinks (*The Role of Providence in the Social Order*, p. 24).

However, no less unironical a thinker than Kant gives some very strange instances of apparently providential design. For example, Kant is impressed by the operation of the ocean currents in connecting the Arctic regions with the temperate: 'Nature's care arouses most admiration, however, by carrying driftwood to those treeless regions, without anyone knowing exactly where it comes from. For if they did not have this material, the natives would not be able to construct either boats or weapons, or dwellings in which to live' ('Perpetual Peace', p. 110).

Future historians will have similar problems in deciding the seriousness of sociobiology, no doubt.

[30] H. Blumenberg, 'Paradigmen zu einer Metaphorologie', pp. 70–1.

that the third, and so forth, till the last that moveth the instrument that strikes the clocke.[31]

An important part of the significance of the watch or machine analogy in the seventeenth and eighteenth centuries was to suggest that the adjustment of interacting causes to produce an overall benevolent effect gave good reason to see the world as providential in its general character, thereby bypassing the need to identify providence with particular interventions against the course of nature.[32] Bossuet's successors, who saw not just the material world but history itself as unfolding without the need for particular divine intervention, embraced his suggestion that it is in the passions of men that the secret of the providential character of history lies. The passions are the motivating force for historical change. As Turgot puts it in the middle of the eighteenth century:

> Empires rise and fall; the laws and forms of government succeed one another; the arts and sciences are discovered and made more perfect. Sometimes arrested, sometimes accelerated in their progress, they pass through different climates. Interest, ambition and vain glory perpetually change the scene of the world, inundating the earth with blood. But in the midst of these ravages man's mores [les moeurs] become sweeter, the human mind becomes enlightened, and the isolated nations come closer to each other. Commerce and politics reunite finally all the parts of the globe and the whole mass of human-kind, alternating between calm and agitation, good and bad, marches constantly, though slowly, toward greater perfection.[33]

If the passions are potentially destructive, they are also vital and animating; moreover, providentially, it is their *unintended consequences* that are the means by which men are led to develop from barbarism to civilization. It is the way in which the passions are ordered, balanced and set in play one against the other that is the secret key to history – and, in the process, the passions themselves come to be changed:[34]

> Men's passions, even their furies, have led them, without their knowing where they are going. I think I see an immense army whose movements are all directed by a mighty genius. At the sight of the military signals, at the tumultuous noise of trumpets and drums, whole squadrons deploy, even the horses are full of a fire which has no purpose, each group marches on across the obstacles without knowing the issue, only the chief perceives the effect of so many combined movements: in the same way the blind passions have multiplied ideas, enlarged knowledge, and made minds more perfect, owing

[31] G. De Malynes, *A Treatise of the Canker of England's Common Wealth* (London, 1601), pp. 95–6, quoted in R. Brown, *The Nature of Social Laws*, p. 43. For the idea of an economic machine see also R. Meek, 'The Rise and Fall of the Concept of the Economic Machine', and A. Hirschmann, *The Passions and the Interests*.
[32] See R. Brown, *The Nature of Social Laws*, p. 123.
[33] Turgot, 'A Philosophical Review of the Successive Advances of the Human Mind', p. 41.
[34] See the discussion of the 'passions and the interests' in Ch. 3 above, pp. 65–7.

to the lack of a reason whose day had not yet arrived and which would have been less powerful if it had governed earlier.[35]

Thus, without individuals being aware of it, Providence enables good consequences to follow from aspects of human nature that are, apparently, bad.[36] Voltaire brings the idea of the watch-maker God and of the special, providential role of the passions together explicitly in his *Traité de métaphysique*:

> It is with this mainspring [sc. the passions] that God, called by Plato the eternal geometer, but whom I call here the eternal engineer [*machiniste*], animated and embellished nature: the passions are the wheels which set all these machines in motion.[37]

In this context, the analogy with the machine is positive: it denotes the purposeful relationship between the Creator and his creation, on the one hand, and the benevolent organization and adjustment of parts to one another, on the other. The idea that the universe consisted of a harmonious adjustment of parts was, of course, immensely reinforced by the development of Newtonian physics and the discussion of its significance – Newton's own conception of the universe as requiring the occasional intervention of God was described by Leibniz as a 'watch that the Creator has to wind up from time to time'. The point to note is this. The Newtonian conception of the universe made no reference to the *immanent* operation of purpose, but the particular forces that Newton identified were related to one another in a manner that ensured that the universe (or, at least, the solar system) was in *balance*. Thus the 'adjustment' by which the Creator's purpose was supposed to be revealed lay in the simplicity and

---

[35] Turgot, 'On Universal History', pp. 69–70.
Compare Marx's use of the military analogy in *Das Kapital* for the emergence of collective power in the labour process:

> Just as the offensive power of a squadron of cavalry, or the defensive power of a regiment of infantry, is essentially different from the sum of the offensive or defensive powers of the individual cavalry or infantry soldiers taken separately, so the sum total of the mechanical forces exerted by isolated workmen differs from the social force that is developed, when many hands take part simultaneously in one and the same undivided operation, such as raising a heavy weight, turning a winch, or removing an obstacle ... Not only have we here an increase in the productive force [*Produktivkraft*] of the individual, by means of co-operation, but the creation of a new productive force, namely, the collective power of masses [*Massenkraft*]. (*Das Kapital*, Vol. 1, p. 343 [Eng. trans., pp. 355–58].)

[36] Rather later, Kant was to take up the same idea of the transforming power of the passions in a famous passage of his 'Idea for a Universal Natural History with a Cosmopolitan Purpose' (1784):

> Nature should thus be thanked for fostering social incompatibility, enviously competitive vanity and insatiable desires. Without these desires, all man's excellent natural capacities would never be raised to develop ... The natural impulses ... the sources of the very unsociableness which cause so many evils, at the same time encourage man towards new exertions of his powers and thus towards a further development of his capacities. (p. 45)

[37] Voltaire, *Traité de métaphysique* (1734), Ch. 8. Lovejoy gives a slightly different quote as from *Dieu et les hommes*.

harmony of the laws themselves. An explicitly 'Newtonian' account of society that makes this point clear is given by Montesquieu in his discussion of the 'principle of monarchy' in the *Spirit of the Laws*:

> It is with this kind of government as with the system of the universe, in which there is a power that constantly repels all bodies from the centre, and a power of gravitation that attracts them to it. Honor sets all the parts of the body politic in motion, and by its very action connects them; thus each individual advances the public good, while he only thinks of promoting his own interest.[38]

III Vico

Commentators have very often seen Vico (1668–1744) as the founder of the conception of history as unfolding development that we find in Hegel and Marx. According to Isaiah Berlin, for example, Vico is 'for better and for worse' the 'pioneer' of this view.[39] That *The New Science* (1725) is a novel work in very many ways is indisputable, but it seems to me that much of its originality is a product of the eclectic way in which it combines various contemporary and ancient ideas, rather than (whatever Vico himself may claim) embodying the consistent working out of a single, unprecedented insight. Vico's professed intention for his 'new science' is that it should be a 'demonstration, so to speak, of what providence has wrought in history, for it must be a history of the institutions by which, without human discernment or counsel, and often against the designs of men, providence has ordered the great city of the human race.'[40] While this conception of history makes the idea of 'unintended consequences' fundamental, it does so in a way that incorporates important elements of contemporary providentialism, as well as of Augustinianism, ancient cyclical theories and foundation myths.

Vico, like Bossuet, makes a clear distinction between gentile history and the history of the Jews. However, while Bossuet allows that providence intervenes specifically in both cases, Vico restricts special intervention to the history of the Jews.[41] Gentile history thus shows in pure form the adjustment of means to ends that is characteristic of providence generally. Since providence has for its end, 'its own immeasurable goodness', whatever it institutes must be directed to 'a good always superior to that which men proposed to themselves' and this is 'the preservation of the

---

[38] *The Spirit of the Laws*, Bk III, Ch. 7, p. 25.
[39] *Vico and Herder*, p. 35.
[40] *The New Science*, para. 342, p. 60.
[41] 'For besides the ordinary help from providence [that is, the benefit of Divine benevolence in the ordering of the world] which was all that the gentiles had, the Hebrews had extraordinary help from the true God, which was their reason for dividing the whole world of nations into Hebrews and gentiles' (para. 312, p. 48).

human race'.[42] Even to the gentiles, in Vico's view, God's goodness expresses itself materially. To look at gentile history is instructive, Vico believes, but the point is not the contrast between its wretchedness and transitoriness and the glory of the heavenly city. Rather, when we look at the way in which God provides gentile nations with customs and institutions appropriate to their (in many cases cruel and barbarous) natures, we shall find a realization in social terms of the Argument from Design and a refutation of materialism and naturalism:

> These proofs will become luminous and distinct when we reflect with what ease the institutions are brought into being, by occasions arising often far apart and sometimes quite contrary to the proposals of men, yet fitting together of themselves ... And [the reader] will find that he has thereby proved to the Epicureans that their chance cannot wander foolishly about and everywhere find a way out, and to the Stoics that their eternal chain of causes, to which they will have it the world is chained, itself hangs upon the omnipotent, wise, and beneficent will of the best and greatest God.[43]

Vico sees this demonstration in the way in which, from simple origins, complex and purposive effects result, and in the contrast between the ends intended by agents and the ends brought about by their actions. Such reversals take place, as Vico points out, not in the world of inanimate nature but as a result of the freely chosen actions of human beings. The 'unintended consequences' at issue are, he claims, not the entropic side-effects that chance and uncertainty introduce to undermine the realization in the material world of human intentions but a special kind of finality. Towards the end of the book, Vico enumerates some of what he considers to be the most striking ways in which such reversals are brought about:

> Men mean to gratify their bestial lust and abandon their offspring, and they inaugurate the chastity of marriage from which the families arise. The fathers mean to exercise without restraint their paternal power over their clients, and they subject them to the civil powers from which the cities arise. The reigning order of nobles mean to abuse their lordly freedom over the plebeians, and they are obliged to submit to the laws which establish popular liberty. The free peoples mean to shake off the yoke of their laws, and they become subject to monarchs. The monarchs mean to strengthen their own positions by debasing their subjects with all the vices of dissoluteness, and they dispose them to endure the slavery of stronger nations. The nations mean to dissolve themselves, and their remnants flee for safety to the wilderness, whence, like the phoenix, they rise again.[44]

Although Vico claims that his examples show that providence works in the best possible way, those that he offers, it must be said, do not show

[42] Ibid., paras. 343–4, p. 60.
[43] Ibid., paras. 344–5, pp. 60–1.
[44] Ibid., para. 1108, pp. 382–3.

any particularly extended concatenation of particular causes: men simply take on projects that fail and then pay the price in the revenge or resistance of others. The fact that nobles who 'abuse their lordly freedom' should bring about popular liberty is no more notable or counterintuitive than the observation that gamblers, in trying to get the money to live luxuriously, more usually lose what they originally have and are forced to live even more poorly. No doubt, if one were committed to a providentialist view, one could see this as a case of bad things leading to good. But there is nothing implausible or incomplete about a non-teleological, purely individualistic account of these same events. Nevertheless, unlike Bossuet, Vico does not countenance God's particular intervention in history (apart from in the exceptional cases mentioned above) and so it is clear that he goes further in pursuing the application of general providentialism to history than any of his predecessors had done.

IV The Four Stages Theory

But Vico is a symptom of the emergence of a new view of history, rather than the initiator of it.[45] Much more significant for its influence on contemporaries was the appearance of a schema of historical development that was to become something like a prevailing orthodoxy among the thinkers of the French and the Scottish Enlightenment: the so-called Four Stages Theory.[46]

According to the theory, human society develops through four economic stages: hunting, pasturage, agriculture and commerce. These succeed each other in a fixed sequence. Furthermore, at each stage, the economic form of the society in question is thought of as being prior to, and (to some degree) determinant of, its institutions and customs. Finally, the theory was a theory of progress in a double sense: a picture of economic advance which is at the same time a moral one.[47]

Each of these elements is clearly of considerable relevance to the theory of ideology – indeed, the Four Stages Theory apparently represents a striking anticipation of two of the most characteristic features of Marx's historical materialism: the progression of society through definite economic 'modes of production' and the 'primacy' of economic life in determining the wider structure of society.[48] Furthermore, the fact that such a novel theory should appear in France and Scotland apparently simultaneously (in unpublished lectures by Turgot and Smith of around 1750, if Ronald

---

[45] Although the details of the dissemination of Vico's ideas are a matter of dispute, it is beyond doubt that *The New Science* was almost unknown for most of the eighteenth century.
[46] Meek, *Social Science and the Ignoble Savage* and 'The Scottish Contribution to Marxist Sociology'.
[47] As Walter Bagehot describes Smith's version of the theory, it was an attempt to show 'how, from being a savage, man rose to be a Scotchman' (W. Bagehot, *Biographical Studies*, quoted in D. Reisman, *Adam Smith's Sociological Economics*, p. 138).
[48] See particularly, Meek, 'The Scottish Contribution to Marxist Sociology'.

Meek is correct) and that it should have gained adherents so swiftly[49] itself seems to indicate that 'the time must in some sense and for some reason have been ripe for these events, and the way must have been prepared for them by certain earlier events.'[50]

Meek is certainly right to see the Four Stages Theory as distinctive and novel. There had, it is true, been many earlier narratives of different 'ages' of mankind, descriptions of the way in which the customs and ways of life of different peoples diverged, and accounts, more or less speculative, of the transition from the isolated, primitive life of man in the 'state of nature' to the organized life of the *polis* or 'civil society'. But they are quite different from the idea that (as Meek puts it): 'the key factor in the process of development was the mode of subsistence'.[51]

To appreciate its novelty, we need only compare the discussion in Montesquieu's *Spirit of the Laws* (1748) that comes closest to anticipating the Four Stages Theory. This is the treatment in Book XVIII of 'Laws in the Relation they bear to the Nature of the Soil'. There, it is true, Montesquieu does discuss the variation of laws and customs in relation to different 'modes of subsistence' – for example, those peoples who do and those who do not 'know the use of money' or those who do and those who do not cultivate the land. But there is no suggestion that there is any kind of necessary progress from one mode of subsistence to another – nor that it is the mode of subsistence that, ultimately, plays the determining role in relation to other institutions.[52]

---

[49] Meek mentions five authors – Kames and Dalrymple in Scotland, Quesnay, Helvétius and Goguet in France – who made public use of the theory in the 1750s. (*Social Science and the Ignoble Savage*, pp. 91, 99.)

[50] Ibid., p. 91.

[51] Ibid., p. 2.

[52] The question of Montesquieu's view of history – or, rather, the absence from Montesquieu of a view of history as an unfolding development – is addressed by Becker, who considers it to be characteristic of the eighteenth century in general:

> Professor Vaughan points out that Montesquieu was troubled with difficulties which the idea of the progressive unfolding of institutions would easily have disposed of, and is at a loss to understand why Montesquieu did not make use of the idea, since all the elements of it were there, in his own manuscript, staring up at him from the table. Very true it is that the idea was there in his own manuscript. But the significant thing is that Montesquieu made little use of it, that no one (Leibniz excepted) made much use of it. The idea was present in the eighteenth century, but no one made it welcome; it wandered forlornly about in the fringes of consciousness, it timidly approached the threshold, but it never really got across. (*The Heavenly City of the Eighteenth-Century Philosophers*, p. 97.)

If I have understood correctly what Becker means by the 'idea of the progressive unfolding of institutions', then it seems to me that this is precisely what the Four Stages Theory – schematic and unsophisticated as we might think it to be – amounted to. The question, therefore, is not, as Becker supposes: Why did the eighteenth century not take up the idea of a progressive unfolding of institutions? but: Why did they not do so prior to Turgot and Smith, yet adopted it so swiftly thereafter?

Becker's answer to his own (I believe, spurious) question is that the eighteenth century writers 'were not primarily interested in stabilizing society, but in changing it. They did not ask how society had come to be what it was, but how it could be made better than it was' – which seems to me to be obviously untrue. Meek's explanation for the adoption of the Four Stages Theory – the growth of interest in the nature of 'primitive' man – also appears speculative at best.

From the point of view of the theory of ideology, it is the connection between economic life and other institutions, customs and ideas that is of the greatest significance. Meek records a number of instances of such a claimed connection on the part of the thinkers of the Scottish Enlightenment. Thus Ferguson asserts that ' . . . forms of government take their rise chiefly from the manner in which the members of a state have been originally classed.'[53] The historian Robertson maintains that:

> . . . in every inquiry concerning the operations of men when united together in society, the first object of attention should be their mode of subsistence. Accordingly as that varies, their laws and policy must be different.[54]

and:

> Upon discovering in what state property was at any particular period, we may determine with precision what was the degree of power possessed by the king or by the nobility at that juncture.[55]

While John Millar gives an account of the role played by 'differences of situation' at the beginning of his *Origin of the Distinction of Ranks*:

> The variety that frequently occurs in these, and such other particulars, must have a prodigious influence upon the great body of a people; as, by giving a peculiar direction to their inclination and pursuits, it must be productive of correspondent habits, dispositions, and ways of thinking.[56]

These passages are certainly extremely striking – the more so to the modern reader because they are apparently written in the empirical language of causal science, rather than being speculative reconstructions based on an *a priori* providentialist teleology.[57] But it must be said that they remain isolated and programmatic occurrences within the authors' works. Neither Ferguson, Robertson nor Millar support such general

---

[53] *An Essay on the History of Civil Society*, p. 226, quoted in R. Meek, 'The Scottish Contribution to Marxist Sociology', p. 38.

[54] W. Robertson, *History of America* (1777), Vol. I, p. 324, quoted in R. Meek, 'The Scottish Contribution to Marxist Sociology', p. 37.

[55] W. Robertson, *The History of the Reign of the Emperor Charles V* (1769), Vol. I, p. 222, quoted in R. Meek, 'The Scottish Contribution to Marxist Sociology', pp. 37–8.

[56] J. Millar, *Origin of the Distinction of Ranks* (1771), quoted in R. Meek, 'The Scottish Contribution to Marxist Sociology', p. 40.

[57] This is not to suggest that, for these authors, the empirical approach would have been thought to be incompatible with teleology. In Viner's view:

Eighteenth-century British social philosophy was in fact soaked in teleology. I know of no British writer before Bentham who frankly renounced teleology, and of no important writers except Mandeville and David Hume – and perhaps Thomas Hobbes – who could plausibly be interpreted on the basis of their actual writings as not honestly accepting it. There is no logical conflict between teleology and automatism if ends or design have been built into the mechanism itself, as was universally affirmed. (*The Role of Providence in the Social Order*, p. 24.)

claims with any very extensive range of examples of correspondences between economic life and other institutions and customs beyond what is to be found already in Montesquieu; nor do they address the problem of identifying a mechanism in society by which these connections might come into being. For a more extensive empirical investigation of the connection between economic life, political institutions, customs and ideas, we must turn to Adam Smith.

V Adam Smith: Unintended Consequences and the 'Invisible Hand'

Adam Smith must occupy the central place in any account of ideas about unintended consequences in eighteenth-century social theory. Not only does Meek make a good case for him as the co-originator (with Turgot) of the Four Stages Theory, but he was – was he not? – the prophet of the Invisible Hand. Yet the place of the idea of unintended consequences in Smith's social theory is somewhat different than the received image of him as a *laissez-faire* ultra-individualist would suggest.[58]

Smith was certainly a providentialist in his general view of society, as he makes clear in the *Theory of the Moral Sentiments*. According to Smith, there is no contradiction between the scientific perspective of efficient causes and the providential one of teleology:[59]

In every part of the universe we observe means adjusted with the nicest artifice to ends which they are intended to produce; and in the mechanism of a plant, or animal body, admire how every thing is contrived for advancing two great purposes of nature, the support of the individual and the propagation of the species. But in these, and in all such objects, we still distinguish the efficient from the final cause of their several motions and organizations. The digestion of the food, the circulation of the blood, and the secretion of the several juices which are drawn from it, are operations all of them necessary

---

[58] If there were to be a prize for the author on politics whose work is most consistently misrepresented, Smith should surely win it (with de Tocqueville and Rousseau as runners-up). Stephen Leacock's version of the economists' received wisdom is wittier than most:

> Adam Smith! Adam Smith!
> Listen what I charge you with.
> Didn't you say
> In the class one day
> That selfishness was bound to pay?
> Of all your doctrines that was the pith
> Wasn't it, wasn't it, wasn't it, Smith?
> (Stephen Leacock, *Hellements of Hickonomics*)

To which question the only answer is 'No'.

[59] Adam Smith, *The Theory of Moral Sentiments*. It has been suggested that there is some incompatibility between the 'selfish' view of man presented by Smith in *The Wealth of Nations* (1776) and the 'sociable' view of *The Theory of the Moral Sentiments*. I see no evidence for this and will treat the two works as continuous with one another.

for the great purposes of animal life. Yet we never endeavour to account for them from those purposes as from their efficient causes, nor imagine that the blood circulates, or that the food digests of its own accord, and with a view or intention to the purposes of circulation or digestion. The wheels of the watch are all admirably adjusted to the end for which it was made, the pointing of the hour. All their various motions conspire in the nicest manner to produce this effect. If they were endowed with a desire and intention to produce it, they could not do it better. Yet we never ascribe any such desire or intention to them, but to the watch-maker, and we know that they are put in motion by a spring, which intends the effects it produces as little as they do. But though, in accounting for the operations of bodies, we never fail to distinguish in this manner the efficient from the final cause, in accounting for those of the mind we are very apt to confound these two different things with one another. When by natural principles we are led to advance those ends, which a refined and enlightened reason would recommend to us, we are very apt to impute to that reason, as to their efficient cause, the sentiments and actions by which we advance those ends, and to imagine that to be the wisdom of man, which in reality is the wisdom of God.[60]

Perhaps the most striking feature of this passage to the modern reader is that Smith makes no distinction between 'organism' and 'mechanism': he invokes simultaneously the organic analogy between society and an animal body and the mechanical one between society and a watch. Indeed, he speaks (in a way that would seem to be plainly oxymoronic to later thinkers) of the '*mechanism* of a plant, or animal body'. What is common to both analogies is the adjustment of causal processes in such a way that, when set in motion within the system, they bring about a concatenation of effects that can be recognized as purposive. In the case of society, the 'efficient' causality comes from human beings' 'sentiments and actions' – sentiments that are 'rational', yet not the product of individuals' reason. The editors of *The Theory of Moral Sentiments* refer this aspect of Smith's thought back to the Stoic view of nature as a cosmic harmony and point out that 'Phrases that occur in Smith's account of this Stoic conception are echoed when he expresses his own opinion.'[61] However this may be,[62] Smith's choice of analogies and, above all, his application of them to the organization of society identify his conception of cosmic harmony as one that is also very much of his own time.

But although Smith's general conception of society is strongly providentialist, his account of particular cases of unintended consequences is far from embodying uniformly the naive optimism that asserts that 'everything is for the best in this best of all worlds'. Indeed, without splitting hairs, it is possible to identify six different kinds of unintended consequence that play a significant role in Smith's writings:

[60] *The Theory of Moral Sentiments*, II.ii.3.5, p. 87.
[61] Ibid., p. 7.
[62] It is worth recalling Blumenberg's strictures regarding the dangers of an anachronistic interpretation of the ancient idea of the *machina mundi* (see note 30 above).

1 *Unintended consequences that are in the interests both of the original agent and of others* The clearest example of this is the 'principle of authority': Smith's account of the way in which our disposition to sympathise more easily with those who are our social superiors sustains *de facto* authority.[63] This is an example of a straightforwardly beneficial unintended consequence: as Smith understands it at least, it is in our individual interests to support the social order and so our natural disposition to do so is both in our interests and in the interests of our fellow-citizens.[64]

2 *Unintended consequences that do not go against the interests of the original agent and that are in the interests of others* It is my contention that the two examples – the one in *The Theory of Moral Sentiments*, the other in *The Wealth of Nations* – which Smith refers to explicitly as products of the 'invisible hand' are of this kind.

In *The Theory of Moral Sentiments*, Smith uses the phrase in connection with the distributive consequences of the unequal allocation of resources. This unequal allocation does allow the rich to consume more than the poor, he concedes. But how much more the rich consume in fact depends not on their desires but on their physical capacity, which, fortunately, is severely limited ('The homely and vulgar proverb, that the eye is larger than the belly, never was more fully verified . . . ')[65] Thus the rich:

> . . . are led *by an invisible hand* to make nearly the same distribution of the necessaries of life, which would have been made, had the earth been divided into equal portions among all its inhabitants, and thus without intending it, without knowing it, advance the interest of society, and afford means to the multiplication of the species.[66]

The rich consciously pursue their own interest (try to maximize their consumption) and succeed in doing so (although this does not lead them to consume as much as they suppose that they would like to). In this, they advance, Smith claims, the interests of the poor. (Smith's argument, it must be said, seems fairly obviously specious. To be sure, consumption by the rich 'benefits' the poor to the extent that the poor receive more than

---

[63] See Chapter 3, pp. 95–9 above.

[64] Although he considers this to be an example of the arrangement of human sentiments to produce an effect equivalent to that which might have been produced by rational reflection, Smith does not think that the disposition to obedience is always rational: it can also help to support tyranny (and he is clear that there is no inference from this fact to the idea that tyranny is either rational or justified). Our sentiments should not be thought of, in Smith's view, as being somehow above or immune to reason, a point that he illustrates in his discussion of the Greek practice of infanticide:

> When custom can give sanction to so dreadful a violation of humanity, we may well imagine that there is scarce any particular practice so gross which it cannot authorise. Such a thing, we hear men every day saying, is commonly done, and they seem to think this is a sufficient apology for what, in itself, is most unjust and unreasonable conduct. (*The Theory of Moral Sentiments*, V.2.15, p. 210.)

[65] Ibid., IV.1.10, p. 184.

[66] Ibid., IV.1.10–11, pp. 184–5, my emphasis.

they would have done had they not been employed at all. Yet the rich *do* consume more than the poor, even if it is, as Smith, implausibly, claims, only 'little more'. So it follows that the distribution of the 'necessaries of life' that comes to the poor is only 'nearly the same' as would have resulted from an initial equal division of resources. Read in this way, the 'benevolence' seems to consist in the poor not being as badly off as they might have been, not in the more pertinent sense that they are as well off as they could be.)

A similar phenomenon is being described when Smith uses the expression 'invisible hand' in *The Wealth of Nations*. In this case, Smith is discussing the way in which individuals decide to invest. Smith's starting point is that the industry of every society is limited by 'what its capital can maintain':

> No regulation of commerce can increase the quantity of industry in any society beyond what its capital can maintain. It can only divert a part of it into a direction into which it might not otherwise have gone; and it is by no means certain that this artificial direction is likely to be more advantageous to the society than that into which it would have gone of its own accord.[67]

On the contrary, Smith believes, there is good reason to leave matters to the individual, acting in pursuit of his own advantage, for ' ... the study of his own advantage naturally, or rather necessarily leads him to prefer that employment which is most advantageous to society.'[68]

In explaining how it is that the individual pursues what is most advantageous to society, Smith brings forward two very different kinds of consideration.

The first has to do with the fact that, left to themselves, individuals will prefer, other things being equal, to invest their capital at home rather than abroad. In investing, Smith argues, the investor benefits not only himself but those whom he employs. So this tendency to invest at home is beneficial to his fellow-citizens, while not harmful to himself.

The second consideration put forward by Smith is that 'every individual who employs his capital in the support of domestic industry, necessarily endeavours so to direct that industry, that its produce may be of the greatest value'. But, since 'the annual revenue of every society is always precisely equal to the exchangeable value of the whole annual produce of its industry, or rather is precisely the same thing with that exchangeable value' it follows that 'every individual necessarily labours to render the annual revenue of the society as great as he can.'[69] In other words, if each maximizes, all maximize.

It is in the conjunction of these two considerations that the 'invisible hand' manifests itself:

[67] *The Wealth of Nations*, Bk IV, Ch. 2, p. I, 477.
[68] Ibid.
[69] Ibid., Bk IV, Ch. 2, p. I, 477.

By preferring the support of domestic to that of foreign industry, he intends only his own security; and by directing that industry in such a mannner as its produce may be of the greatest value, he intends only his own gain, and he is in this, as in many other cases, led by an invisible hand which was no part of his intention.[70]

From the point of view of 'unintended consequences', the two kinds of consideration are very different. In the first case, there is a separately identifiable beneficial consequence from the decision of individuals acting in their own self-interest – the fact that the investment then leads to the employment of domestic resources, to the benefit of the society at home.[71] The second consideration, however, is, arguably, not an unintended *consequence* at all: it is not a separate event following from certain actions but a feature of the overall situation at the time when those actions take place. In this case, all that Smith appears to be claiming is that, if each individual maximizes value for themselves, then society, considered as the sum of individuals, will maximize value as a whole. This (and a few similar passages) is presumably the source for Smith's reputation as the founder of red-in-tooth-and-claw *laissez-faire* – unfortunately for him, since they seem to embody the 'fallacy of composition' in the most naive and crude form. It is simply not true that we can each maximize our own well-being atomistically, without effects on others and *their* ability to maximize *their* well-being.[72]

What is plain in both examples of the 'invisible hand' mentioned by Smith is that, although in each case the original agent is pursuing his own interests, the unintended consequence is not such as to amplify his success: the beneficial effects are the effects that his self-regarding actions have on others.

3 *Unintended consequences that go against the interests of the original agent*

---

[70] Ibid.

[71] One should point out that Smith's argument here would be held by modern economists to be invalid – or, rather, to hold only under some very restrictive assumptions, of which he is not, apparently, aware. For investment at home to benefit the domestic economy by 'setting in motion' resources, it must be true that those resources are currently lying idle (or are underused): it is no 'benefit' if, in preferring to invest at home, the investor 'crowds out' the use of resources that would otherwise be employed more profitably in other ways.

Furthermore, the 'benefit' is obviously relative to a restrictive choice of alternatives. Imagine two countries, A and B, with investors X and Y. If each has a non-rational preference for investing at home then A will benefit from X's investment and B will benefit from Y's investment – but that is not to say that both would not have been even better off if X had invested in B and Y in A.

[72] On the very next page, indeed, we find Smith's clearest anticipation of Mrs Thatcher's approach to economics: 'What is prudence in the conduct of every private family, can scarcely be folly in that of a great kingdom' (*The Wealth of Nations*, p. I, 478).

It should be pointed out in mitigation – if not exoneration – of Smith here that he is talking about maximizing *value*, by which he means the quantity of 'labour commanded' by the economy. At any one time, he takes this to be fixed (which is, strictly speaking, true, but neglects the important point that the kind of 'artificial' reallocation of resources from one use to another that he deplores can in principle lead to an increase of welfare produced by the same quantity of labour).

but that are in the interests of others The most striking example of this kind of unintended consequence that Smith considers comes when he discusses the decline of baronial power. Smith's argument in *The Wealth of Nations* (an extended form of an argument taken from his friend Hume) is that the 'great proprietors' committed a kind of class suicide. Before the development of commerce and manufacture in the towns, those who owned the land, Smith says, had no outlets through which they could exchange its surplus product. As a result, the great proprietor 'consumes the whole in rustic hospitality at home', building up a great house and paying for a retinue.[73] The barons' distribution of the economic surplus to their servants and retainers in this way was the source of their political power.[74] Any attempt by the crown to strengthen its own authority and to establish 'order and good government' was bound to fail, Smith believes, 'because it could not alter sufficiently that state of property and manners from which the disorders arose'.[75]

What finally did undermine baronial power was a concatenation of self-reinforcing tendencies that followed the development by the great proprietors of an appetite for luxury goods. The towns grew in order to supply them with such goods. With the rise of the towns, however, there was now an outlet for surplus agricultural produce. In response to this increased demand, farms were enlarged and the 'occupiers of land . . . reduced to the number necessary for cultivating it'.[76] The surplus agricultural population was thus removed from the land to the towns, there to become artisans and merchants, no longer dependent upon some feudal lord. For all of these reasons, the balance of power inevitably shifted in favour of the towns (and the crown) and against the great proprietors, and so what started as an attempt by the lords simply to increase their own consumption, ended by undermining their power altogether:

> Having sold their birth-right, not like Esau for a mess of pottage in time of hunger and necessity, but in the wantonness of plenty, for trinkets and baubles, fitter to be the playthings of children than the serious pursuits of men, [the great proprietors] became as insignificant as any substantial burgher or tradesman in a city. . . .
>
> A revolution of the greatest importance to the public happiness, was in this manner brought about by two different orders of people, who had not the least intention to serve the public. To gratify the most childish vanity was the sole motive of the great proprietors. The merchants and artificers, much less ridiculous, acted merely from a view to their own interest, and in pursuit of their own pedlar principle of turning a penny where a penny was to be got. Neither of them had either knowledge or foresight of that great

---

[73] *The Wealth of Nations*, Bk III, Ch. 4, p. I, 433.

[74] 'Upon the authority which the great proprietors necessarily had in such a state of things over their tenants and retainers, was founded the power of the ancient barons' (Ibid., Bk III, Ch. 4, p. I, 435).

[75] Ibid., Bk III, Ch. 4, p. I, 437.

[76] Ibid., Bk III, Ch. 4, pp. I, 438–9.

revolution which the folly of the one, and the industry of the other, was gradually bringing about.[77]

Smith makes clear that this outcome represents more than simply an (unintended) shift of power from barons to towns: it is a 'revolution of the greatest importance to the public happiness'; in other words, a benefit to society as a whole that can reasonably be seen as part of the benevolent operation of providence.

4 *Unintended consequences that are in the interests of the original agent but that go against the interests of others* The clearest examples of this sort of unintended consequence come in Smith's discussions in *The Wealth of Nations* of monopoly. The effects of monopoly are generally pernicious, Smith believes, in raising market prices above their natural price and so attracting resources into channels where they are not used to best advantage. Monopoly, Smith says, is always ' . . . a great enemy to good management, which can never be universally established but in consequence of that free and universal competition which forces everybody to have recourse to it for the sake of self-defence.'[78] There is thus a clear contrast between the 'advantage which the monopoly procures to a single order of men' (who can flourish without being efficient) and the ways in which it is 'hurtful to the general interest of the country'.[79]

An even more important (if less clear-cut) example of an unintended consequence of this kind is the effects, as Smith sees them, of the division of labour. The idea of a continuously increasing division of labour is the central unifying theme of *The Wealth of Nations*: it is the motor of human progress and to that extent Smith is committed to a view of it as benevolent to all. Nevertheless, Smith is in no doubt as to its pernicious side-effects, which he describes vividly:

> In the progress of the division of labour, the employment of the far greater part of those who live by labour, that is, of the great body of the people, comes to be confined to a few very simple operations; freqently to one or two. But the understandings of the greater part of men are necessarily formed by their ordinary employments. The man whose whole life is spent in performing a few simple operations, of which the effects too are, perhaps, always the same, or very nearly the same, has no occasion to exert his understanding, or to exercise his invention in finding out expedients for removing difficulties which never occur. He naturally loses, therefore, the habit of such exertion, and generally becomes as stupid and ignorant as it is possible for a human creature to become.[80]

Dramatic though these effects are, however, they do not, apparently, in

---

[77] Ibid., Bk III, Ch. 4, pp. I, 439–40.
[78] Ibid., Bk I, Ch. 11, Pt 1, p. I, 165.
[79] Ibid., Bk IV, Ch. 7, Pt 3, p. II, 139.
[80] Ibid., Bk V, Ch. 1, Pt 3, Art. 2, pp. II, 302–3.

Smith's view, outweigh the good effects of the division of labour itself – not least because they are not wholly irremediable. It is notable that the passage quoted comes in a section discussing 'the education of youth' and concludes ' . . . this is the state into which the labouring poor.. must necessarily fall, *unless government takes some pains to prevent it*' (my emphasis).

5 *Unintended consequences that go against the interests both of the original agent and of others* In general, Smith argues, monopoly benefits one group at the expense of the broader interests of society. But, in the case of Great Britain's relationship with its American colonies, other factors are also at work. Were the monopolistic restriction on trade with the American colonies lifted, Smith argues, both mother country and colony would benefit; it would be in everyone's interest if Great Britain were to agree to part 'good friends' from the American rebels.[81] But, as Smith himself recognizes, this prescription is wholly unrealistic for reasons of vanity, for 'Such sacrifices, though they might frequently be agreeable to the interest, are always mortifying to the pride of every nation . . .'[82]

Politicians naturally lack the far-sightedness to enforce the general interest against the vanity and the misconceptions of the citizens, who see only the immediate benefits from the particular trade, while not appreciating how much greater those benefits would be if only no attempt was made to steer and control them:

> To found a great empire for the sole purpose of raising up a people of customers, may at first sight appear a project fit only for a nation of shopkeepers. It is, however, a project altogether unfit for a nation of shopkeepers; but extremely fit for a nation whose government is influenced by shopkeepers.[83]

Here, then, it is the short-sightedness of politicians pursuing what they mistakenly believe to be the general interest (rather than the particular interests of a particular section of society) that leads to unintended consequences harmful to that interest.

6 *Unintended consequences that go against the interests of the original agent without affecting the interests of others* This is the most traditional – and hence, from the point of view of this chapter, perhaps, the least interesting – form of unintended consequence: the bad results that follow for individuals from their inability to perceive their own best interests.[84] The clearest example that Smith gives is the way in which leases were kept

---

[81] Ibid., Bk IV, Ch. 7, Pt 3, p. II, 132.
[82] Ibid., Bk IV, Ch. 7, Pt 3, p. II, 131.
[83] Ibid., Bk IV, Ch. 7, Pt 3, p. II, 129.
[84] A feature of human nature discussed forcefully by Hobbes, for example:

> For all men are by nature provided of notable multiplying glasses, (that is their passions and Self-love,) through which every little payment appeareth a great grievance; but are destitute of those prospective glasses, (namely Morall and Civil Science,) to see a farre off the miseries that hang over them, and cannot without such payments be avoided. (Hobbes, *Leviathan*, p. 239.)

short in the (supposed) interest of the proprietors of land – who were, as Smith points out, 'anciently the legislators of every part of Europe'. But, Smith says, 'Avarice and injustice are always shortsighted, and [the proprietors did not foresee how much this regulation must obstruct improvement, and thereby hurt in the long-run the real interest of the landlord.'[85]

The detailed accounts that Smith gives of so many different kinds of unintended consequence are evidence of his close historical and sociological observativeness. But the fact that, as he makes clear, many unintended consequences are not beneficial might be thought to throw doubt on how appropriate it is to call him a providentialist. Providentialism, after all, is supposed to show how things (particularly, apparently bad or morally indifferent things) have good consequences. Yet several of the examples just discussed are cases in which Smith clearly believes that the unintended consequences are bad, not just for the agents themselves, but for society as a whole.

I do not think that there is necessarily any conflict, however. Smith thought of himself as a kind of 'physician' to the body politic, a body which may be either healthy or sick (and will become more or less so depending on whether the therapy to which it is subjected is appropriate or not). For Smith, the mark of a *healthy* social organism is that the unintended consequences of social actions undertaken within it are beneficial; if it is sick, they are not. Societies are healthy if they are organized in ways that are 'natural'.[86] If monopolies and other restrictions on trade and competition are prohibited, capital is left to find its own best use, and, in general, individuals permitted (indeed, required) to make their own way then society's innate vigour will be maximized. In that case, there are beneficial unintended consequences (the examples of the 'invisible hand') and even negative side-effects (above all, the effects of the division of labour) are not wholly irremediable. On the other hand, in societies governed by arrangements that he considers to be 'artificial' – characterized by rigid attempts to intervene and control – the side-effects of social action are pernicious and enervating.

A very clear statement of this contrast can be found in *The Theory of Moral Sentiments*. Smith contrasts there the approach that seeks to work in accord with society's own nature, with what he calls the 'spirit of system'. The 'man of system', as Smith describes him:

> . . . seems to imagine that he can arrange the different members of a great society with as much ease as the hand arranges the different pieces upon a chess-board. He does not consider that the pieces upon the chess-board have

---

[85] *The Wealth of Nations*, Bk III, Ch. 2, p. I, 416.
[86] A term which for Smith, as for most of his contemporaries, has a clearly affirmative moral dimension. It was only Hume (in his essay 'On Suicide') who called into question the idea that something could happen in nature and yet be called 'unnatural'.

no other principle of motion besides that which the hand impresses upon them; but that, in the great chess-board of human society, every single piece has a principle of motion of its own, altogether different from that which the legislature might chuse to impress upon it.[87]

In *The Wealth of Nations*, Smith returns to this theme and takes the opportunity of making the medical analogy explicit in terms of a contrast between his own views regarding the health of society and those of the physiocrat Quesnay, a former doctor:

Some speculative physicians seem to have imagined that the health of the human body could be preserved only by a certain precise regime of diet and exercise, of which every, [even] the smallest violation necessarily occasioned some degree of disease or disorder proportioned to the degree of the violation. Experience, however, would seem to show, that the human body frequently preserves, to all appearances at least, the most perfect state of health under a vast variety of different regimens ... Mr. Quesnai [*sic*], who was himself a physician and a very speculative physician, seems to have entertained a notion of the same kind concerning the political body ... He seems not to have considered that in the political body, the natural effort which every man is continually making to better his own condition, is a principle of preservation capable of preventing and correcting in many respects the bad effects of a political oeconomy ... In the political body ... the wisdom of nature has fortunately made ample provision for remedying many of the bad effects of the folly and injustice of man; in the same manner as it has done in the natural body, for remedying those of his sloth and intemperance.[88]

Smith's overall providentialist view still leaves room for a critical contrast between the 'natural' – that which allows the individual constituents of society to follow their own 'principles of motion' – and the 'artificial' organization of society: although he is an optimist, he does not believe that all things *inevitably* turn out for the best. Smith, no less than Rousseau, believes that it is up to human beings to adopt the 'natural' way of doing things.

VI The Problem of Development

As we have seen, Smith does not distinguish between the adjustment of parts to one another that is characteristic of 'machines' and the organization of an organic being. In this respect he was not fundamentally different from his contemporaries in France or Germany. On the other hand, he does make use of a specifically organic contrast (between the sick and the healthy) in order to distinguish those societies that are well ordered from

---

[87] *The Theory of Moral Sentiments*, VI.ii.2.18, pp. 233–4.
[88] *The Wealth of Nations*, Bk IV, Ch. 9, pp. II, 194–5.

those that are not. Yet the contrast between forms of political life that are bad and 'artificial' and those that are good and 'natural' would soon come to be identified, not with sick or healthy *organisms*, but with the difference between the organic realm and the mechanical realms *as such*.

When, in 1797, Hegel wrote (or, at least, wrote down) the short fragment that has become known as 'The Oldest System Programme of German Idealism'[89] his use of the term 'mechanical' was wholly pejorative:

> ... I wish to show that there is no *Idea* of the state, because the state is something mechanical, as little as there is an Idea of a machine. Only what is an object of freedom can be called 'Idea'. So we must go beyond the state! For every state must treat free men as mechanical gear-cogs.[90]

When did this transformation happen and what did it involve?

It will be recalled that the essential feature of the mechanical analogy was the idea of the mutual adjustment of parts in a whole: the idea that, as in a watch (or Newton's model of the solar system) the individual elements and the forces to which they were subject had a character such that their causal interaction would be stable, predictable and good. Such interaction could be understood entirely in terms of the operation of efficient causality, but (as Smith says in *The Theory of Moral Sentiments*[91]) that does not exhaust the matter: the arrangement, which ensures that the parts interact in just the benevolent way that they do, requires us also to think in terms of final causality – an overall purpose. The metaphor of the watch suggests that that adjustment and purpose are something essentially unhistorical: the parts are adjusted to one another once and for all and the process, once set in motion, will repeat itself for as long as the motive power – the 'mainspring' – continues. Parts themselves may, perhaps, wear out, but they do not undergo any change or development after the initial adjustment. On the other hand, the providential view of society, as we find it, say, in Turgot or Smith, is by no means an unhistorical one. Individual 'elements' are not static: the violent passions, for example, lead to a transformation by which they themselves come to be limited and transformed into calmer, more 'polite' forms. Here, then, is the first motivation for the 'organic' analogy: to do justice to the idea of *growth*.

How growth was to be understood – the ways in which it comes about that the seed transforms itself into the plant, the embryo into the adult animal – was a significant problem for eighteenth-century biologists,[92] to

---

[89] Scholars will know that both the date and the authorship of this text are extremely controversial. However, these are currently the best-argued conclusions. See C. Jamme and H. Schneider (eds), *Mythologie der Vernunft*.

[90] *Mythologie der Vernunft*, pp. 11–12.

[91] Quoted at pp. 120–1 above.

[92] The term 'biology' was coined only at the beginning of the nineteenth century to denote a 'vitalistic' approach to the study of the natural world (in contrast to the classificatory aspirations of eighteenth-century 'natural history'). However, I use the term here in its modern sense, to include all those whose interests lie in the life sciences.

which there was no agreed, satisfactory solution. The problem was not merely empirical but conceptual: if growth was to be understood as *development*, then it contained an apparently insoluble antinomy. Somewhat oversimplified, the dilemma can be presented as follows.

1 If a final state (FS) is a *development* from an initial state (IS) then there will be some features of FS by which it differs from IS.

2 But then what relationship do those aspects of FS bear to IS?

3a Are these apparently novel elements to be held to be somehow already present, implicitly, but not apparently, in IS? If so, then they are not really something new.

3b On the other hand, if the novel features of FS are *not* to be found already in IS, then they must be something that is – in relation to the antecedent state – arbitrary, and, hence, unexplained.

4 Thus it seems that either FS is inexplicable in relation to IS or else it is not really a *development* from IS at all.

The dilemma presented itself particularly acutely – both at the level of the individual and of the species – in relation to the development of those aspects of human nature that were, apparently, the most distinctively human: reason, mind, language. Since it appeared to be impossible to give a naturalistic account of the development of the mind as a separate mental faculty, it was necessary either to deny the immateriality of the mind altogether (La Mettrie's *homme machine*) or to accept some form of Cartesian dualism: either way, the world is a world of machines – with or without ghosts inside them.

The assumption on which this argument rests is that explanation involves some kind of continuity between what is to be explained and what does the explaining (the *explanandum* and the *explanans*). A *background belief* regarding explanation is at work here – certainly not an unappealing one. Surely, one might think, there must be something *about* the *explanans* that makes it *explanatory of* those features that are found in the *explanandum*.

This conception of explanation has, in fact, been adopted quite recently by Thomas Nagel in his essay 'Panpsychism'. Nagel's argument is worth reviewing here for it casts considerable light on what was at issue for the eighteenth century.

Panpsychism, Nagel argues, seems to follow from the conjunction of four premises:

1 *material composition*: that agents with mental states are composed of matter that 'had a largely inanimate history' before it found its way into us

2 *non-reductionism*: mental states are not physical properties

3 *realism*: but mental states *are* properties of organisms

4 *non-emergence*: there are no truly emergent properties of physical systems.

For present purposes, the interesting premise is premise (4). Nagel argues for this as a consequence of his view of causality. Against a 'correlation' or 'phenomenalist' view of causality, Nagel claims that true causes necessitate their effects in a way that is, in principle, comprehensible, and that, if we are to be able to comprehend that necessity, there must be some feature of the cause that explains why it should have the effect that it does. This is what the correlation view of causality fails to provide:

> ... it is obvious that when I touch a hot pan it causes pain. There *must* be some kind of necessity here. What we cannot understand is *how* the heat ... necessitates the sensation. So long as we remain at the level of a purely physical conception of what goes on in the brain, this will continue to appear impossible.[93]

Nagel, then, rejects the correlationist view of causality as inadequate because it fails to explain *how* the relation that it identifies is explanatory. Unless there were properties present in the initial state corresponding to the properties of the final state, the final state would bear no intelligible relation to the state by which it was supposed to be being explained, and this is what explanation needs, in Nagel's view. The conclusion, for Nagel, is that the causal relations between body and mind require that there should be in the physical system 'intrinsic properties of the components ... from which the mental properties of the system follow necessarily' – in other words, mental features.[94] Panpsychism follows from this.

Like Nagel, the response of many, if not most, eighteenth-century thinkers to the problem of development was to look for continuity between the initial and the final state. Thus they conceived growth in terms of some form of the doctrine of preformation – what was called, confusingly to modern ears, the doctrine of *evolution*. (Their opponents, the 'epigenetists' believed that a form asserted itself gradually and continually in the course of the animal's development.) According to preformationism, whatever features developed later in an organism could be thought of as present, *in nuce*, in the original – 'encased', as Lovejoy puts it, 'within one another like a nest of boxes'.[95] Preformation, it is clear, is very compatible with the watch-maker analogy. For, though the process is an unfolding, not a repetition, what is going on is simply that a chain of efficient causes makes manifest an organization that had been predetermined at the very

---

[93] 'Panpsychism', p. 187.
[94] Ibid.
[95] *The Great Chain of Being*, pp. 243–4.

outset of the process: thus it can be represented as both mechanical and organic.

Historical development, as it had been argued for by Turgot and Smith, could be understood as a providential 'evolution' of this kind – although what was developing was not an individual organism but the species as a whole, moving through stages from 'immaturity' to 'maturity'. An explicit statement of this position is to be found on the very first page of Ferguson's *An Essay on the History of Civil Society* (1767):

> Natural productions are generally formed by degrees. Vegetables grow from a tender shoot, and animals from an infant state . . . This progress in the case of man is continued to a greater extent than in that of any other animal. Not only the individual advances from infancy to manhood, but the species itself from rudeness to civilization.[96]

The implication, however, is that the stages through which the species passes *before* the full development of 'civilization' are somehow deficient: an inadequate anticipation of what will come to full realization only later.

VII The 'Organic' against the 'Mechanical': Herder

It is significant that Johann Gottfried Herder (1744–1803), the thinker who first applied the strong contrast between mechanism and organism to the political realm, also rejects the interpretation of history as a process in which 'all preceding generations [should have been made] properly for the last alone, which is to be enthroned on the ruined scaffolding of the happiness of the rest.'[97]

Herder was a student of Kant who started his career as a Protestant pastor in his native Riga. He was a many-sided thinker, a brilliant writer and speaker whose interests ranged over literature and criticism, the origins of language, epistemology and theology, and the biological sciences, as well as history and politics. However, certain central preoccupations run through all of Herder's writings. Both Herder's attempt to rethink the notion of biological development and his account of development in the political realm are a response to the deeply felt problem presented by the paradox of development. Herder believed that it must be possible to show that the mind is both something distinctive within and at the same time an integral natural part of God's creation.

Thus he looked, as Frederick Beiser puts it, for 'a middle path between the extremes of a reductivist materialism and a supernaturalist dualism'.[98]

---

[96] *An Essay on the History of Civil Society*, p. 1.
[97] *Reflections on the Philosophy of the History of Mankind*, Bk VIII, Ch. 5, p. 75. As well as the works of Millar (whose *Origin of the Distinction of Ranks* he reviewed) Herder certainly also knew the writings of Robertson and Ferguson. See R. Pascal, 'Herder and the Scottish Historical School'.
[98] *The Fate of Reason*, p. 128.

He refused to accept the idea that reality should contain two utterly different kinds of substance, one physical and the other mental, but neither was he prepared to fall back into a simple materialism, in which everything is referred back to the laws of motion of an essentially inert matter. Instead, his starting point is a metaphysical conception that is intended to be both naturalistic and non-reductive: the concept of *Kraft* (power).

What Herder means by *Kraft* is complicated (and his arguments in defence of it conspicuously thin),[99] but it is possible to identify six central features.

1 *Matter*   *Kraft* is more fundamental than 'matter'. Indeed, Herder appears to regard matter as a product of *Kräfte*: the latter are not simply forms that animate an inert material but are in some sense internal to, and, ultimately, generative of, matter.[100]

2 *Mind*   Mind, too, is an effect of *Kräfte*. But it is not to be thought of as opposed to body. On the contrary, mind is an effect of the body taken as a unified whole: the mind, in Herder's view, has just as much right to be said to be 'in' the sense-organs as in the brain. Mind is that aspect of organic being that is not just active and reactive, but self-aware.[101]

3 *Development*   *Kräfte* are capable of growth and development. This is neither the simple unfolding of preformationism, nor the realization of a pre-established fixed form. For Herder, growth is – or, at least, can be – real *genesis*.

4 *Dynamism*   *Kräfte* are complex and conflictual. Although they form a unity, they are not uniform or unvarying. On the contrary, they are dynamic and, potentially, negative. However, with time they come into balance with one another.[102]

---

[99] Herder seems to be an early example of that persistent tendency in German philosophy to regard it as a sufficient argument in favour of a philosophical position to point out the attractiveness of the conclusions that can be drawn from it – if it is true.

[100] Herder asserts that 'order arose out of chaos by means of divine implanted *Kräfte*' (*Reflections on the Philosophy of the History of Mankind*, Bk XV, Ch. 2, p. 87).

[101] As H. B. Nisbet puts the point, ' . . . Herder was by nature predisposed in favour of some sort of philosophical monism. He was always inclined to envisage the whole universe as an ultimate unity. But while later (materialistic) monists have affirmed the oneness of everything by denying, within the traditional dualism, that one of its two poles (in this case, mind or spirit) has any separate existence, Herder preserves both matter and spirit by reducing them to the higher common factor of *Kraft*' (*Herder and the Philosophy and History of Science*, p. 4).

[102] This aspect is part of what made Herder so influential on that literary and social movement called the *Sturm und Drang* (Storm and Stress). See R. Pascal, *The German Sturm und Drang*. As Berlin sums the matter up:

> . . . in general [Herder] considered nature as a unity in which the *Kräfte* – the mysterious, dynamic, purpose-seeking forces, the interplay of which constitutes all movement and growth – flow into each other, clash, combine, coalesce. These forces are not causal and mechanical as in Descartes; nor insulated from each other as in the *Monadology* of Leibniz; his notion of them owes more to neo-Platonic and Renaissance mysticism, and, perhaps, to Erigena's *Natura naturans* than to the sciences of his time. (*Vico and Herder*, pp. 176–7.)

It is worth noting, though, that the idea of *Kräfte* as real, negating forces also owed something to Herder's teacher Kant's early defence of contradiction: *Versuch, den Begriff der negativen GröBe*

5 *Understanding* The operation of *Kräfte* – or at least some of them – is intelligible. Because we ourselves are a system of *Kräfte*, it is open to us to understand them from the inside. In so doing, we gain access to those 'powers' which alone could make causal processes more than a blind and unreasonable sequence of intrinsically unconnected events.

6 *Unity* Finally, organic wholes, formed out of *Kräfte*, form unities in some strong sense. What that 'inner unity' amounts to is clearest in relation to consciousness: consciousness is not an *effect* in the mind of an *event* in a sense-organ, but is something that unites the apparently separate parts into a single entity. The doctrine of *Kräfte* could do justice, Herder believed, to the unity necessary (he supposed) to organic life and to consciousness, without having to abandon the aspiration to a naturalistic explanation of the world.[103]

Herder's account of *Kräfte* corresponds most closely to the position that the eighteenth century would call 'hylozoism'.[104] For the hylozoist, the

---

in der Weltweisheit einzuführen, and to Kant's account of the universe, in the *Allgemeine Naturgeschichte und Theorie des Himmels*, as the product of the interplay of 'attractive and repulsive forces'. (See Beiser, *Enlightenment, Revolution and Romanticism*, p. 194.)

[103] The need for (and the nature of) unity in living beings was, like the problem of development, a burning metaphysical issue in Herder's day. Herder greatly admired Rousseau's *Émile*, and so he certainly knew the following passage from the *Profession of Faith of a Savoyard Priest*:

... for my own part, whatever Locke may say, it is enough for me to recognize matter as having merely extension and divisibility to convince myself that it cannot think, and if a philosopher tells me that trees feel and rocks think, in vain will he perplex me with his cunning arguments ... But if it is true that all matter feels, where shall I find the sensitive unit, the individual ego? Shall it be in each molecule of matter or in bodies as aggregates of molecules? Shall I place this unity in fluids and solids alike, in compounds and in elements? ... If every elementary atom is a sensitive being, how shall I conceive of that intimate communication by which one feels within the other, so that their two egos are blended into one? ... The sensitive parts have extension, but the sensitive being is one and indivisible; he cannot be cut in two, he is a whole or he is nothing; therefore the sensitive being is not a material body. (*Émile*, pp. 242–3.)

The other side is put in a fictional dialogue between Diderot and D'Alembert, *D'Alembert's Dream* (written by Diderot in 1769, but only made public in 1784, after Diderot's death). Diderot defends the idea that matter itself is sensitive – to which D'Alembert (supposedly) objects:

D'ALEMBERT: While not understanding the nature of sensitivity or matter, I can see that sensitivity is a simple quality, one and indivisible, and incompatible with any divisible object or *suppositum*. (*D'Alembert's Dream*, p. 160.)

Diderot counters that this objection is purely metaphysical: that there is no reason to think that the supposed 'continuity' of an organic being differs in principle from the 'contiguity' characteristic of a swarm of bees: what we think of as a single unit, is always divisible – although the way that the 'swarm' functions cannot be for that reason reduced to claims about the operation of the parts.

Herder (despite his pluralistic conception of *Kräfte*) was on D'Alembert's rather than Diderot's side in this dispute.

[104] Herder himself might dispute the application of the term, however: 'hylozoism' is, literally, the doctrine that there is life in matter. Herder's position is that both mind and matter are themselves the effects of *Kräfte*. Again, the label of 'pantheism' (frequently applied to Herder) is misleading if it is taken to imply that God exists *only* as embodied in his creation. Herder (a Lutheran pastor) appears to me to take a more orthodox view of the relationship between God

solution to the problem of development is to argue that the connection between an initial state and the final state that emerges from it does not lie in the *material* character of FS but in the *mental* character of IS. Herder's position is thus very close to Nagel's 'panpsychism'. He would have agreed with Nagel that causation requires something more than correlation. But he would have thought that developmental processes involving the interplay of *Kräfte* could meet that requirement without there being in any conventional sense a *correspondence* between cause and effect. In Herder's view, the point about organic beings is that they *organize themselves*:

> Bearing in mind these transformations, these living operations in the egg of the bird or in the womb of the mammal, I feel we speak imprecisely if we talk of seeds that are merely *evolving*, or of an *epigenesis* by which the members are superadded externally. It is *Bildung* (genesis), an effect of growing, inward *Kräfte*, brought together in a mass by Nature in order that they might manifest themselves.[105]

This is, of course, the crucial point from the point of view of the theory of ideology: it is only if society is like an organism in this respect that the organic analogy supports the idea of society as a self-maintaining system. But, in fact, Herder does not emphasize this aspect in his account of society, although what he does have to say does not seem to be incompatible with it.

Three aspects of Herder's biologism bear most directly on his political philosophy: his assertion of the importance of the ideas of *diversity*, of *balance* and of *equality*. Herder gives a pluralistic twist to Leibniz's idea that, when closely inspected, the organic world shows every tree, every leaf and every other organism to have minute differences in structure that establish its individuality. The interaction of *Kräfte* in the developing organism is not merely a source of conflict: just as the universe can be seen as an 'equilibrium of contending *Kräfte*', forming itself from chaotic multiplicity into a stable and self-sustaining harmony, so, too, the characteristic of an organic being is its inner balance. But the condition for such a balance to be achieved is that each of the individual elements must be able to express its own distinctive nature.[106] Thus Herder's use of the

---

and his creation. Nisbet suggests that 'pananimism' is the 'least misleading term' to describe Herder's view (*Herder and the Philosophy and History of Science*, p. 11).

[105] J.G. Herder, *Sämtliche Werke*, edited by B. Suphan (Berlin, 1877–1913), XIII, p. 173, quoted in F. M. Barnard (ed.), *Herder on Social and Political Culture*, p. 273.

[106] This is, to my knowledge, the very first appearance of an idea that, taken up by Humboldt (in the concept of *Eigentümlichkeit*) and passed on to John Stuart Mill, was to have the greatest consequences for liberalism. In the central part of *On Liberty*, Mill uses the organic analogy to assert the distinctiveness of the good for each individual and, hence, the possibility of a harmonious flourishing of the social whole without the need for directive intervention by the state. Herder, it is interesting to note, makes almost exactly this point in the *Reflections*:

As man is the most artfully complicated of creatures, so great a variety of genetic character

organic analogy represents an almost complete inversion of its traditional meaning: while in earlier uses (for example, in the fable of Menenius Agrippa) the point of the organic analogy was to vindicate the hierarchical subordination of society to a superior directing princple, for Herder, the characteristic of a living being is its internal unity and its free and uncoerced cooperation: 'every creature is in all its parts one living cooperating whole'.[107] Each part realizes its intrinsic character and sets its own ends:[108]

The end of anything that is not just a lifeless means must lie in itself.[109]

Herder was not, however, the first to express the contrast between those forms of political organization that do, and those that do not, respect the good of each individual member as a contrast between 'living' continuity and 'lifeless' contiguity. Rousseau, in his article on 'Political Economy' for the *Encyclopédie*, was making just this contrast as early as 1755:

The body politic can be considered more specifically as an organised body, alive and resembling that of man ... The citizens are the body and the members which make the machine live, move and work, and which, if the animal is in a state of health, one could not wound in any part without the painful impression carrying to the brain.

The life of the one with the other is the self which is common to all, the reciprocal sensitivity and the internal correspondence of all the parts. If this communication should cease, the formal unity were to evaporate, and the contiguous parts to belong to one another by no more than juxtaposition, the man is dead or the state is dissolved.

The body politic is thus also a moral being which has a will; and this general will, which always tends towards the conservation and the well-being of the whole and of each part, and which is the source of laws, is, for all of the members of the state, in relation to it and to one another, the rule of what is just and unjust ...[110]

---

occurs in no other. Blind imperious instinct is wanting in his delicate frame; but in him the varying currents of thought and desires flow into each other, in a manner peculiar to himself. Thus man, from his very nature, will clash but little in his pursuits with man; his dispositions, sensations and propensities being so infinitely diversified, and, as it were, individualized. What is a matter of indifference to one man, to another is an object of desire: and then each has a world of enjoyment in himself, each a creation of his own. (*Reflections on the Philosophy of the History of Mankind*, Bk VIII, Ch. 3, p. 59.)

[107] *Reflections on the Philosophy of the History of Mankind* (1784–91). Quoted in F. M. Barnard (ed.), *Herder on Social and Political Culture*, p. 261.

[108] Isaiah Berlin writes: 'The use of organic metaphors is at least as old as Aristotle; nobody had used them more lavishly than mediaeval writers; they are the heart and centre of John of Salisbury's political tracts, and are a weapon consciously used by Hooker and Pascal against the new scientific-mechanical conceptions. There was certainly nothing novel in this notion; it represents, on the contrary, if anything, a deliberate return to older views of social life.' (*Vico and Herder*, pp. 149–50.) Berlin misses the originality of the sense with which Herder is now using the metaphor of the organic – and of the contrast with the 'mechanical' that he introduces for the first time.

[109] *Reflections on the Philosophy of the History of Mankind*, Bk XV, Ch. 1, p. 8.

[110] J.-J. Rousseau, Article 'Économie Politique' I, 241–2.

But Herder (unlike Rousseau, who still refers to the healthy body politic as a 'machine') introduces a pejorative sense of 'machine'.[111] Machines have the characteristics of instrumentality, homogeneity and repetitiveness. They use the material that they need for their operation without consideration for that material's intrinsic character and impose their own ends upon it regardless. Where the machine is a state, the costs are borne by the individuals who are thereby condemned to one-sidedness and mutilation. Thus Herder writes in his *Yet Another Philosophy of History* (1774):

Hence it must follow that a large part of this so-called new civilization is actually a piece of mechanism. More closely examined, this mechanism is in fact the essential characteristic of the new spirit ... [New] methods rendered superfluous forces which were formerly necessary and which now (for every unused force decays) are lost in the mists of time. Certain virtues pertaining to science, war, civil life, navigation, government, are no longer needed, since these have been mechanized, and the machine can be controlled by one single person with one single thought, one single sign.[112]

But it is in his *Reflections on the Philosophy of the History of Mankind* (1784–91) that Herder introduces his contrast between natural and 'mechanical' forms of society in most detail:

These patched-up fragile contraptions known as state-machines are wholly devoid of inner life. There is no sentiment, no sympathy of any kind linking their component parts. Just like Trojan horses they move together or against each other. Without national character, they are just lifeless monsters.[113]

For Herder, it is the absolute monarchies that are the most 'mechanical' states, ordered by the will of a single individual, epitomized in the idea of *sovereignty*. They lack the shared consciousness – the 'national character' – that would give them the unity that is characteristic of living beings. The subjects of mechanical states are condemned to an eternal, senseless, torment, which they can escape only by destroying themselves:

Since we are told by the political scientist that every well-constituted state must be a machine regulated only by the will of one, can there conceivably be any greater bliss than to serve in this machine as an unthinking member?

---

[111] Herder does not always use the term 'machine' pejoratively – but that is the leading sense.
[112] J. G. Herder, *Yet another Philosophy of History*, quoted in F. M. Barnard (ed.), *Herder on Social and Political Culture*, p. 196.
[113] J. G. Herder, *Sämtliche Werke*, edited by B. Suphan (Berlin, 1877–1913), XIII, pp. 384–5, quoted in F. M. Barnard, *Herder's Social and Political Thought*, p. 59.

Or, indeed, contrary to our better knowledge and conscience, to be whirled around all our lives on Ixion's wheel, with no comfort other than that of performing the final office of infanticide upon our free and self-determining soul in order to find happiness in the insensibility of a machine?[114]

Thus for Herder, as for Rousseau, the 'false consciousness' of human beings in an oppressive and inhumane society is consequence, symptom and cause of the fact that the society itself is a 'false society', lacking the animating threads that would enable its victims even to be aware of what it is that they lack: 'it is the first germ of freedom to feel that one is *not* free, to recognize the fetters that restrain one'.[115]

Herder's contrast between mechanical and organic forms of social life finds its place within an account of historical development that is a mixture of the conventional and the radically innovative. His explanation of reality as constituted by the interplay of opposed *Kräfte* is complemented by a providential account of both nature and history. Providence expresses itself, Herder claims, not as a 'spider' invisibly tugging the web of events this way or that or as a 'poltergeist in the order of things'[116] but in the way in which history overall incorporates the perfection that comes from realizing all possibilities.[117] As Herder puts it:

Everything came to life upon our earth that could live upon it: for every organization carries within itself a combination of manifold forces, which restrict one another, so that a maximum of them could survive.[118]

Thus the diversity of peoples and cultures is an essential part of that providential perfection.

Herder emphasizes that the forms taken by human beings (both physically and socially) vary greatly from time to time and from place to place. Each individual culture is like a plant which – responding to its environment – grows in a certain direction, blooms and perishes. While variations and adaptations take place *within* the various organisms out of which the species is composed, Herder is clear that humanity is, in the

---

[114] *Reflections on the Philosophy of the History of Mankind*, Bk VIII, Ch. 5, p. 77, translation modified. The 'political scientist' referred to might have been one of the so-called 'Cameralists'. The following passage could have been what Herder had in mind:

A properly constituted state must be exactly analogous to a machine in which all the wheels and gears are precisely adjusted to one another; the ruler must be the foreman, the mainspring of the soul – if one may use the expression – which sets everything in motion. (Justi, *Gesammelte Politische und Finanzschriften*, quoted in R. Plant, *Hegel*, p. 115.)

[115] J. G. Herder, *Sämtliche Werke*, edited by B. Suphan (Berlin, 1877–1913), VIII, pp. 201–2, quoted in F. M. Barnard, *Herder's Social and Political Thought*, p. 94.

[116] *Reflections on the Philosophy of the History of Mankind*, Bk XV, Ch. 5, p. 112.

[117] 'The principle of plenitude', as Lovejoy calls it. (See note 30 above.)

[118] *Reflections on the Philosophy of the History of Mankind*, Bk XV, Ch. 5, p. 112, translation modified.

end, all one species.[119] Nevertheless, the history of the human species has this peculiarity: that each nation forms part of a 'chain of development [*Bildung*]'.[120] To this extent, Herder keeps within the boundaries of the Enlightenment in seeing the history of the human race as forming an overall progress.

However, Herder's theory of history is not a simple account of the steady accumulation of knowledge and the increase of human powers of control. Although he *does* believe that they have increased, the growth of knowledge and control – like any other one-sided development – brings with it a corresponding loss in other areas: 'The more we divide our mental powers by refinement, the more the inactive powers decay.'[121] It is only when all our powers are engaged that man's *active* nature can come to fulfilment. Yet nor did Herder agree with Rousseau's *Discourse on the Arts and Sciences* that fragmentation was the inevitable (and unacceptable) price of the growth of knowledge. For Herder, the history of human progress is like the history of the universe as a whole: an account of how contending *Kräfte* moderate each other and come into balance and harmony, so that the 'preserving' forces come with time to dominate:

> All destructive *Kräfte* in nature must, as time goes by, not only submit to the preserving *Kräfte*, but also, in the end, themselves serve the realization of the whole . . . As the storms of the sea are more rare than its regular winds, so there is a benevolent natural ordinance in the human race, *that many fewer destroyers than preservers are born into it.*[122]

For Herder, no less than for his more orthodox Enlightenment contemporaries, the modern world held out the possibility of an advance in moderation and civilization. It is possible, Herder believed, for human beings to achieve happiness and fulfilment at every stage of history, provided that their society takes a form that allows them to be themselves: he was no 'primitivist'. It was simply that the repressive, absolutist states of contemporary Germany (and France) would have to be replaced before *Humanität* – a properly integrated, active humanity – could flourish.[123]

---

[119] It is inevitable that we look at Herder's 'biological anthropology' with hindsight, in the light of modern Darwinism. In general, Herder endorses the modern definition of speciation (the members of a species are those who are capable of mating and producing fertile offspring). Thus he rejects Kant's idea that mankind is made up of different *races*. He also believes that variations among human beings (darker skins for those dwelling in tropical regions) are adaptive. On the other hand, he is clear that such characteristics are heritable rather than environmental (dark-skinned parents will have dark-skinned children, even in northern climates). Thus (lacking the Darwinian account of genetic variation and random selection) he supposes that certain, dramatic, environmental changes cause heritable changes in man (and other animals).

[120] *Reflections on the Philosophy of the History of Mankind*, Bk XV, Ch. 3, p. 100.

[121] Ibid., Bk VIII, Ch. 5, p. 73.

[122] Ibid., Bk XV, Ch. 2, pp. 87–9.

[123] For the important role played by the concept of *Humanität* in Herder's politics (and, in particular, in the welcome that Herder gave to the French Revolution) see F. Beiser, *Enlightenment, Revolution and Romanticism*, Ch. 8.

VIII The 'Organic' against the 'Mechanical': Kant and Schiller

Kant (from whom Herder drew so many of his own ideas) wrote a very hostile review of the *Reflections* – motivated in part, apparently, by personal resentment against Herder, whom he blamed for the poor reception of the *Critique of Pure Reason*.[124] Kant attacks the idea of *Kräfte* for failing to solve the problem that it sets itself: that of providing a genuine *explanation* of organic development. Nevertheless, when Kant came to work out his own views on the organic realm, the underlying similarity of his position to Herder's is more striking than their differences. In the *Critique of Judgement* (1790) Kant set out to give a rigorous account of how the organic realm differed both from inorganic nature and from the products of human activity – mechanical artefacts or works of art. Although order and systematicity were characteristic of the organic realm, they were not exclusive to it. The differentiating feature of organic nature was its self-maintaining and self-reproducing character.

Kant's view is that organic nature represents an objectively insoluble problem. Organic beings are a part of the natural world and, to that extent, can be explained according to the ordinary laws of empirical causality, but what is most essential to them – their *organized* character – can neither, Kant believes, be analysed away as a merely subjective projection of purpose onto objective reality[125] nor be given an empirical explanation:

> In a thing that we must judge as a natural purpose (an organized being), we can no doubt try all the known and yet to be discovered laws of mechanical production, and even hope to make good progress therewith, but we can never get rid of the call for a quite different ground of production for the possibility of such a product, viz. causality by means of purposes. Absolutely no human reason (in fact no finite reason like ours in quality, however much it may surpass it in degree) can hope to understand the production of even a blade of grass by mere mechanical causes.[126]

---

[124] See F. Beiser, *The Fate of Reason*, Ch. 5. Beiser points out that Herder is indebted at many points to Kant's own earlier ideas. Thus one could suppose that Kant's attack on Herder was made more vehement for being aimed at his own, pre-Critical past.

[125] 'Organized beings are then the only beings in nature which, considered in themselves and apart from any relation to other things, can be thought as possible only as purposes of nature [*Naturzweck*]' (*Critique of Judgment*, Sect. 65, p. 222).

[126] *Critique of Judgment*, Sect. 77, p. 258. In this passage Kant appears to be asserting that what modern science takes for granted is impossible, not just in practice, given the current state of knowledge, but in principle, so it is unfortunate that when he canvasses a position that corresponds to the modern theory of evolution (not, of course, that he calls it by that name) Kant presents his objections only very cryptically. According to Kant, 'Epicureanism', which takes 'Blind chance . . . as the explanatory ground, not only of the agreement of the developed products [of nature] with our concepts of their purpose, . . . but even for the determination of the causes of this production in accordance with the laws of motion' is explanatorily empty: 'nothing is explained, not even the illusion in our teleological judgments' (*Critique of Judgment*, Sect. 72, p. 240). His objection seems to be the one familiar from Smith's discussion in *The Theory of Moral*

His strictures against attempts to explain the organic realm notwithstanding, Kant endorses the theory of epigenesis, as presented by J.F.
Blumenbach, whom he praises both for his contribution to the 'proof' of
the theory but also for the way in which he limits 'a too presumptuous
employment of it'.[127]

Kant's extended account of the differences between organism and
mechanism takes up Herder's idea of the contrast between the *internal*
purpose of the former and the *external* purpose of the latter. An organism
as a 'natural purpose' is such that its parts 'as regards their presence and
their form . . . are only possible through their reference to the whole.'[128]
That is to say, each part must be explained as being the way that it is
because of the relation that it has to the whole of which it is a part. But,
although this gives a contrast between *organism* and *mechanism*, it is not
exclusive to the organic realm. Internal purposiveness could be just as
much a characteristic of a deliberately produced work of art (the form
given to a successful work of art by an artist, Kant believes, relates its
parts with the same kind of inner necessity). What is distinctive about an
organic being is that it is truly *self*-producing. In an organism, we must,
Kant says, take the 'concept of the whole' as if it were the cause of the
way in which the parts develop and are combined:

> In this case, then, the connection of *effective causes* may be judged as an *effect
> through final causes*.
>
> In such a product of nature, every part not only exists *by means of* the
> other parts, but is thought as existing *for the sake of* the others and the whole
> – that is, as an (organic) instrument. Thus, however, it might be an artificial
> instrument, and so might be represented only as a purpose that is possible in
> general; but also its parts are all organs reciprocally *producing* one another.
> This can never be the case with artificial instruments, but only with nature
> which supplies all the material for instruments (even for those of art). Only

Sentiments: that any explanation of organized beings must explain not only the operation of
efficient causes within the organism but also deal with the 'determination of the causes of this
production' – the question of how it should be that just such causes should produce just such
effects.

This is a point that Kant refers to frequently in the first *Critique* as the requirement to seek a
ground of causality – in other words, to look for an explanation for a (causal) explanation that
shows why it should be true. Famously, however, for Kant, although it is a question that we can
(indeed, must) pursue, it is one that, in the study of nature, we cannot answer.

The Darwinian 'Epicurean', of course, believes that, to the extent that this search for a 'ground'
is a genuine explanatory requirement at all, it can be met: it is chance (and the differential survival
of more or less successful adaptations) that leads to the emergence of *organized* beings, whose
parts then interact according to efficient causality in the apparently purposive way that they do.

[127] *Critique of Judgment*, Sect. 81, p. 274. Thus, Herder and Kant seem to have reached a very
similar position, for, as Nisbet writes:

> In Part II of the *Ideen*, . . . Herder ended up by employing in practice the very epigenesis,
> with its doctrine of successive growth by convergence upon a centre, which he had rejected
> in theory in Part I before reading Harvey, Blumenbach and Wolff. (*Herder and the Philosophy
> and History of Science*, p. 205.)

[128] *Critique of Judgment*, Sect. 65, p. 219.

a product of such a kind can be called a *natural purpose*, and this because it is an *organized* and *self-organizing being*.[129]

Thus, for Kant, a true organism combines the characteristics of *unity* (each part is the way that it is because of its relation to the whole) with the power to *produce*, *preserve* and *propagate* itself. In this, Kant says, it is quite unlike a merely mechanical artefact — even a purposefully organized one, such as a watch:

> . . . a watch wheel does not produce other wheels; still less does one watch produce other watches, utilizing (organizing) foreign material for that purpose; hence it does not replace of itself parts of which it has been deprived, nor does it make good what is lacking in a first formation by the addition of missing parts, nor if it has gone out of order does it repair itself — all of which, on the contrary, we may expect from organized nature. An organized being is then not a mere machine, for that has merely *moving* power, but it possesses in itself *formative* power of a self-propagating kind which it communicates to its materials though they have it not of themselves; it organizes them, in fact, and this cannot be explained by the mere mechanical faculty of motion.[130]

The fact that parts in an organic whole develop in the way that they do for the sake of the whole is, for Kant as much as for Herder, quite compatible with the corresponding idea that each part is an end in itself:[131] in an organism 'everything is a purpose and, reciprocally, also means'.[132]

The *Critique of Judgment* is the *locus classicus* for the discussion of the distinction between organism and mechanism and none of the later German Idealist and Romantic writers was uninfluenced by it. However, although Kant does explore the analogy between the organic realm and the political, he himself (unlike Herder) does not go so far as to claim that social life is, in fact, organic.[133] A contrast still remains: the well-ordered

---

[129] Ibid., Sect. 65, p. 220.

[130] Ibid., Sect. 65, pp. 220–1.

[131] The idea that things — actions, lives, institutions — should be *both* means *and* ends seems to be one of German Idealism's most valuable contributions to moral thought:

> It is not enough to take steps which may some day lead to a goal; each step must be itself a goal and a step at the same time. (Eckermann, *Gespräche mit Goethe*, 18 Sept. 18 1823.)

This point is wilfully ignored by those — Talmon and Popper are only the most notorious — who, for their own polemical purposes, conflate Romantic and Idealist organicism with twentieth-century 'totalitarianism'.

[132] *Critique of Judgment*, Sect. 66, p. 222.

[133] In the first part of the *Critique of Judgment*, Kant (surely with Herder's *Ideen* in mind) selects the way in which a state is represented as a 'mere machine (like a hand mill) if it is governed by an individual absolute will' as an example of symbolism (*Critique of Judgment*, Sect. 59, p. 198) and, in the second part, in a famous footnote, Kant goes on to endorse the organic analogy for a sovereign state:

> In a recent complete transformation of a great people into a state [it is assumed that Kant here is referring to the American Revolution — M. R.] the word *organization* for the

state is organized so that both parts and whole exist for the sake of each other, but Kant does not suggest that even the well-ordered state has the power of self-organization and self-preservation that, he claims, is characteristic of true organisms.

Fichte, Kant's admirer and would-be successor, makes just this claim in his *Foundations of Natural Right according to the Principles of the Wissenschaftslehre* (1796):

> In the organic body every part continually preserves the whole, and is itself, inasmuch as it preserves the latter, thereby preserved: in just this way does the citizen relate to the state.[134]

At this point, the line between the metaphorical and the literal use of the idea of organism as applied to the social system seems to have disappeared and we have, for the first time, the idea of the well-adjusted society as automatically and actively self-reproducing. For Herder, the 'mechanical' state is self-reproducing (we are 'whirled around all our lives on Ixion's wheel') but only in the way that a watch is: its elements fit smoothly into each other because each element has been ground down into uniformity and homogeneity. But the mechanical state is incapable of the kind of natural self-repair that is characteristic of organisms: it is coordinated but easily broken.

Thus the idea of the 'mechanical' state can be seen to bring together those two elements that we have so far been tracing separately: the idea of false consciousness and the idea of society as a systematic order. There is 'false consciousness' in the mechanical state, in the form of a 'loss of identity': the self that lives in it is cut off from its true nature. Yet it is also systematic – although negatively so. Even bad societies are systematically self-maintaining, albeit unhealthily and oppressively.

Both elements are given clear expression in one of the seminal political texts of German Romanticism: the sixth of Schiller's *Letters on the Aesthetic Education of Man* (1795). Schiller takes up the idea that, in the modern world, the growth of empirical knowledge, the division of labour and the separation of ranks all mean that man has become specialized and divided, with the result that the 'totality of the species' (*Totalität der Gattung*) becomes impossible to recover from its 'fragments' (*Bruchstücke*), the individual members:

> Once the increase of empirical knowledge, and more exact modes of thought, made sharper divisions between the sciences inevitable, and once the increasingly intricate clockwork of the states necessitated a more rigorous separation of ranks and occupations, then the inner connection [*Bund*]

---

regulation of magistracies, and even of the whole body politic, has often been fitly used. For in such a whole every member should surely be purpose as well as means, and, while all work together toward the possibility of the whole, each should be determined as regards place and functioning by means of the Idea of the whole. (Sect. 65, p. 225.)

[134] *Grundlage des Naturrechts nach Prinzipien der Wissenschaftlehre*, p. 203.

of human nature was severed too, and a disastrous conflict set its harmonious powers at variance [*entzweite*] . . .

This disorganization, which was first started within man by art and learning, was made complete and universal by the new spirit of government [*Geist der Regierung*] . . . That polyp-nature of the Greek states, in which every individual enjoyed an independent life, but could, when the need arose, grow into the whole organism, now made way for an ingenious clockwork, in which out of the piecing together [*Zusammenstückelung*] of innumerable but lifeless parts, a mechanical kind of collective life ensued. State and Church, laws and customs [*Sitten*], were now torn asunder; enjoyment was divorced from labour, the means from the end, the effort from the reward. Everlastingly chained to a single little fragment of the whole, man himself develops into nothing but a fragment; with his ear filled everlastingly with the monotonous sound of the wheel that he turns, he never develops the harmony of his being, and, instead of putting the stamp of humanity upon his nature, he becomes nothing more than the imprint of his occupation and of his specialist knowledge.[135]

As the society itself is not harmonious, nor is the individual: for Schiller, as for Rousseau, man in modern society lacks a true identity. The self-division of man in a society that lacks inner unity makes him all too easily its victim. A society composed of such individuals can maintain itself by a process of repetition, but it does not develop. While Greek society had the ability to grow back when damaged, this regenerative capacity (its 'polyp-nature') has been lost by the merely mechanical organization of the modern state. No wonder, then, that, for Schiller and his successors, God can no longer be regarded as a benevolent watch-maker. For Romantic political thought, it is the free and organic character of creation that is the truest sign of its providential character:

Most shallow and superficial in truth is that physical science which would consider the system of nature, with all the marvels of beauty and majesty wherewith its Maker has adorned it, as nothing more than a piece of lifeless clockwork . . . If . . . to meet the needs of men's limited capacity, we must when speaking of the Creator, employ such trifling and childish similes, then of all human avocations and pursuits that of the gardener will serve best to illustrate the divine operations in nature. Almighty and omniscient, however, He has Himself created the trees and flowers that he cultivates, has Himself made the good soil in which they grow, and brings down from heaven the balmy spring, the dews and rain, and the sunshine that quicken and mature them into life and beauty.[136]

Whether (and how) the social machine can be restored to its organic nature is the fundamental problem preoccupying Romantic politics.

---

[135] *Letters on the Aesthetic Education of Man*, Sixth Letter, pp. 33–5.
[136] Friedrich Schlegel, *Philosophie des Lebens*, 6th Lecture, pp. 163–4.

5

Hegel

In Hegel, we have for the first time an author whose theory integrates the two background beliefs behind the theory of ideology. Hegel's legacy includes both a series of fertile ideas regarding the nature of false consciousness in modern society and a fully worked-out account of the role of unintended consequences in history.

Hegel's earliest writings take up the Schillerian idea of the mutilation of the individual in a 'false' society and the theme of loss of identity continues to govern the forms of false consciousness that he deals with in the *Phenomenology of Spirit* (1807) and elsewhere.

In general, false consciousness, for Hegel, involves two elements.

1 There is a failure on the part of individuals to appreciate the nature of their own agency, or of the higher agent, *Geist*, of which they are embodiments.

2 The lack of that recognition leads to a distorted or in some way inadequate relationship between agents and their products: recognition is the necessary condition for transforming the relationship.

Other kinds of false consciousness – misperceptions and defective attitudes – are explained as part of this overarching schema of loss of identity and failure of recognition.

Hegel's philosophy of history includes all three kinds of unintended consequence distinguished in the previous chapter. For Hegel, history is *providential*: its essential meaning is given from the point of view of *Geist* – 'spirit'. It is *progressive*: *Geist* 'comes to itself' through a series of stages.

Finally, it is composed of self-maintaining elements (each stage is held together by an inner principle). Moreover, the idea of the 'cunning of reason' offers an account of how an individual agent, acting freely, may bring about purposes that go beyond his own original intentions and that he himself fails to understand fully.

I Division and Nature

The framework within which Hegel presents these doctrines is rationalist as well as Providentialist. Reason governs the order of the universe in general and of history in particular. Thus the good life for the individual consists for Hegel, as much as it does for Plato, in a life lived in accordance with reason. History consists in the working out of the possibility of such a life – the development of the individual and society to the point at which the individual can identify rationally with society. False consciousness arises because of the division of the self from this wider kind of unity; unintended consequences come about because the agents by and through whom the rational and providential purposes of history are realized do not (indeed cannot) recognize the full significance of their actions.

Hegel's very first publication – the essay, *The Difference Between the Fichtean and the Schellingean Systems of Philosophy* (the '*Differenzschrift*' of 1801) – locates the origins of philosophical systems in the need to re-establish unity in human life:

> Division [*Entzweiung*] is the source of the need for philosophy . . .[1]

As culture itself has become divided, according to Hegel, so it is the responsibility of philosophy to try to repair that breach. Philosophies are attempts on the part of *Geist* (the collective mind in which we all, as individuals, participate) to restore its own 'divided harmony' and, at the same time, symptoms of that division.[2] In language clearly derived from Herder and Schiller, Hegel contrasts two kinds of state. The modern state, Hegel argues, is dominated by the understanding rather than by reason. The unity of such a *Verstandesstaat* is merely mechanical and its citizens are isolated and passive. Healthy states, by contrast, like organisms, contain within themselves a source of unity that cannot be reduced to the merely subsuming or atomistic principles of the understanding – a state that *could* be fully apprehended in that way would be *eo ipso* a false society:

> But this understanding-state [*Verstandesstaat*] is not an *organization* but a *machine*; the people is not the organic body of a rich and common life, but an

---

[1] *Differenz des Fichteschen und Schellingschen Systems, Werke*, II, p. 20.
[2] 'In culture [*Bildung*] that which is a form of appearance of the Absolute has isolated itself from the Absolute and become fixed as something independent.' (Ibid.)

atomistic and lifeless multiplicity, whose elements are absolutely opposed substances. On the one hand, they are a set of points – rational beings – and, on the other, a manifold of materials, modifiable by reason (or, as it is in this case, understanding). They are elements whose unity lies in a concept and whose combination is an unceasing dominion.[3]

At the outset of his career, Hegel saw philosophy as part of a movement of radical political transformation. The *Ältestes Systemprogramm* had announced itself as the harbinger of a new kind of philosophy, one which would provide the symbolic foundations for a future egalitarian society, based on the 'absolute freedom of all minds [*Geister*] that carry the intellectual world within themselves and seek neither God nor immortality outside'.[4] In the *Differenzschrift*, Hegel calls for reason, in the form of speculative philosophy, to fight against the domination of the state and religion by the 'understanding' and by 'common sense' ('*der gesunde Menschenverstand*'). By the time of the *Phenomenology of Spirit* (1807), however, philosophy's role was a secondary one: to bring to consciousness that which had already been achieved, implicitly, by *Geist*.[5]

Nevertheless, as Hegel's position on the political spectrum swung from radical anti-statism to conservative apologetics, he never doubted that it was the role of philosophy to comprehend and try to overcome division – whether the division be the result of the fundamental irrationality of the existing political order or simply a failure to recognize that order's rational character.

For Hegel's mature philosophy, the whole of reality – both nature and history – is a single, self-differentiating unity, manifesting in its different forms and levels one great, pure structure: that of the *Idea* (a modern equivalent, as Hegel himself claims, of the Greek conception of the cosmos as animated by the *logos*). Nature itself is an alienated form of the Idea:

Nature is the son of God, although not as the Son, but as abiding in otherness – the divine Idea as held fast for a moment outside divine love. Nature is *Geist* alienated from itself; *Geist* is *released* into nature: a Bacchic god unrestrained and unmindful of itself. In nature, the unity of the notion [*Begriff*] is concealed.

A Thinking [*denkende*] consideration of nature must consider how . . . the Idea is present in each level of nature itself; alienated from the Idea, nature is only the corpse of the understanding. Nature is the Idea, however, only implicitly. Hence Schelling called her a petrified – others, indeed, a frozen –

---

[3] Ibid., p. 87.
[4] C. Jamme and H. Schneider (eds), *Mythologie der Vernunft: Hegels 'ältestes Systemprogramm des deutschen Idealismus'*, p. 12.
[5] This past existence is an already attained possession of the universal *Geist*, which is the substance of the individual and so, although it appears as external to him, constitutes his non-organic nature. *Bildung*, in this respect, seen from the side of the individual, consists in acquiring what is thus present, absorbing his non-organic nature into himself, and taking possession of it. (*Phänomenologie des Geistes*, p. 27.)

intelligence; God, however, does not remain petrified and dead: the very stones cry out and raise themselves to *Geist*.[6]

The language of this passage – the reference to *alienation* and to the 'Bacchic god' – reveals how much Hegel's philosophy owes to the emanationist ideas regarding the One and the Many of neo-Platonism and pagan mysticism.[7]

Specific problems, such as that of the nature of the individual, the unity of society and the operation of unintended consequences find a place in Hegel's system as part of this metaphysics of loss and recovery. Indeed, Hegel makes it clear that he regards his speculative philosophy as a rational, non-metaphorical continuation of the mystical tradition:

> It should be mentioned here, regarding the significance of the speculative, that it means the same as what was formerly called, in connection with religious consciousness and its content, the *mystical*. Nowadays, when people speak of *mysticism*, this is usually taken to be equivalent to what is mysterious and incomprehensible ... But, first, it must be said that the mystical is only

---

[6] *Enzyklopädie der philosophischen Wissenschaften* II, *Werke*, IX, para. 247, p. 25. '*Denken*' and '*Begriff*' are important technical terms for Hegel. For an explanation of their significance, see my *Hegel's Dialectic and its Criticism*, especially Ch. 3.

[7] The role of the myths of Dionysus and Osiris as allegories for the theme of the One and the Many are given a superb discussion in Edgar Wind's *Pagan Mysteries in the Renaissance*, pp. 133–5. Wind also makes some useful points regarding the importance of neo-Platonic ideas for Hegel and Schelling (pp. 192–6).

One metaphor illustrates how deeply the theme of dispersal and fragmentation permeated German thought. In his *Aesthetica in nuce* ('*A Rhapsody in Cabbalistic Prose*' (1762)) Hamann writes:

> Speak that I may see you! This desire was fulfilled by the creation, which is a discourse from one creature to another; for one day speaks to another and one night announces itself to the next. Its password runs through every climate to the end of the world and in every dialect its voice is to be heard. But wherever the guilt lies (outside us or within) we have nothing but riddles [*Turbatverse*] and *disjecti membra poetae* for our use. (*Aesthetica in nuce*, p. 198.)

The phrase *disjecti membra poetae* (*etiam disjecti membra poetae* – 'Even in his dismembered state, the limbs of a poet') is from Horace, and it seems to have been taken up from Hamann into Romantic discourse as a standard metaphor. Herder speaks of all the beings of organic nature as appearing as '*disjecti membra poetae*', and the phrase is also used by the Romantic physicist admired by Benjamin, J. W. Ritter.

Hölderlin comes very close to the metaphor in his *Hyperion* (and brings it together with the Rousseauian theme of the fragmentation of individuals in contemporary society):

> I can think of no people as torn apart as the Germans. Craftsmen are to be seen, but no human beings ... masters and men, but no human beings. Is it not like a field of battle where hands and arms and other limbs lie scattered in pieces while the blood of life drains away into the soil? (F. Hölderlin, *Hyperion*, quoted in R. Plant, *Hegel*, p. 19.)

Although Hegel does not, to the best of my knowledge, use the phrase, many of his metaphors also come extremely close to it. A hundred years after Hamann, Karl Marx could use the phrase casually in relation to the division of labour:

> Modern manufacture wherever it arises ... either finds the *disjecta* [*sic*] *membra poetae* ready to hand, and only waiting to be collected from its dispersal ... or it can easily apply the principle of division by exclusively assigning the various operations of handicraft production ... to particular workers. (*Das Kapital*, Vol. 1, p. 385 [Eng. trans., p. 399–400].)

a secret for the *understanding*, because the latter has *abstract identity* as its principle. The mystical . . . is the concrete unity of those determinations which the understanding only takes as true in separation and opposition.[8]

II Development

That Hegel should have been defending ideas such as these at a time when the empirical sciences were advancing as never before may seem to be a bizarre anachronism: as unlikely as a gothic cathedral in a supermarket car park. But, in certain central respects, Hegel's philosophy was a response to the most immediate issues of contemporary metaphysics, not just a throwback to a lost world of mysticism and speculation.

Hegel's version of the neo-Platonic doctrine of the One and the Many provides an answer to the paradox of development, identified in the previous chapter. That problem was what relationship there might be between an initial state and a final state such that the final state could nonetheless be said to be a *development* from the initial one. A development, on this view, involves more than just a *change* from one state to the next. There must be an intelligible continuity, so that the later stage can be *explained by* the earlier one. Hegel accepts this requirement. It is met, he believes, by the central claim of speculative philosophy: the doctrine of 'determinate negation'.[9] Speculative philosophy (in contradiction to the doctrine of 'evolution') shows that there can be a 'logic' of development in which the product is more complex than the starting point:

> . . . the emergence of the philosophical Idea in its development is not a *change*, a becoming something other, but equally an internalization, a process of self-deepening in its own self, its progression makes the previously general, less determinate Idea more determinate in itself . . . The further development of the Idea or its greater determinacy are one and the same thing. The most *extensive* is also the most *intensive*. The extension as a development is not a scattering and dispersal, but, equally, a comprehension which, the more powerful and more intensive with the extension, enriches and furthers this comprehended content.[10]

The development of the Idea in pure form is a process in which each stage is richer and more complex than its starting point; nevertheless, the succeeding stage is wholly implicit within the preceding one. The development of the complex from the simple is only truly intelligible as the science of the pure Idea. It is in tracing this development *a priori*, in 'Thought', that philosophy provides the kind of exposition – both rigorous and intelligible – that is, Hegel believes, the goal of philosophical reasoning.

---

[8] *Enzyklopädie der philosophischen Wissenschaften* I, *Werke*, VIII, para. 82, *Zusatz*, p. 178.
[9] This topic is explored in detail in *Hegel's Dialectic and its Criticism*. See Chapters 2 and 3 especially.
[10] *Vorlesungen über die Geschichte der Philosophie* III, *Werke*, XX, pp. 476–7.

Only in Thought is all foreignness transparent, invisible; *Geist* is free here in absolute fashion.[11]

In nature itself, however, the Idea is 'petrified'. While nature embodies the rational order of the Idea, it does so in a way that makes that order a kind of fixed programme (a 'formal cause') which it applies to material reality 'from outside', willy-nilly. Thus development in nature is not fully intelligible and, for this reason, in Hegel's view, it is not free. True freedom, for Hegel, requires that there should be a relationship of necessitation connecting the antecedent conditions with whatever event or action is to be counted as free. Otherwise, the latter would be simply random and inexplicable. This necessitation must be an 'internal' – that is to say, intelligible and rational – one. If not, the relationship between an event and its antecedents is that the latter are a kind of alien 'fetter'. This is the point of Hegel's (apparently bizarre) claim that freedom requires *neither* necessity *nor* contingency:

> ... nature is not free, but is only necessary and contingent. For necessity is the inseparability of different terms which yet appear as indifferent towards each other; but because this abstract state of externality also receives its due, there is contingency in nature – external necessity, not the internal necessity of the notion.[12]

Since the *Begriff* is 'outside itself' in nature, there can be no fully intelligible relationship between its forms and the reality within which they are realized:

> The *contradiction* of the Idea, arising from the fact that, as Nature, it is external to itself, is more precisely this: that, on the one hand, there is the *necessity* of its forms which is generated by the notion ... while, on the other hand, there is their indifferent *contingency* and indeterminable irregularity.[13]

Development, according to Hegel, is a matter of both '*Ansichsein*' (the 'in itself' – '*potentia*') and '*Fürsichsein*' (the 'for itself' – actuality). It is the drive of the *an sich* to develop itself that leads to growth and change.[14] Because, in the natural world, the *an sich* remains separated from the *für sich*, so the individual organisms (which are, in one sense, the subject of the developing process) lack true identity and continuity from one to another. The *Begriff* realizes itself in a multiplicity of individuals, but the species itself does not develop. In *Geist*, however, *an sich* and *für sich* can coincide:

---

[11] Ibid., XVIII, p. 42.
[12] *Enzyklopädie der philosophischen Wissenschaften* II, *Werke*, IX, para. 248, p. 30.
[13] Ibid., para. 250, p. 34.
[14] 'Thus it is in the seed of the plant ... It has the drive to develop itself; it cannot tolerate merely being *an sich*' (*Vorlesungen über die Geschichte der Philosophie I*, *Werke*, XVIII, p. 41).

In the case of natural things, the subject, which was the beginning, and that which exists as its conclusion – the fruit, the seed – are two individuals ... The seed in nature, after it has made itself other, returns to unity. Likewise in *Geist*; that which is *an sich* becomes *for Geist* and, in this way, *Geist* becomes for itself. The fruit, the sprout, is not *for* the first seed, but only *for us*. In *Geist*, however, ... that for which the other is is the same as that other. It is only in virtue of this that *Geist* is with itself in its other [*bei sich selbst in seinem Anderen*]. The development of *Geist* is emergence and self-explication, but, at the same time, a coming to itself.[15]

Thus it follows for Hegel that, although there is growth in nature – individual organic beings organize and preserve themselves according to their innate pattern – there can be no true (that is to say, fully intelligible) *development*:

Metamorphosis pertains only to the notion as such, since only its alteration is development.[16]

III History and Freedom

In the realm of *Geist*, however, things are quite different:

[*Geist*] is consciousness, free because beginning and end coincide in it.[17]

It is the process of *Geist*'s coming to self-knowledge as an individual that gives the world as a whole its meaning. *Geist* is striving to reach a state at which it is both '*an und für sich*':

This being with itself of *Geist*, this coming to itself, can be expressed as its highest, absolute goal. It is only this that it wills and nothing else. Everything that happens in heaven or on earth – happens eternally – the life of God and everything that occurs temporally, only strives towards this: that *Geist* knows itself, makes itself objective, finds itself, becomes *für sich*, merges with itself. *Geist* is bifurcation and alienation, but only in order to be able to come to itself.[18]

Thus history, for Hegel, has crucial metaphysical significance as being the sphere in which this process can be accomplished:

World-history, we see, is just the unfolding [*Auslegung*] of *Geist* in time, as nature is of the Idea in space.[19]

[15] Ibid.
[16] *Enzyklopädie der philosophischen Wissenschaften* II, *Werke*, IX, para. 249, p. 31.
[17] *Vorlesungen über die Geschichte der Philosophie I*, *Werke*, XVIII, p. 41.
[18] Ibid., pp. 41–2.
[19] *Vorlesungen über die Philosophie der Geschichte*, *Werke*, XII, pp. 96–7 [Eng. trans., p. 72].

History, however, does not just embody the order of the Idea externally but represents the record of *Geist*'s endeavours to attain that point at which it can be '*bei sich selbst in seinem Anderen*' – that is to say, *free*:

> Philosophy teaches that all the qualities of *Geist* exist only through freedom; that all are but means for attaining freedom; that all seek and produce this and this alone.[20]

History is strongly providential. In it we can trace out the realization of a good purpose – namely, the development of *Geist* towards self-recognition and freedom:

> Thus we maintain that the destiny of the world of *Geist*, and ... the *final cause of the world* [*Endzweck der Welt*] is *Geist*'s consciousness of its freedom, and, *ipso facto*, the actuality of that freedom.[21]

Geist is fully free only when it is aware of its own nature, and history is comprehensible to the extent that it can be seen as a series of attempts on the part of *Geist* to come to that awareness. Hegel would surely have agreed with Schelling's comparison of history to an epic poem whose two sides express the *Iliad* of *Geist*'s self-externalization and the *Odyssey* of its return to its own self.[22]

Only philosophy can reconstruct the development of the Idea in full rigour, but the logic of history – the working-out in logical order of the forms taken by *Geist* as it tries to bring itself to the point of self-knowledge – can be comprehended in retrospect. What brings these two kinds of comprehension together in Hegel's system is the *Phenomenology of Spirit*: the 'science of the appearance of knowledge' [*Wissenschaft des erscheinenden Wissens*], which, by allowing the individual to trace through the forms of *Geist*, is supposed to initiate him thereby into the realm of pure speculative thought ('absolute knowledge').

Thus history has significance for Hegel in three ways.

1 First, there is its intrinsic purpose – *Geist*'s struggle to achieve self-knowledge.

2 Second, there is the 'science' of history – history as understood by philosophy in retrospect, as an intelligible embodiment of the pure forms.

3 Finally, there is the phenomenological role of historical understanding itself, in initiating the individual into speculative metaphysics.

[20] Ibid., p. 30 [Eng. trans., p. 17].
[21] Ibid., pp. 32–3 [Eng. trans., p. 19].
[22] Schelling, 'Mythologie und Religion', quoted in B. Lypp, *Ästhetischer Absolutismus und politische Vernunft*, pp. 202–3.

It is within this comprehensive framework of Idealist philosophy that the specific features of Hegel's conception of history must be understood.

Development in nature, where the *an sich* and *für sich* are separate, Hegel claims in the *Lectures on the Philosophy of History*, 'takes place in an immediate, unopposed, unimpeded manner; between the *Begriff* and its realization ... nothing can intrude.'[23] But in the sphere of *Geist* it is different: here the process of development is not merely a matter of a 'simple essence' [*einfache Wesenheit*] realizing itself in external reality, but of *Geist* overcoming the resistance of aspects of its own self:

> *Geist* is opposed to itself: ... it has to overcome itself as the truly hostile obstacle to its own self; development that is a smooth emergence in the natural world, is, in *Geist*, a hard and unending struggle against itself. What *Geist* desires is to attain its own *Begriff*, but it conceals that from itself; it is proud and self-satisfied in this self-alienation.[24]

Thus, in Hegel's view, history is a realm of conflicts and reversals, not, as one might assume, because the smooth working-out of logical processes is disrupted by randomness and contingency – that, in fact, is the characteristic of nature – but because history is truly a *drama* in which different aspects of a principle contend with one another and resolve themselves into ever more complex and sophisticated forms.

The history of *Geist* embodies itself in a series of individual cultures – the *Volksgeister* – which grow and die like individual plants:

> The life of a people ripens a certain fruit, for its activity is aimed at the completion of its own principle. But this fruit does not return to the bosom of the people that conceived and bore it; on the contrary, it becomes a poison-draught to it. It cannot leave it alone, for it has an insatiable thirst for it; to taste the drink means its own downfall – and, at the same time, the rise of a new principle.[25]

Here again, however, it is the disanalogy rather than the analogy between history and organic nature that is important: as individual cultures grow and die, they do so, unlike plants, not as particular examples of a species – realizations of the essentially timeless form that they embody – but as conscious expressions (and, therefore, developments) of the *form itself*. Thus one culture passes on to its successor a different (and higher) form, in a way that (in Hegel's view) the essentially repetitive processes of organic nature do not.

Each particular culture is, Hegel claims, a single substance – a living

---

[23] *Vorlesungen über die Philosophie der Geschichte, Werke*, XII, p. 76 [Eng. trans., p. 55].
[24] Ibid.
[25] Ibid., p. 104 [Eng. trans., p. 78].

'individual totality', from which no part can be viewed in isolation.[26] We should think of each culture as a whole that is held together by a single principle that penetrates and permeates every aspect of it:

> ... each stage [of the development of the *Weltgeist*], being different from every other one, has its specific and particular principle. In history, such a principle becomes the determination of the spirit — a particular *Volksgeist*. It is here that it expresses concretely all the aspects of its consciousness and will, its total reality; it is this that imparts a common stamp [*das gemeinschaft-liche Gepräge*] to its religion, its political constitution, its social ethics [*Sittlichkeit*], its legal system, its *mores* [*Sitten*], but also to its science, its art, its technical skill. These special peculiarities must be understood as deriving from that general peculiarity, the particular principle of a people. Conversely, it is from the factual details present in history that the general character of this peculiarity is to be discerned.[27]

E. H. Gombrich, who quotes the above passage in full in his *In Search of Cultural History*, gives what is, to my mind, an exemplary commentary on it:

> I like to picture the content of this all-important paragraph diagrammatically as a wheel from the hub of which there radiate eight spokes. These spokes represent the various concrete manifestations of the national Spirit, in Hegel's words "all the aspects of its consciousness and will". They are the nation's religion, constitution, morality, law, customs, science, art and technology. These manifestations which are visible on the periphery of my wheel must all be understood in their individual character as the realizations of the *Volksgeist*. They all point to a common centre. In other words, from whichever part on the outside of the wheel you start moving inwards in search of their essence, you must ultimately come to the same central point. If you do not, if the science of a people appears to you to manifest a different principle from that manifested in its legal system, you must have lost your way somewhere.[28]

Of course (with Hegel, surely, one could not expect otherwise) the metaphor of the wheel is an interpretative oversimplification. In particular, it suggests that in each culture the different aspects of cultural life are of equal weight. But this is not the case. In fact, part of the distinctiveness of a particular manifestation of *Geist* is that, within it, one or other aspect of culture comes to the fore, while another recedes into the background: thus

---

[26] ... the constitution [*Verfassung*] of a people, with its religion, art and philosophy (or, at least, with its conceptions and Thoughts [*Vorstellungen und Gedanken*] – its culture [*Bildung*] generally) ... forms *one* substance, one *Geist*. A state is an individual totality; it is not possible that any single aspect of it, however important – the political constitution, for example – can be extracted independently, examined and assessed by an isolated examination directed at it alone. (Ibid., pp. 64–5 [Eng. trans., pp. 45–6].)
[27] Ibid., pp. 86–7 [Eng. trans., pp. 63–4].
[28] *In Search of Cultural History*, pp. 9–10.

the Greeks were a people of art, religion and philosophy, the Romans of law and technology, and so on. But the point that Gombrich makes – that each area of culture, in Hegel's view, could be said to 'correspond' to every other, without there being any single area that is explanatorily primary – is crucial.[29]

Hegel's theory of history combines Providentialism – the idea that history as a whole embodies a purposive development – with an account of social unity. Hegel employs the by now familiar contrast between organism and mechanism to describe the difference between adequate and defective forms of such unity. Societies should not be merely mechanisms, reproducing themselves according to the formal laws of the understanding. Nations that live according to merely mechanical principles are moribund, according to Hegel: 'This habit (the watch has been wound up and continues of its own accord) is what brings natural death.'[30] Vital societies, like organisms, on the other hand, are given unity by being expressions of an inner principle (an aspect of the all-animating Idea). But, unlike organisms, they are attempts to articulate that principle to themselves (to become *für sich*). This is why the most vital historical forms are evanescent: as they are born and develop, so they are bound to come into conflict with other aspects of the logic of *Geist*.

Hegel's theory is 'Idealist', we might say, in two senses: ontologically, in that his grasp of the historical process is informed by the conviction that the whole of reality is, ultimately, the Idea, but also sociologically, to the extent that what really determines the character of a society is the principle – the form and stage of *Geist* – that is embodied in it. According to Hegel's sociological idealism, what matters most in historical development is the categories within and through which the world is understood; as these change, so, too, does society. As he puts it in the *Encyclopedia*:

> [All] development [*Bildung*] reduces itself to a difference in categories. All revolutions, in the sciences, no less than in world history, derive from the fact that *Geist*, for its own understanding and self-awareness, in order to possess itself, has now changed its categories, and grasped itself more deeply, inwardly and unitarily.[31]

The categories frame our engagement with the world, and determine the form that our cultural activities – and this, for Hegel, includes economic life – can take. Hegel, of course, believed that his sociological idealism was a consistent application of his metaphysics (just as Marx would claim that historical materialism was a part of philosophical materialism). The

---

[29] Thereby, it confutes a common Marxist misinterpretation of Hegel. The Marxist, as a materialist, believes that economic life (the 'base') determines the cultural and ideological superstructure that corresponds to it. Thus it is typical for Marxists to assume that Hegel, as an Idealist, maintains the contrary thesis, namely that the base is determined by the superstructure. But Hegel's Idealism in fact denies explanatory primacy to any isolable part of the social whole.

[30] *Vorlesungen über die Philosophie der Geschichte, Werke*, XII, p. 100 [Eng. trans., p. 74].

[31] *Enzyklopädie der philosophischen Wissenschaften* II, *Werke*, IX, para. 246, *Zusatz*, pp. 20–1.

'common principle' that informs a society's culture is itself an aspect of the Idea. Yet sociological idealism does not require metaphysical idealism; as Gombrich has argued, 'Hegelianism without metaphysics' has been something like a ruling orthodoxy in the study of cultural history.[32]

IV *Geist* and the Individual

Seen from the standpoint of *Geist*, then, history is a purposeful and (in Hegel's sense) *logical*, development through stages. How does this relate to the individuals and groups whose actions are the immediate cause of historical change? According to Hegel, it is through the passions that the purposes of Providence articulate themselves.

> This may be called the *cunning of reason* – that it sets the passions to work for itself.[33]

This famous quotation is potentially misleading, however, to the extent that it suggests that *Geist* uses the passions for the realization of its purposes in the same way that a human being might make use of an animal's desires for some human purpose. The carrot and the stick – the desire for food and the fear of pain – by which we direct the donkey have no intrinsic relationship to the purpose to be achieved. Even if the end is the donkey's own good – say to lead it to a field with new pasture – the means employed and the reason for their employment are not comprehended by the donkey and so the purpose is not truly the donkey's own. One agent sets the incentives in response to which another agent acts and, in this way, controls it.

Bossuet's account of the Providential character of history, in fact, corresponds closely to this model. According to Bossuet, God intervenes

---

[32] Gombrich identifies 'Hegelianism without metaphysics' in the work of the founding heroes of *Kulturgeschichte*, Burckhardt and Wölfflin – from whom he quotes a typical example:

> To *explain* a style cannot mean anything but to fit its expressive character into the general history of the period, to prove that its forms do not say anything in their language that is not also said by the other organs of the age. (H. Wölfflin, *Renaissance and Baroque*, quoted in E. H. Gombrich, *In Search of Cultural History*, p. 25.)

On which Gombrich comments:

> Not that Hegelian metaphysics were accepted in all their abstruse ramifications by any of these historians any more than they were by Burckhardt. The point is rather that all of them felt, consciously or unconsciously, that if they let go of the magnet that created the pattern, the atoms of past cultures would again fall back into random dustheaps. (*In Search of Cultural History*, p. 25.)

Contemporary attempts to identify the essential features of our culture in terms of what is characteristic of 'modernity' or 'post-modernity' are clearly continuations of this tradition.

[33] *Vorlesungen über die Philosophie der Geschichte*, *Werke*, XII, p. 33 [Eng. trans., p. 49].

to alter the character of human beings' passions according to his purposes.[34] For Hegel, on the other hand, *Geist* does not control the passions in this way. When Hegel speaks of the role of the 'passions' in history, he is not concerned with a kind of brute desire but with the conscious and reflective pursuit of ends. To this extent, action is not just a matter of forces pushing individuals but something *cognitive*:

> Agents have finite ends and particular interests in their activity – but they are knowing, Thinking beings. The content of their purposes is permeated by universal, essential determinations regarding *right, the good, duty*, etc. For mere desire, the wild and raw will, falls outside the scene and sphere of world-history.[35]

Geist has purpose but it does not act, in the conventional sense, *wilfully*: its purposes, that is to say, lie in its nature and that nature, Hegel insists, is discoverable. Does this mean, then, that *Geist* is not an agent? Not according to Hegel. *Geist* acts in the sense of being goal-directed and in aiming to come to self-awareness – to attain being *an und für sich*. But it does not have the power of arbitrary choice. Thus *Geist* is not an agent in precisely the same way as an individual human being and so cannot threaten our freedom in some of the ways that another human being might do. To that extent, it is possible for the individual to act rationally in such a way as to make the purposes of *Geist* his own. It is wrong, therefore, Hegel believes, to claim that the overarching purposes of *Geist* use individuals merely as a means:

> When we speak of something as a 'means', we represent it, in the first place, as merely external to its purpose – that does not take part in the latter . . . Human beings, least of all, however, relate to the rational end in that wholly external sense, as means . . . On the contrary, men are ends in themselves according to that rational end itself.[36]

The 'universal determinations' of *Geist*, however, are in a process of development through time. History is the site of colossal collisions between existing codes of law and custom and new conceptions of value and principles of action, quite different from those that had sustained the current system. Yet these, too, may be embodiments of *Geist*'s self-realization: it is the *world-historical individual* who succeeds in grasping that fact:

---

[34] 'God . . . holds every heart in his hands. At times he bridles man's passions, at others he gives them free rein; and that is how he moves all of mankind. Should he wish to see a conqueror, he will spread terror before him and will inspire him and his armies with invincible boldness. Should he wish to see legislators he will send them his spirit of wisdom and foresight; he will cause them to forestall the evils that can befall a state and lay the foundations for public tranquility . . .' (*Discourse on Universal History*, pp. 373–4).
[35] *Vorlesungen über die Philosophie der Geschichte, Werke*, XII, p. 28 [Eng. trans., p. 44].
[36] Ibid., p. 50 [Eng. trans., p. 33].

This universal is a moment of the productive Idea, a moment of truth striving and driving for itself. The historical individuals – the world-historical individuals – are those in whose purposes there lies such a universal.[37]

The passions, for Hegel, are a link between the logic of *Geist* and its perception by human beings. The world-historical individual is privileged in this way, for he has an apprehension – intuitive, rather than reflective – of the nature of his age and his action is guided by it. The characteristic end of a world-historical individual is at once both private (or, rather, egotistic) and public: the desire for exclusive political power (Caesar) or for military glory (Alexander, Napoleon). Although he may appear merely to be advancing his own private interests, however, the way that he does so is informed by his awareness of the development of *Geist*:

Such individuals had no consciousness of the Idea as such in pursuing their ends; on the contrary, they were practical, political men. But they were at the same time Thinking men, who had an insight into what was necessary – what was *timely* [*an der Zeit*] ... World-historical individuals, the heroes of an age, must thus be recognized as the perceptive ones [*die Einsichtigen*]; their words and deeds are the best things of their age.[38]

What is distinctive about the world-historical individual is not the fact that he pursues aims that are intrinsically different from those of others (Caesar's enemies had precisely the same ones) but his perception of what is involved in achieving those objectives in the circumstances of the time. The world-historical individual is more sensitive than others to the development of *Geist* – in particular, to the presence of new and vital forms of it.

Hegel describes world-historical individuals as drawing upon 'the inward *Geist* that remains subterranean but which, impinging on the external world as upon a shell, breaks it in pieces'.[39] It is for this reason – that they are in touch with *Geist* in its most advanced form, not for their personal *charisma* – that such individuals are natural leaders; the source on which the world-historical individual draws is already an implicit part of the life of their fellow-men.[40] The world-historical individual is able to use the force of *Geist* to amplify his own effects on others:

[37] Ibid., p. 29 [Eng. trans., p. 45].
[38] Ibid., p. 30 [Eng. trans., p. 46].
[39] Ibid.
[40] Although Hegel's examples of 'world-historical individuals' – Caesar, Alexander, Napoleon – are all great military-political leaders, the kind of apprehension of *Geist* that they have is not confined to the political realm. In the *Encyclopedia*, Hegel makes clear that he believes that it is possible to apprehend the truth of the Idea intuitively, in 'experience' (although this is not the highest form of awareness of it), for which he takes Goethe as his example:

A great mind [*ein grosser Sinn*] is great in its experience ... The great mind of a Goethe, for example, looking into nature or history, has great experiences, catches sight of what is rational and gives expression to it. (*Enzyklopädie der philosophischen Wissenschaften* I, *Werke*, VIII, para. 24, *Zusatz*, pp. 20–1.)

... this advanced *Geist* is the inward soul of all individuals, but as unconscious inwardness, which the great men make conscious for them. This is why others follow these soul-leaders, for they feel the irresistible force of their own inner *Geist* that they encounter in them.[41]

It is the force of *Geist*, Hegel believes, that determines the fate of civilizations. If the *Geist* is strong within it, then a civilization can overcome material weakness and hardship, just as the Greeks overcame the Persians at Thermopylae. On the other hand, once a *Volk* has achieved its purpose, it falls back into a calm routine and becomes self-satisfied and vulnerable. When one civilization supersedes another, as Rome did Carthage or Greece, the explanation lies as much in the enervation of the latter as in the vitality of the former.

Thus, at the collective level, Hegel's theory of history is highly deterministic: all *Volksgeister* grow, flourish and are superseded, as *Geist* itself passes from one form to another. Yet, because the way that this inflexible schema asserts itself is cognitive – a matter of perception on the part of the individual – it is in principle quite compatible with the view that the individual is autonomous and *responsible* in his formation of ends and choice of action.[42] It is simply that some individuals have a deeper awareness of the nature of the context within which they act than others.

Hegel's theory of the cunning of reason is an account of the coordination of two kinds of subject: *Geist* and the individual. Explanation at the level of *Geist* amplifies and completes explanation at the level of the individual agent by placing the actions of individuals into a context of wider significance. However, that does not show that individual explanation is invalid or that the individual's choices are unreal or redundant. What it does do is to contradict a reductive picture of individuals as inevitably following the dictates of simple material forces. It is because individuals' reasoning contains an apprehension in an obscure form of the structures of *Geist* that we can play our part in *Geist*'s 'coming-to-itself'.[43]

[41] *Vorlesungen über die Philosophie der Geschichte, Werke*, XII, pp. 30–1 [Eng. trans., p. 46].

[42] 'This is the seal of the absolute and sublime destiny of man – that he knows what is good and what is evil, that his destiny is to will either the good or the bad, and that he can be responsible ... Only the animal is truly innocent.' (*Vorlesungen über die Philosophie der Geschichte, Werke*, XII, pp. 50–1 [Eng. trans., p. 34].)

[43] Shlomo Avineri has argued that Hegel's account of the world-historical individual is inconsistent. He presents three quotations to support his view:

(a) The historical men, world-historical individuals, are those who grasp ... a higher universal, make it their own purpose, and realize this purpose in accordance with the higher law of the spirit ... The world-historical persons, the heroes of their age, must therefore be recognized as its seers.

(b) Caesar was motivated not only by his own private interest, but acted instinctively to bring to pass that which the times required.

(c) Such individuals have no consciousness of the Idea as such. They are practical and political men. We thus find Hegel describing the world-historical individual as, alternatively, (i) wholly conscious of the idea of history and its development, (ii) only instinctively conscious of it, and (iii) being wholly unaware of it.

With all the possible allowance for the varieties of expression and nuance, no adequate

While it is true that individuals do not fully understand the ramifications of *Geist*, that need not be a bar to their freedom, for, of course, finite individuals – even free ones – never could comprehend the *full* significance of their actions. By acting in a certain way, the individual brings about the purposes of *Geist* as an unintended consequence of the rational pursuit of his own ends: *Geist* does not *manipulate* individuals.

V False Consciousness: the *Phenomenology of Spirit*

Hegel's theory of history, then, is an account of the way in which change is brought about by individuals taking actions whose significance they do not fully comprehend. But it would be somewhat misleading to speak of Hegel as 'bringing together' thereby the idea of false consciousness with historical providentialism and social organicism. On the contrary, from Hegel's point of view, both sets of ideas are themselves products of his fundamental metaphysics: the story of the loss and recovery of *Geist*.[44] Thus the primary form of false consciousness at work in Hegel's philosophy is what I called in Chapter 2 a distortion of identity of a cosmic or metaphysical kind: the fact that *Geist* lacks the unified self-presence that comes when it knows itself in its otherness. As its title makes clear, the *Phenomenology of Spirit* is Hegel's compendium of these forms of division, loss and distortion.

The name 'Phenomenology' was introduced into German philosophy by J. H. Lambert in his *Neues Organon* (Leipzig, 1764) of which the fourth part was entitled '*Phänomenologie oder Lehre von dem Schein*' ('Phenomenology or doctrine of appearance'). Lambert, an astronomer, was much struck by the importance for science of the contrast between how things are and how they seem to be.[45] Generalized, this idea is a powerful theme in subsequent German philosophy, informing both Kant's 'Copernican

---

explication can be given to what must in the last resort be viewed as contradictory statements.
(S. Avineri, 'Consciousness and History: *List der Vernunft* in Hegel and Marx', pp. 111–12.)

I disagree. I have no doubt that Hegel's view is (ii) – that individuals are intuitively but not fully reflectively aware of *Geist*. Neither quotation (a) (which is, in fact, a patch-work arranged by Avineri) nor quotation (c) contradicts that. The German word in (a) that Avineri translates as 'seers' is '*Einsichtigen*' – literally, 'those who have insight' – and this matches very well the idea of the world-historical individual perceptively making a purpose his own without being reflectively aware *that* he is so doing. In other words, quotation (a) is perfectly compatible with (ii). As for quotation (c), the German has it that these men did not have '*Bewußtsein der Idee überhaupt*': that is, although their consciousness was informed by the Idea, they were not aware of it as being the Idea as such. So quotation (c) cannot be taken to support view (iii) rather than (ii). Thus Hegel's view seems to me to be plainly consistent.

[44] The 'loss' of unity is, at the same time, a progress and so, like the Fall of Man in the Christian story, turns out to be, in the end, a gain.

[45] Lambert is credited with being one of the first to infer the structure of our galaxy from the perceived image of the Milky Way – a brilliant example of the practical employment of such a contrast.

Revolution' and Hegel's *Phenomenology*. As Novalis was to put it: 'Truthful presentation of error is indirect presentation of truth.'

Since the *Phenomenology* is not a work of history but an attempt to retrace the forms of consciousness in a 'logical' fashion[46] it would be an oversimplification to identify particular ideas to be found in it with specific sociological or psychological phenomena. Nevertheless, the 'shapes' through which consciousness is described as passing in its progress towards self-knowledge include almost all the different forms of false consciousness identified in Chapter 2. It is worth mentioning some of those conceptions individually, if only for the fact that they would prove so resonant with later authors.

For the Marxist tradition, the *Phenomenology* is, in Marx's words, 'the true birth-place and secret of the Hegelian philosophy'.[47] Bringing together as it does ideas of false consciousness with those of labour, self-expression and the need for mutual recognition, it prepares the way, in Marx's view, for a critique of alienation that goes beyond Hegel.[48]

At the level of the individual, Hegel identifies a variety of different ways in which the self comes to be detached from (that which appears to it as) otherness. At the beginning of the *Phenomenology*, in the chapter on Lordship and Servitude (*Herrschaft und Knechtschaft*), Hegel asserts the necessity for mutual recognition as a condition for self-consciousness. Recognition of the individual as more than just a natural being, he argues, requires that its life be put at risk.[49] Such recognition, however, cannot come about where one agent looks upon another simply as the means to satisfy his appetites and his power over that other is absolute.[50] Thus it is the *labour* of the slave (whose submission is the outcome of the life-and-death conflict), rather than the enjoyment of the master, that contains within itself the condition for true self-recognition.

---

[46] At the very end of the *Phenomenology*, Hegel makes the contrast between this and empirical history itself in the following terms:

> The goal – absolute knowledge, or *Geist* knowing itself as *Geist* – is reached by the recollection of the *Geister*, as they are in themselves ... Their preservation, from the point of view of their freely appearing existence in the form of contingency, is *history*; from the point of view of their comprehended organization [*begriffne Organisation*], however, the science of the appearance of knowledge [*Wissenschaft des erscheinenden Wissens*]. (*Phänomenologie des Geistes*, p. 564.)

[47] *Economic and Philosophical Manuscripts*, p. 383.

[48] The *Phenomenology* is therefore concealed and mystifying criticism, criticism which has not attained self-clarity; but in so far as it grasps the alienation of man – even though man appears only in the form of mind – *all* the elements of criticism are concealed within it, and are often prepared and worked out in a way that goes far beyond Hegel's own point of view. (Ibid., p. 385.)

[49] The individual that has not risked his life can be recognised as a *person*; but it has not attained the truth of this recognition as that of an independent self-consciousness. (*Phänomenologie des Geistes*, p. 145.)

[50] Self-consciousness is in and for itself [*an und für sich*] to the extent that and by the fact that it is in and for itself for another; that is, that it exists only as something that is *recognised* ... The unfolding of the concept [*Begriff*] of this spiritual unity [*geistige Einheit*] in its reduplication is presented by the movement of recognition [*Anerkennen*] ... (Ibid., p. 143).

But without recognition by another the self cannot truly have its own identity.[51]

The *Phenomenology* contains accounts both of social division and of individuals' 'false consciousness'. In the case of the former, this manifests itself characteristically in the presence of different kinds of irreconcilable claim, the most famous example being the case of Antigone. Both private piety and public duty, Hegel believes, represent an aspect of *Geist* and each is in its own way a rational and valid claim. Yet, at this incomplete stage of *Geist*'s development, there is no way to acknowledge both claims – much less to reconcile them – and so the result is *tragic*.[52] The tragic individual such as Antigone is subject to false consciousness, not because she acts *irrationally*, but because she faces a situation in which whatever she does is wrong: she is condemned to guilt.[53] It is society itself that is antinomical, because it contains within its essence these inconsistent claims.

Later in the *Phenomenology*, Hegel argues that it is characteristic of that stage of the development of *Geist* that he calls '*Geist* alienated from itself' [*der sich entfremdete Geist*] that the individual should seek to escape into a kind of 'false freedom'.[54] The characteristic self in this world is the self of *vanity* [*Eitelkeit*], a self that sees the vanity of everything but that is – like the *amour-propre* of Pascal and Rousseau – itself vain. Unbeknown to itself, it requires its own alienation from reality in order to preserve its identity. Its characteristic figure is Diderot's 'Rameau's Nephew', who, light and witty, floats over everything without being able to find meaning in any of it.[55] Like Pascal's victims of *amour-propre*, the vain self pursues the goods

---

[51] '. . . thus the labouring consciousness comes hereby to the intuition of independent being as belonging to itself' (Ibid., p. 149). Clearly, this chapter is far more complex than the brief points mentioned here can do justice to. In particular, Hegel himself would not have endorsed the apparent implication, congenial to Marxists, that true recognition requires that each should engage in material labour and none should live solely on the labour of others.

[52] But the ethical essence [*das sittliche Wesen*] has divided itself into two laws, and consciousness, as an undivided attitude towards the law, is only assigned to one of them . . . For [self-consciousness], insofar as it becomes a self for itself and moves into action, rises out of its simple immediacy and itself posits *division* . . . So by this action it becomes *guilt*. For it is its deed and the deed of its ownmost essence. And the guilt takes on the significance of a *crime*: for, as a simple ethical consciousness, it has aligned itself with the one law, declined the other, and violated the latter by its deed. (*Phänomenologie des Geistes*, p. 334.)

[53] As Adorno puts it, '*Es gibt kein richtiges Leben im Falschen*' ('One cannot live right in falsehood') (*Minima Moralia*, p. 42).

[54] The world of this *Geist* falls apart into two: the first is the world of reality, or its own alienation; the second, however, that which it, rising up over the former, builds itself in the ether of the pure consciousness. The latter, which is opposed to that alienation, is for that very reason not free from it, but is, rather, merely the other form of that alienation, which consists of having consciousness in two worlds and which includes both of them. (*Phänomenologie des Geistes*, p. 350.)

[55] [This consciousness] is the self that is for itself, that does not just know how to judge everything persuasively, but knows how to express wittily the contradiction in the fixed essence of reality, and in the fixed categories of judgement . . . It knows, then, how to express each moment against the other, indeed the inversion of all of them; it knows better what everything is than it knows itself, whatever its nature may be . . . This vanity requires the vanity of all things, in order to draw from them its consciousness of self; hence it produces the vanity itself and is the soul which supports it. (Ibid., p. 375.)

of this world only to discover that they are without intrinsic meaning –
that whatever meaning they have comes from the self's vanity.[56] The vain
self lacks a true identity because it cannot recognize itself in what is other
than itself.

VI *Schein*

However, one theme that is not dealt with in detail in the *Phenomenology*
is even more important for the theory of ideology. This, surprisingly, given
the title of the book, is the idea of *Schein* itself.

Schein, it is no exaggeration to say, is the central concept of German
Idealist aesthetics: 'The beautiful has its life in *Schein*', as Hegel puts it in
the *Lectures on Aesthetics*.[57] In its etymological origins, *Schein* signifies both
illusory appearance (as in Lambert) and that lustrous quality, at once
superficial and mysterious, that might be rendered in English as 'sheen' or
(as Coleridge does) 'translucence'. It is *Schein* that makes works of art (and
beautiful natural objects) something more than just material things.
Herder, in his *Plastik* (1778), suggests an etymological connection between
Schein and beauty: '*Schönheit* (beauty) takes its name from *Schauen*
(looking) and from *Schein*.'[58]

The concept is closely connected to the idea (promoted especially by
Goethe, Schelling and, following them, Coleridge) that true art is *symbolic*
(rather than allegorical).[59] Symbolic art is transcendent, in the sense of 'pointing
beyond itself', but it has no definitely assignable content.[60] As used by German
Idealism, *Schein* is illusory only to the extent that our perception of an
object in which *Schein* is manifest is somehow elusive or indefinite: although
art is the realm of *Schein* this is not because art depicts a realm of objects
and events that may not exist. *Schein*'s elusiveness is, rather, the index of
the character of art as a kind of 'occluded manifestation' of a higher reality.

For Hegel, *Schein* is a product of the beautiful object's character as a
vehicle for the manifestation of truth. Insofar as the Idea 'exists externally
for consciousness and the *Begriff* is in immediate unity with its external
appearance' it is, according to Hegel, 'not just true but beautiful'.[61] Thus

---

[56] Power and wealth are the supreme ends of its exertions ... they are the actually
acknowledged powers. However, this recognition and acceptance is itself vain; and just by
taking possession of power and wealth it knows them to be without a self of their own, knows
rather that *it* is the power over them, while they are vain things. (Ibid.)
[57] *Vorlesungen über die Ästhetik I*, *Werke*, XIII, p. 17.
[58] J. G. Herder, *Plastik*, *Sämtliche Werke*, VIII, 10. Schiller was the first to use the expression
'*schöner Schein*'.
[59] A symbol ... is characterized by a translucence of the Special in the Individual or of the
General in the Especial ... Above all, by the translucence of the Eternal through and in the
Temporal. (S. T. Coleridge, *The Statesman's Manual*, p. 30.)
[60] 'If the symbolic expresses anything apart from the presentation then it does so in indirect
fashion' (J. W. Goethe, 'Über die Gegenstände der bildenden Kunst', p. 461).
[61] *Vorlesungen über die Ästhetik I*, *Werke*, XIII, p. 151.

the beautiful is 'the sensible translucence of the Idea' ('*das sinnliche Scheinen der Idee*').[62]

The idea of *Schein* — the attribution of spiritual significance to natural objects and artefacts – has close affinities with that of 'fetishism', discussed in Chapter 3. Fetishism, as understood by Hume and de Brosses, is the attribution of a non-natural property (animation, divinity) to a natural material object. It is an illusion which embodies a kind of category mistake. Although the susceptibility to such illusions is to be explained emotionally (and those emotions, in turn, socially) according to Hume, the error itself is purely cognitive.

Hegel's account of *Schein* is significantly different from Hume's Enlightenment theory, however. Although *Schein* is not part of what Hegel would call the 'natural being' of objects (say, those properties that would figure in a physicist's account of the world) it is not, for that reason, something purely subjective: a *projection* onto the world by the individual. On the contrary, Hegel's metaphysics leaves open, as naturalistic philosophies such as Hume's do not, a third possibility: that *Schein* is an actual (in that sense, *vis-à-vis* the individual subject, objective) expression of a higher subject, *Geist*.

Hegel believes that the Idea realizes itself (as we would say) *objectively* in the beautiful object: it is as much part of the object as its physical constitution (although, of course, it requires a particularly constituted perceiver to discern it; if we try to detect it by purely physical methods then we shall fail). Thus *Schein* is illusory, for Hegel, not because the subject is *mistaken* in attributing it to the object but because the subject fails to recognize its true source.

But, just as *Schein* is both illusion and reality, so art is also both true and untrue. For the character of the Idea cannot be properly expressed in any sensible medium; it can be fully grasped only in the domain of speculative philosophy: pure Thought.[63] As *Geist* has developed towards truth, beauty has shown itself to be less and less adequate as a form of expression for the Idea: in the end, art is left behind in favour of philosophy.[64]

The connection between these two ideas is made clear when we consider Hegel's solution to a problem of German Idealist and Romantic aesthetics which we might call 'Winckelmann's Paradox'. For Winckelmann and his successors (Herder, Goethe, Schiller, Hölderlin, the Schlegels and Karl Marx, to name only a few of the most prominent thinkers who accepted the paradox's premises) it appeared deeply puzzling that the art of the

---

[62] Ibid.

[63] In symbols the truth is still dimmed and veiled by the sensible element; it is only entirely manifest to the consciousness that is in the form of Thought; the meaning is only the Thought itself. (*Wissenschaft der Logik*, I, 211.)
See my *Hegel's Dialectic and its Criticism*, especially Chs 4 and 5.

[64] 'Thought and reflection have soared above beautiful art' (G. W. F. Hegel, *Vorlesungen über die Ästhetik I*, Werke, XIII, p. 24).

Greeks should remain an unsurpassed ideal of beauty, and yet that their own age should be incapable of recapturing whatever it was that had given Greek art its magic. The paradox was that Greek art was in a sense both open to the modern age (still capable of being appreciated) and closed (incapable of imitation). In Marx's words:

> ... the difficulty lies not in understanding that the Greek arts and epic are bound up with certain forms of social development. The difficulty is that they still afford us artistic pleasure and that in a certain respect they count as a norm and as an unattainable model.[65]

Hegel agrees that, even nowadays, Greek art is supremely beautiful, and offers his own explanation for this apparent paradox. The reason for the inimitable beauty of Greek art, he maintains, is that it was the objective embodiment of a particular stage of *Geist*, one in which *Geist* had not yet discovered the universality that would bring it into conflict with the world of the senses. The continued 'existence' of *Schein* (its openness to modern perception) is a result of the fact that, at a later stage of *Geist*, *Geist* includes aspects of its own earlier self: although *Geist* has now, Hegel believes, achieved universality, part of that universality lies in its ability to appreciate (even if it can no longer legitimately confine itself to) particularity. In consequence, those who now look back on Greek art from a higher stage can be moved by what it articulates (for it really is a feature of the statues and architecture that they so much admire) without being able to express themselves in the same way.

VII The Overcoming of 'False Consciousness'

Like Plato, Hegel believes that philosophy is not merely a contemplative study: as the mind achieves understanding, so, too, it is practically reconciled to the rationality of that which it understands – philosophical understanding transforms the individual's attitude towards the reality of which he is a part. The highest form of this understanding, Hegel believes (once again, like Plato), is speculative and *a priori*: the product of the mind's ascent to the realm of 'pure Thought'. In philosophy, the individual can achieve a fully transparent understanding of reality, to the extent that reality is knowable at all.

Yet (and here he is quite *unlike* Plato) Hegel also believes that this process of philosophical understanding involves an interplay between two kinds of subject: individual consciousness and the collective subject, *Geist*. It is only when *Geist* (at the interpersonal level) has achieved a certain point of completion that it is open to the individual to come to know itself in its relation to *Geist* (and in coming to this awareness to bring *Geist* itself

---

[65] *Grundrisse der Kritik der politischen Ökonomie*, p. 31 [Eng. trans., p. 111].

thereby to its very final point). Thus true understanding is possible only when history (and, hence, society) has taken on a rational form. If recognition by the individual is the key to transforming practical relationships, it is also true that such recognition is possible only once a transformation has taken place on the supra-individual level.

With its emphasis on the need for the practical transformation of society as a precondition for the elimination of false consciousness, this view is naturally highly congenial to the Marxist version of the theory of ideology. It is clear, however, that it also leaves a number of awkward questions. If it is *necessary* for *Geist* to have achieved a certain form for false consciousness to be overcome, why is that not also *sufficient*? Why do we need *both* a practical transformation of society *and* recognition on the part of the individual? Is a rational society only the precondition for a philosophical understanding of the world? Hegel's answer would appear to be that, while such a stage of *Geist* is *intrinsically* rational, philosophy is nevertheless required for it to be demonstrated to be so. But then does this mean that everyone must be a speculative philosopher in Hegel's ideal society in order to be rationally reconciled to it? If not, it seems that Hegel is forced (like Plato) to divide society once again into two parts: the one, like Plato's philosopher-rulers, composed of those who know the rationality of the state, and the other of non-philosophers, who may be legitimately coerced in the name of that rationality.

Hegel's philosophy, then, brings together the two intuitions which, I claim, make the theory of ideology appear to be so plausible: the idea of the self-maintaining character of the social order and the idea of false consciousness. But it does so in the context of an idealist metaphysical system that represents the apotheosis of rationalism and providentialism. The challenge implicitly facing his successor, Marx, is to do justice to those background beliefs in the context of an avowedly secular – materialistic and scientific – account of society.

6

Marx

With Marx, the theory of ideology becomes explicit in two respects. The first, but less important, is that Marx is the first writer to use the term 'ideology' to denote those forms of consciousness by means of which societies that would not receive the spontaneous and rational compliance of their members are able, nevertheless, to maintain themselves. Secondly, however, it is Marx who makes the first conscious attempt to separate the ideas of unintended consequences and of false consciousness from any framework of optimistic providentialism or of theologically inspired jeremiads against the corruption of human nature.

It will be the argument of this chapter that Marx did not have a *theory* of ideology in the full sense – an empirically well-specified account, that is, connecting *explanans* and *explanandum* by means of a plausible explanatory connection. On the contrary, I shall argue, Marx has no fewer than five different (and, for the most part, mutually incompatible) models of ideology: five distinct outlines of the mechanism by which ideological phenomena are to be identified and explained.

Interpreters of Marx's mature writings divide into two main groups. On the one hand, there are those who see *Das Kapital* as continuing the themes and preoccupations that are to be found in Marx's early writings (principally, the concern with alienated labour and its overcoming). On the other, there are those who emphasize that a break took place in Marx's thought in the mid-1840s, after which he abandoned Hegelian conceptions of loss and recovery in favour of an approach modelled closely on the natural sciences. The account that will be presented in this chapter diverges from both of these interpretations. I have no doubt that around 1845 Marx did indeed make a radical break with many of his earlier conceptions and convictions. I shall argue, however, that the two principal strategies for reconstructing Marx's theory of ideology along lines strictly parallel to the natural sciences – the interpretation of the idea of a correspondence between base and superstructure in terms of functional explanation and the contrast between essence and appearance – fall short of what is needed to sustain it. Thus, in my view, the presence of a form of quasi-Hegelian collectivism in Marx's mature work is neither a rhetorical hangover nor a result of Marx's continuing commitment to his earliest ideas but a theoretically motivated return. It is a reflection of and response to the fact that an austere self-restriction to the ontological and methodological assumptions of the natural sciences is insufficient to make good the claims about the nature of social life and the role of ideas to which Marx is fundamentally committed.

I The Emergence of the Theory of Ideology

Although the background beliefs informing the theory of ideology and the body of theoretical reflection supporting them came down to Marx through what was for the most part an idealist and theologically inspired tradition of thought, the name 'ideology' itself did not. Despite attempts to relate the origin of the term to Bacon's doctrine of *idola* – his account of the illusions to which human reason characteristically falls victim – it is beyond doubt that the term 'ideology' in the nineteenth century has its origins in the French *philosophe* and supporter of the Revolution, Destutt de Tracy.

Destutt de Tracy (or Antoine-Louis-Claude, comte de Destutt de Tracy, to give him his full name) was an exceptionally interesting figure.[1] An aristocrat with a military background, he moved in liberal and enlightened intellectual circles in the years prior to the Revolution. As an aristocrat and a moderate Destutt de Tracy was arrested under the Terror and sentenced to death, a fate that he escaped only because of the fall of Robespierre on the day before he was due to go to the guillotine. (It is said of him – as it has, no doubt, been said of many others – that his hair turned white overnight as a result of this experience.) Destutt de Tracy was a political and, in particular, educational reformer who took his intellectual inspiration from Locke and Condillaç. Like them, he rejected any version of the doctrine of innate ideas – indeed, any idea of a fixed human nature. But Destutt de Tracy went further than Locke, using empiricist epistemology to support (what we might nowadays call) the sociology of knowledge. If human beings developed their ideas in response to their environment, and if human nature was essentially malleable, then it followed that each set of social circumstances would produce a particular type of individual with characteristic ideas and conceptions of the world:

[1] He has also been the beneficiary of an exemplary biography, by E. Kennedy, to which I am much indebted.

different circumstances, a different type. This, said Destutt de Tracy, was the proper object of study for those whose interest was the human mind. Unlike the 'metaphysical' philosophers, who aimed to establish normative results concerning the structure and limits of human knowledge on the basis of an unchanging human nature, *idéologie* would simply set out to discover the positive determinants of ideas and their systematic connections.

Thus *idéologie* was explicitly opposed to the philosophy of Kant (although Destutt de Tracy does call the Kantians the 'truest friends of liberty and reason in Germany').[2] Kant's ideas, he asserts,

> . . . are actually only Platonic, Cartesian and Leibnizian ideas turned over in a thousand different ways, presented under different names, and always founded on the abuse of abstract principles.[3]

If the Kantians are to be cured, he believes, then they will require a stiff shot of empiricism:

> I send them back unceremoniously to Condillac's *Traité de Systèmes*, which makes quick work of them.[4]

But if, to Destutt de Tracy, the German philosophers looked like a throwback to an already superseded kind of metaphysics, they themselves – to the extent that they were aware of Destutt de Tracy at all – were no more impressed with him: in his discussion of Locke's view of the origin of complex ideas in experience, Hegel remarks that:

> The French in particular have taken up this and continued it; their *idéologie* contains nothing beyond this.[5]

Given Destutt de Tracy's allegiance to a positive approach to the study of ideas in society and his rejection of the 'metaphysical' assumptions of the Kantians it may seem surprising and ironic – to say the least – that

[2] Letter to Droz. Quoted in E. Kennedy, *A Philosophe in the Age of Revolution: Destutt de Tracy and the Origins of 'Ideology'*, p. 120.
[3] *De la métaphysique de Kant*. Quoted in ibid., p. 118.
[4] Ibid.
[5] *Vorlesungen über die Geschichte der Philosophie III, Werke*, XX, p. 219. Although he was certainly unsympathetic to *idéologie*, Hegel seems not to have been wholly uninformed about it. His only other mention of it (known to me) also comes in the *Lectures on the History of Philosophy*, where he remarks that the Scottish philosophy (of whom Adam Smith is the 'best known' and Dugald Stewart 'the last and least significant') was taken up in France and that it is from this that 'what the French call *idéologie*' takes its starting point. Since there are, in fact, remarkable similarities between Stewart's *Elements of the Human Mind* and Destutt de Tracy's *Élémens de l'idéologie*, the possibility of such a direct link cannot be discounted (*Vorlesungen über die Geschichte der Philosophie III, Werke*, XX, p. 286).

when, half a century later, Marx came to write the *German Ideology*[6] Kant himself should be castigated as an 'ideologist'.[7] How did this apparent reversal in the meaning of the term come about and what did it amount to?

The answer, it is clear, lies in Napoleon Bonaparte. The *idéologues* (Napoleon is supposed to have invented the name himself) had originally been allies of Napoleon, under whose patronage they hoped to realize their projects for educational reform. But, as the First Consul's political ambitions increased in grandeur (and as he sought in consequence to make his peace with the Church) it became apparent that the *idéologues'* hopes that he would realize the secular and enlightened ideals of the Revolution, but in a more moderate and rational form than the Jacobins, were misplaced. After he became emperor, Napoleon appears to have developed something like an obsession with the *idéologues*. Here, for example, is an extract from a speech made to the *Conseil d'État* in 1812:

> We must lay the blame for the ills that our fair France has suffered on *ideology*, that shadowy metaphysics which subtly searches for first causes on which to base the legislation of peoples, rather than making use of laws known to the human heart and the lessons of history . . .
>
> When someone is summoned to revitalize a state he must follow exactly the opposite principles. History depicts the human heart, and it is in history that we must discover the advantages and disadvantages of different forms of legislation. Such are the principles of which a great empire's Council of State must never lose sight. To this must be added the courage to face any test and the readiness to die in the defence of sovereign, throne and laws.[8]

In other words, 'ideology' is an attempt to come to principles of law and legislation abstractly – that is, theoretically – rather than through the kind of practical wisdom that comes from the study of history or from direct political engagement (it is clear, of course, whom Napoleon has in mind as the embodiment of such wisdom). 'Ideology' seems to have served him as

---

[6] *The German Ideology* was composed between November 1845 and June 1846. Notoriously, it failed to find a publisher and was left by Marx to the 'gnawing criticism of the mice' (not just a picturesque metaphor, as it turns out: some parts of the surviving manuscript have indeed been eaten away). Although it was presented as a joint work with Engels, the main theoretical ideas and key formulations are Marx's.

[7] We find again in Kant the characteristic form which French liberalism, based on real class interests, assumed in Germany. Neither he, nor the German burghers whose whitewashing spokesman he was, noticed that these theoretical ideas of the bourgeoisie had as their basis material interests and a *will* that was conditioned and determined by the material relations of production. Kant, therefore, separated this theoretical expression from the interests it expressed; he made the materially motivated determinations of the will of the French bourgeois into *pure* self-determinations of '*free will*', of the will in and for itself, of the human will, and so converted it into purely ideological conceptual determinations and moral postulates. (*The German Ideology*, p. 99.)

[8] *Réponse à l'adresse du Conseil d'État*, 20.xii.1812. Quoted in E. Kennedy, *A Philosophe in the Age of Revolution: Destutt de Tracy and the Origins of 'Ideology'*, p. 215.

a convenient term of abuse for all those who presumed to question his decrees and decisions from any kind of reflective vantage-point.[9]

The word had passed into German before 1830 and was in the dictionaries in its pejorative sense by 1838.[10] A letter to Marx from his father, Heinrich, written in 1837, refers to Napoleon's quarrel with the *idéologues* as an instance of the emperor's tyrannous character. So, did Marx himself acquire the term from any particular source or did he take it from the common stock of political language at the time? One possible influence was that prominent mediator between France and Germany, Heinrich Heine. Heine used the term 'ideology' quite frequently and (although he was not the first to use the phrase 'German ideology') he made the connection between ideology and the character of contemporary German intellectual and political life explicitly: the Germans, he wrote, were ideologists because they lived in a world of speculation, detached from the real practical events that were changing politics in other countries (above all, in France):

> As far as the Germans are concerned, they need neither freedom nor equality. They are a speculative people, ideologists, thinkers before and after the event, dreamers who live only in the future, never in the present.[11]

This quotation, written as early as 1828, comes from a book published as *Reisebilder* (*Pictures of Travel*), which Marx is assumed to have known.[12] So copious are the echoes of Heine in Marx's early writings and so closely does his own characterization of the specifically German features of the 'German ideology' – abstract speculation, distance from practical engagement – correspond to Heine's that it seems to me overwhelmingly probable that Heine must take the main credit for Marx's use of the term.

However, a particular episode relating to his doctoral dissertation makes

---

[9] A letter written to Jefferson by John Adams in 1813 mentions this sense of *ideology* as having been invented by Napoleon to designate impractical schemes.

Napoleon was aware, however, that the *idéologues* had secular and scientific intentions – although he considered them dangerous:

> Your *idéologues* destroy all illusions and the age of illusions is for individuals as for peoples the age of happiness. (Talleyrand's Memoirs, quoted in E. Kennedy, *A Philosophe in the Age of Revolution: Destutt de Tracy and the Origins of 'Ideology'*, p. 189.)

[10] See the article *'Ideologie'* in *Geschichtliche Grundbegriffe*, III, pp. 131–69 (pp. 141–2).

[11] Heine, *Englische Fragmente*, p. 211. Heine makes great comic play with this *topos*. In the *On the History of Religion and Philosophy in Germany* he speaks of the practical French being so busy with their Revolution that they did not have time to dream, and so they had to get the Germans to do it for them. But he did not invent the joke. Hegel (whom Heine knew personally and admired) says as much in his discussion of Kant's philosophy in the *Lectures on the History of Philosophy*. Unlike the French, who turn their radical ideas into revolutionary actions, the German tumult, Hegel says, remains in the Germans' heads, and 'the German head does not disturb its nightcap and goes to work inside itself' (*Vorlesungen über die Geschichte der Philosophie III*, *Werke*, XX, p. 332).

[12] S. S. Prawer describes 'the fragment of a novel Marx began in 1837' as 'heavily dependent on Sterne's *Tristram Shandy* and Heine's *Pictures of Travel*.' (*Karl Marx and World Literature*, p. 15). Later, in Paris, Marx and Heine were to become friends and collaborators.

it apparent that Marx himself was not aware that he was part of a process
of linguistic innovation. In an article in the (East German) *Deutsche
Zeitschrift für Philosophie* for 1970, H. Oertel drew attention to a passage in
Marx's doctoral dissertation (completed in 1841) in which Marx quoted
from Epicurus in his own translation:

> Nicht der Ideologie und der leeren Hypothesen hat unser Leben Not,
> sondern das, daß wir ohne Verwirrung leben.[13]

Oertel remarks that 'the negative content that Epicurus gives to the
word "ideology" shows itself clearly here'[14] and he goes on to identify
another passage from Epicurus, noted by Marx in the preliminary studies
for his dissertation, which seems to reinforce his reading:

> The fantasies of the mad and dream-images are also true; for they are a
> motivating force; that which does not exist, on the other hand, is not a
> motivating force.[15]

However, Oertel has taken Marx's translation to be accurate, and, as it
turns out, Marx seems to have been under a double misapprehension
about the passage. The Greek word ἰδιολογίας that Marx translates as
'ideology' would have meant in fact something more like private or
personal opinion (as in our 'idiosyncrasy' or 'idiolect'). As H.-C. Rauh
pointed out against Oertel, Marx would appear to have translated Epicurus
'in the light of German-French everyday language'.[16] But, beyond that, it
turns out that the edition from which Marx was working was itself
unsatisfactory and, instead of ἰδιολογίας it should have read ἤδη ἀλογίας.
There seems, then, to be no reason to revise the view argued for in earlier
chapters that the conception of ideology as we find it in Marx and his
successors is something characteristically modern.

II The Critique of Religion

Before the composition of *The German Ideology*, the term 'ideology' clearly
had little significance for Marx.[17] However, while the term was not an

---

[13] 'It is not ideology and empty hypotheses that our life needs, but this: that we should live
without confusion' (H. Oertel, 'Zur Genesis des Ideologiebegriffs', p. 208).
[14] Ibid.
[15] Taken from Diogenes Laertius, Book X, quoted ibid., p. 209. There is, Oertel points out, a
striking echo of this passage in *The German Ideology*:

> The fog-figures [*Nebelbildungen*] in the brains of men are necessary sublimates of their
> material, empirically determinable life-process, associated with material presuppositions.

[16] H.-C. Rauh, 'Zur Herkunft, Vorgeschichte und erste Verwendungsweise des Ideologiebegriffs
bei Marx und Engels bis 1844', p. 698.
[17] Apart from the doctoral dissertation, Oertel mentions two other early instances of Marx using
the word 'ideology' (or its cognates): in the article that he wrote on the law against the 'theft' of

important one for the young Marx, the critique of false consciousness certainly was. As is well known, Marx associated himself as a young man with that group of left-wing philosophers and social critics called the 'Young Hegelians', and the process of coming to terms with (and, in the end, distancing himself from) them governed much of his early intellectual development. Two preoccupations of the Young Hegelians, both arising from the interpretation of Hegel, run through this process: the relationship between philosophy and practice and the criticism of religion. The issues are as follows.

First, if it was true (as Hegel had claimed) that *Geist* had reached a point of completion, what role then remained for philosophy? Was it (as Hegel himself appeared to believe) that the historical conditions had been achieved under which speculative philosophy could flourish freely? In that case, as was explained at the end of the previous chapter, historical development would only have provided the necessary, but not the sufficient, condition for a fully rational social order: only by means of philosophy would it be possible for that implicitly rational order to be *comprehended as* rational (and hence for it to become rational explicitly). But then was it to be assumed that the explicit rationality of the social order was to be reserved for only a portion of the members of society – those philosopher-rulers who, like Plato's 'guardians', alone had access to the truths of speculative philosophy? In that case, in what sense could the non-philosophers be said to be 'rationally reconciled' to their society? Or should it be supposed – astonishing as it might appear – that all the citizens in Hegel's realized state would be speculative philosophers? Hegel did not appear to offer any clear solution to this problem.

The second issue concerns the relationship between philosophy and religion. For Hegel, the issue was a precarious and controversial one. While he himself emphasized the consonance between his philosophy and the Christian religion, the objection was frequently raised against Hegelianism that it was an implicit secularization of Christianity in violation of its true character. (1) To make God equivalent to *Geist*; (2) to make *Geist* fully knowable to reason, and (3) to argue that the full self-realization of *Geist* required consciousness of *Geist*'s nature on the part of human beings appeared to violate, respectively, (1) the personal character of the Christian God, (2) the role of revelation in religious belief and (3) the Christian doctrine of Creation as an act of gratuitous divine benevolence (for if God requires man for His completion, then He has a reason that is not wholly unselfish for creating him). Was Hegelian philosophy compatible with Christianity or did it amount to a radical critique of it?

As Young Hegelianism developed, both these themes would come

---

wood and in *The Holy Family*. The latter comes in the context of a reference to Napoleon, whose 'scorn for industrial *hommes d'affaires*', Marx asserts, 'was the complement to his scorn for ideologists'. Thus Marx, unlike his father, here seems to be taking Napoleon's evaluation of the *idéologues* at face value. (*The Holy Family*, p. 123.)

together. Having started out as loyal and would-be orthodox disciples of Hegel, the group came, following David Friedrich Strauss's *Life of Jesus* (1835), to emphasize the implicitly anti-religious elements in Hegelianism, setting the inner principle of 'reason' and the nature of *Geist* as the essence of humanity against the claims of faith, transcendence and religious revelation. In this way the Young Hegelians moved more and more to an attitude towards Hegel that set the 'essential', rational Hegel against his orthodox, conservative self. To this was added the further claim that, in contradiction to Hegel's own views, the rational aspects of Hegelianism still required realization in contemporary society – and that the means to do this was the criticism of religion. Thus the Young Hegelians moved from orthodox Hegelianism, via a critical reinterpretation of Hegel, to a position critical both of Hegel in particular and of philosophy in general.[18]

It was with this position – embodied in the writings of Ludwig Feuerbach in the early 1840s – that Marx associated himself. He puts forward his own version of these views in his 'Towards a Critique of the Hegelian Philosophy of Right. Introduction'.[19] This short piece is a compressed masterpiece of vehement rhetoric, seething with antithesis and chiasmus. Yet it contains all the elements of an account of 'necessary false consciousness'.

Marx's starting point is that:

For Germany, the critique of religion is essentially completed . . .[20]

Thus Marx's problem is how, in German conditions, to go beyond the critique of religion. His first step is to explain the significance of that critique, as he understands it – why 'the critique of religion is the prerequisite of every critique'.[21] The critique of religion is important, he says, because the refutation of error in the sphere of religion is the necessary means to combat error in the non-religious realm:

Error in its profane form of existence is compromised once its celestial *oratio pro aris et focis* [prayer for hearth and home – M. R.] has been refuted.[22]

By 'error in its profane form' Marx here means not just false beliefs about the world but 'false consciousness' in its broad sense: human beings' false attitudes – to their surroundings and to themselves – and their inability to form true identities for themselves. The reality of contemporary mankind reflects itself in the world of religion, while, on earth, man fails

---

[18] A more nuanced treatment of this development is to be found in L. Stepelevich's *Introduction* to his collection *The Young Hegelians*.
[19] This introduction (the full work remained in draft form) was published in February 1844 in the *Deutsch-Französische Jahrbücher* (edited in exile by Marx himself and Arnold Ruge).
[20] 'Towards a Critique of the Hegelian Philosophy of Right: Introduction', p. 131.
[21] Ibid.
[22] Ibid.

to recognize himself (and, because man fails to recognize himself, he is therefore not who he ought to be).[23]

Religion is a product of human activity. But that activity is the activity of man in society and so it is a reflection of a particular society:

> This state, this society, produce religion, which is an inverted world-consciousness, because they are an inverted world.[24]

The implication is that only an 'inverted', secular world would produce the world of religion as its offshoot. But religion is not simply an image or a reproduction of existing, profane reality. It is also, Marx says, a theory about and justification of that reality – and a realm in which the individual can realize himself, given that realization in the profane world is not possible.[25] Thus religion (1) reflects reality and (2) justifies it, as well as (3) providing consolation by offering individuals the possibility of a pseudo-self-realization. These three functions of religion are, respectively, (1) neutral in relation to the existing order (presenting a transposed image of profane reality), (2) supportive of it theoretically (by legitimating it) and (3) supportive of it practically (by satisfying partially those who would otherwise be radically dissatisfied). Beyond these three functions, Marx also at one point appears to concede that religion can have a critical function:

> The wretchedness of religion is at once an expression of and protest against real wretchedness.[26]

However, he does not explain, even metaphorically, how religion can play this critical role, and it seems that his views are better embodied in his (very famous) next two sentences:

> Religion is the sigh of the oppressed creature, the heart of a heartless world and the soul of soulless conditions. It is the opium of the people.[27]

If anything is to play the role of protest against existing conditions it is, it would appear, not religion itself but the critique of religion. The secret

---

[23] Man, who has found only his own reflection in the fantastic reality of heaven, where he sought a supernatural being, will no longer be disposed to find only the semblance of himself, only a non-human being, here where he seeks and must seek his true reality . . . Religion is, in fact, the self-consciousness and self-esteem of man who has either not yet gained himself or has lost himself again. (Ibid.)

[24] Ibid. Note that Marx is here echoing Hegel's *topos* from the *Phenomenology* of the '*verkehrte Welt*' (the inverted world).

[25] Religion is the general theory of this world, its encyclopedic compendium, its logic in popular form, its spiritualistic *point d'honneur*, its enthusiasm, its moral sanction, its solemn complement, its universal basis of consolation and justification. It is the fantastic realization of the human being because the human being has attained no true reality. (Ibid.)

[26] Ibid.

[27] Ibid.

of religion is that it is profane in origin. The critique of religion exposes that secret and connects religion back to its unacknowledged origins.[28]

Thus the criticism of religion is an attempt to strip reality back to its essential core: an essential core that characteristically conceals itself ('a condition which requires illusions'). It is the critique (and practical transformation) of this form of social existence which is, of course, Marx's real project and for which the criticism of religion has merely prepared the ground:

> Criticism has plucked the imaginary flowers from the chain, not so that man shall bear the chain without fantasy or consolation, but so that he shall cast off the chain and gather the living flower. The critique of religion disillusions man so that he will think, act, and fashion his reality as a man who has lost his illusions and regained his reason, so that he will revolve about himself as his own true sun. Religion is only the illusory sun about which man revolves so long as he does not revolve about himself.[29]

Once this has been done, philosophy ('in the service of history') must move on to another task: 'to unmask human self-alienation in its secular forms'.[30]

The word 'ideology' does not appear in this highly compressed discussion (the passages quoted come from barely more than a page), and Marx presents his claims either as simple and unsupported assertions or, at best, as metaphors whose presuppositions he does not explore in any detail. Yet it is already possible to see in outline the central claims made by the theory of ideology:

1 Religion is *false consciousness*. Although religion *reflects* profane reality, it is *false* to the extent that it carries with it the belief that it is not a reflection that takes its content from another realm but something autonomous: a transcendent reality in its own right. Moreover (although Marx does not explain how) it does not just reflect the profane realm: it justifies it.[31] Furthermore, religion offers a kind of surrogate satisfaction (the narcotic pleasures of an 'opium').

2 Religion maintains a profane world that is false (the '*verkehrte Welt*'). In particular, it conceals man's own self-division from himself and enervates him so as not to feel the dissatisfaction with his own world that he rationally should do.

---

[28] The abolition of religion as the illusory happiness of the people is a demand for their true happiness. The call to abandon illusions about their condition is the call to abandon a condition which requires illusions. (Ibid.)

[29] Ibid., pp. 131–2.

[30] Ibid., p. 132.

[31] An obvious possible mechanism is the following. Because the social order corresponds to the religious order (the latter is, after all, in fact a reflection of the former) and the religious order is believed (falsely) to be eternal, the social order is taken (again falsely) to be an expression of that eternal order – hence, natural and immutable.

3 Finally, religion is a necessary product of this false world: it results from a 'condition which requires illusions'.[32]

At this stage of his intellectual and political development Marx was already well on his way to separating himself from the Young Hegelians. He had a clear view as to the limitations of the critique of religion and, indeed, of criticism in general as a form of political action. He believed that any analysis of society and politics must proceed from the nature of civil society and he vehemently rejected the Hegelian idea that social life is an expression of some non-material underlying force or principle. Furthermore, he associated himself explicitly with the political programme of communism and argued that it was for philosophy to ally itself with the proletariat.[33] However, there were certain, things that Marx had not yet done. He had not distanced himself from Feuerbach, whose criticism of Hegel he took over more or less without question.[34] Nor did he have a view of history as a series of economically determined epochs, each governed by a particular 'mode of production'.

The years from 1843 to 1845 (when *The German Ideology* was finished) were certainly the most turbulent and intellectually fertile of Marx's life. They included his move from Germany to Paris and then to Brussels, the beginning of his collaboration with Engels and (not coincidentally) the start of his lifelong immersion in the study of political economy. By the end of this period (which also saw the composition of the 'Paris Manuscripts' of 1844) some very noteworthy changes had occurred in Marx's thinking.

The first such change is in his attitude towards philosophy. He is now explicitly hostile to it. So far from regarding philosophy as a potential weapon in the hands of the proletariat, Marx has come to identify it as

---

[32] Although the condition 'requires illusions', it is not clear that Marx believes that religion is there *because* contemporary society is a condition that requires illusions.

[33] Just as philosophy finds its material weapons in the proletariat, so the proletariat finds its spiritual weapons in philosophy ... Philosophy cannot be actualized without the abolition [*Aufhebung*] of the proletariat; the proletariat cannot be abolished without the actualization of philosophy. ('Towards a Critique of the Hegelian Philosophy of Right: Introduction', p. 142.)

[34] At this stage, Marx's view was that it was necessary to go beyond 'religious criticism' such as Feuerbach's – a task that, as we have seen, he regarded as essentially completed – but he did not identify any internal inadequacy in that criticism itself. Thus the sketches for Marx's critique of Hegel's *Philosophy of Right* contain remarks such as the following:

Hegel at all times makes the Idea the subject and makes the proper and actual subject, like 'political sentiment', the predicate. But the development proceeds at all times on the side of the predicate. (*Critique of Hegel's 'Philosophy of Right'*, p. 11.)

But such a 'reassignment' of subject and predicate (and Feuerbach's own critique of Hegel really amounts to little more than this) is not sufficient to escape from the metaphysics of idealism. The metaphysical structure of Hegel's philosophy is that of a monistic subject from which the predicates of reality emerge as part of a self-differentiating process. Whether this subject is called the 'Idea' or 'Man' is not the most important issue. The real difficulty for a self-proclaimed materialist is how it could be supposed that such a 'development on the side of the predicate' should be possible at all.

part of the realm of religion and mystification that requires criticism – ideology. The Young Hegelians – Feuerbach, in particular – are no longer seen as limited but in their own way effective critics of religion and Hegelianism but are themselves criticized harshly for being still, however unconsciously and unintentionally, trapped within the limits of Hegel's philosophy.[35] More positively, Marx now holds to an economically determined theory of history that is very close to the 'historical materialism' whose classic statement was given in the Preface to *A Contribution to the Critique of Political Economy* of 1859. The division of labour, he argues, both develops those productive forces with which men produce their means of subsistence and, at the same time, necessitates the division of society into antagonistic classes. Each stage of the division of labour is associated with a characteristic 'mode of production', a 'form of ownership' within which a particular class is 'dominant'. It is from these 'real premises', as Marx calls them, that his account of ideology in *The German Ideology* departs.

III The 'Reflection' Model

Like 'Towards a Critique of the Hegelian Philosophy of Right. Introduction', *The German Ideology* is full of polemical assertions of the priority of material life over the world of religion, thought and speculation. But it also contains two analogies that could, in outline at least, serve as mechanisms for the explanation of the connection between material life and ideas. The first of these is embodied in the following famous passage:

> If in all ideology men and their circumstances appear upside-down as in a *camera obscura*, this phenomenon arises just as much from their historical life-process as the inversion of objects on the retina does from their physical life-process.
>
> In direct contrast to German philosophy, which descends from heaven to earth, here we ascend from earth to heaven. That is to say, we do not set out from what men say, imagine, conceive, nor from men as narrated, thought

---

[35] German criticism has, right up to its latest efforts, never quitted the realm of philosophy. Far from examining its general philosophic premises, the whole body of its inquiries has actually sprung from the soil of a definite philosophical system, that of Hegel. Not only in their answers but in their very questions there was a mystification. This dependence on Hegel is the reason why not one of these modern critics has even attempted a comprehensive criticism of the Hegelian system, however much each professes to have advanced beyond Hegel. Their polemics against Hegel and against one another are confined to this – each extracts one side of the Hegelian system and turns this against the whole system as well as against the sides extracted by the others. To begin with they extracted pure unfalsified Hegelian categories such as 'substance' and 'self-consciousness', later they desecrated these categories with more secular names such as 'species', 'the Unique', 'Man', etc. (*The German Ideology*, p. 40.)

Marx could almost have had his own earlier self in mind. The 'Theses on Feuerbach', Marx's exceptionally interesting attempt to resume his views on philosophy, also date from this period.

of, imagined, conceived, in order to arrive at men in the flesh. We set out from real, active men, and on the basis of their real life-process we demonstrate the development of the ideological reflexes and echoes of this life-process. The phantoms formed in the human brain are also, necessarily, sublimates of their material life process, which is empirically verifiable and bound to material premises.[36]

Let us call this the *reflection model* of ideology. The idea is that ideology relates to material life as images do to reality in a *camera obscura* or on the retina of the human eye: each individual item in reality is reproduced accurately, but in reverse. The apparent advantage of the reflection model is that it seems to give a clear sense to the claim that ideology is 'false consciousness': ideology is not just a reflection of material life but an *inversion* of it.

Yet brief consideration of the analogy shows that, as it stands, Marx's account is inadequate. I shall make three objections, of which the first is the most fundamental. It is this.

1 It is indeed true that the images on the human retina are 'upside-down'. But does this mean that human beings do not perceive the world about them accurately? Of course not. The fact is that, as far as human perception is concerned, 'upside-down' is the right way up for images to be on our retinas. And this points the way towards the problem with Marx's analogy. Marx's analogy appears to give a sense to the idea that ideology is 'false consciousness' by describing *all* ideological consciousness as reversed or inverted. But this leaves no room for the contrast between 'true' consciousness and 'false' consciousness and, for this reason, the notion of false consciousness loses the purchase it needs: initial appearances to the contrary, Marx's analogy gives no sense to the idea that ideology is 'false consciousness'.

This criticism is made on the most natural reading of the passage: namely, that Marx is here suggesting that inversion is characteristic of consciousness in general. But, one might say, is it not possible that Marx means only that portion of consciousness that is 'ideological'? In that case, there is indeed a basis for the contrast between true and false consciousness (ideology is contrasted with non-inverted consciousness). But then the criticism becomes that Marx has given us no basis to suppose that ideological consciousness is formed in any way differently from the way that non-ideological consciousness is produced. So how does it come to be upside-down?

2 The second objection does not come from the image of the '*camera obscura*' itself but from the phrase later in the quoted passage in which Marx continues the analogy by speaking of the ideological 'reflexes and echoes' of real life-processes. Ideological ideas are, he goes on to say,

'phantoms' and 'sublimates' in their relationship to the real world. All of these metaphors carry with them an important implication: that ideological thought is *the effect of* real processes, but that it is itself insubstantial, without material reality or causal power. In other words, it is what philosophers call *epiphenomenal*: something that is an effect of a process but which does not have further effects itself. If this is Marx's considered view, then it is, clearly, disastrous for the theory of ideology. For the point of the theory of ideology was to explain how it was that certain forms of thought served to sustain particular societies. Thus these forms of thought are, by assumption, not ineffective, but have very important causal effects: namely, helping to maintain a particular social and economic order.

3 Finally, there is a general objection to the parallel that Marx makes between the relationship of mind to matter, on the one hand, and of ideology to material life, on the other. It is not obvious why we should accept this parallel. Is the implication that ideology is immaterial and material life non-intellectual? But this plainly contradicts Marx's basic position. Not only is it odd for an avowed materialist to suggest that ideas are something basically insubstantial, but, more important, it conflicts with one of Marx's most fundamental views: the idea that economic life, so far from being unconscious or unreflective, is the central part of man's cognitive engagement with external reality. Marx, then, gives us no good reason to suppose that ideology relates to material life as mind does to matter.

As it stands in *The German Ideology*, the reflection model, then, is not satisfactory. The parallel with the relationship between mind and matter fails to explain how it should be that ideology is a form of *false* consciousness. Nor does it help us to understand how such a mirroring or reflecting relationship should happen to hold between economic and non-economic life. In fact, as an explanation, it advances very little beyond the idea of religion as the inverted consciousness of an inverted world asserted in 'Towards a Critique of the Hegelian Philosophy of Right: Introduction'.

IV The 'Interests' Model

But even in the *German Ideology* itself there is another model at work. While the reflection model drew on the parallel between the ideological process and a traditional, realist account of perception (the immaterial mind mirrors passively a mind-independent reality), the *interests model*, as I shall call it, develops from a more pragmatist approach to epistemology. That Marx was (at this time, at least) attracted to such views is apparent from the 'Theses on Feuerbach'. In the second thesis Marx writes:

> The dispute over the reality or non-reality of thinking that is isolated from practice is a purely *scholastic* question.

While, in the fifth thesis, he continues:

> All social life is essentially *practical*. All mysteries which lead theory to
> mysticism find their rational solution in human practice.[37]

From this point of view, the most significant aspect of ideas is not their
relationship to a mind-independent reality but that they are the products
of practical activity, and that this practical activity is itself guided by
interests. The materialistic view of history to which this leads does not,
Marx says, 'in every period . . . look for a category' (a reasonable summary
of Hegel's view of the determinants of history and society). On the
contrary, the materialistic view of history, he says, remains on the 'real
ground' of history:

> . . . it does not explain practice from the Idea but explains the formation of
> ideas from material practice; and accordingly it comes to the conclusion that
> all forms and products of consciousness cannot be dissolved by mental
> criticism, by resolution into 'self-consciousness' or transformation into
> 'apparitions', 'spectres', 'fancies', etc. but only by the practical overthrow of
> the actual social relations which gave rise to this idealistic humbug.[38]

The problem with the interests model does not lie in the view that ideas
are the product of interests itself, which is, of course, a very plausible one
(although it is more difficult to determine just what proportion of our ideas
are products of interests in this way – surely not all of them? – and to
explain just how it is that interests should assert themselves in the process
by which ideas are formed). The problem is that ideological ideas are not
simply ideas formed in the pursuit of interests. They are, in fact, supposed
to be ideas that go against the interests of those who hold them (and in
this way further the interests of others). How do ideas of this kind come
to be accepted?

Marx's answer starts from the assertion that 'the ideas of the ruling
class are, in every epoch, the ruling ideas' – that is, he claims,

> . . . the class which is the ruling *material* force of a society is at the same
> time its ruling *intellectual* force. The class which has the means of material
> production at its disposal, has control at the same time over the means of
> mental production, so that thereby, generally speaking, the ideas of those
> who lack the means of mental production are subject to it.[39]

But this is not a satisfactory solution. Marx now seems to have switched
to a view of those who live under the domination of the ruling class as
passive victims, taking their ideas from those who control the 'means of

[37] 'Theses on Feuerbach', pp. 121, 122.
[38] *The German Ideology*, p. 58.
[39] Ibid., p. 64.

mental production' like obedient chicks, with no critical reflection on their part as to whether the ideas are either true or in their own rational interests. This, it seems, is an almost paranoid view. Why should one suppose that the ruling class is capable of promoting its interests effectively, forming its ideas in response to those interests, whereas the dominated classes simply accept whatever is served up to them? Marx does, however, attempt to make his claim slightly more plausible by what he has to say about the nature of mental production. It is, he says, the most significant development in the division of labour that mental and manual labour become separated:

> Division of labour only becomes truly such from the moment when a division of material and manual labour appears. (The first form of ideologists, *priests*, is concurrent.) From this moment onwards consciousness *can* really flatter itself that it is something other than consciousness of existing practice, that it *really* represents something without representing something real; from now on consciousness is in a position to emancipate itself from the world and to proceed to the formation of 'pure' theory, theology, philosophy, ethics, etc.[40]

The separation between mental and manual labour, Marx maintains, does not really lead to the formation of autonomous ideas: the ideologists who produce ideas are still part of the ruling class whose interests their ideas represent. Nevertheless, it offers an explanation as to why such ideas should be accepted by those, the dominated classes, whose interests they go against: they are accepted because they are (apparently) disinterested. The ideologist, on this view, is like a bribed referee: able to influence the outcome of the game the more effectively for the fact that he is (falsely) believed to be impartial.

Is the ideologist, then, engaged in deception? Does he know the partiality of his ideas but presents them nonetheless as if they were neutral and disinterested? On the contrary. According to Marx, the ideologist is *sincere* – and, because he sincerely believes in the independence and objective validity of his own ideas, he is able to persuade others to accept them as such all the more effectively. Here, however, is the problem. How are we to suppose it to be true that the ideologists should both be constrained so that they produce ideas in the interests of the ruling class of which they are, appearances to the contrary, a part *and* that they (and those who accept the ideas from them) remain sincerely unaware of the nature of this connection – so much so that what they believe about the source of their ideas is, in fact, the exact opposite of what is really the case? If the reason that the ideologists believe that the ideas they produce are disinterested is that they do indeed produce independently, then how does that subterranean dependence whose existence Marx claims nevertheless assert itself (and why are they not aware of it)?

[40] Ibid., pp. 51–2.

V The Correspondence Model

My third model for the theory of ideology draws on the preface that Marx wrote in 1859 for his *Contribution to the Critique of Political Economy*. This preface has been widely regarded as the canonical statement of doctrine of 'orthodox' Marxism, latterly by G. A. Cohen in his *Karl Marx's Theory of History: a Defence*, to which I shall refer in detail in what follows. Cohen's work is of very great significance, for it takes up the challenge of trying to demonstrate that Marx can redeem the claims he makes for his theory of history *without* the need for special assumptions regarding the kinds of entities or forms of explanation employed. Ideas that in Hegel are derived as a consequence of the ontological distinctiveness of *Geist* – such as the idea that history follows a path through stages and the understanding of societies as systems, held together by some inner principle – can be defended, Cohen tries to show, on assumptions that are unobjectionable from the point of view of scientifically informed secular materialism. There are indeed very many statements in Marx's mature writings that suggest that he would have chosen to see his own enterprise in just those terms and, to this extent, Cohen's work provides an ideal opportunity to test how successfully a theory of ideology might be accommodated within such limits.

In the Preface to the *Contribution* Marx writes that:

> With the change of the economic foundation the entire immense superstructure is more or less rapidly transformed. In considering such transformations, a distinction should always be made between the material transformation of the economic conditions of production, which can be determined with the precision of natural science, and the legal, political, religious, aesthetic or philosophic – in short, ideological forms in which men become conscious of this conflict and fight it out.[41]

In other words, apparently, ideology should be understood as part of the 'superstructure' which corresponds to the economic 'base'. But, although the sense of the passage just quoted appears to be to make an identification between superstructure and ideology, not every interpreter of Marx has been convinced. Cohen himself explicitly distinguishes between the superstructure and ideology:

> The superstructure consists of legal, political, religious and other non-economic *institutions*. It probably includes universities, but it does not include knowledge, for knowledge is not an institution.
>   Ideology, on the other hand, is also not an institution but, like science, a set of ideas.[42]

---

[41] *A Contribution to the Critique of Political Economy*, p. 21.
[42] *Karl Marx's Theory of History*, pp. 45–6. J. Larrain has taken a similar position.

However, the idea that there is a clear line to be drawn between institutions and the ideas that are found in them such that the former can be identified without essential reference to the latter seems dubious. Can one separate the Christian Church from its belief in God? It is true that Marx does distinguish a few lines earlier between the 'legal and political superstructure' and the 'definite forms of social consciousness',[43] and so one might think that the references in the passage quoted are similarly distinct. But I am not persuaded, and, indeed, even if there is ideological social consciousness outside the superstructure, I do not see why this should mean that the superstructure is not ideological as well.

There is, however, a more serious objection against trying to interpret Marx's conception of ideology within the context of the base–superstructure distinction. That is that the distinction fails to include one of the most important ingredients in Marx's notion of ideology, namely, the sense in which ideology is held to be *false consciousness*. From the fact that a characteristic superstructure can be found to 'correspond' to every base it does not follow that there is anything necessarily 'false' about ideological consciousness. The ideology just 'does the job', as it were, of helping to maintain the base in question; the sense of 'falsehood' (that is, worthiness of criticism) applies, if at all, not to the superstructure as such but to the economic base to which it corresponds.

In what follows I shall, his own reservations notwithstanding, start from Cohen's analysis of the base–superstructure distinction as the most defensible form of the correspondence model of the theory of ideology. The central feature of Cohen's interpretation is his casting of the idea that base and superstructure correspond to one another in terms of functional explanation. In his book, Cohen first presents this interpretation of the notion of correspondence in terms of another part of Marx's theory, the correspondence between relations of production and forces of production, but what he has to say holds, *mutatis mutandis*, for base and superstructure as well:

> When Marx says production relations *correspond* to productive forces, he means the former are appropriate to the latter, and we may impute to him the further thought that the relations are as they are *because* they are appropriate to productive development.[44]

We see here, then, the two elements that are central to functional explanation, in Cohen's view.

1 The first condition of one phenomenon, A, being functionally explained by another, B, is that A should be appropriate to (be good for, promote) B.

[43] *A Contribution to the Critique of Political Economy*, p. 21.
[44] *Karl Marx's Theory of History*, p. 136.

But the second condition is equally necessary:

2 That A should have come about *because* it is good for B.

Thus it may be the case, for example, that the fact that I do not clean my kitchen provides conditions that are appropriate to the well-being of the mice who infest it (conditions that are *functional for* the mice). But there is a functional *explanation* here for my failing to clean the kitchen *only if* it is also the case that the needs of the mice are, in some way, responsible for my behaviour as the cause of my slovenliness.

Why should we impute this second condition to Marx? To take the case of religion, we saw above that Marx clearly believes that religion is 'good for' (helps to preserve) the world that gives rise to it. Moreover, that world *needs* religion (it is a 'condition that requires illusions'). But does that imply that religion is there *because* the world needs it? Not necessarily. Consider Robinson Crusoe. The food and fresh water on Robinson's island are good for him. Nor would he survive unless the food and fresh water were there. But, although we can infer from the fact that Robinson Crusoe is alive on his island that there must be food and fresh water, this does not mean that they are there *because* they are good for Robinson.

At least some of Marx's mature suggestions have a very similar structure. Take the division of labour. The division of labour separates individuals from one another with the effect that they lack a perspective from which they might understand the labour process as a whole. In consequence, the individuals in question are less likely to see the alternatives to the division of labour and to the mutilating effects that it has. This is 'good for' the division of labour in the sense of helping to preserve it. Yet it does not follow that these 'good' effects of the division of labour are there because they are good for it. They are simply side-effects of a system of production that, incidentally, they serve to sustain. Yet, if such explanations were all that there were to the theory of ideology then there would obviously be something lacking. It would be simply a happy accident (from the point of view of the existing social structure) that the division of labour should happen to produce the effects that it needs, just as it is a happy accident for Robinson Crusoe that he should have been washed up on a fertile island. Only if the second condition is also true and the ideas that help to sustain society are there because they help to sustain it can we see the ideas in question as a systematic part of the way that unequal societies are able to maintain themselves.

I now want to develop two lines of criticism of the attempt to develop a theory of ideology based on the interpretation of 'correspondence' as a form of functional explanation, relating to its first and second elements respectively.

The first focuses on the notion of 'appropriateness'. What does it amount to? Cohen again gives his clearest explanation of the notion in the context of the claimed correspondence between forces and relations of production, which he defines as follows:

> To say that an economic structure *corresponds* to the achieved level of the productive forces means: the structure provides maximum scope for the fruitful use and development of the forces and obtains *because* it provides such scope.[45]

The phrase Cohen uses, 'provides maximum scope for', is of great importance. The structure which corresponds, he is saying, is the one which provides *the best* ('maximum') means of promoting the use and development of the productive forces. This is evidently an immensely strong claim. Putting it into the context of the discussion of ideology, it amounts to saying that, of all the possible kinds of legal, political, aesthetic and religious institutions that a society *could* have, it has just those ones which are best for it.[46] Let us call this the 'strong interpretation' of the idea of functional relation. There is, I suggest, no reason to object to the strong interpretation on logical grounds, but, as a matter of empirical fact, it seems quite implausible.

But there is another way of understanding the functionalist claim. Instead of the strong thesis that the superstructure which corresponds to the base is the one which promotes the base maximally, we could say that a superstructure corresponds to the base provided, simply, that it promotes it. In that case there will, presumably, be a set of superstructures, all of which meet the sufficient condition of promoting the base to some degree.[47]

At this point, however, the question arises: what do we mean here by 'promote' (or by the alternative phrases Cohen uses such as 'is good for', 'is in the interests of', 'furthers the development of', or 'is appropriate to')? The answer may well turn out to be: not very much. The argument is this.

Take two states of affairs, A and B, which are mutually compatible (if A comes about then so can B: it is not the case that A implies not-B or that B implies not-A). Imagine, too, that there is some further state, C, which is excluded by A (if A, then not-C) and which in turn excludes B (if C, then not-B). If that is so, then the occurrence of A will lead to the satisfaction of one of the necessary conditions for B (namely, that C should not occur). To this extent, A is plainly good for B and so may be said to 'promote' it. To make the example more concrete, we might take the idea (a commonplace in Marxist writing) that racism (or sexism) promotes capitalism, the reasoning being that racism (or sexism) divides the working

---

[45] Ibid., pp. 278–9.
[46] Consider the parallel with Darwinism. Darwinism tells us (for example) that the tiger's stripes are *good for* it by enabling it to conceal itself in the jungle. But, surely, it would be *even better* for the tiger if it could – absurd though the supposition may be – make itself invisible at will. (I take this example from Jo Wolff.)
[47] Only one member of that set will meet the strong condition: of being the one that promotes the base *the most*.

class and hence excludes its political mobilization which would, in turn, lead to the overthrow of capitalism.[48] Examples like this are all too easy to come up with. To deny them one would have to deny that there are significant incompatibilities between forms of economic life and systems of thought – that Greek art could go with the feudal economy, or that Renaissance politics would be compatible with late twentieth-century international capitalism, for example.[49] And this, of course, none of Marxism's serious competitors would ever claim.[50]

Another example will make clear how weak the condition for something being good for or in the interests of something else has by now become. Perhaps it would benefit the Children of Israel to be Pharaoh's slaves if, by being Pharaoh's slaves, they were kept from starvation.[51] But, in fact, the Children of Israel would be much better off if they were free.[52] And, of course, in practical fact, there almost always is some possible alternative situation to our own in which we would be even worse off than we are now: surely that is not enough to say that such situations are 'good for' us?[53]

At this point, it is clear, the notion of benefit has been stretched so far that it threatens to lose its sense entirely and the theory to become incapable of confirmation or refutation. A parallel example – and it is not, given the background to the theory of ideology in the providentialist tradition, an entirely unrelated one – shows the dangers. Take the belief that reality is disposed according to the ordinances of a benevolent creator. Early Christian writers were apt, according to Viner, to apply this view to the distribution of natural resources in relation to economic activity. Thus when complementary natural resources lay close to one another (for

[48] In other words, racism (A) excludes a united and mobilized working class (C) which would exclude capitalism (B). Thus A is good for B.

[49] The argument is this.
   Say that feudal economic life is incompatible with Greek art. (If there is Greek art then there is no feudal economics.) But, we may presume that Greek economic life (the economic system that the Greeks happened to have) excludes the simultaneous presence of feudal economics. Therefore Greek economic life (A) excludes feudal economic life (C) which would exclude Greek art (B). Hence Greek economics is 'good for' Greek art. QED.

[50] Thus Hegelianism (with or without 'metaphysics') asserts that there is indeed a characteristic relationship between the different parts of society at a single epoch.

[51] A (being slaves) promotes B (the welfare of the Children of Israel) by excluding C (starvation) which excludes B.

[52] Not, of course, if we are to believe the Bible, that the Children of Israel always saw things this way themselves.

[53] The two senses of benefit canvassed so far might be interpreted as (roughly) (1) 'as good as it could be' and (2) 'better than it might be'. They correspond to extreme positions. But, perhaps one might say, neither of these are the natural senses of 'benefit'. Intuitively, the suggestion is, someone is benefitted if and only if he is better off than one would have expected him to be otherwise – not 'as well off as he could possibly have been' or 'better off than he might conceivably have been'. As far as the way that we use the term 'benefit' in practice goes, the suggestion carries weight, but it highlights the problem rather than solves it. For what shall we take the relevant counterfactual to be? Unless we can establish rigorously which of all the possible alternatives to measure the person's welfare against (which state we should otherwise have expected him to be in) the notion of benefit cannot be given a determinate interpretation. I do not see how this could be done.

example, deposits of iron ore in the vicinity of forests) this was taken as evidence of the operation of divine goodness. But such goodness was no less apparent to them in cases where the resources lay separated from one another, for this, they argued, would have the effect of encouraging trade and, hence, the peaceful intercourse of one part of mankind with another.[54]

Marxists are adept at just the same kind of reasoning. Too often, as Jon Elster has pointed out, they have been content to protect their theory from refutation by switching the time-horizon: if a belief explicitly supports the ruling class then it is in the ruling class's interests; if it seems to work against the ruling class, however, then it is assumed to be (somehow) in their interests in the long term. It is such 'frictionless speculations' which have, as Elster says, brought the theory of ideology 'into deserved ill-repute'.[55]

In sum, the alternatives for the understanding of the functional relation appear to be: accept the strong interpretation by which to say that A is appropriate to B is to say that it is the best possible alternative for B (but this is empirically absurd) or face the fact that the weaker interpretation may be so weak that it says no more than that a particular state excludes another state that would be even worse. At the least, the notion requires more specification than Cohen or other defenders of Marxism have given it.

Interpreted in its weak form, the functional thesis defines only a set of compatible forms of consciousness that are appropriate to a particular economic 'base', and this, as we have seen, is not something that other approaches to social theory – the Hegelian one, for example – would deny. But the second element in the idea of functional explanation is quite distinct: it is the idea that the superstructure has come to be the way that it is *because* it is good for the base. Even if Marxism lacks a distinctive conception of what being 'good for' that base amounts to, this claim ensures that Marxism does not collapse back into the other theories it so vehemently opposes. However (on Cohen's own admission) it is at this point that Marxism has the least evidence on its side.

We shall look at this second element in the structure of functional explanation first from the point of view of the evidence that would be required to establish it. Let us concede that the case we are dealing with is one where it has been established that a certain ideology (A) is 'good for' or 'appropriate to' the base (B). Let us call the fact that ideology A obtains *Fact I* and the fact that A is good for B *Fact II*. The question we then have to answer is whether Fact I is true because of the truth of Fact II or whether it is simply that the two facts are independently true. If the former, then the second element in the structure of functional explanation is satisfied and the ideology is explained by the base.

What evidence would be needed to establish such a relation? Cohen,

---

[54] See Viner, *The Role of Providence in the Social Order*, pp. 35–8.
[55] *Making Sense of Marx*, p. 460

who calls this kind of explanation 'consequence explanation', argues in *Karl Marx's Theory of History* that:

> The confirmation of consequence explanations and laws raises no unusual problems. To stick to simplifying statement, the law-statement (and hence the explanation it would support) is confirmed by instances satisfying its major antecedent and consequent, and disconfirmed by instances satisfying its major antecedent only. A complication arises in assessing whether the major antecedent is satisfied, since it attributes a dispositional property. We therefore confront the problem of counterfactuals, but not in any novel way.[56]

In other words, Cohen is saying, consequence explanation does not have to contradict the very simplest empiricist account of the relationship between evidence and theory. If we have two phenomena, X and Y, and we want to know if Y has come about *because of* X, then we should look on cases where there is both X and Y as confirming the supposition and cases where there is X but not Y as disconfirming it. Simple enough. But there are reasons to doubt Cohen's confidence. Consider the structure I outlined:

Fact I:
    An ideology, A, exists.
Fact II:
    A benefits the base, B.[57]
The consequence law:
    Fact I comes about *because of* Fact II. That is: Fact II, *hence* Fact I.

Thus Fact II is the major antecedent and the consequence law would, if we are to follow Cohen, be disconfirmed in the case that the major antecedent, Fact II, is true but the consequence, Fact I, is not. But how, one might ask, could one ever determine that Fact II were true without Fact I also being true? How could we tell that it is true that one state is good for another state when that first state itself doesn't obtain?

But, Cohen will say, this objection is beside the point. The reason that the explanation appears to be unfalsifiable is that I have taken it to be a matter of some particular ideological belief. In that case, it does indeed seem peculiar that I should be able to confirm that something is true about that particular but that the particular itself should not exist. But that is not what is at stake. We are not concerned just with some particular state of affairs – the holding of some particular belief in some particular context – but rather with the laws that make that explanation valid *in* that particular case. The laws in question allow for the explanation of *certain kinds* of belief held in *certain kinds* of situation in terms of the benefit they would

---

[56] *Karl Marx's Theory of History*, p. 265.
[57] One possible objection, which I shall do no more than mention here, is that the entities involved in explanation are not 'things' – forms of consciousness or states of society – but facts – relational and dispositional truths about those things. There are those who have their doubts about the legitimacy of explanations of this kind.

bring, and in this we are in precisely the same situation as with any other scientific hypothesis: we can definitely confirm hypotheses about such benefits in general, Cohen would argue, even though there may be cases in which those kinds of belief do not obtain.

At this point we move to the real difficulty: what is the scope of this supposed law? Would it be (this would be the most general possibility) that *whenever* a form of consciousness, A, would benefit a social structure, B, then that form of consciousness will obtain – that the South African whites will believe *whatever* would favour apartheid? In any circumstances, however, an almost incalculable number of beliefs *would* benefit the established social order. (For example: that the minds of the government are under the direct control of invisible superior and benevolent beings landed from an alien civilization beyond the stars; that science has established that those who occupy subordinate positions in society are happier and live longer than those who command; that managers under-stand the needs of economic life in a way that their subordinates could never comprehend for themselves.) Are we to take it that whenever we could hypothesize plausibly such a belief but it does not in fact obtain the theory of ideology is empirically disconfirmed? Surely no one would want to defend the theory of ideology in that absurd form. Yet it is more difficult to determine just what the advocate of the theory of ideology *would* want to claim. If we concentrate our attention only on those observed cases where the form of consciousness is *prima facie* beneficial to the social structure, then the theory of ideology does indeed become unfalsifiable, for the evidence used to assess it is restricted to just those cases in which, by assumption, it is observationally confirmed.

Cohen gives the following claim as an example of the sort of consequence explanation that he has it in mind to defend:

> the bourgeois media report industrial conflicts in a style which favours the capitalist class *because* that style of reportage has the asserted tendency[58]

Now what is the scope of the law of which this is supposed to be an instance? Is it a generalization just about the reporting of industrial disputes or about reporting in general (*all* reporting favours the capitalist class)? Is it about privately owned media or about the media in general? Is it about any forms of discourse about the world produced in contexts paid for by those whose aim is to make a profit? Unless this is determined in advance, the observation that an industrial dispute is reported in a way that favours the employers is useless: if the theory of ideology is to be tested by observation, then the scope of the conjecture must be determined in a way that is independent of the test.[59]

[58] *Karl Marx's Theory of History*, pp. 271–2.
[59] Clearly, the difficulties regarding evidence are compounded by the fact that in this case we are not dealing with a relationship between 'natural kinds' (lightning – thunder, fire – smoke) but between two kinds of fact, one of which is 'dispositional' (that the existence of A *would benefit* B), and the difficulty is reinforced because, as was argued earlier, the notion of 'benefit' is left so imprecise.

The discussion so far has been presented in terms that correspond to the empiricist account of 'induction' – the idea that theories are vindicated by the accumulation of confirming instances in the absence of unexplained contrary evidence. However, this is an abstraction from the real processes of science; informally at least, much scientific reasoning employs a kind of 'inference to the best explanation' – theories are accepted because it is agreed that there is something that requires an explanation and that the candidate theory does better than any other at explaining it.[60] To take an example: the tiger's stripes seem to be a clear case of something that needs explanation – it is very hard to believe that it just happened to have them. The question, then, is: of the possible explanations of the tiger's stripes available, which deals best with the phenomenon? For us, of course, it is Darwin's theory of evolution.

Might the interpretation of the theory of ideology as a form of functional explanation not be argued for in the same way? I do not think that this helps its cause. For it is certainly not the case that the theory of ideology is the only candidate that would explain the (supposed) phenomena: as we have seen, Hegelianism too (with or without 'metaphysics') claims to give an account of how it should be that there is a 'correspondence' between different areas of a culture. How, then, to judge between them? At this point, it is important to note that we require more of explanations than that they should simply 'fit' the phenomena. It is also necessary that the kind of entities the theory postulates should be plausible, likewise the mechanism that connects them. In the absence of such a plausible mechanism, even the most empirically 'obvious' hypotheses are to be treated with suspicion.[61]

What sort of mechanism does the theory of ideology have to suppose? Once again, a comparison with the parallel case of Darwinian biology may help to clarify matters.

As a simple beginning, one might divide the Darwinian theory into four main elements:

1 the observation that species have certain peculiar characteristics

2 the hypothesis that those characteristics further the welfare of the species in the environment in which it finds itself

3 the hypothesis that the species has those characteristics precisely *because* they further its welfare

---

[60] This form of reasoning has been called '*Jewish modus tollens*' ('If not p, *what?*').

[61] Surely no child with a globe has failed to observe the way in which the continents appear to 'fit together', despite the fact that they are separated by thousands of miles of ocean. Furthermore, evolutionary biologists have long been puzzled by the presence of related species on separate continents (hence a variety of theories regarding 'land bridges', now lost, were put forward). The most 'obvious' explanation for both of these phenomena – that the continents *really did* once fit together – was not even considered seriously, however, for it appeared to be absurd to suppose that continents, of all things, should be able to move around the globe – until, that is, the development of the theory of tectonic plates.

4 the hypothesis that there exists a mechanism – natural selection – which ensures that, over time, species come to acquire characteristics which further their welfare.

Darwin was, of course, a practising field naturalist. But the observations of particular characteristics which he made did not, of themselves, lead to the further hypotheses. Indeed, they hardly needed to: the hypothesis of the adaptation of species was already universal among eighteenth- and early nineteenth-century observers, while hypothesis (3) – the idea that species have the characteristics they do *because* they are beneficial – is just what the Christian view of nature as the product of a benevolent Creator implies. So the whole weight of Darwinism falls (as he himself makes perfectly clear) on the fourth element – the process of natural selection as the mechanism behind 'evolution'.

But there is something rather paradoxical about this. On the one hand, natural selection is what differentiates Darwin's theory of evolution, yet natural selection was not part of his observed data. Darwin observed the adaptation and variation of species and *hypothesized* the process of natural selection as the best explanation for its development. Indeed, the mechanism behind natural selection itself – the principle of genetic variation – was not known to Darwin.

Cohen has gone so far as to suggest that we should detach the idea that species have the characteristics that they do because those characteristics are functional for the species from the theory of natural selection. The role of natural selection, Cohen argues, is that it helps to explain why (1) to (3) above are true:

> In our view, Darwin's theory is . . . among other things, a compelling account of why functional explanations apply in the biosphere. It is possible to know *that* x explains y, and yet find it puzzling that x *should* explain y, through failure to see *how* x explains y. Among Darwin's achievements was an attractive theory of how the fact that a facility would benefit a species helps to explain its acquisition.[62]

Cohen's position is this. Scientific explanations, he believes (and I wholeheartedly agree with him on this point), are offered in the context of a background of ontological beliefs. It is these beliefs and commitments by which we judge whether a purported explanation can be accepted as truly explanatory:

> All explanation operates against a background of theoretical presupposition to which candidate explanations which satisfy structural and confirmational criteria must conform.[63]

Cohen illustrates this point with reference to Newton's laws of motion:

---

[62] *Karl Marx's Theory of History*, p. 271.
[63] Ibid., p. 264.

The presuppositions of early modern physics, for example, included a
principle forbidding action at a distance, and Newton's laws of motion,
despite their theoretical economy and predictive success, were not regarded
as explanatory, even by Newton, because they were thought to violate the
constraint on explanation the principle imposed. The restrictive presupposition was in time abandoned, so that Helmholtz could write in the mid-
nineteenth century: 'To understand a phenomenon means nothing else than
to reduce it to the Newtonian laws. Then the necessity has been satisfied in
a palpable way.' In earlier days Newton's laws were structurally sound but
were considered materially inadequate for explanation.[64]

In other words, the 'background beliefs' behind a theory include beliefs
about the nature of what is under investigation and the mechanism by
which the phenomena to be explained are connected. That it should do
justice to such beliefs is a condition for what we take to be a satisfying
explanation: the theory of natural selection explains how it is that the
functional explanation of biological phenomena can meet these conditions.
But there is something puzzling here too, as Cohen's example from
Newton makes clear. If it is the case that the background beliefs condition
what we require from an empirical explanation, what is to govern our
background beliefs themselves? An examination of what lay behind the
adoption of the theory of evolution will show more clearly what is at stake.

The discovery of evolution is usually represented in one of two ways.
Either the theory is presented as a brilliant and original intellectual leap
on the part of a great scientist which has been so well confirmed that it
now seems to us to be only common sense, or else it is depicted as a
relatively obvious notion which was ignored by Darwin's predecessors
because the weight of religious dogma made it too painful to consider. In
both cases, part of the point of the story is to explain why it is that (in
contrast to the great contemporary discoveries in mathematics, physics and
chemistry) the theory of evolution does not now strike people as being
obscure or counterintuitive. However, neither of these apparently diametr-
ically opposed accounts is correct. The hypothesis of evolutionary change
from one species to another had, in fact, been canvassed many times before
Darwin. It was rejected not for reasons of religious orthodoxy but for *a
priori* philosophical reasons. Of Darwin's predecessors, no one had thought
through the issues more clearly than Kant.

In Kant's view we have to accommodate two contending principles. On
the one hand we are forced to reject the idea of preformation – the idea
that whatever structured product emerges from a biological process of
generation that structure must have been prefigured or preformed in the
parent that gave rise to it. That, he says, simply does not account for the
known facts about breeding, in particular, the possibility of hybrids. On
the other hand, however, we cannot see how 'lifeless' matter can give rise
to what is structured and self-maintaining:

[64] Ibid.

That crude matter should have originally formed itself according to mechanical laws, that life should have sprung from the nature of what is lifeless, that
matter should have been able to dispose itself into the form of a self-
maintaining purposiveness . . . [is] contradictory to reason.[65]

To this, of course, the scientist may well retort: if the theory of evolution
contradicts what philosophers believe about causality, well, so much the
worse for them! This is understandable, but we should be careful of being
too contemptuous of the metaphysics of causality. The received view about
causation had an extraordinarily long history among philosophers of all
persuasions.

Berkeley referred to the 'old known axiom' that 'nothing can give to
another that which it hath not itself'[66] while Descartes, in his proof of the
existence of God in the Third Meditation, makes use of the principle that
'there must be at least as much reality in the cause as in the effect'. In fact,
the principle can be traced all the way back to Aristotle: 'The cause which
prompts something to partake of a certain quality always partakes of that
quality to a greater extent.'[67]

We dismiss background beliefs from our notion of the requirements of
explanation at our peril. Yet the processes by which they are derived and
justified remain deeply obscure.

Perhaps the proper conclusion would be to describe Darwin's break-
through as a philosophical one, though in a negative sense – in his
ignorance of (or, at least, his willingness to ignore) the received view about
the nature of causal processes which had inhibited his predecessors. In
Darwin's predecessors the background belief that the genesis of a complex
phenomenon cannot be given an adequate causal explanation by reference
to an originating cause more simple than itself was too strong to allow
them to accept a phenomenon which was, in a sense, staring them in the
face.

Now the theory of ideology clearly has important parallels to Darwinism.
Like Darwinism, the theory of ideology does not just claim that there exist
certain beliefs in society which maintain the social structure; it says that
those beliefs are there *just because* they maintain the social structure. The
correlative question is: how do they come to be there? For Darwinism, the
answer is by natural selection – genetic inheritance, differential survival,
and so on. Although we do not observe these processes in detail, there are
enough reasons for confidence in their existence for us to accept them as a
general explanation of the changing characteristics of species through time.
And it is this that allows us to justify our belief in species as having the
characteristics they have because those characteristics are good for them
(to be more precise, because they are good for those genes, of which

---

[65] *Critique of Judgment*, sect. 81.
[66] Berkeley, *Three Dialogues*, quoted in E. Craig, *The Mind of God and the Works of Man*, p. 42
[67] *Posterior Analytics* I.2, *Metaphysics* II.1, quoted in P. Bayle, *Historical and Critical Dictionary*,
p. 406

individual animals are the bearers and of which the species is the collective instantiation). According to Cohen, the case of social theory is exactly the same:

> The background against which consequence explanation is offered in biology or anthropology or economics is a conception of species or societies or economic units as self-maintaining and self-advancing . . .[68]

This is an absolutely crucial passage. If, indeed, it is legitimate to see 'societies or economic units' as self-maintaining, then we shall have a strong presumption in favour of the existence of the kind of mechanism that must be supposed by the theory of ideology. As we have now seen *in extenso*, however, this background belief is not part of an unchanging heritage of human thought about society but made its appearance within the relatively short period from Herder and Schiller to Hegel. But what would justify a materialist making such an ontological assumption about the nature of society?

Would we have to identify a process akin to the process of natural selection before it could be rationally maintained? Not necessarily, Cohen believes. He maintains that it is not in all cases necessary to support claims made for functional explanation in social theory with the kind of 'elaborating explanation' that Darwinism provides for the functional explanations presented in biology:

> . . . in the absence of such [an elaborating] theory we shall still observe provocative correlations between the requirements of living existence and the actual endowments of living things, correlations fine enough to suggest the thesis that they have those endowments because they minister to those requirements. We can rationally hypothesize functional explanations even when we lack an account which, like Darwin's, shows how the explanations work . . . [The] fact that functional explanations may reasonably be proposed, in the light of suitable evidence, but in advance of an elaborating theory, is very important for social science and for history. For functional explanations in those spheres often carry conviction in the absence of elaborative context.[69]

Cohen is clearly right to assert that we do not – should not – limit our explanations to cases where we can support them by means of an elaborating explanation. Consider how we explain individuals and their capacities. I know that if I were lucky enough to be able to spend some months in France my French would improve. My accent would be less foreign and my ability to find the words I need would become more fluent. Such explanations are so well accepted as to be practically banal, but we have, in fact, very little idea of the *mechanism* (assuming that there is one) which lets human beings operate in this way. Psychologists have recently

[68] *Karl Marx's Theory of History*, p. 264.
[69] Ibid., pp. 285–6.

made some progress in explaining the physiology behind learning and memory, and we may expect them to make a good deal more in the near future. But no one would pretend that, at this stage, such explanations are anything other than incomplete. Yet it is not as if we feel the need to wait for some elaborating explanation about brain physiology before we take our everyday generalizations about learning and other mental capacities to be justified. We are sufficiently confident that human beings do indeed work this way without needing to know in detail *how* they do it.

Could we not, then, use just the same reasoning in the case of society? If societies *do* develop beliefs which serve social interests as and when those interests require such beliefs, why should we make our acceptance of that fact dependent on an account of how they do it? In fact, the argument would go, that may be just the wrong way round to do things. If societies generate the beliefs which are necessary to their operation, then this is a sign that they are like organisms: they have the capacity to operate in ways which maintain themselves. It is only a prejudice towards atomism which makes us think that reduction to the level of individuals is the prerequisite for an explanation in terms of society to be acceptable.

But there is an absolutely crucial dissimilarity between human beings and societies. Societies and the way they operate are a matter of dispute in the way that – at the simple level – human beings are not: we do not have a commonly agreed 'folk sociology' to match the 'folk psychology' by which we explain people's everyday beliefs and actions. Again we see the precariousness of the relation between ontology and evidence. On the one hand, we look for explanations in terms which are appropriate for the objects in question; on the other, our ideas about the nature of the objects themselves respond to the evidence we have about the way they behave. Thus, given the paucity of the evidence, the suggestion that we should use the idea of society as a self-maintaining system as the *starting point* for social theory carries far less force than the corresponding idea of individuals as cognitively developing rational agents has in psychology.

Cohen's general point – that 'provocative correlations' should lead us to hypothesize functional explanations even in the absence of elaborative context – is, in my view, entirely valid, but he is too sanguine about this as a defence of the claims of Marxist social theory for three reasons.

1 First, as I have argued, the theory of ideology is not well enough specified for us to have good empirical evidence on its basis.

2 Secondly, it is not the case that there are no powerful competing accounts of the phenomena to be explained.

3 Finally, it is not just that we happen to lack, as yet, a fully satisfactory account of the elaborating explanation for the functional claims: we do not even have a clear idea of what such an explanation would look like.

Cohen suggests that:

There are traces in Marx of a Darwinian mechanism, a notion that thought-systems are produced in comparative independence from social constraint, but persist and gain social life following a filtration process which selects those well adapted for ideological service.[70]

But there are two objections to be made to this as a way of meeting the demand for an elaborating explanation. The first is that in the sphere of ideology the correlation (if it is one) between, say, bourgeois individualism and the development of capitalism is far too immediate to allow time for the sort of random mutation and 'filtration' characteristic of the Darwinian struggle for life.

A counter to this objection would be to suppose that the ideas already exist as part of the common stock of the culture. What the filtration process explains in this case is not how the ideas are *generated* but how they come to be *accepted*. Here we come to the second objection, however, for at this point the theory of evolution and the theory of ideology diverge. The crucial feature of the latter is that ideologies are accepted by those whose interests they go against. Can the evolutionary model offer the basis for an explanation of such 'perverse' phenomena?

The distinctive characteristic of Darwinian evolutionary theory is that it explains the emergence of features (the giraffe's long neck or the tiger's stripes) in virtue of their transmission from one generation to the next: over time, those traits are selected which are most successfully transmitted.[71] Transmission itself, in turn, is determined by (1) survival (the organism must live to maturity in order to breed) and (2) reproduction (it must mate and breed successfully).

Overall, the theory of evolution states that traits are selected that are good for transmission. Nevertheless, those traits that are 'good' for transmission (are most easily inherited) are not necessarily 'good' in a more general sense (either for the individual animal or for the species). Although in nature transmissibility tracks what we may generally think of as being 'good' for the animal remarkably well, this is a substantive claim on Darwinism's part. As Stephen Jay Gould puts the point, '"Survival of the fittest" is not a tautology'.[72] The most striking biological examples of divergence between fitness and transmission arise when traits are developed solely for the purpose of reproductive competition.

In general, mating competition provides a restricted context in which traits can be selected for transmission that are also good in a more general sense (the combat of males lets them show their strength, etc.). Most reproductive competition takes place on a symbolic or mimetic level (stags joust, peacocks display) and this has its own evolutionary advantage (it is

---

[70] Ibid., p. 291.
[71] This is an oversimplification. It should read something like 'of the available features' – and the question of what determines 'availability' is highly contentious.
[72] *Ever Since Darwin*, p. 43. If we were to substitute 'most transmissible' for 'fittest' then the proposition *would* be tautological.

obviously wasteful if males kill each other in the combat for a mate). But there is also the danger that reproductive advantage can become detached, as it were, from the context that originally gave it point. Thus features may evolve that are, judged strictly by the benefit that they bring the organism from the point of view of its survival, perverse or dysfunctional. (Gould discusses the example of the 'Irish Elk', whose antlers grew larger and larger solely, he argues, as a result of the 'escalation' of reproductive competition between males.)[73]

Does this help us in the understanding of ideology? When it comes to ideas, evolutionary explanation would have it that those ideas will survive that continue to be selected and transmitted. Unlike the biological case, however, the reason why ideas will be selected will be the perceived advantage that they bring to the thinker (if there is a quasi-Darwinian mechanism in culture, it must act *through* the belief-system of the individual thinker, not in spite of it). Thus, for ideas to be selected that *go against* the real interests of the thinker, there must be either some failure of rationality on the thinker's part (which would itself, of course, require an evolutionary explanation) or else some cognitive deficiency in the situation with which the thinker is faced – a discrepancy, for instance, between real and perceived interests. This is, in fact, a common situation. We all know institutions (educational institutions and penal institutions come to mind especially) that encourage the development of attitudes and forms of behaviour that are against the interests of those who hold them when they come to leave those institutions.

However, the fact that a discrepancy between real and perceived interest does arise in some cases is far from showing that (or how) capitalism creates a framework such that individuals *in general* voluntarily and in virtue of the normal mechanisms of belief-formation accept ideas that go against their interests. An evolutionary foundation for the theory of ideology would have to give an account of the evolution of perverse sub-systems for the generation of ideological ideas equivalent to the biologist's account of the origin of the 'sub-system' of mating competition that leads to such phenomena as the Irish Elk's excessive horns. Here, the first objection comes back into play: how could this take place quickly enough to produce the kind of immediate response to social 'needs' that the theory of ideology requires? While an evolutionary account might explain how categories come to be selected for that are in the interests of some group or of 'society', taken in a suitably general way, in my view, it does not, as it stands,

---

[73] Ibid., Ch. 9. If species were always 'on a knife-edge' in their environment then they would not be able to afford those extra energies that go into extravagant forms of reproductive competition and so the latter would not evolve. Nevertheless, the fact that there is sufficient latitude in the environment for such features to have evolved does not mean that a species is not evolutionarily disadvantaged by perverse forms of reproductive competition. The margin that the species has to deal with exogenous changes in the environment or with the competition of other species is reduced, making it more liable to extinction. That, Gould claims, is what happened to the Irish Elk.

provide a convincing explanation of how ideas are formed and accepted by subordinate classes that are in the interests of the ruling class alone.

In conclusion, the correspondence model, interpreted as a form of functional explanation, presents the prospect of an account of ideology that (like Darwin's theory of evolution) is secular and materialist in its ontological commitments. It supports the claim that Marxist social theory is scientific in just the way that the natural sciences are scientific – no special forms of explanation need to be admitted in virtue of the supposedly distinctive nature of the *Geisteswissenschaften* (which is not to say, of course, that Cohen thinks that the social sciences are *just like* the natural sciences). But, unlike Darwinism, the 'conception of societies as self-maintaining and self-advancing' that the base–superstructure account of ideology assumes is not supported by a plausible elaborating explanation. Nor is the confirming evidence for the theory sufficiently compelling for us to be justified in adopting that conception of society in its absence.

VI Essence and Appearance

The fourth model of ideology that I identify in Marx, like the correspondence model, appeals to the analogy between Marxist theory and the natural sciences. However, while the attribution of the correspondence model to Marx requires a considerable amount of reconstruction, this model has its basis in Marx's own account of the nature of scientific procedure. Marx writes in the third volume of *Das Kapital*:

> It should not astonish us, then, that vulgar economy feels particularly at home in the alienated outward appearances of economic relations, in which these *prima facie* absurd and complete contradictions appear and that these relationships seem the more self-evident the more their internal relationships are concealed from it, although they are understandable to the popular mind. But all science would be superfluous if the outward appearance and the essence of things coincided.[74]

To the extent that ideology is a matter of false consciousness, on this model, the illusions involved are not false beliefs about reality but stem from the fact that reality itself is false. The surface of social reality is not a simple one on which items present themselves as they really are. On the one hand, objects have properties which are not immediately apparent (their 'internal relationships'); on the other hand, these relationships are what, in fact, governs the behaviour and appearance of reality as it presents itself (the 'alienated outward appearances'). Such a contrast between essence and appearance, says Marx, is characteristic of 'all science'.

Some such contrast does indeed seem obvious and unproblematic: we

---

[74] *Das Kapital*, 3, p. 825 [Eng. trans., p. 817].

do posit internal properties (the molecular structure of materials, for example) as an explanation for their behaviour (that they bend, break or dissolve in certain circumstances) and such properties are quite distinct from the immediately observable properties of the material. But Marx goes beyond this: his claim is not just that the outward appearance of things is insufficient to explain their properties; it is actually *false*. In discussing the way in which, in capitalist society, labour is sold to capitalists as a commodity, in exchange for wages, Marx writes:

> Hence we may understand the decisive importance of the transformation of the value and price of labour-power into the form of wages, or into the value and price of labour itself. This phenomenal form, *which makes the actual relation invisible, and, indeed, shows the direct opposite of that relation*, forms the basis of all the juridical notions of both labourer and capitalist, of all the mystifications of the capitalist mode of production, of all its illusions as to liberty, of all the apologetic shifts of the vulgar economists.[75]

Thus we see Marx making three claims:

1 that we should see reality as layered, having a surface appearance governed by an underlying structure

2 that to make such a distinction is characteristic of the scientific approach to reality in general

3 that the phenomenal form conceals the real relations and falsifies them (it 'makes the actual relation invisible and indeed shows the opposite of that relation').

The objection is that claims (1) and (2) (which are plausible) do not, as Marx appears to assume, entail (3). According to claims (1) and (2), the way that we see the world is not, immediately, adequate for us to explain the way that the world is. But that does not make our perception of the world *false*. The truth is, surely, that we simply lack a theory. Yet Marx's claim (3) is much stronger: reality (at least, social reality under capitalism) presents itself in a way that mystifies those who live in it. Marx goes on to make an explicit connection between what he takes to be the mystifying effect of the wage form and the general character of science:

> ... in respect to the phenomenal form, 'value and price of labour', or 'wages', as contrasted with the essential relation manifested therein, viz., the value and price of labour-power, the same difference holds in respect to all phenomena and their hidden substratum. The former appear directly and spontaneously as current modes of thought; the latter must first be discovered by science.[76]

---

[75] Ibid., 1, p. 562 [Eng. trans., pp. 591–2], my emphasis.
[76] Ibid., 1, p. 564 [Eng. trans., p. 594].

As it stands, the claim that the 'hidden substratum' must first be discovered by science does not substantiate the claim that the phenomenal form 'shows the exact opposite of the real relation'. The fact that the appearance of reality should fail to carry with it or lead us to a scientific explanation of its underlying structure does not make that appearance misleading or in other ways 'false'. If I taste a banana, its taste (the taste by which I, quite correctly, identify it *as* a banana) does not, admittedly, lead me to understand the biochemical processes that explain why it tastes the way that it in fact does. But it would be wrong to say, therefore, that the 'surface appearance' – the taste – was 'concealing' that true explanation. The point is that our perceptual engagement with reality is not, in the first instance, a theoretical one; so the fact that appearances do not 'reveal' what will be discovered by theory should not be taken as in any way a criticism of the appearances or the immediate perceptual judgements based upon them.

In what sense, then, might one say that surface appearances could be 'false'? The most detailed discussion that Marx provides of a case where the surface of reality presents itself as 'false' is to be found in the section of the chapter on Commodities in *Das Kapital* called 'The Fetishism of Commodities and the Secret Thereof'.[77]

The word 'fetishism' that Marx uses recalls, of course, de Brosses (whom he himself had certainly read). In de Brosses' original sense, the fetishist is someone who attributes to an object in the world a quality that it in fact lacks, for reasons which have to do with the fetishist's own 'false consciousness'. The mechanism of deception is thus a psychological one – a failure of rationality on the part of the individual (for instance, the fear of natural processes may lead him to believe, against evidence, that the forces governing such processes will respond to personal appeal). Marx's conception of commodity fetishism, however, is rather different:

> It is as clear as day that man, by his activity, changes the form of the materials of nature in a way that is useful to himself. The form of wood, for instance, is altered when a table is made out of it. Yet, nevertheless, the table remains *wood*, a common everyday thing. But, as soon as it steps forth as a *commodity*, it transforms itself into a sensible-supersensible [*sinnlich übersinn-liches*] thing.[78]

In other words, the commodity is not simply a material object – not even a purposefully selected and transformed one – but something that has social significance. This by itself, of course, is not enough to show that the

---

[77] As Cohen points out, commodity fetishism is not the only kind of fetishism with which Marx is concerned – indeed, he claims, it is not even the most significant. However that may be, it is certainly the example that Marx treats in the greatest detail and, in my view, offers the best opportunity to analyse what his claims amount to.

[78] *Das Kapital*, 1, p. 85 [Eng. trans., pp. 81–2]. Note, too, the echo of Hegel's conception of the work of art as the '*sinnliche Scheinen der Idee*'.

object is deceptive: an arrow, say, which we use as a sign-post does not have the significance of pointing the way *intrinsically* (physically or as a direct result of how it has been formed). Nevertheless, the fact that the arrow only has that significance socially does not mean that it does not really have it, that we are wrong to ascribe that significance to it. In what, then, does the deceptive character of the commodity consist? Marx explains the nature of this enigma as follows:

> The secret of the commodity-form thus simply consists in this: that it reflects back to men the social character of their own labour as objective character-istics of the products of labour themselves, as social natural properties of these things [*gesellschaftliche Natureigenschaften dieser Dinge*]; hence also the social relationship of the producers to their collective labour [*Gesamtarbeit*] as a social relationship between objects, existing externally to the producers.[79]

Thus, Marx is claiming, two separate facts or properties are here distorted. First, the 'social character' of human beings' labour appears (falsely) as an objective character of the products themselves, and, secondly (in consequence of the first fact, as he asserts), the producers' own relationship to the collective labour process in which they participate seems to inhere in objects independent of the producers themselves. The key question, then, is what this 'social character' that is apparently a property of the products themselves amounts to. Only if we have a convincing interpretation of this phrase can we determine in what sense it is that the ascription of that property to the commodity is false or deceptive.

Is it the sheer fact that the commodity *is* a commodity – a use-value that also has an exchange-value? This suggestion must be rejected, if only for the simple reason that the belief that the product is a commodity is in no way a false or deceptive belief (any more than it is deceptive to believe that the arrow *is* a sign-post). Similarly, it cannot be something concealed from the producers that commodities *do* as a matter of fact exchange for one another in certain proportions: it is hard to see how anyone could live their lives within a market society without having an adequate understanding of facts of this kind (enough, at least, to be able to buy something to eat).[80]

As Marx plainly argues, however, it is not such first-order facts about commodities but a second-order one that is the source of deception: it is not *that* commodities can be exchanged with one another in certain ratios but *the reason why* they exchange in the ratios that they do that is the 'hidden secret':

---

[79] Ibid., 1, p. 86 [Eng. trans., p. 83].
[80] As Marx, indeed, acknowledges:

> What, first of all, practically concerns producers when they make an exchange is the question how much of some other product they get for their own; in what proportions the products are exchangeable. (*Das Kapital*, 1, p. 89 [Eng. trans., p. 86].)

When these proportions [sc. the exchange-ratios – M. R.] have, by custom, attained a certain stability, they appear to result from the nature of the products, so that, for instance, one ton of iron and two ounces of gold appear to be of equal value as naturally as a pound of gold and a pound of iron, in spite of their different physical and chemical qualities, appear to be of equal weight. The character of having value, when once impressed upon products, obtains fixity only by reason of their acting and re-acting upon one another as quantities of value. These quantities vary continually, independently of the will, foresight and action of the producers. To them, their own social action takes the form of the action of objects, which rule the producers instead of being ruled by them.[81]

In this case, a surface appearance is said to be 'false' to the extent that it suggests or promotes a theoretical explanation that is false (or bars the way to one that is true). I have argued that (Marx's own assertions about the discrepancy between essence and appearance to the contrary) this is by no means the general case in scientific explanation: bananas taste the way that they do without suggesting any particular biochemical explanation for their taste. On the other hand, it would be wrong to deny altogether that there are cases when things misleadingly 'look a certain way'. Thus, to take the most celebrated example, it looks as if the sun goes round the earth. The reason is that the natural (although, as it turns out, incorrect) inference from the fact that the sun moves relative to other items within the perceptual field (which themselves stay stationary in relation to one another) is that the sun really is in motion and that those other objects are stationary. The case of commodity fetishism as Marx presents it runs parallel to this 'geocentric' illusion. Those who suffer from commodity fetishism in this respect do not suffer from a practical inability to conduct economic transactions in terms of values but from a theoretical deficiency in understanding what, ultimately, determines those values. The object perceived is deceptive to the extent that the immediate evidence suggests a naive (and, indeed, false) theory about its etiology. But the illusion is not a direct perceptual illusion or failure of recognition. The idea that products have their values intrinsically is not so much an economic illusion (an illusion that in some way limits the capacity of agents to engage in economic transactions) as a theoretical illusion about the economy (a misconception regarding the way that the economy as a whole works).

Why should producers have this illusion? The real reason, Marx believes, why products exchange in the ratios that they do is the determination of the magnitude of value by labour-time. This law 'forcibly asserts itself like an overriding law of nature [just as the] law of gravity asserts itself when a house falls down'. Yet the exchange-relations themselves do not make this apparent. They are, Marx says, 'accidental and ever-changing'. It is for this reason, he claims, that the determination of the magnitude of value by labour-time is 'a secret hidden beneath the

---

[81] Ibid.

apparent motions of the relative values of the commodities'.[82] In other words, (1) the surface of reality as it appears is too turbulent for us to recognize the currents which, at a deeper level, are working to determine those surface phenomena, and (2) the turbulent surface invites another, superficial but false, explanation. But neither part of this claim appears convincing. After all, the phenomena of meteorology are extremely complex but one would hardly say that the complexity of the weather *obscured* analysis of its underlying causes. Moreover, to take the second part of the claim, it is by no means clear why an observer should be disposed to infer that commodities have their values intrinsically from the fact that the movement of their values is volatile. In fact, it seems to me that the opposite inference is more natural. If it is true that commodities' values change apparently randomly, as Marx claims, surely that would make one more inclined to assume that values were *not* intrinsic to commodities but the effect of external forces (like the movement of leaves in a breeze, say)?

As explained above, Marx's account of commodity fetishism contains two kinds of illusion: (1) illusions regarding the social character of the products of labour and (2) illusions regarding the relations between the producers themselves. Marx's account of the second kind of illusion is very similar in structure to the first.

As social production comes to be organized individualistically, so, in consequence, Marx asserts, the character of labour itself changes: it takes on, he says, 'a two-fold social character'.[83] It is now not merely the case that the labourer must labour usefully: he must labour usefully to satisfy the wants that are signalled to him through the market. Thus, implicitly, the market commensurates his labour with the labour of every other producer – his own labour has its value in relation to the way in which others perform the same labour. This two-fold character of the labour of the individual producers, says Marx:

> ... appears to them, when reflected in their brain, only under those forms which are impressed upon that labour in everyday practice, in the exchange of products – the socially useful character of their own labour appears under the form of the condition that the product must be useful (for others, that is) and the social character of the equality between the different kinds of labour appears in the form of that which all these physically different articles that are the products of labour have in common: namely, their character of being *values*.[84]

Here again, then, we have an illusion of the second rather than the first order: the individual producers are aware of the role of the market in determining the way in which they labour. In this they are quite correct. But they also believe (falsely) that it is the market that makes their labour

[82] Ibid., 1, p. 89 [Eng. trans., pp. 86–7].
[83] Ibid., 1, p. 87 [Eng. trans., p. 84].
[84] Ibid., 1, pp. 87–8 [Eng. trans., p. 84].

useful (rather than it being recognized as a contingent fact about this form of production that their socially useful labour takes on a market-determined form). We can see, then, that Marx considers the illusion regarding the nature of commodities and the illusion about the nature of the labour process to be complementary.

1 In the case of commodities, it is

    a believed falsely that commodities have their values intrinsically;

whereas, in fact,

    b the values of commodities are determined extrinsically, by the social labour expended upon them.

2 In the case of the labour process, it is

    a believed falsely that individual labour is socially useful only derivatively, in virtue of the market value of its products;

whereas, in fact,

    b labour has that character intrinsically, as part of the collective labour of society.

Society generates such false beliefs spontaneously, Marx claims – the world of commodities 'veils rather than reveals', he says, the social character of private labour and of the relations between the individual producers.[85] That the true source of the value of commodities lies in the labour expended in their production is, Marx maintains, a matter of simple scientific truth. So, too, is the fact that the social character of private labour consists in the equalization of that labour under the auspices of the market. But, Marx says, knowledge of these facts does not dispel such false appearance:

> The recent scientific discovery that the products of labour, so far as they are values, are but material expressions of the human labour spent in their production, marks, indeed, an epoch in the history of the development of the human race, but by no means dissipates the objective illusion [*gegenständlichen Schein*] through which the social character of labour appears to be an objective character of the products themselves. What is true only of the particular form of production with which we are dealing, the production of commodities, namely, that the specific social character of independent private acts of labour consists in their equality by virtue of being human labour, which character assumes in the product the form of value – this fact appears to the producers, notwithstanding the discovery above referred to, to be just

[85] Ibid., 1, p. 90 [Eng. trans., p. 87].

as real and final, as the fact that, after the discovery by science of the component gases of air, the atmosphere itself remained unaltered.[86]

Yet Marx's analogy fails. While he is right to say that the discovery of the component gases of air leaves the atmosphere unchanged, this is beside the point. Admittedly, it is absurd to think that a scientist's discovery about an object should change the object itself, but that is not the issue: the question, rather, is whether, having now discovered the truth about that object, individuals will still continue to entertain their previous false beliefs about the object. It is not a question of whether the atmosphere itself changes but whether what we believe about it does.

The atmosphere is something that we 'perceive', if we can be said to do so at all, by interacting with it (that is, breathing). This activity (like the tasting of the banana) is wholly untheoretical. So it is not in the least surprising that a theoretical discovery about the atmosphere will leave that practical engagement 'unaltered'. On the other hand, the false beliefs that Marx alleges that we have about the economy – that the value of commodities is intrinsic to them and that the social character of labour derives from the exchange of commodities – are false beliefs of a theoretical character. Why should we assume that these beliefs will persist in the face of contrary evidence? If fetishism really is a theoretical illusion, then there seems to be no reason to suppose that the discovery of the truth will not dispel the illusion.

In the light of the failure of this analogy, one phrase that Marx uses in the passage quoted above is particularly revealing. 'Objective illusion' (*gegenständlicher Schein*),[87] with its echo of Hegel, indicates that the theory of the fetishism of commodities has its ancestry not just in Enlightenment theories of religious illusion but also in the Idealist theory of *Schein*. *Schein* for the Idealists, it will be recalled, is not a cognitive illusion but a perceptible characteristic inherent in objects. Thus *Schein*, like fetishism, is not dissipated by an intellectual discovery on the part of the perceiver; it has its source in the activity of a higher kind of agency.

The failure to make good the claims of the theory of fetishism by means of the analogy with the natural sciences should make us take such language seriously. In the next section, we shall examine how far an interpretation of Marx that confines itself strictly to what is licensed by the parallel with the natural sciences should be supplemented (or, indeed, supplanted) by a collectivist or quasi-Hegelian reading of *Das Kapital*.

VII A Hegelian Marx?

The essence and appearance model as it was presented in the previous section trades on the analogy with the explanations of natural science in

[86] Ibid., 1, p. 88 [Eng. trans., pp. 85–6].
[87] He uses it again at p. 97.

order to provide an account of how it is that the individuals who live in
capitalist society are deceived about the nature of their labour and of the
value that their products have. But, although the contrast between essence
and appearance itself is quite legitimate, it does not explain why appearances should be *false* (rather than merely untheoretical). We are left with
the claim that capitalist society is a distinctive kind of *deceptive object*,
although the essence–appearance analogy as it stands gives no explanation
of why that should be so.

In the face of this failure it seems reasonable to wonder whether the
abandonment of Hegel might not have been too radical. Might there not
be a way of adopting at least some of the key features of Hegel's account
of history and society without having to commit oneself to all of the idealist
metaphysics within which they are embedded? As we shall see, there are
indeed very clear signs that the mature Marx was committed to ideas that
are incompatible with the image of him as a methodologically individualistic social scientist promoted by Cohen and other 'analytical Marxists'.

To argue that such themes are present in Marx's mature writings is not
to claim that the 'Darwin of the social world' is not there also. Nor do I
wish to imply that the 'analytical Marxists' are unaware of the existence of
Hegelian elements in Marx's work.[88] Cohen's interpretation of Marx, however, is explicitly defensive and, to this extent, he clearly feels free to
neglect or reject themes which might be incompatible with the central thrust
of his argument. Since I regard that defence as unpersuasive, it seems to
me important to give more sustained attention to these other elements.

The crucial deficiency of the 'base and superstructure' approach was its
failure to provide a plausible 'elaborating explanation' for the 'conception
of . . . societies or economic units as self-maintaining and self-advancing'.[89]
A 'Hegelian' or collectivist reading of Marx would, in a sense, turn that
difficulty on its head. If societies really *are* self-maintaining systems then
this is as much a basic truth about societies as the fact that human beings
are agents who act on the basis of their beliefs and desires; there is no
need for an elaborating explanation to persuade us to accept that fact.

The interpretation of *Das Kapital* to be presented in this section
attributes three main features to capitalism.

1 The capitalist system is a quasi-Hegelian self-reproducing and self-
   maintaining process. The subject that realizes itself in the course of this
   process is capital itself.

2 The capitalist system is both *deceptive* and *defective*. It presents itself to
   those who live within it in a way that conceals its true nature from them.
   But, beyond that, it is also defective in the sense that the labour process
   violates the true or intrinsic nature of labour itself.

[88] Elster, in particular, emphasizes their presence.
[89] *Karl Marx's Theory of History*, p. 264.

3 Capitalism is a system of a dual kind; it is held together by a negative principle, but, like Schiller's modern 'clockwork-state' or the *Verstandes-staat* denounced by the Young Hegel, it also contains within itself (although it keeps suppressed) the possibility of a more affirmative kind of unity.

Yet, if these Hegelian elements are indeed present in Marx's mature writings, what relationship do they have to his commitment to scientific materialism? There are, it seems, only three ways in which the two strands might be related.

1 that one or other is not meant seriously: either the parallel to the natural sciences or the apparent Hegelian collectivism are mere rhetorical flourishes to be ignored

2 that, although Marx does indeed adopt both strands, he was not fully aware of this fact and would have rejected his commitment to one or other of them as inconsistent had he become aware of it

3 that Marx believed that the two strands were consistent.

As a matter of interpretation, it seems that (3) is the most likely position for Marx to have taken. However, this belief seems to be plainly false. In particular, as I have argued, the parallel to the natural sciences does, while the Hegelian collectivist interpretation does not, require an elaborating explanation to justify the ontological commitment to the view of social systems as self-maintaining. Thus it seems right to keep the two interpretations separate from one another, whatever Marx himself may have believed about the relations between them.

The explicit evidence for the mature Marx's view of his relationship to Hegel comes from two main sources, neither of which is particularly extensive. The first is in the *Grundrisse*, the work written by Marx in 1857–8 and generally regarded as a first version of *Das Kapital*. As part of this text there exists a draft Introduction whose discussion of the 'Method of Political Economy' contains an account of Marx's differences with Hegel.

Marx introduces this discussion by means of a contrast between his own conception of method and what one might call a commonsense empiricist conception. 'It seems to be correct', Marx writes, 'to begin with the real and the concrete, the real presupposition'.[90] Yet this is not so, he asserts, for the most immediate categories that one might frame on the basis of observation – for instance, that of the 'population' – are themselves 'an abstraction' when one leaves out the divisions out of which they are composed. To put his point another way, to attempt to develop generalizations from what is observed by abstracting from specific differences leads to emptiness: for an explanation, something more is needed.

---

[90] *Grundrisse der Kritik der politischen Ökonomie*, p. 21 [Eng. trans., p. 100].

According to Marx, this further element is that the abstracting process of observation must be complemented by a synthetic process of construction. The result, instead of being the 'chaotic representation' that is immediately given to observation, will now be structured and intelligible – a 'rich totality of many determinations and relations'. Scientific thought, then, should move from the concrete to the abstract and back to the concrete again – but in a different form:

> The concrete is concrete because it is the concentration [*Zusammenfassung*] of many determinations, hence unity of the diverse [*Einheit des Mannigfaltigen*]. It appears in thought, therefore, as a process of concentration, as a result, not as a point of departure, even though it is the point of departure in reality and hence also the point of departure for intuition and conception [*Anschauung und Vorstellung*].[91]

From this point of view, Marx's criticism of Hegel is complementary to his rejection of empiricism. While empiricism moves only from the concrete to the abstract, according to Marx, Hegel, he alleges, is prey to the opposite illusion: that of believing that the process of developing complex structures out of simple categories is itself the ultimate nature of reality:

> Hegel thus fell into the illusion of conceiving the real as the product of thought concentrating itself, probing its own depths, and unfolding itself out of itself, by itself, whereas the method of rising from the abstract to the concrete is only the way in which thought appropriates the concrete, reproduces it as the concrete in the mind. But this is by no means the process by which the concrete itself comes into being.[92]

The Hegelian idealist is misguided because he takes 'the movement of the categories as the real act of production ... whose result is the world' –

> ... and this is correct insofar as the concrete totality is a thought-totality, a thought-concrete, *in fact* a product of thought, of comprehension [*des Denkens, des Begreifens*]; but it is by no means a product of the notion [*des Begriffs*], thinking and revealing itself outside or above intuition and conception [*Anschauung und Vorstellung*]. Rather, it is the product of the transformation of intuition and conception into thought.[93]

To go by the *Grundrisse* Introduction, Marx does not believe that scientific materialism is incompatible with a Hegelian presentation of the movement of Thought as a developing process, starting from a simple category that is progressively deepened and made more complex. The

---

[91] Ibid., pp. 21–2 [Eng. trans., p. 101].
[92] Ibid., p. 22 [Eng. trans., p. 101].
[93] Ibid.

error does not lie in the movement of the categories itself but in the Hegelian's conception of what the status of that movement is.

Naturally, evidence from the *Grundrisse* needs to be treated with some caution – it was written a decade before the publication of the first volume of *Das Kapital* and never completed. However, this account of Marx's views regarding his methodology is confirmed by a second piece of evidence: the Postscript that Marx himself wrote to the second edition of *Kapital*, Volume 1 (published in 1873). Marx there notes (with his customary heavy irony) his reviewers' inability to make up their minds as to whether his method is 'English-deductive' or 'German-metaphysical'. In explanation, Marx goes on to quote at length the (in other respects, highly gratifying) review from the *European Messenger* of St Petersburg. The reviewer contrasts the realism of Marx's approach to political economy in *Das Kapital* with what he takes to be the idealism of the form in which it is there presented. At the end of this long excerpt, Marx remarks:

> While the writer pictures what he takes to be actually my method, in this striking and (as far as concerns my own application of it) generous way, what else is he picturing but the dialectical method?[94]

Marx then offers an explanation for the apparent discrepancy between the mode of presentation of *Das Kapital* and its underlying approach – an explanation that echoes very clearly the account of method given in the *Grundrisse* Introduction. The misunderstanding, Marx claims, comes from a perhaps understandable but superficial comparison between his own dialectical method and that of Hegel. Because the method of presentation [*Darstellungsweise*] employed in *Das Kapital* involves the independent development of categories as a self-sufficient sequence, he explains, it may look as if it is, like Hegel's, idealist. In fact, however, this impression arises because the inquiry that preceded that presentation is left out of consideration. In contrast to Hegel, who mistakes the process of thought-development for the *logos* underlying all of reality, Marx asserts that thought is always, ultimately, derivative from external reality:

> Of course, the mode of presentation must differ in form from the mode of inquiry. The latter has to appropriate the material in detail, to analyse its different forms of development, to trace out their inner connections. Only after this work is done, can the actual movement be presented correspondingly. If this is done successfully, and the life of the material is reflected ideally, it may appear as if it were a matter of an *a priori* construction.
>
> My dialectical method is not only different from the Hegelian, but is its direct opposite. To Hegel, the process of thought (which, under the name of

'Idea' he transforms into an independent subject) is the demiurge of reality, the latter forming merely its outward appearance. With me, on the other hand, the ideal is nothing other than the material, transferred and translated in men's heads.[95]

Thus Marx, like Hegel, believes that a scientific presentation involves the ordered development of categories; unlike Hegel, he believes that those categories are derivative, not primitive. Yet, relatively clear though this conception of method is, it must be said that it leaves two very serious problems.

1 First, it assumes that it is permissible to make use of a form of presentation in which simple categories are transformed into complex ones, without recourse to idealist metaphysics.

Even if one concedes, as Marx does, that the thought-determinations involved are, ultimately, the products of abstraction from reality, some account must be given of what makes this process of 'determinate negation' (Hegel's term for the process by which simple categories generate complex ones) rational – what legitimates the claim that one category develops out of another.[96]

2 Futhermore, accepting for the sake of the argument that such a development in thought is permissible, the question still remains whether it corresponds to reality sufficiently to be explanatory of development in the external world.

For Hegel's speculative metaphysics, the question of the correspondence between thought and reality does not arise (or, rather, it has been settled at a much earlier stage: once Thought has embarked upon the *Logic*, it is assumed to be operating in the realm of 'Absolute Knowledge', in which it 'knows itself to be the whole of reality'). But, unless such a correspondence can be assumed, then in what sense is the developed 'concrete in thought' an *explanation* of the immediately given reality of which it is supposed to be a reconstruction? For Hegel, it is not just in philosophy that the Idea develops. The development of categories in the realm of pure Thought represents the developing character of *Geist* in the world. Is Marx committed to some similar kind of correspondence?

When Marx comes to apply this conception of method in practice in the *Grundrisse*, the resonances of Hegelianism are unmissable. Indeed, many of the concepts – positing [*setzen*], mediation [*Vermittlung*], moments [*Momente*], semblance [*Schein*], reflexion [*Reflexion*] – come straight from

[95] Ibid., 1, p. 27 [Eng. trans., pp. 24–5].
[96] It was the argument of Chapter 2 of *Hegel's Dialectic and its Criticism* that this categorial development is actually implausible except in the context of Hegel's metaphysics.

Hegel. Just as the theme of the *Science of Logic* is the self-complicating, circular development of the Idea, so the *Grundrisse* traces the way in which *capital* posits itself, changes form, mediates itself in otherness and so, finally, recovers itself.[97]

Capital is self-realizing or self-validating value [*sich selbst verwertender Wert*]. As it circulates and transforms itself, it draws into its orbit and gives form to the apparently independent ingredients of economic life – for instance, the process of production,[98] and labour itself.[99] It is this process that is the true, underlying source of the motion that takes place on the surface of capitalist production: the exchange and circulation of commodities.[100]

In all of this, there is a clear relationship of priority between the process of production and the individual members of society: the latter are in all cases subordinated to the former:

> Individuals are subsumed under social production; social production exists outside them as their fate; but social production is not subsumed under individuals, manageable by them as their common wealth.[101]

In short, the *Grundrisse* presents an account of capitalist production as a self-unfolding process with capital as its subject. It is the process itself – not just the categories in terms of which it is analysed – that is dynamic and self-transforming. Yet it should be said that the *Grundrisse* were, of course, only a rough draft (Marx even cautions himself at one point regarding the 'idealistic manner of presentation' that he employs in it).[102] Thus the test

---

[97] Capital, however, is now posited [*gesetzt*] as it is in all of its moments [*Moments*], in which it appears now as money, now as commodity, now as exchange-value – posited, that is, as value that does not just preserve itself formally but as *realizing value* [*verwertender Wert*], value that relates itself to itself as value ... Capital is thus posited as value in process [*prozessierender Wert*] but which is capital in each of its moments. (*Grundrisse der Kritik der politischen Ökonomie*, p. 435 [Eng. trans., p. 536].)

[98] Capital has been regarded until now as a simple process of production. But this process is, viewed from the side of its form [*der Seite der Formbestimmtheit nach*], a process of self-realization [*Selbstverwertungsprozess*]. (Ibid., p. 217 [Eng. trans., pp. 310–11].)

On the previous page Marx describes capital as 'a production relation that has been reflected into itself' [*ein in sich reflektiertes Produktionsverhältnis*].

[99] ... capital cannot confront capital if capital does not confront [*gegenübersteht*] labour, for capital is only capital as non-labour; in this contradictory relation. Thus the concept and the relation of capital itself would be destroyed ... As capital it can posit itself only by positing labour as not-capital, as pure use-value. (Ibid., p. 199 [Eng. trans., p. 288].)

[100] Circulation, therefore, does not carry within itself the principle of self-renewal. The moments of the latter are presupposed in relation to it, not posited by it ... Circulation, therefore, which appears as that which is immediately present on the surface of bourgeois society, exists only in so far as it is constantly mediated. Looked at in itself, it is the mediation of presupposed extremes. But it does not posit these extremes. Thus, it has to be mediated not only in each of its moments, but as a whole of mediation, as a total process itself. Its immediate being is therefore pure semblance [*Ihr unmittelbares Sein ist daher reines Schein*]. It is the phenomenon of a process taking place behind it. (Ibid., p. 166 [Eng. trans., p. 255].)

[101] Ibid., p. 76 [Eng. trans., p. 158].

[102] Ibid., p. 69 [Eng. trans., p. 151].

for how far such a position may legitimately be ascribed to the mature Marx is how far there is evidence in its favour in *Das Kapital* itself.

In fact, there is a considerable amount here too to confirm this interpretation. Although the organization of *Das Kapital* is rather different from the *Grundrisse*, the structure of the book is again very strikingly similar to that of Hegel's work. Just as Hegel's *Logic* starts from the 'indeterminate immediacy' of the category of Being before embarking on its ascending spiral through existence, essence and the notion towards the final, most rich, determination – the Idea itself – so Marx opens his account with a very simple category, the commodity, and continues to add more and more complex determinations – exchange, money, labour-power, surplus-value – culminating in the full complexity of capitalist accumulation.

Nor is this just a matter of the order of exposition. In his (rather infrequent) general statements on the ontology of social life in *Das Kapital*, Marx is far from endorsing individualism. To return to the review from the *European Messenger*, mentioned above, one passage seems particularly significant. The reviewer is here describing (to Marx's own approval) the difference between Marx's view of economic life and that of economists in former times:

> The old economists misunderstood the nature of economic laws when they likened them to the laws of physics and chemistry. A more thorough analysis of the phenomena shows that social organisms differ among themselves as fundamentally as plants or animals. Nay, one and the same phenomenon falls under quite different laws in consequence of the different structure of those organisms as a whole, of the variations of their individual organs, of the different conditions in which those organs function, etc.[103]

In accepting this description of his work, Marx appears to be committing himself to an organic ontology of society and a holistic conception of the relationship of parts to that social organism.[104]

The text of *Das Kapital* gives further evidence to support this account. There is, first, the concept of *capital* itself. Here again (if not quite as frequently as in the *Grundrisse*) Marx depicts capital as a dynamic, self-realizing subject. Indeed, precisely the same definition of capital as in the *Grundrisse* – capital is *der sich selbst verwertender Wert* – is presented several times.[105] Capitalist production, Marx says, is not just a process

---

[103] *Das Kapital*, 1, p. 26 [Eng. trans., p. 24].
[104] It should be said, though, that, although Marx endorses *systemic holism*, he rejects a perspective of historical teleology; to this extent, even on this interpretation, his conception of history is clearly anti-Hegelian.
[105] For example:

> ... the life-process of capital consists only in its motion as self-realizing value [*in seiner Bewegung als sich selbst verwertender Wert*]. (*Das Kapital*, 1, p. 329 [Eng. trans., p. 339].)

> The circulation of money as capital is, on the contrary, an end in itself, for the realization of value [*die Verwertung des Werts*] only exists within this renewed movement. (Ibid., p. 167 [Eng. trans., pp. 169–70].)

whose outcome is goods and profit but one which produces and reproduces the capital relationship itself.[106]

As in the *Grundrisse*, Marx specifically asserts the priority of that relationship over the individuals who participate in the production process – workers and capitalists. For instance, Marx claims that, whenever a substantial rise in wages might imperil 'the constant reproduction of the capital relationship', it is checked:

> It cannot be otherwise in a mode of production in which the worker exists to satisfy the need for the realization of existing values [*Verwertungsbedürfnisse vorhandner Werte*], instead of, on the contrary, material wealth existing to satisfy the developmental needs of the worker.[107]

The capitalist – although he is, of course, the material beneficiary of this process – is, in fact, no more in control of it than is the worker. He is, Marx says, 'personified capital'; his action is only a 'function of the capital that has been given will and consciousness in him'. Although the capitalist is like a miser – a 'fanatic for the realization of value' [*Fanatiker des Verwertung des Werts*] – his personality results from his position within the social system. Marx describes the capitalist's relationship to the system of which he is a part in terms that clearly echo Herder and Schiller:

> ... what appears in [the miser] as an individual mania is, in the capitalist, the effect of the social mechanism, in which he is only a gear-wheel [*nur ein Triebrad*].[108]

It is not only capital but production itself that Marx appears to view collectivistically. He employs a variety of organic and corporeal terms to express this view: production involves the 'production-organism' [*Produktionsorganismus*],[109] the 'social body of labour' [*gesellschaftlicher Arbeitskörper*][110] or the 'productive combined body' [*produktiver Gesamtkörper*].[111] Marx even takes up what he calls the 'fatuous fable' of Menenius Agrippa (see p. 106 above) to describe how 'the individual is himself divided, and transformed into the automatic motor of a fractional operation'.[112]

---

[106] Capitalist production, seen in context as a process of reproduction, thus produces not just the commodity, not just surplus-value; it produces and reproduces the capitalist relationship [*das Kapitalverhältnis*] itself – on the one hand, the capitalist, on the other, the wage-labourer. (Ibid.)

[107] Ibid., p. 649 [Eng. trans., pp. 680–1].

[108] Ibid., pp. 618–19 [Eng. trans., pp. 648–9].

[109] Ibid., p. 407 [Eng. trans., p. 441].

[110] Ibid., p. 430 [Eng. trans., p. 445].

[111] Ibid., p. 350 [Eng. trans., p. 363].

[112] Remembering Schiller's description of the 'polyp-nature' of Greek society, no doubt, Marx then comments in a footnote:

> In corals, each individual is, in fact, the stomach of the whole group. It supplies the group with nourishment – unlike the Roman patrician who removes it. (Ibid., pp. 381–2 [Eng. trans., p. 396].)

In the chapters on 'The Division of Labour and Manufacture' and 'Machinery and Modern Industry' Marx frequently refers to the 'collective labourer' [*der Gesamtarbeiter*], whose unity and productivity (under the direction of capital) he contrasts with the impotence and fragmentation of the individual labourer,[113] while in the section on the 'Fetishism of Commodities' he refers several times to the subsidiary role of individuals in relation to 'social collective labour' [*die gesellschaftliche Gesamtarbeit*].[114] From the point of view of the collective labourer, the labour process is a combination of fragmented parts that owe their form ultimately to the role which they play in the process seen as a whole: the 'division of labour' is not just a paraphrase for the idea of the division of tasks between individual labourers but is an account of the sub-division of an otherwise unified whole:

> When an individual appropriates natural objects for his livelihood, no one controls him but himself. Afterwards he is controlled by others . . . As in the natural body head and hand wait upon each other, so the labour-process unites the labour of the hand with that of the head. Later on they part company and even become deadly foes. The product ceases to be the direct product of the individual, and becomes a social product, produced in common by a collective labourer.[115]

We have seen, then, that Marx makes use of a rich array of analogies – Hegelian and organic – in *Das Kapital* to express the dynamic, self-reproducing nature of the process of capitalist production and of the deformity and subordination that it imposes upon the workers who produce within it. Those who wish to defend Marx on methodologically individual-ist assumptions will no doubt argue that these analogies are no more than metaphorical flourishes, hangovers from earlier days and inconsistent with Marx's overall commitment to a materialist account of social life. Yet this response cannot be given much weight. To meet the standards of methodological individualism, Marx would have had to have given his readers an adequate elaborating explanation for the self-reproducing character of society and this he has conspicuously failed to do. It is in appearing to legitimate the absence of such an account that the Hegelian element fits so appropriately into Marx's mature thought.

From the Hegelian point of view, societies are expressions of the *Volksgeist* and have this purposive self-preserving character as much as (indeed, more than) plants or animals. Thus, to the extent that the mature

---

[113] The one-sidedness and even the deficiency of the detail-labourer become perfections when he is part of the collective labourer. (Ibid., pp. 369–70 [Eng. trans., p. 383].)

[114] For example:

> The complex of these private labours forms social collective labour . . . the private labours actually act as members of the collective labour only through the relations in which exchange places the products of labour and, hence, the producers themselves. (Ibid., p. 84 [Eng. trans. p. 86].)

[115] Ibid., p. 531 [Eng. trans., pp. 557–8].

Marx remained indebted to a Hegelian and holistic ontology of social life, it is understandable that he should have seen no reason to give an elaborating explanation for the view that societies or economic units are 'self-maintaining or self-advancing': it simply follows from that ontological commitment.

While Hegel's description of the self-unfolding of the Idea is, ultimately, an affirmative one, Marx's depiction of the circulation process of capital is highly critical: the society governed by the self-reproducing circuit of capital is itself a false society.[116] In what does this falsehood consist? The theory of fetishism when seen in the light of Marx's Hegelianism provides some of the answers.

1 First, the society is deceptive: the circulation process dissimulates itself.

It encourages false beliefs such as that what has value derivatively has that value intrinsically (the illusion of commodity fetishism) and that something intrinsically social (namely, the collective labour process) exists only in virtue of the individuals' acts of exchange. Only through exchange do producers show themselves as 'elements of the social collective labour [*Glieder der gesellschaftlichen Gesamtarbeit*]'.[117] Yet it is not just that capitalism is deceptive.

2 The circulation process of capital also imposes a false form on social reality.

Because commodity production takes place as a process by which the producers 'do not come into contact with one another until they exchange their products', it follows, Marx claims, that:

> the specific social character of their private labour does not show itself except in this act of exchange. In other words, the private acts of labour actually assert themselves as elements of the social collective labour [*Glieder der gesellschaftlichen Gesamtarbeit*] through the relations which exchange establishes between the products of labour and, through them, between the producers. To the latter, therefore, the social relations between their private acts of labour manifest themselves as what they are – that is, not as the

---

[116] In a famous letter of 1858 he describes the work that he is engaged in writing (in this case the *Grundrisse*) as a

> ... critique of the economic categories, or, if you like, the system of bourgeois economy critically presented. It is a presentation [*Darstellung*] of the system and simultaneously, through this presentation, a criticism of it. (Letter to F. Lassalle, 22 February, 1858, in *Selected Correspondence*, p. 103.)

Thus Marx believes (1) that the critique of the categories of economic life is *eo ipso* a critique of the account of economic life given within the received categories of political economy and (2) that in presenting those categories scientifically he will, at the same time, be criticizing them.

[117] *Das Kapital*, 1, p. 87 [Eng. trans., p. 84].

immediate social relationships of persons in their labour but as material relationships between persons and social relationships between things.[118]

In what sense is this a matter of illusion or false consciousness? To the extent that social production takes place on the basis of individuals labouring independently, their activities being coordinated through the imperatives of a system of market exchanges, then production is indeed, Marx says, a matter of 'material relationships between persons and social relationships between things'. Hence such a perception is not misguided; it reflects the reality of a form of economic life in which the members of the collective body labour in isolation, rather than cooperating as part of a system of 'immediate social relationships'. It is, then, this form of society itself that is to be counted as *false*.

What is thereby distorted and violated, the Hegelian interpretation maintains, is the nature of social labour. If labour *appears to be* atomized and individualized (to be collective only as a result of the activity of capital) then this is because it *really is* atomized and individualized. The social relationship of the producers to their *Gesamtarbeit* appears as 'a social relationship between objects, existing externally to the producers'[119] because, in appearing this way, 'the social relations between their private acts of labour manifest themselves *as what they are* – that is, not as the immediate social relationships of persons in their labour but as material relationships between persons and social relationships between things.'[120]

The ultimate secret of capital is that it is itself a form of social labour – social labour alienated and absorbed into itself by the circulation process of capital. The producers are oppressed by a power that they themselves have created:

> Capital is dead labour that, like a vampyre, only animates itself by sucking living labour into itself, and that lives all the more, the more of it that it absorbs.[121]

This is why:

> As man is dominated in religion by the products of his own head, so he is dominated in capitalist production by the products of his own hand.[122]

Capitalism is a form of collective life that fragments the organic unity of the social production organism and that subordinates collective labour to an infernal system in which:

[118] Ibid.
[119] Ibid., p. 86 [Eng. trans., p. 83].
[120] Ibid., p. 87 [Eng. trans., p. 84], my emphasis.
[121] Ibid., p. 247 [Eng. trans., p. 257].
[122] Ibid., p. 649 [Eng. trans., pp. 680–1].

. . . the automaton itself is the subject, and the workers are merely conscious organs of the automaton, and together with them, subordinated to the central moving-power.[123]

The reappearance of *topoi* from Herder, Schiller and Hegel (all of whom Marx read avidly) in *Das Kapital* is thus more than just vivid metaphor. The ideas that these metaphors and images express – the priority of the collective over the individual, the individual's fragmentation and isolation, and the substitution of oppressive and mechanical forms of social unity for immediate and organic ones – represent central elements in Marx's view of the systematic nature of capitalist society. Marx's return to Hegelianism represents a reversion to an ontological model that is at odds with his simultaneously expressed intention to prosecute the critique of political economy as a science that is scientific in just the same way as the natural sciences. But the inconsistency is not *unmotivated*. The mature Marx's Hegelianism is no mere hangover of residual elements but represents a response – conscious or not – on his part to the problem he faced in giving theoretical expression to his two background beliefs: that society is a system that sustains itself automatically and that it does so (at least in large part) by the false consciousness of those whom it oppresses.

VIII Unified Labour?

The consequences of Marx's Hegelianism are not simply for his account of the capitalist system itself. Implicit in his account of the falsehood of capitalist society – his depiction of the capitalist production process as a usurpation by capital of the *Gesamtarbeit* of society – there is a corresponding conception of the true and essential nature of social production.

For Hegel, men become reconciled when they live in a society in which *Geist* has attained a point of completion such that it is possible for individuals to know themselves as members of *Geist* and to realize that their own rationality, will and personality come to fulfilment in it. For Marx, of course, it is not simply a matter of coming to recognize the rationality of a social system that already exists.

Under the hegemony of capital, labour, according to Marx, has taken on a 'two-fold character' – the usefulness of the worker's labour is now determined, he asserts, by its place within a network of exchange relations which establish its value in relation to other kinds of labour. The relations between workers are 'material relationships between persons and social relationships between things' instead of being 'the immediate social relationships of persons in their labour'.[124]

Implicitly, then, human beings are members of a unified subject – social

---

[123] Ibid., p. 442 [Eng. trans., p. 458].
[124] Ibid., p. 87 [Eng. trans., p. 84].

collective labour. Yet this subject has been usurped by a collective subject of a false and oppressive kind: capital. Just as Schiller's fragmented individuals are ground beneath the gear-wheels of a mechanical social order at the cost of the organic unity that would realize their full collective potential, so those who labour under capitalism are condemned to follow its dictates.

Thus the condition for reconciliation is that this false subject should be practically overthrown and the true subject – collective labour – that is latent within capitalism restored. The false collective subject must be destroyed in order to allow the true collective subject to reunite itself. This takes place as a necessary result of the development of capitalism itself, Marx believes.

As the productive forces developed by capitalism grow, so, too, Marx claims, does the 'mass of misery, oppression, slavery, degradation, exploitation'. A stage is reached, however, at which the intrinsic social character of production comes increasingly into conflict with the private form under which it is organized under capitalism. The monopoly of capital becomes a 'fetter' on production and 'the centralization of the means of production and the socialization of labour at last reach a point where they become incompatible with their capitalist shell.' At this point, the shell 'bursts asunder' and the 'expropriators are themselves expropriated'.[125]

It is significant that the most extended discussion in *Das Kapital* of the nature of what is to replace capitalism also comes in the section on the Fetishism of Commodities, immediately following Marx's account of the illusions and deformations caused by the production of commodities. Marx moves on to compare capitalist production with other forms of production. He starts with Robinson Crusoe ('since political economy loves *Robinson-ades*')[126] whose productive activity he describes as rational and transparent:

> In spite of the variety of his productive functions, he knows that his labour in whatever form is but the activity of one and the same Robinson. Necessity itself compels him to apportion his time accurately between his different kinds of work . . . His stock-book contains a list of the objects of utility that belong to him, of the operations necessary for their production; and, lastly, of the labour time that definite quantities of those objects have, on average, cost him. All the relations between Robinson and the objects that form his self-created wealth are here so simple and clear that even Herr M. Wirth should be able to understand them without particular mental exertion.[127]

Production for Robinson, Marx says, is a purely administrative operation: the end is known, as are the resources available and the techniques by which the end could be attained. The choices facing him are thus simple ones. Marx then moves from 'Robinson's island, bathed in light' to

[125] Ibid., p. 791 [Eng. trans., p. 837].
[126] Ibid., p. 90 [Eng. trans., p. 88].
[127] Ibid., p. 91 [Eng. trans., p. 88].

discuss the 'dark ages of mediaeval Europe' and the patriarchal organization of production that we find, he says, 'on the historical threshold of all civilized peoples'[128] before alighting on:

> ... a community of free individuals, carrying on their labour with the means of production in common, in which the labour-power of all the different individuals is consciously applied as the combined labour-power of the community.[129]

Here, says Marx,

> All the characteristics of Robinson's labour are ... repeated, but with this difference, that they are social, instead of individual ... The social relations of the individual producers to their labour and to the products of their labour remain here transparently simple, in production as well as in distribution.[130]

The thought that a complex modern economy could present no problems that were different in principle from the problems faced by an individual producer producing for his own subsistence is simply incredible. As Alec Nove has rightly pointed out, given 'the vast scale and innumerable interdependencies of the modern industrial economy [the organization of production] will not and cannot be "simple".'[131] Even if the end of the individual's production is knowable, we have no right to assume the same regarding socialist production in an advanced society. Not only is the problem of assessing needs and desires on such a scale inconceivably more complicated than it is for a single individual, but decisions must be made regarding the objective weight to be given to each individual's subjective perception of need (this includes the problem of making interpersonal comparisons of welfare) and opportunities must be given for tastes to develop and change. Furthermore, even if, *per impossibile*, *we* could determine in a finite time what the end of production should be, it does not follow that it would then be simply a matter of choosing which of the available techniques to employ to achieve it: the allocation of labour involves the same kinds of question regarding the appropriate weight to give to subjective preferences as do consumption decisions. Furthermore, in any rational economy, there must be some incentive for producers to change their techniques of production – to innovate.[132] of the 'social

---

[128] Ibid., p. 91 [Eng. trans., pp. 88–9].
[129] Ibid., p. 92 [Eng. trans., p. 90].
[130] Ibid., pp. 92–3 [Eng. trans., pp. 90–1].
[131] *The Economics of Feasible Socialism*, p. 33.
[132] It is not necessary to labour these points here, for Nove has pursued them with patient reasonableness and informed passion. But it is worth noting how far this naive misconception regarding the simplicity and transparency of collective organization permeates the Marxist tradition. Nove cites the following examples, as he says, 'at random':

'Everything will be done quite simply without the so-called value' (Engels). 'Communist humanity will create the highest form of the administration of things, where the very

Gesamtarbeit', the latent collective subject, by means of the 'immediate social relationships' they enter into in their labour.

Yet the character of this connection to social *Gesamtarbeit* remains mysterious. What knowledge of the standpoint of *Gesamtarbeit* could the individual producers be supposed to have, and how would they get it? In what sense is that social decision-making power which, Marx says, consciously applies 'the combined labour of the community' that of the producers themselves? Just as Hegel leaves it open how it is that the individual comes to identify himself rationally with *Geist* (does everyone have to be a philosopher to recognize himself in it?) so Marx offers no account of how these two subjects – the individual producer and the social *Gesamtarbeiter* — are supposed to communicate with one another.

We have seen, then, that Marx, throughout his career as a social thinker, was committed to the idea that class societies in general and capitalism in particular are characterized by some form of false consciousness and that he believed that this pervasive false consciousness was an indispensable part of the reason why such societies can survive. But Marx has no consistent, single way of making that point. In this sense, he has no *theory* of ideology, only a series of models by which he hopes to capture and make plausible that basic commitment. What is worse, it would appear that in his most mature writing he is committed to two views: the idea that the contrast between surface appearance underlying reality is characteristic of science in general, on the one hand, and the idea that capital is a kind of self-realizing subject whose surface manifestations dissimulate its real character, on the other. Marx puts the two views together, no doubt without being aware of doing so, and this allows him to help himself to Hegelian conclusions while maintaining – falsely – that they involve no ontological commitments beyond those that would be made by any reasonable scientist.

----

problem of collective and individual [decision-making] will disappear as the human beings of the future will do what is called for by the dry figures of statistical calculation. Administration of men will vanish for ever' (Bukharin). 'The function of control and accountancy, becoming ever more simple, will be performed by each in turn' (Lenin). 'To organize the whole economy on the lines of the postal service . . . all under the leadership of the armed workers, that is our immediate [*sic*] aim' (Lenin). 'Capitalism has simplified the work of accounting and control, has reduced it to a comparatively simple system of bookkeeping, that any literate person can do' (Lenin). (Ibid., pp. 32–3.)

We know all too well how 'really existing socialism' has attempted to realize such organization in practice: either by unaccountable *dirigeisme* or by attempts to restore decisions over production to direct, face-to-face forms of social interaction; Bolshevik authoritarianism or infantile disorder.

7

Critical Theory

The previous chapter identified the dilemma facing the theory of ideology: either it must make good its claim to be scientific in the same way as, for example, biology, and give a proper underpinning to the notion of 'correspondence' (in which case, the theory must identify a mechanism connecting ideology to the social structure) or else it must be prepared to acknowledge and defend an explicit discontinuity between the social and the natural sciences.

Marx himself seems to come down on both sides of the issue. The models for the theory of ideology which are to be found in his work are conceptually quite distinct, however, and a choice between them has to be made. The analytical Marxists, as we have seen, opt for ontological parsimony. Yet their attempts to purge Marx's theory of Hegelian elements do so at the cost of being able to offer plausible foundations for the theory of ideology.

In this chapter we shall examine three strategies to be found in the writings of the so-called Frankfurt School that go in the other direction, starting with the dispute between Theodor Adorno and Walter Benjamin regarding the concept of the 'aura'. Although the two men were friends and regarded themselves as intellectual collaborators, the dispute that took place between them in the 1930s reveals a fundamental difference regarding the ontology of social life.[1] Adorno's writings take up and extend

---

[1] A note on chronology. Benjamin was born in 1892 and died in 1940; Adorno was born in 1903 and died in 1969. Benjamin's essay 'The Work of Art in the Age of its Mechanical Reproducibility' was published in 1936 in the journal of the *Institut für Sozialforschung* (of which Adorno was at the time a leading member – after the war, he was to be its co-director). The principal works of Adorno to which I shall refer are the *Negative Dialektik*, published in 1966, and the *Ästhetische*

Marx's conception of capitalism as a self-reproducing totality to produce the most thoroughgoing, consistent and philosophically sophisticated version of Marxist Hegelianism ever developed. Benjamin's work, on the other hand, contains a novel approach to the theory of ideology. Neither Hegelian nor reductively materialist, his highly original conception of experience offers an account, in outline at least, of the philosophical underpinnings of the correspondence between base and superstructure. Moreover, Benjamin's writing also contains a critique of the rationalist view of the self which, as I have argued, has dominated not just Marxism but the entire Western tradition of thought about false consciousness.

I The 'Aura'

The concept of the aura was introduced by Benjamin as a way of characterizing that quality of numinousness, traditionally thought to be characteristic of authentic (and original) works of art. As he writes in 'The Work of Art in the Age of its Mechanical Reproducibility':

> We define the aura of [a natural object] as the unique phenomenon of a distance, however close it might be. If, while resting on a summer afternoon, you follow with your eyes a mountain range on the horizon, or a branch which casts its shadow over you, you experience the aura of those mountains, of that branch.[2]

The aura is, in the first place, a quality of our experience of objects, not necessarily restricted to the products of artistic creation. In the case of the work of art, this exalted quality (what Benjamin calls its 'cult-value') is closely tied to its religious or quasi-religious aspect – a remnant of the association between art and religion characteristic of pre-modern society:

> The definition of the aura as a 'unique phenomenon of distance however close it may be' represents nothing but the formulation of the cult value of the work of art in categories of space and time perception. Distance is the opposite of closeness. The essentially distant object is the unapproachable one.[3]

However, the 'desacralizing' processes of modern civilization – the development of industrial capitalism and the attendant rise of the masses – have, hand in hand with the purely technical fact of the increasing mechanical reproducibility of the art-work itself, diminished human

---

Theorie, which was published posthumously. Nevertheless, as Adorno himself always emphasized, the views expressed in those works expand but do not revise the positions taken by him in the 1930s (and, indeed, before).

[2] 'Das Kunstwerk im Zeitalter seiner technischen Reproduzierbarkeit', p. 479.

[3] Ibid., p. 480n.

beings' power to see and respond to this quality. Thus, the *uniqueness* of the work of art becomes increasingly questionable, and leads to the decline of its cultic function:

> [The contemporary decay of the aura] rests on two circumstances, both of which are related to the increasing significance of the masses in contemporary life. Namely, the desire of contemporary masses to bring things 'closer' spatially and humanly, which is just as ardent as their bent towards overcoming the uniqueness of every reality by accepting its reproduction . . . To pry an object from its shell, to destroy its aura, is the work of a perception whose 'sense of the universal equality of things' has increased to such a degree that it extracts it even from a unique object by means of reproduction.[4]

At first sight, this may appear as simply a Marxist version of the conventional conservative lament for the erosion of high culture. But Benjamin does not *disapprove* of this desacralizing process. Given that the auratic values of uniqueness and authenticity were themselves, in fact, a perceptual legacy from the work of art's cultic function, it follows that their elimination will open the way to a political form of art – a transition which he welcomes:

> . . . for the first time in world history mechanical reproduction emancipates the work of art from its parasitical dependence on ritual . . . But the instant the criterion of authenticity ceases to be applicable to artistic production, the total function of art is reversed. Instead of being based on ritual, it begins to be based on another practice – politics.[5]

Benjamin fails to make clear what this political form of art might amount to, and it is on this point that Adorno's objection to his analysis is first raised. On one level, the objection is that Benjamin's dismissal of the aura is too extreme: open as the traditional work of art is to criticism, to sweep aside its auratic qualities entirely leaves no basis for any distinction between art and propaganda. As Adorno was to put it in his *Ästhetische Theorie*:

> The deficiency of Benjamin's grandly conceived *theory of reproduction* remains that its bipolar categories do not allow differentiation between the conception of art which has been fundamentally *disideologized* and the abuse of aesthetic rationality for mass-exploitation and domination.[6]

Yet there is more at stake here than Adorno's preference for Schoenberg over Brecht. It is the fact that Adorno interprets the concept of aura from the point of view of a would-be materialist transformation of Idealist

---

[4] Ibid., p. 479.
[5] Ibid., pp. 481–2.
[6] *Ästhetische Theorie*, p. 90.

aesthetics that provides the key to his theoretical disagreement with Benjamin. To understand this transformation, we must look at Adorno's critique of Hegel.

II Adorno's Transformation of Idealism

There are two possible approaches that a materialist critic of Hegel might take. One is to argue that Hegel's dynamic and developmental conception of reality is indissoluble from the Idealist framework within which it is presented by Hegel himself, from which it follows that to reject the Idealist framework implies adopting a quite different conception of the nature of reality and of the forms of explanation that are appropriate to it. This, in effect, is the position taken by the analytical Marxists.[7] On the other hand, it is also possible to think (as the young Hegelians did) that Hegel's philosophy contains a truth in mystified or inverted form of which it is itself unaware and that the first step towards recovering that truth is to invert Hegel's own inversion.

Adorno holds the latter view. As he puts it at the beginning of the *Negative Dialektik*, only if Hegel's philosophy contains 'experiences which are – against Hegel's own emphases – independent of the Idealistic apparatus' can philosophy be something more than an *ex post facto* theory of science.[8] Thus the key to Adorno's relationship to Hegelianism lies in his attempt to produce a 'materialistic transformation' of Hegel by 'reading back' the concept of *Geist* as an enciphered representation of *society*: 'Beyond the philosophy of identity's magic circle, the transcendental subject can be deciphered as society, unconscious of its own self'.[9] Putting it in its most succinct form, Adorno writes: 'The World-Spirit is, but it is no such thing'.[10] In other words, the idea of *Geist* corresponds to something important about the nature of history and society, but to represent that subject as the realization of reason in history is to distort its nature.

What is concealed by the 'enciphering' of society in the concept of *Geist* is the oppressive nature of capitalist society, Adorno claims. It is true that the social process acts as a collective subject, operating in a way that goes beyond the intentions of the individuals who compose it. Yet the nature of this process in relation to individuals is repressive and antagonistic – an 'order of compulsion'. The idea of *Geist* is in every sense an *idealization*, for it represents what is really an antagonistic process as if it were the embodiment of harmony and reconciliation. Part of the purpose of 'negative dialectic' is to reverse that idealization and to expose the bogusness of its claims to universality:

---

[7] It is also the position argued for in *Hegel's Dialectic and its Criticism*.
[8] *Negative Dialektik*, p. 19.
[9] Ibid., p. 179.
[10] Ibid., p. 298.

The compulsive order of reality, which Idealism projected into the realm of the subject and of *Geist*, is to be translated back out of it . . . .The prior universality [of the process of production] is both true and false: true because it forms the 'ether' which Hegel calls *Geist*; untrue because its 'reason' is, as yet, no such thing, and its universality the product of particular interest.[11]

The Idealist representation of society under the form of *Geist* is encouraged by the form taken by society itself: it is the fact that social labour in a society of generalized commodity exchange (that is, capitalism) becomes independent of and in that sense prior to individuals that makes for the correspondence between the Idealist concept of *Geist* and the structure of society. Yet, for Adorno, the priority of the collective is a violation of the autonomy of the individual; it is (whether recognized as such by the individual or not) a form of compulsion:

Idealism which distilled [the abstract law-governedness of exchange] into its Absolute Spirit, at the same time enciphers the truth that the phenomena encounter this mediation in the form of a mechanism of compulsion. *That* is what is concealed behind the so-called problem of constitution.[12]

Adorno does not, however, just reverse the affirmative tinge that Hegel gives to the description of social reality by presenting it as part of the self-realization of *Geist*. He also thinks that a materialistic critique of Hegel requires a challenge to Hegel's account of *Geist*'s structure: in particular, Adorno rejects the monistic claim at the heart of Hegel's metaphysics that *Geist* is the source of all reality. *Geist*, Adorno counters, is not an ontological first cause, the 'ground of grounds'. It is only one pole in a social labour process cleft between mental and manual labour:

Geist is no isolated principle but one *moment* in social labour – that which is separated from the corporeal.[13]

Just as the structure of *Geist* is the product of a self-differentiating process, so, too, Adorno believes, capitalist society is essentially a series of expressions taken on by social labour. It follows from this that economic life and culture are not to be treated as an edifice (as the 'base' and 'superstructure' metaphor would suggest) but as the two extreme poles of a self-reproducing social totality. For Adorno, the social process is a totality of 'mediations', not subject to the kind of causal explanation to be found in the natural sciences. He makes the point in strikingly Hegelian language in one of his letters to Benjamin:

[11] Ibid., p. 22.
[12] Ibid., p. 57.
[13] *Drei Studien zu Hegel*, p. 270.

... I consider it methodologically unfortunate to treat individual striking features from the realm of the superstructure 'materialistically', by putting them into relation with corresponding features of the base, immediately and even causally [*unvermittelt und gar kausal*]. The materialistic determination of cultural characteristics is only possible as mediated by the *totality* [*Gesamtprozess*].[14]

It is apparent, then, Adorno's transformation of Hegel's concept of *Geist* incorporates both of the central claims made by the Hegelian interpretation of *Das Kapital*: the claim that capitalist society is defective and the claim that it is deceptive. On the one hand, the collective subject dominates individuals; social labour is alienated and takes the form of a social subject – capital – that dominates the individuals who are, in the end, the means by which it reproduces itself. But the idea of *Geist* also reflects the deceptiveness of the social process – its monistic ontology is encouraged by the way in which the priority of the universal over the particular *appears* to be the result of the innate creativity of that collective subject (when, in fact, it is only the *result* of the form taken by social labour under capitalism).

Given his general reading of Hegel's metaphysics and social theory, it is unsurprising that Adorno should interpret the concept of aura in terms of an application of the Marxist account of social labour to the Hegelian concept of *schöner Schein*.[15] *Schöner Schein*, according to the Idealists, results from the role of the authentic work of art as a symbolic presentation of a transcendent realm – a channel or a window through which to have access to what is universal. For Hegel, of course, that is its limitation. Art is a form of sensible manifestation of *Geist*, but one which is (for that very reason) occluded and imperfect: it cannot do justice to the true, universal character of the Idea.

The work of art, like the commodity whose use-value lies in consumption, is a product of social labour, Adorno argues. Ultimately, it is social labour that both transforms material reality and confers meaning on it (although that 'meaning' does not in all cases have an explicit, linguistic character). Under the regime of alienated social labour, the production of commodities for use has come to take on the purely instrumental character of a *Stoffwechsel* – a 'material exchange' – and the function of labour as a source of meaning has been lost. In this way, social labour is transformed into a narrowly economic concept, instead of being seen as the process that gives the social totality its structure. Production in the sphere of art lies outside the main process by which society reproduces itself physically, and so, although artistic production carries within it many of the deceptions and deformities characteristic of commodity production in general, it still

---

[14] Letter to Benjamin, 10 November 1938, *Über Walter Benjamin*, pp. 138–9.
[15] Rolf Tiedemann, the editor of the collected works of both Benjamin and Adorno, and the author of a doctoral thesis on Benjamin written under Adorno's supervision, asserts the connection explicitly in an encyclopaedia article: 'the "*schöner Schein*", as ascribed to art by Idealist aesthetics, rests on auratic *Schein*'. (R. Tiedemann, 'Aura'.)

retains a trace of the freedom that has been eliminated from production elsewhere and this manifestation of *Geist* (understood in the sense of society) is the source of art's *Schein*, its ability to 'point beyond itself':

> That by which works of art, as they become appearance, are more than what they are: that is their *Geist*.[16]

Insofar as it is the outcome of a labour-process that has not been deprived of its capacity to confer meaning onto its products, *Schein* represents an implicit criticism of the alienation of production elsewhere in society:

> Magic itself, when emancipated from its claim to be real, is an element of enlightenment; its *Schein* desacralizes the desacralized world. That is the dialectical ether in which art today takes place.[17]

Although art is detached from the processes of social labour by which society physically reproduces itself, the processes that are embodied in artistic production are expressive of society in a way that material production no longer is. Thus art has a general social significance just because of its apparent isolation:

> The relation of works of art to society is comparable to Leibniz's monad. Windowless – that is to say, without being conscious of society, and in any event without being constantly and necessarily accompanied by this consciousness – the works of art . . . represent society.[18]

In this way, the work of art's character as *Schein* is, in Adorno's apparently paradoxical phrase, both true and false; *Schein* is something deceptive because it creates the illusion that the aesthetic quality of the work of art is a property that is intrinsic to it, without relation to non-aesthetic reality. Yet, in fact, it is *Schein*, the product of the underlying process of social labour, that creates the link between the work of art and society in general:

> But *Geist* is not simply *Schein*. It is also truth. It is not only the fraudulent image of an independent entity but also the negation of all false independence.[19]

Thus, just as *Schein* points beyond itself to a transcendent realm, according to the German Idealists, so, for Adorno, it is the sign of the 'immanent universality' of the art object. But in this case what art is pointing to is not a domain of Platonic universals, but a historical process:

[16] *Ästhetische Theorie*, p. 134.
[17] Ibid., p. 93.
[18] *Introduction to the Sociology of Music*, p. 211.
[19] *Ästhetische Theorie*, pp. 165–6.

Such immanent universality of the individual is objective as sedimented history.[20]

Adorno believes that the task of interpretation is to reconstruct the activity that has given an object its meaning – its 'sedimented history'. Interpretation aims to recover the 'immanent universality' of apparently isolated phenomena, like the 'monadic' work of art, by revealing the social processes of which *Schein* is the outcome. Indeed, this is characteristic not just of Adorno's aesthetics but of his approach to philosophy in general. In his discussion of Husserl's claim that phenomenology gives access to a region of essential truths which could be directly known by what he calls the 'intuition of essence', Adorno seeks to reinterpret the claim in the light of his own doctrine of the constitutive role of society *qua* transcendental subject:

> 'Intuition of essence' is the name for the physiognomic way of regarding intellectual [*geistige*] matters. It is legitimated by the fact that the intellectual realm is not constituted by the consciousness which is directed towards it cognitively. It it constituted, rather, well beyond the individual who originates it, in the collective life of *Geist*, and is objectively grounded according to its immanent laws.[21]

Given the fact that immanent universality results from the operation on the object of a meaning-conferring social process, philosophy should attempt to retrace and thereby in a sense re-animate the latter. The particular task of philosophical aesthetics is to 'save' the *Schein* of works of art through the theoretical reconstruction of the sedimented layers of *Geist*'s activity:

> ... no work of art has its content other than by the *Schein* in its own form. The central part of aesthetics would, thus, be the salvation of the *Schein*, and the emphatic justification of art, the legitimation of its truth, depends on this salvation.[22]

But the fact that even authentic art (art that manages to retain its *Schein*) remains limited to a demarcated sphere of life makes it – like religion in the 'Towards a Critique of Hegel's Philosophy of Right. Introduction.' – at best an imaginary flower on the chains of society: a model of emancipation that distracts from the real bondage of social production at the same time as providing a contrast with it. In setting art in its social context, aesthetic theory has a dual role, therefore: to use the *Schein* of autonomous art to provide a critique of heteronomous economic life while, at the same time, criticizing the ideology of art for art's sake.

This is why Adorno opposes Benjamin's acceptance of the decline of

---

[20] *Negative Dialektik*, p. 165.
[21] Ibid., p. 89.
[22] *Ästhetische Theorie*, p. 164.

the aura so vehemently. The elimination of *Schein*, he believes, would be a sign that cultural production, too, had been reduced to a part of 'ordinary' economic life and that socially meaningful art had been abandoned in favour of the 'culture industry', which reproduces the existing social system by satisfying its members' emotional needs as cold-heartedly and instrumentally as, traditionally, capitalism has satisfied their material needs. In that case, art would no longer have a critical role at all: the emancipatory baby would have gone out with the ideological bath-water.

Plainly, there is a clear line of continuity from Hegel's aesthetics, through Marx's theory of fetishism, to Adorno's aesthetics, as the following five points make clear:

1 *Non-material property*   In each case a material object is invested with a non-material property or power (for Hegel and Adorno, *schöner Schein*; for Marx the power of exchanging at a value).

2 *Agency*   The object has that non-material property as the result of an agency that has operated upon it. (For Hegel, this is *Geist*; for Marx, the social labour embodied in the object; for Adorno, *Geist* and social labour are equivalent.)

3 *Objectivity*   Perceivers who recognize the non-material property are not simply deluded or misguided, all three authors claim: it really is present in the object. (This is the difference between Hegel, Marx and Adorno and Enlightenment theorists such as Hume or de Brosses.)

4 *Deceptiveness*   Perceivers *are* deluded to the extent that they fail to recognize the agency that is the true source of the non-material property. In the Hegelian account of the nature of art perceivers believe that *schöner Schein* comes from the individual genius of the artist, rather than from the role of the artist as a vehicle for *Geist*; in the case of the fetishism of commodities, they believe falsely that the non-material property is intrinsic to the object in question; according to Adorno, *Schein* is deceptive to the extent that it obscures the social origins of art's meaning.

5 *Defectiveness*   The whole phenomenon arises because the agent is inadequate or incomplete in some way. For Hegel, *schöner Schein* is a product of *Geist* at a stage when it is not fully realized; for Marx and Adorno, commodity fetishism and artistic *schöner Schein* are products of a situation in which social labour has become fragmented under the domination of capital.

Adorno's aesthetics are intended to take up the quasi-Hegelian conception of capitalism as a self-articulating totality to be found in outline in *Das Kapital*: their objective is to extend and complete Marx's account rather than to compete with it. Yet in taking up and transforming Hegel's concept of *schöner Schein*, Adorno avoids a difficulty that Marx's account of the fetishism of commodities had failed to deal with. The illusions that Marx describes – that commodities have their values intrinsically and that social labour is useful only derivatively, in virtue of the market value of its products – are not perceptual qualities but *false beliefs* attaching to the commodity. If it is true that capitalism is a *deceptive object* then it is plausible to think that such false beliefs will be objectively encouraged (just as the apparent motion of the sun encourages geo-centrism). But, although Marx talks about 'the objective illusion [*gegenständlichen Schein*] through which the social character of labour appears to be an objective character of the products themselves',[23] it is not plausible to claim that these beliefs will remain unaffected by contrary knowledge. (In other words, Marx's version of point (1) above fails to substantiate point (3).) Insofar as *schöner Schein* is a perceptible quality attaching to objects as a result of the action of an agency, however, this is not a problem for Adorno's theory: perceptible qualities are, typically, knowledge-independent.

Adorno's idea of social labour as an objective source of meaning implies a view of commodity fetishism that is at least rather different from (if not clearly incompatible with) that presented in *Das Kapital*. On this view (which is also to be found in Lukács's *History and Class-Consciousness*) the fetishism of commodities does not so much consist in the *attribution* to the commodity of a property that it would naturally lack as the *elimination* of an immediate quality that it *ought to* have: the significance that objects should acquire as a result of social labour but which alienated labour under capitalism is incapable of conferring on them. The characteristic of commodity fetishism on this view is *reification* – the reduction of what is vital or meaning-bearing to something merely thinglike.

Adorno's theory has the attraction – and the questionableness – typical of Hegelian theories. It offers a comprehensive solution to a number of the most central problems of the Marxist theory of ideology. It offers an account of the relationship between material production and the realm of ideas that does not have to treat the one as a mere reflex or echo of the other. Moreover, like Hegel's doctrine of the cunning of reason, it offers an explanation of how agents can be dominated by processes that go beyond their own foresight and intentions, without depicting them as simply passive or manipulated. Finally, it offers an account of the objectivity of illusion: of how *Schein* results from a supra-individual agency. Yet these answers come at a philosophical price – that of accepting a central, overarching concept of social labour whose implications are not fully clear.

As a materialist, Adorno must deny that natural processes are intrinsically meaningful because nature itself has a purpose independent of human activity, so what can he mean when he says that history is 'sedimented' in phenomena? How can a materialist say that an object literally 'bears in itself' anything other than a causal natural history? Social labour, on the

[23] *Das Kapital*, 1, p. 88 [Eng. trans., pp. 85–6].

materialist understanding, transforms an object physically. It also represents the realization of a purpose on the part of the person who performs that transformation – and this purpose or intention can be recognized by an observer who sees the product. But how is the collective life of *Geist* supposed to 'sediment' itself in the product? It is at this point that Adorno fails to give a clear answer. Instead of answering the question of how meaning processes can have this quasi-natural 'objectivity' in relation to individuals, he slips back into Idealist terminology that conceals the dilemma. The purpose of 'negative dialectic', he says, is to free the 'mediations' which whatever is given immediately conceals within itself.[24] But what, precisely, is the philosophical status of a 'mediation'? Is it a *causal*, a *logical*, or a *semantic* relation? For Hegel, of course, it embraces all three: mediations are 'moments', as he puts it, in the fundamental rational structure of reality. But Adorno, who rejects Hegel's assumption of an Absolute Subject, has no right to assimilate the three in a way that depends on this assumption. And yet, if he does not, he has no way of explaining the crucial feature of his notion of *Geist*: its ascription to processes of meaning the objectivity usually reserved for material causal processes.

It is his transformation of the Idealist doctrine of *Geist* which provides the intellectual substance behind Adorno's criticism of Benjamin. A letter written to Benjamin in the last year of Benjamin's life, in 1940, makes this clear:

> You write in *Baudelaire* . . . 'To perceive the aura of an appearance means to invest it with the ability to raise its gaze.' This differs from earlier formulations by the use of the concept of *investment*. Is it not an indication of that aspect which, in *Wagner*, I made fundamental to the construction of phantasmagoria, namely, the moment of *human labour*. Is not the aura, perhaps, the trace of the forgotten human element in the thing, and does not therefore this form of forgetting relate to what you see as experience? *One is almost tempted to go so far as to see the foundation in experience, underlying the speculations of Idealism, in the endeavour to retain this trace* – in those things, indeed, which have become alien.[25]

This letter – characteristic in the manner of its attempt to lead Benjamin back towards Adorno's own ideas – gives expression to the two central elements in Adorno's theory I have stressed: Adorno's association of the aura with the concept of social labour and his interpretation of the Idealist doctrines of *Schein* and of *Geist* in terms of the latter. For Adorno, it is labour, the 'forgotten human element', that gives significance to the objects that aesthetic theory sets out to interpret.

Adorno himself certainly considered his letter to be of theoretical significance, since he reproduced it in a collection he published called *Über*

---

[24] *Negative Dialektik*, p. 48.
[25] Letter to Benjamin, 29 February 1940, *Über Walter Benjamin*, p. 160; my emphasis.

Walter Benjamin. But even more illuminating, in my view, is Benjamin's reply, written only months before his death. For, in that reply, Benjamin quite clearly and explicitly rejects Adorno's proposal:

> But if, indeed, it should be the case that the aura is a matter of a 'forgotten human element', then it is not necessarily that which is present in labour. The tree or the bush which are invested are not made by men. It must be a human element in things which is *not* endowed by labour. On this I would like to take my stand.[26]

In rejecting the equation of meaning and the labour process, Benjamin is distancing himself from what is at the same time the most central and the most dubious element of Adorno's theory. Clearly, Benjamin, at least, believed that he and Adorno had quite different conceptions of the sources of the aura. On the interpretation of his thought to be presented in the next sections, he was absolutely right.

III Benjamin's Marxism

That Benjamin should have regarded himself as a Marxist at all seemed astonishing to those who knew his early work. Nothing could be further removed from what one would normally understand by 'materialism' than Benjamin's early writings, with their predilection for mystical theories of language and unblushingly anti-scientific metaphysics. Nevertheless, in 1931, three years after the publication of *The Origin of German Tragic Drama*, the obscure masterpiece which he had intended as his habilitation thesis, we find him writing about it to the Swiss editor, Max Rychner, in the following terms:

> ... what I did not know at the time of its composition became more and more clear to me soon after: that, from my very particular position on the philosophy of language, there exists a connection – however strained and problematic – to the viewpoint of dialectical materialism.[27]

Benjamin was never in a position to pursue the life of independent scholarship for which alone he regarded himself as suited, and one effect of this has been to create an image of him (like Kafka, whom he so much admired) as a helpless victim, a kind of frail and exotic butterfly, blown on the gales of Europe between the wars. One should treat this with a considerable degree of caution, however. At least where his work was concerned, Benjamin was self-assured, even calculating. Nor was he ever the withdrawn, other-worldly figure that his fascination with the forgotten by-ways of intellectual history might lead one to imagine. From his school-

---

[26] Letter to Adorno, 7 May 1940, in W. Benjamin, *Briefe*, p. 849.
[27] Letter to Max Rychner, 7 March 1931, in W. Benjamin, *Briefe*, p. 523.

days he showed a strong commitment to radical political activity. Though it was, no doubt, his love-affair with Asja Lacis, the Soviet communist whom he met on Capri, which brought him to think more seriously about Marxism than before, there is no reason at all to suppose that even that forceful personality could have manipulated Benjamin's work into a direction which he himself did not want it to take.

Working on his own left Benjamin heavily dependent for intellectual companionship on three friends, all major figures in their own right: Gershom Scholem, Bertolt Brecht and Theodor Adorno, and the relationship to these three adds a further biographical complication to the question of Benjamin's Marxism. Inevitably, it has been their perspectives – above all, those of Scholem and Adorno, the devoted guardians of Benjamin's literary legacy and tireless promoters of his reputation – which have dominated later interpretations. Yet, genuine and close as his relationship was with all three men, it did not prevent Benjamin from preserving a certain intellectual distance, and even, at times, playing one off against the other. What is more, Benjamin knew well that all three had reservations about his Marxism – reservations which, of course, only increased his innate caginess.

Brecht and Scholem – opposed to each other in every other way imaginable – were equally dismissive of the idea of Benjamin as a Marxist. Scholem spoke of Benjamin's 'Janus face'; he was, Scholem said, caught in theoretical vacillation: 'torn between his sympathy for a mystical theory of language and the necessity, felt equally strongly, to combat it from within the framework of a Marxist world-view'.[28] Brecht – typically – was even more trenchant. His comment on Benjamin's 'Marxist' essay, 'The Work of Art in the Age of its Mechanical Reproducibility': 'All mysticism, from an attitude against mysticism. This is how the materialist view of history is adapted! It is quite dreadful.'[29]

Whereas Brecht and Scholem reject the idea of Benjamin as a Marxist out of hand, Adorno's attitude is much less simple. It is true that Adorno did not take Benjamin's early ideas to be inherently incompatible with Marxism. On the contrary, he made the idea of their reconciliation his own. Yet he was by no means convinced by Benjamin's own attempts to bring the two together. In the letters by which the two men kept in touch through their years in exile in the 1930s, Adorno repeatedly expressed the fear that Benjamin, under the influence of Brecht, was sacrificing the dialectical subtlety of his early work in favour of a simplistic 'vulgar-Marxism'. In the face of this, Adorno took his own task to be 'to hold your arm steady until Brecht's sun has sunk once more into exotic waters'.[30]

Adorno's passionate engagement with Benjamin's work was, notoriously,

[28] Walter Benjamin: die Geschichte einer Freundschaft, p. 260.
[29] Bertolt Brecht, Arbeitsjournal, 25 July 1938, quoted in W. Benjamin, Gesammelte Schriften, vol. I.3, p. 1025.
[30] Letter to Benjamin, 18 March 1936, in T. W. Adorno, Über Walter Benjamin, p. 134.

to become the source of much bitterness. As the German New Left rediscovered Benjamin in the 1960s, suspicions were raised that Adorno had used Benjamin's financial dependence on the Institute for Social Research and his subsequent control over access to Benjamin's unpublished writings to promote that side of Benjamin's work which was most congenial to his own ideas. Exaggerated though many of these accusations were, there can be no doubt that Adorno's intellectual relations with Benjamin were marked with something of the intensity, possessiveness, and difficulty of those between master and disciple. To write, as Adorno once did to Benjamin, claiming to speak as 'the advocate of your own intentions', cannot have made his criticisms any easier to bear.

Brecht, Scholem and Adorno notwithstanding, we should not suppose that Benjamin simply drifted into Marxism for personal and political reasons, or in response to contemporary events in Germany, without proper consideration of what was involved intellectually. In support of this, I shall argue, first, that there are important continuities between Benjamin's early 'theological' and his later would-be Marxist thought, and, second, that the latter did indeed entail a substantial and significant intellectual disagreement with Adorno (of the depth of which Adorno himself does not seem to have been aware, either at the time or later).

Most important of the continuities between Benjamin's early and mature thought is his allegiance to a distinctive form of Kantian philosophy. He enunciates this first in an early essay (written as a twentieth birthday present for Gershom Scholem) called 'On the Programme of the Philosophy to Come'. Here Benjamin argues that Kant's philosophy is to be accepted, but criticized. What is to be accepted, he thinks – and this, I believe, is a matter on which he never changed his mind – is the fundamental turn given to philosophy by Kant; what Kant himself calls his 'Copernican revolution' – a turn away from purporting to investigate the nature of reality directly, towards an investigation of our *experience* of that reality. Yet, fundamental though Benjamin considers Kant's turn to the question of experience to be, he is critical of what he takes to be the restricted conception of experience – as if to experience were simply to catalogue sense-images under formal, general rules – which Kant himself presupposes. This critical encounter with Kant leads to what Benjamin proclaims to be contemporary philosophy's prime task: 'to undertake the foundation of a higher conception of experience, under the auspices of Kantian thought'.[31] Scholem, in his touching and revealing memoir of Benjamin, recalls a conversation from that time in which Benjamin explained his point more vividly:

He spoke of the breadth of the concept of experience which this meant, and which, according to him, included the mental and psychological links between man and the world in areas not yet reached by knowledge. When I made the

[31] 'Über das Programm der kommenden Philosophie', p. 160.

point that, in that case, the mantic disciplines would be legitimately included in this conception of experience, he replied with an extreme formulation: A philosophy which does not include the possibility of divination from coffee-grounds cannot be true.[32]

Thus, even at his most mystical and apparently anti-scientific, Benjamin's chief concern is Kantian; that is to say, he wants to articulate the distinctiveness of certain kinds of experience – the allegorical world of the *Trauerspiel*, for example, or the struggle against myth in Greek tragedy – which a scientifically oriented culture dismisses or takes to be insignificant. But this does not mean that their claims must be treated as cognitively valid; the experiences are important in their own right, not as alternatives to scientific knowledge. It is the shared framework of experience, not the idea of social labour, that is the 'forgotten human element' referred to by Benjamin in his letter to Adorno on the aura.

The emphasis on the concept of experience is the key to Benjamin's relation to Marxism in general and, more particularly, to the theory of ideology, for it is the means by which he confronts the question of what connects different areas of a culture, allowing us to see a common identity in their apparent diversity. While for Hegel, and the Hegelian Marxist Adorno (as well as those cultural historians whom Gombrich describes as subscribing to 'Hegelianism without Hegel'), cultures are differentiated totalities, unified by the fact that they emanate from a single centre, Benjamin poses the question in terms of the relation between 'base' and 'superstructure'.

In a highly significant fragment from the *Passagen-Werk* (the study of life and art in nineteenth-century Paris that he worked on but failed to complete during the 1930s) Benjamin proposes his own answer to this problem of the nature of the determination of the ideological superstructure:

At first sight it seems as though Marx only wanted to establish a causal connection between superstructure and base. But his remark that the ideologies of the superstructure mirror relationships in a false and distorted manner goes beyond this. The question is, in fact: if, in a certain sense, the base determines the thought- and experience-content of the superstructure, yet this determination is not a simple mirroring, how (leaving aside the question of its causal origin) is it to be characterized? As its expression. The economic conditions under which society exists come to expression in the superstructure.[33]

The question of Benjamin's relation to Marxism can thus be brought into focus in the form of a specific problem: how the existence of such an 'expressive' relationship between base and superstructure can be accom-

[32] *Walter Benjamin: die Geschichte einer Freundschaft*, p. 77.
[33] *Das Passagen-Werk*, vol. 1, p. 495.

modated within the framework of his conception of experience. The
solution Benjamin proposes emerges most perspicuously in a short piece,
'On the Mimetic Faculty', written in 1933. Here, once again, Benjamin
pursues his challenge to the flattened, Enlightenment conception of
experience. Even in the modern world, he claims (and Freud is just as
important a witness to this as Marx) human beings show a disposition to
structure their experience according to what he terms 'non-sensible
resemblances' – resemblances, that is, in which similarity is not just a
matter of 'mapping' or visible correspondence, and which may appear
bizarre or even occult when measured against the standards of a world-
view for which that is the only kind of experience imaginable.

Scholem (for whose reaction to the piece Benjamin waited with
particular eagerness) regarded it as another instance of the Janus face – a
return (welcome to his mind) to the mystical stance of the early writings;
it lacked, he said, 'even the slightest hint of a materialist view of
language'.[34] But that is not how Benjamin himself saw things. Admittedly,
the essay is quite at odds with modern scientific reductionism. But there
is another sense in which the intentions behind 'On the Mimetic Faculty'
might reasonably be described as materialist, as a kind of Marxist-
Kantianism. What the essay attempts to do is to undermine a perspective
from which certain phenomena must either be dismissed, or, if they are
acknowledged, treated as in some way occult or transcendent. Nowhere
does Benjamin come closer to the ideas of Wittgenstein than here. Only
because the 'enlightened scientific' conception is taken as a norm are
certain experiences made to seem supernatural; they are treated as such
just because they go beyond the presupposed scientific perspective.

In a very interesting letter to Adorno's wife, Gretel, Benjamin drew a
parallel between this essay and an essay of Freud's on telepathy (the essay,
I believe, now forms the second of the *New Introductory Lectures on
Psychoanalysis*).[35] What impressed Benjamin was that, in this essay, Freud,
like himself, takes seriously a phenomenon often dismissed; not treating
telepathy as something occult, but seeing it, rather, as a type of perception,
operating at a level not normally appreciated or acknowledged.

Mimetic experience is what allows us to identify 'correspondences'
between different areas of social life ('similarity is the *organon* of experience', Benjamin writes in the *Passagen-Werk*), and makes plausible the
idea of an expressive relationship between economy and ideology. The

[34] *Walter Benjamin: die Geschichte einer Freundschaft*, p. 259.
[35] The letter thanks Gretel Adorno for sending a 'psycho-analytic almanac', and expresses the
hope that she herself had read the 'contribution by Freud on telepathy and psychoanalysis'.
Benjamin mentions that he recognizes in Freud's view that 'telepathy' is the 'phylogenetic
precursor' of language his own thoughts in 'On the Mimetic Faculty'. Freud treats telepathy as a
kind of mimetic communication in which the subjects are not consciously aware of the channels
by which communication is taking place between them. I have not been able to trace the almanac
in question, but, of Freud's writings on telepathy, it is the treatment in the *New Introductory
Lectures* (written down by Freud but never delivered as lectures) that matches this description
best.

expressive relationship obtains because similarities have been transmitted by society's members (without, of course, their being aware of it) at the deepest, collective, levels of their experience. The task of the social theorist is to reawaken that experience from its sedimentations and incrustations. Phenomena which seem the most dissonant and obscure – the interior exteriors of the *passages* themselves, the passion for roulette, the vogue for panoramas – may turn out to be the most revelatory. What Novalis once said of poetry is also true of Benjamin's *Urgeschichte*: the more personal, peculiar and temporal a phenomenon is, the closer it may stand to the centre.

Needless to say, this approach makes the concept of experience bear an enormous weight; there is, inevitably perhaps, a certain element of circularity. The 'unseen affinities', referring, as they do, to a subterranean level of awareness, are not such as, immediately and unambiguously, to strike the uninstructed observer; and yet it is their existence which provides Benjamin's concept of experience with its only possible verification. Proof, thus, necessarily makes reference to the reader's own intuition – a point which Benjamin acknowledges in language quite strikingly reminiscent of Wittgenstein: 'Method of this work: literary montage. I have nothing to say – only to show.'[36] Yet there is always the worry that what are shown as the latent significance of cultural phenomena are, in point of fact, no more than subjective associations, made plausible by the shared political commitment of author and reader.

Furthermore, the necessary reference to intuition places a severe limit on how far Benjamin's 'cultural Marxism' can be given expression in terms of the sort of scientifically oriented discursive theory characteristic of Marx's own 'economic Marxism'. If Benjamin's writing often seems 'impressionistic' or unsystematic then this is because its central purpose – the eliciting of correspondences – cannot be carried out in methodical fashion. Hence, it is hard to see how he could, in principle, have responded to Adorno's criticism that his treatment of his material was insufficiently theoretical: ' ... the work is located at the cross-roads between magic and positivism. This place is bewitched. Only theory can break the spell: your own fearless, good speculative theory.'[37]

What then of the decline of the aura? If the doctrine of the aura is read as corresponding to the Idealist concept of *Schein*, it follows that the disintegration of the aura implies the loss of art's potential for intrinsic meaning. So the political art, by which Benjamin hopes auratic art will be replaced, can, it would appear, be no more than instrumental. It will be purely a means to generate the appropriate, 'proletarian' emotional responses.

But from Benjamin's own point of view the alternative is not so simple. There is a parallel here to his rehabilitation of allegory in *The Origin of Tragic Drama*. There Benjamin rejected the opposition between the

---

[36] *Das Passagen-Werk*, vol. 1, p. 574.
[37] Letter to Benjamin, 10 November 1938, in T. W. Adorno, *Über Walter Benjamin*, p. 140.

'intrinsic' meaningfulness of symbolic art and the 'conventional' meaning of allegory, for allegory, he claimed: '. . . is not a technique of image-play, but *expression*, as language is expression, indeed, as script is.'[38] Similarly, in 'The Work of Art in the Age of its Mechanical Reproducibility' he ascribes a distinctive experiential quality (what he calls, in contrast to 'cult value', 'exhibition value') to post-auratic art. Thus, for Benjamin, it seems that the work of art in the age of mechanical reproduction *can* escape what appears to Adorno as an exhaustive alternative: it need be neither *Schein* nor pure propaganda. While Adorno, like the German Idealists from whom he took over the concept, makes *Schein* into the identifying characteristic of authentic art, Benjamin envisages a future form of art that, like the world of Baroque allegory, will be intrinsically meaningful but not based on *Schein*.

Benjamin is usually seen as a brilliant (if somewhat mystical) aphorist, rather than the proponent of an original and consistent social theory. Yet, his 'Marxist-Kantianism' does, it seems to me, have claims to be treated as equal in significance to the more familiar Marxist-Hegelianism represented by Adorno. In particular, it takes up implicitly the challenge of relating base and superstructure in a way that is wholly original. Benjamin proposes a mechanism for the way in which the 'superstructure' corresponds to the 'base' (the 'unseen affinities' generated through the mimetic dimension of experience) which is wholly unlike the quasi-Darwinian one associated with functional explanation. We might describe Benjamin's conception of 'non-sensible resemblances' as a form of 'tacit knowedge' – the mimetic capacity that it brings into play amounts to a perceptual capacity operating at that level that Freud described as the 'pre-conscious'.

Given that the Marxist tradition has been split between those who have wished to establish the continuity between the explanations of Marxist sociology and the natural sciences and those, like Adorno, who have maintained its affinity with Hegel, it is not perhaps surprising that Benjamin's Marxism, which fits into neither model, should not have been appreciated. But the idea that what connects different parts of a culture is a kind of tacit knowledge has played a role outside the borders of Marxism, in social anthropology in particular.

It can be found, for example, in the writings of the most celebrated anthropologist of modern times, Claude Lévi-Strauss. Lévi-Strauss's conception of myth is (needless to say) complex and controversial. At times he has encouraged an interpretation of himself as a kind of Chomsky of *la pensée sauvage*: isolating from the diversity of particular myths a few invariant structures that form the basic grammar of mythical thought.[39]

---

[38] *Der Ursprung des deutschen Trauerspiels*, p. 338.
[39] But, as Dan Sperber among others has noted, this cannot be the end of the story. Although we need to know the grammar of a language before we can settle the meaning of what is being said by means of it, its meaning does not *consist in* its grammar. So, by analogy, even if we accept that Lévi-Strauss has identified the grammar of myth, this still leaves the question of what myths *mean* (*Rethinking Symbolism*, Ch. 3).

However this may be, the role of correspondences in Lévi-Strauss's account of social life becomes apparent when he turns his attention to the problem of intercultural comparison. In the collection of his essays published as *Structural Anthropology*, for example, Lévi-Strauss offers an account of how we might contrast English with French or Chinese styles of cookery, using an analysis of whether certain key contrasts (between hot and bland food, native and foreign ingredients, and so on) are made salient within them or not. He concludes with a bold suggestion:

> Once we have defined these differential structures, there is nothing absurd about inquiring whether they belong strictly to the sphere considered or whether they may be encountered (often in transformed fashion) in other spheres of the same society. And, if we find these structures to be common to several spheres, we have the right to conclude that we have reached *a significant knowledge of the unconscious attitudes of the society or societies under consideration.*[40]

The best way to understand such statements (and on this point I find myself very much in agreement with the view of the matter of the French anthropologist Dan Sperber) is as a claim about the tacit knowledge that is specific to a particular society: despite not being able to express that knowledge in explicit or theoretical terms, the members of a culture share the capacity to 'map' one area of their experience into another one in such a way that they can recognize (though not articulate) its appropriateness. Speculations of this sort remind us that Lévi-Strauss at one point described his enterprise as a contribution to 'the theory of superstructures'.[41] They remind us, too, that he regarded himself as an 'inconstant disciple' of Émile Durkheim.[42] According to Durkheim, religion (and thus, by extension, myth) is 'something eminently social'.[43]

The way that religion plays this role, according to Durkheim, is by expressing in sacred form the structures of society:

> Above all, it is a system of ideas with which individuals represent to themselves the society of which they are members and the obscure but intimate relations which they have with it. This is its primary function; and, though metaphorical and symbolic, this representation is not unfaithful. Quite on the contrary, it translates everything essential in the relations which are to be explained.[44]

---

[40] *Structural Anthropology*, p. 87; my emphasis.
[41] *The Savage Mind*, p. 130.
[42] *Structural Anthropology*, dedication.
[43] Religious representations are collective representations which express collective realities; the rites are a manner of acting which take rise in the midst of assembled groups and which are destined to excite, maintain or recreate certain mental states in these groups. (*The Elementary Forms of Religious Life*, p. 10.)
[44] Ibid., p. 225.

Although religion and its cosmology may appear to be an attempt to come to terms with the frightening and alien realities of the physical world, that is not so; indeed, if it were, then it would be mysterious as to how it could survive when it is so obviously inadequate.

This aspect of Durkheimianism was to become orthodoxy among anthropologists,[45] although the mechanism by which the social relations represented are supposed to be connected to the realm in which they are expressed remains as obscure in Durkheim as in Marx's own claim about the correspondence between base and superstructure.[46] For Mary Douglas, for example, the role of culture as an expression of social structure is fundamental. As she writes in *Purity and Danger*:

> Any culture is a series of related structures which comprise social forms, values, cosmology, the whole of knowledge through which all experience is mediated ... *The rituals enact the form of social relations and, in giving these relations visible expression, they enable people to know their own society.*[47]

For Douglas, social beliefs (for example, regarding pollution and sexual danger) are best regarded as 'symbols of the relation between parts of society, ... mirroring designs of hierarchy or symmetry which apply in the larger social system.'[48]

However, both Douglas and Lévi-Strauss treat the fact (as they suppose it to be) that human beings share such 'unconscious attitudes' or that they have the capacity to give their social relations 'visible expression' in rituals or institutions as a starting point for ethnographic investigation. It is not a belief whose presuppositions they explore. Neither author explains what such claims assume about the nature of human beings and their cognitive capacities. What is involved in the idea that human beings act socially in such a way as to manifest 'common structures' in a variety of contexts? It is here, it seems to me, that we encounter just those problems to which Benjamin's 'Marxist-Kantianism' – his assertion of the existence of a mimetic capacity operating alongside the regular and familiar processes of reasoning – was supposed to represent a solution.

Not that one should underestimate its difficulties. One cannot deny that Adorno was right to argue that the objectivity of Benjamin's theory rests

---

[45] Thus Edmund Leach (who is, in fact, very critical of the 'prejudice in favour of equilibrium' embodied in the Durkheimian approach) writes:

In sum, then, my view here is that ritual action and belief are alike to be understood as forms of symbolic statement about the social order. (*Political Systems of Highland Burma*, p. 14.)

[46] According to Durkheim, the connection was supposed to lie in the existence of the *conscience collective* and the priority of the latter over the individual consciousness: cultures cannot fail to express the content of the *conscience collective* and the *conscience collective*, in turn, cannot but embody the form of the social structure. However, this assumption seems to be no less of an ontologically questionable (and empirically unfalsifiable) assertion than the Hegelian conception of *Geist* that it resembles so markedly.

[47] *Purity and Danger*, p. 128; my emphasis.

[48] Ibid., p. 4.

on the claim of a shared, pre-discursive level of collective experience, and it may be that this historicized version of the Kantian 'transcendental subject' will prove just as problematic as Adorno's attempt to invoke the concept of social labour as a surrogate of Hegel's *Geist*. However, if it were sustained, then it would fill the explanatory lacuna that otherwise disqualifies the base-superstructure model of ideology.

IV Anti-Rationalism and False Consciousness

Benjamin's conception of experience underpins his account of the connection of base and superstructure. But it is significant, too, for the way that it involves an account of false consciousness quite different from the rationalist conceptions that have dominated Western thought about false consciousness, Marxism included. For Benjamin, emancipation is not about increasing the discretionary power of the rational self or attaining a position of 'transparency' at which the will of the individual producer and that of the *Gesamtarbeiter* will coincide. In Benjamin's view, the characteristic feature of the experience of modernity is its impoverishment and it is the possibility of remedying this that is the focus of his critique of capitalism. Rationalism, so far from giving a satisfactory theory of false consciousness, is itself a form of false consciousness, Benjamin believes.

Benjamin gives his most explicit account of what is involved in this conception of experience in the essay 'On Some Motifs in Baudelaire', which was published in the *Zeitschrift für Sozialforschung* in 1939.[49] While Benjamin continued to resist Adorno's interpretation of 'The Work of Art in the Age of its Mechanical Reproducibility', by which the elimination of the aura entails the reduction of art to propaganda, he does indeed appear in this later essay to take a more explicitly critical attitude towards the decline of the aura.

The concern to lay hold of a 'true' or 'authentic' conception of experience, 'as opposed to the kind that manifests itself in the standardized, denatured life of the civilized masses',[50] was a major preoccupation of philosophy, aesthetics and sociology, Benjamin notes, in the late nineteenth and early twentieth century. The majority of this literature, however, loosely labelled 'the philosophy of life', was either wholly unhistorical or consciously reactionary (indeed, in several cases – Benjamin mentions Klages and Jung but he could just as well have added Heidegger – its authors even made common cause with fascism). Benjamin sets out to develop a progressive and historical form of this critique of experience and to use it to establish the distinctiveness of Baudelaire's understanding of

---

[49] The essay was published only after an earlier version had been rejected by the Institute and a long correspondence involving Benjamin, Adorno and Horkheimer, in particular. See *Gesammelte Schriften*, vol. I.3, pp. 1064–188.
[50] 'Über einige Motive bei Baudelaire', p. 608.

modernity. In the essay, Benjamin draws heavily on Bergson, Proust, Freud (specifically *Beyond the Pleasure Principle*) and Valéry, although his views on experience and its relation to modernity are also clearly indebted to Nietzsche, Simmel and Rilke, as well as owing something to Klages and Stefan George, on the political Right, and to the Surrealists on the Left.

Benjamin's starting point is a short discussion of Bergson's *Matière et Mémoire*. What interests Benjamin is less the relationship between matter and memory that is signalled in the title itself than the role played by the structure of memory for experience. Insofar as memory is a matter of tradition, it is a part of collective existence, *mémoire pure*, in Bergson's terms. In this respect, according to Benjamin:

> It is less the product of facts firmly anchored in memory than of a convergence in memory of accumulated and frequently unconscious data.[51]

But Bergson takes this *mémoire pure* to be a timeless characteristic of the human mind, when it is, in fact, Benjamin claims, a reaction to a particular kind of experience – 'the inhospitable, blinding age of big-scale industrialism'.[52]

As is well known, Proust, whom Benjamin discusses next, based his own account of experience on Bergson, but he substituted the idea of the *mémoire involontaire* for Bergson's *mémoire pure*. In so doing, Proust took the first step towards turning this account of experience into a critique of rationalism, for the *mémoire involontaire* is an experience of the past whose richness (and, indeed, pleasure) is accessible only indirectly, not through the voluntary powers of the mind. Thus its source lies 'somewhere beyond the reach of the intellect', in 'some material object (or in the sensation which such an object arouses in us), though we have no idea which one it is.'[53] However, Benjamin argues, Proust's own treatment of the two types of memory is as unhistorical as Bergson's. Proust regards the possibility of discovering the object that corresponds to the *mémoire involontaire* as a matter of chance – stumbling upon the pass-word that will release the treasures of the past. Benjamin, however, claims that the way in which certain aspects of experience have come to be covered over is a specific feature of the modern world. It is the fact that modern man is 'increasingly unable to assimilate the data of the world around him'[54] that leads to the retreat of his inner life to such an extent that it can be released only as part of a *mémoire involontaire*.

He contrasts the *mémoire involontaire*, as the way in which the isolated, modern individual can come back into contact with aspects of his own past, to a situation in which there is 'experience in the strict sense'. In this

[51] Ibid., 607–53, p. 609.
[52] Ibid., p. 609.
[53] *A la recherche du temps perdu*, quoted in 'Über einige Motive bei Baudelaire', p. 610.
[54] Ibid.

case, there is no such absolute antithesis between individual and collective, voluntary and involuntary memory:

> ... certain contents of the individual past combine with materials of the collective past. The rituals with their ceremonies, their festivals ... kept producing the amalgamation of these two elements of memory over and over again. They triggered recollection at certain times and remained handles of memory for a lifetime. In this way, voluntary and involuntary recollection lost their mutual exclusiveness.[55]

Benjamin's account of the process by which voluntary and involuntary memory came to be separated draws on Freud's *Beyond the Pleasure Principle*. In that particularly idiosyncratic and eclectic work, Freud gives an unusual account of the relationship between perception, consciousness and memory. To what one might call empiricist common sense, perception is the source by which we accumulate items of conscious awareness and memory is the container in which we deposit some of them to be recalled, if possible, at will. Freud, however, presents a view which has consciousness and memory working in opposite directions:

> Becoming conscious and leaving behind a memory trace are processes incompatible with one another within one and the same system.[56]

'Memory' here is that pattern of imprinting that determines the structure of the individual's unconscious, not just the storehouse for the impressions of the past – in other words, involuntary memory. From this point of view, Freud claims, it is the function of consciousness to protect against the intrusion of the outside world into memory, to 'abreact' what would, if absorbed into the personality, tend to destroy it.[57] Benjamin applies this idea to the critique of contemporary life. Insofar as the modern world confronts the individual in a way that is threatening (either as a direct physical threat to bodily integrity or a psychic one – an 'overload' of the perceptual capacities) he will react more and more, Benjamin suggests, by a form of consciousness that 'lives in the moment' (*Erlebnis*) but which does not enter the continuing pattern of life (*Erfahrung*). Where discontinuities rule in one area of life (in industrial production) they will be reproduced mimetically elsewhere: thus the *Erlebnis* of the worker at his machine corresponds to the shock-*Erlebnis* of the passer-by in the crowd

---

[55] 'Über einige Motive bei Baudelaire', pp. 607–53, p. 611.
[56] Freud, *Jenseits des Lustprinzips*, quoted in 'Über einige Motive bei Baudelaire', p. 612.
[57] For a living organism, protection against stimuli is an almost more important function than the reception of stimuli; the protective shield is equipped with its own store of energy and must above all strive to preserve the special forms of conversion of energy operating in it against the effects of the excessive energies at work in the external world, effects which tend towards an equalization of potential and hence towards destruction. (Ibid., p. 613.)

that Baudelaire depicts in the *Fleurs du mal* and to the experiential discontinuities of modern, machine-like gambling (the roulette-wheel).[58]

Baudelaire's poetry is thus a heroic attempt to articulate what one might call the *sensational* quality of modern life. It embodies an *Erlebnis*, as Benjamin puts it, to which Baudelaire has given the weight of an *Erfahrung*. Baudelaire has shown, Benjamin says, the price to be paid for the sensation of modernity: 'the disintegration of the *aura* in the shock-*Erlebnis*'.[59] Both Baudelaire and Proust are witnesses to the fate of experience in the modern age: in different respects, they document the way in which the most significant layers of experience have been banished from a form of existence in which voluntary memory is dominant. Instead of an integrated *Erfahrung* in which the involuntary aspects of memory support and enrich the voluntary, the involuntary memory has retreated until it inhabits a domain of magic, mystery and secrecy − symbols of the way that the wealth of his own experience has become inaccessible to modern man.

In the essay on Baudelaire, Benjamin asserts the existence of a close connection between *mémoire involontaire* and the idea of the aura. The decline in the latter represents at the same time a loss of the former. The aura, in fact, is defined in terms that recall De Brosses' and Hume's analyses of fetishism:

> 'Perceptibility', as Novalis puts it, 'is a kind of attentiveness.' The perceptibility that he has in mind is none other than that of the aura. Experience of the aura thus rests on the transposition of a response common in human relationships to the relationship between the inanimate or natural object and man. The person we look at, or who feels that he is being looked at, looks at us in turn. To experience the aura of a phenomenon means to invest it with the ability to return our gaze. This faculty corresponds to the sources of the *mémoire involontaire*.[60]

It was this very passage to which Adorno was referring in his letter to Benjamin of 29 February 1940, discussed above. As we have seen, Benjamin rejected Adorno's interpretation of the idea that this 'investment' of objects with the capacity to return our gaze is a matter of the 'sedimentation' of labour in the product. But nor is it right to interpret Benjamin as following de Brosses or Hume. The implicit assumption behind such Enlightenment accounts of fetishism is that the 'disenchanted' perception of the natural world − without intrinsic significance and containing only those items that are discoverable by the natural sciences − represents external reality as it is objectively, and that anything beyond that is a form of illusion or subjective 'projection'. But this is not Benjamin's view. The whole thrust of his Kantianism is to refuse the division of experience into a scientifically discoverable 'objective' compo-

---

[58] 'Über einige Motive bei Baudelaire', p. 632.
[59] Ibid., p. 653.
[60] Ibid., pp. 646−7.

nent and a residual, 'subjective' one. Experience and perception modelled on the natural-scientific world-view are not more fundamental from the human point of view than an experience of affinities and correspondences. Benjamin's concern is with the character of *human* experience and the fact that natural objects are always given to us within the human world means that it is not a delusion to experience them *as* having an intrinsic significance.[61] From this point of view, the disenchanted, scientific conception of experience represents not so much an account of the real basis of experience in general as a symptom on the reflective level of the way that in the modern world experience has come to be impoverished in fact.

Like Stendhal, this impoverishment expresses itself for Benjamin in the loss of the power of the imagination. As the powers of voluntary memory are increased, in part through the development of technology (Benjamin cites in particular the development of photography) so, correspondingly, that crucial aspect of the work of art by which it appears to contain an inexhaustible wealth of experience, of which the aura is the emblem, diminishes.[62]

In general, the Baudelaire essay offers two kinds of reason for the decline of involuntary memory. The first lies in the character of the experience faced by the individual subject in the modern world: the tumultuous, shock character of modern capitalism, as embodied in city life and in industrial production. Against this, Benjamin believes, *Erlebnis* can be seen as a kind of defence mechanism.

The second reason for the decline of involuntary memory, however, is the effect of the development of techniques of voluntary memory. As these advance (aided, in particular, by technology) so they displace the unconscious work of the imagination. The model here is the way in which the visual realm has become disenchanted in consequence of the development of photography. By contrast, Benjamin notes the affinity between involuntary memory and the senses of smell and taste (as in Proust's celebrated taste of *madeleine*). The explanation for this, he suggests, is that the sense of smell remains in a certain way peculiarly immune to voluntary recollection:

[61] What would be a delusion, from this point of view, would be to make the assumption that we experience things as significant because they are so, intrinsically, independently of that experience. In Kantian terms, this would be the paralogistic move from transcendental idealism to metaphysical realism.

[62] I am not aware of any evidence that Benjamin knew *De l'Amour*. But Proust apparently did – his account of *mémoire involontaire* is a development of Stendhal's idea of 'crystallization'. So, too, did Valéry, whom Benjamin cites approvingly at this point:

We recognize a work of art by the fact that no idea it inspires in us, no mode of behaviour that it suggests that we adopt could exhaust or dispose of it. We may inhale the smell of a flower whose fragrance is agreeable to us for as long as we like; it is impossible for us to rid ourselves of the fragrance by which our senses have been aroused, and no recollection, no thought, no mode of behaviour can obliterate its effect or release us from the hold it has on us. He who has set himself the task of creating a work of art aims at the same effect. (P. Valéry, *Avant-propos. Encyclopédie Française*, quoted in 'Über einige Motive bei Baudelaire', p. 645.)

The scent is the inaccessible refuge of the *mémoire involontaire*. It is unlikely
that it will associate itself with a visual image; of all sensual impressions it
will ally itself only with the same scent.[63]

Meanwhile, new media increase the scope of voluntary memory and the
techniques of industrial production displace former techniques within
which involuntary memory and *mimesis* were embedded. The paradigm
here is the encapsulation of experience in handicraft skills:

If we designate as aura the associations which, at home in the *mémoire
involontaire*, tend to cluster around the object of a perception, then its
analogue in the case of a utilitarian object is the experience [*Erfahrung*] which
has left traces of the practised hand.[64]

In sum, for Benjamin, the decline of the aura is part of a process which
flattens and reduces experience by bringing it into the realm of the
voluntary and immediate at the expense of involuntary memory. Where
the latter does appear, it manifests itself in the form of an irruption but
constitutes no durable alternative to the impoverishment of everyday life.
In terms of the typology of Chapter 2, the phenomenon is one of false
consciousness in two senses. First, it involves a loss of emotional richness
– a diminution in the quality of experience – and, secondly, it represents a
loss of identity on the part of the subject – a reduction in the individual's
capacity to integrate experience.

Sketchy and speculative though Benjamin's critique of experience is, it
deserves to be treated with great sympathy, for theories of false conscious-

---

[63] 'Über einige Motive bei Baudelaire', p. 641. Interestingly, Dan Sperber has argued for the
central importance of smell to a theory of symbolism on very similar lines. Smells, according to
Sperber, resist taxonomy and semantic organization (what we might call, in Benjamin's terms, the
techniques of voluntary memory). Now, says Sperber, we can divide the retrieval of memorized
information into two: *recognition* ('when in the presence of new information, one remembers that
one already has it') and *recall* – the power of voluntarily bringing to mind an object or experience
'in the absence of an external stimulus'. While it is true that everything that we can recall we can
thereby recognize, it is also the case that recall lags far behind recognition.

Smells are an extreme case in this respect: one recognizes them, but one doesn't recall them
. . . [However,] if olfactory memory fails in the area of direct remembrance (except, perhaps,
for a few exceptionally gifted or trained individuals), its efficaciousness in the area of
recognition is exceptional. One can, at a distance of years, recognize a smell one has only
smelled once, and know first of all that one has smelled it before, then – like a magician who
plucks a long multi-coloured string of handkerchiefs out of a top hat that seemed empty –
one can recover by means of that recognition a whole series of memories that one didn't
know one still had. (*Rethinking Symbolism*, pp. 116–17.)

Sperber's explanation is that the symbolic mechanism is a way of extending memory to areas of
our experience that lie outside the conventional taxonomic system – unable to recall (that is,
represent to itself) its experience, the mind constructs 'not a representation of that object but a
representation of that representation'. In other words, unlike Benjamin, for whom the involuntary
memory remains *sui generis*, a counterpart to voluntary memory with its own mechanism, Sperber
sees the richness of the memory attaching to what cannot be directly recalled as the result of a
mechanism whose function is the continuation of the voluntary memory by other means.

[64] 'Über einige Motive bei Baudelaire', p. 644.

ness that are not based upon a rationalist conception of the human good are rare indeed. While it may not be right, it is not fundamentally misguided in the way that the dominant rationalist tradition is. However, two lines of criticism seem to me to be inescapable.

First, Benjamin gives very little idea of the conditions under which experience could be reintegrated. The examples of *Erfahrung* that he offers are taken almost exclusively from pre-industrial society – the experienced hand of the craftsman or the narrative integration of the story-teller – although it is, of course, important to his political self-understanding as a Marxist that his critique of modernity should be forward-looking. He notes in his essay on Surrealism that a progressive conception of experience must aim towards what he calls *profane Erleuchtung* – a 'profane illumination' in which the mundane experience of reality would be transformed and enriched. But he gives his readers few positive clues, either there or elsewhere, as to how this might be supposed to be possible. Moreover, given the structure of his theory, it is difficult to hypothesize how this omission might be made good.

In each of the examples Benjamin gives – the elimination of experiential aspects of productive activity, the decline of involuntary memory as the result of the development of techniques of memory such as photography, the shock-like temporal structure of modern industry and city life – the impoverishment of experience seems to be inherent in industrial production and its technology, not a contingent result of the way that industrial production is organised under capitalism. Thus what is to say that, even if the proletariat did succeed in seizing power, socialist production would be different? Benjamin remarks on the way in which, in former times, the experience of time was oriented to seasonal events and rituals – but does he think that a socialist society would be able to reintroduce such cycles and festivals, and that, if it did, that would be sufficient to reorient its time-horizons?

In the *Theses on the Philosophy of History* (written, as it appears, in early 1940 and only published posthumously) Benjamin makes it clear that he rejects a conception of socialism that would identify it simply with increased domination over nature. Although he is careful to call the view that he is criticizing 'vulgar-Marxist' (rather than 'Marxist') the charge that he puts forward, namely that '[This vulgar-Marxist] conception of labour amounts to the exploitation of nature, which with naive complacency is contrasted with the exploitation of the proletariat',[65] represents an implicit criticism of Marx's own failure to offer any alternative to the increase of discretionary power as an ideal of the human good. Nevertheless, if Benjamin is (rightly) sceptical about associating socialism with technology-for-technology's sake, he fails to explain (the odd affirmative reference to the new possibilities of experience opened up by the cinema, for example, hardly constitutes such an explanation) how a reintegration of

---

[65] 'Über den Begriff der Geschichte', p. 699.

experience might be possible that did not involve the rejection of the technology of capitalism entirely.

A second line of criticism concerns Benjamin's apparently uncritical attitude towards involuntary memory itself. With Benjamin, the idea of false consciousness has come full circle from St Augustine. Augustine takes it to be a sign of the fallen character of human beings that their powers of voluntary control over their own desires are limited:

> Then (had there been no sin) the man would have sowed the seed and the woman would have conceived the child when their sexual organs had been aroused by the will, at the appropriate time and in the necessary degree, and had not been excited by lust. For we set in motion, at our command, not only those members which are fitted with bones and joints, like the hands, feet and fingers, but also those which are loosely constructed of pliant muscles and tissues . . . We observe, then, that the body, even under present conditions, is an obedient servant to some people in a remarkable fashion beyond the normal limitations of nature; this is shown in many kinds of movements and feelings, and it happens even in men who are living this present troubled life in corruptible flesh. If this is so, is there any reason why we should not believe that before the sin of disobedience and its punishment of corruptibility, the members of a man's body could have been the servants of man's will without any lust, for the procreation of children?[66]

Benjamin, however, sees human beings as limited and impoverished by the very development of such control. What is to choose between them? It may be hard for (many of) us to sympathize with a theory that has provided a theological justification for regimes of sexual relations that have caused such an incalculable amount of guilt and suffering in the course of European history. Nevertheless, Augustine does not simply reject sexual desire as intrinsically bad. The structure of his argument is not: the loss of voluntary control of desires is bad because it leads to sex; but: sexual desire is bad because it is a symptom of (and reinforces) the loss of voluntary control.

The telling point that Augustine still has to make to us is that involuntary memory goes together with involuntary desire, and we should not naively assume that, in abandoning voluntary control over the psyche, this will automatically open the way to forms of life that are rich and experientially integrated. What Benjamin describes affirmatively as an experience rich in mimetic content and affective power can just as easily be seen negatively: instead of the *mémoire involontaire* we have the *idée fixe*; instead of finding oneself in otherness, there is the loss of the ability to free oneself from an alien authority. Benjamin's idea that the development of voluntary memory is primarily a negative psychic by-product of the development of the techniques necessary for the satisfaction of material needs does not recognize the possibility that involuntary memory may be something against which it would be rational to protect ourselves. Without

[66] *City of God*, pp. 587–9.

the power to defend ourselves from what we experience, we may all too easily fall victim to false authorities or pernicious desires. Perhaps the abandonment of voluntary control over the psyche will lead to the kind of corrupt behaviour described in Augustine's story of Alypius and his bloodthirsty obsession with watching gladiators; there are some passions which it is genuinely dangerous to release.

Benjamin would, no doubt, argue that we should not judge the role of involuntary memory by the form it takes within modern industrial capitalism. Just as Proust's *mémoire involontaire* has an exceptional and violent character because the involuntary aspects of memory are otherwise suppressed, so, too, he might argue, the opening up of the non-voluntary aspects of the self is likely to be pernicious in a society in which the self really does need to protect itself. In that context, the compelling – auratic, charismatic – quality that an other can come to take on for the individual is (to use a phrase that was to become a commonplace for the Frankfurt School) an 'identification with the aggressor'.[67] In the absence of the genuine and open love of others, individuals compensate by turning their love onto their leaders.

V Ideology and Anti-Realist Epistemology: Horkheimer and Habermas

Benjamin's reaction to Adorno's interpretation of the concept of social labour is to reject the enterprise of trying to find a materialist analogue for the Idealists' 'transcendental subject' altogether. But this is not the only possible response to its difficulties. Another approach would be to give up Adorno's idea of social labour as an equivalent of Hegel's *Geist*, a source of objective meaning outside the subject, but to retain the idea of the transcendental subject as conditioning the engagement between individuals and mind-independent reality. This strategy, then, associates the theory of ideology with a characteristic epistemology: the doctrine that our encounter with reality is indirect, mediated by a framework of basic categories or concepts. The theory of ideology, on this approach, is centrally concerned with the determinants of that framework. This position has been widespread in twentieth-century neo-Marxism and we shall look at it in the particularly clear and explicit form in which it is presented by two members of the Frankfurt School: Max Horkheimer and (in his early writings) Jürgen Habermas.

The roots of the anti-realist epistemology are to be found in Kant's insistence that the mind plays an active role in cognition. Mind-indepen-

---

[67] Insofar as I can tell, the phrase comes, in fact, from Anna Freud, rather than Sigmund. However, the idea to which it refers – that the weak individual compensates by identifying itself with the strong, even where the strength of the latter is gained at the individual's expense – is very much present in Freud's *Group Psychology and the Analysis of the Ego*.

dent reality cannot be known except as transformed by the 'synthesizing' activity of the subject, applying concepts to the raw material given to us through the senses. As Kant writes in the *Critique of Pure Reason*: 'Thoughts without content are empty, intuitions without concepts are blind.'[68] This novel doctrine made its appearance at the same time as the conviction developed on the part of Herder and others that each culture has its own distinctive identity and value and it is often supposed that there must have been some connection between the two ideas. For Kant himself, the implications of transcendental philosophy are strongly anti-relativist: a single set of twelve categories is common to all finite, rational beings and guarantees the objectivity of our knowledge of a single, common world. But it is easy to see how the model could be taken in a directly opposite direction: if the concepts by which the world is interpreted are supplied by the subject, might they not vary from one subject (or group of subjects) to another? In that case, whatever determined the conceptual scheme which a group adopted would determine its consciousness at the most fundamental level – not this or that particular belief, but the very limits within which beliefs themselves were framed – and each group would live in what was, in effect, its own version of the world.

The connection between transcendental philosophy and the diversity of world-views was not made in Kant's own time or immediately afterwards, however. Those philosophers who considered themselves Kant's most faithful successors, Fichte and Schopenhauer, reasserted and reinforced the idea of the active role of the mind in perception but they did not make it part of any account of cultural variation. As for Hegel, although he was strongly committed to the idea of cultural variation, his epistemology is ultimately an anti-Kantian one: he rejects the dualistic Kantian idea of concepts as a medium or a matrix separating us off from the world as it is in itself.[69]

Marx himself comes close to neo-Kantian anti-realism in the 'Theses on Feuerbach', when he writes that it is the 'chief defect of all hitherto existing materialism' that it considers reality 'only in the form of the object ... but not as sensuous human activity, *praxis*' and that 'the *active side* was developed abstractly by Idealism'.[70] But Marx does not make the connection between the interested character of ideas and the constitutive role of concepts in our engagement with the world explicitly. Indeed, as we have seen, in his mature writings, Marx held a very objectivistic conception of the status of his own activity, one that would be hard to reconcile with the more radical implications of transcendental anti-realism.[71]

[68] *Critique of Pure Reason*, A51/B75.
[69] See, for example, the Introduction to the *Phenomenology of Spirit* and Hegel's discussion of Kant in the *Lectures on the History of Philosophy*.
[70] 'Theses on Feuerbach', p. 121.
[71] This holds whether we interpret his conception of 'science' positivistically (as being scientific in just the same way as any other science) or as involving a commitment to a quasi-Hegelian ontology and methodology – or indeed, as I have argued, as being caught in a tension between the two approaches. There is no support in Marx's mature work that I can see for a conception of science according to which science is always *science-from-a-viewpoint*.

In fact, it seems that Nietzsche's 'perspectivism' is the first full-scale attempt to apply a Kantian or quasi-Kantian epistemology for anti-realist philosophical ends. Nietzsche takes the position that we are cut off from the true nature of reality by the 'apparatus' through which we must try to come to grips with it – and, unlike Kant, he has no confidence that this apparatus itself can act as some kind of guarantor of objectivity.[72] In the late nineteenth and early twentieth centuries, adaptations of Kant along these lines became a 'background belief' in their own right, however, flourishing particularly where neo-Kantian philosophy met and merged into sociology, in the writings of Rickert, Simmel, Mauthner and Max Weber, for example.[73]

The position is clearly articulated in a programmatic essay written by Max Horkheimer in 1937 with the title 'Traditional and Critical Theory'. This essay was acknowledged by the Frankfurt School's members as a classic statement of their programme. Horkheimer starts from a contrast between the realist view that the world is an ensemble of mind-independent facts towards which the thinking subject must take a neutral, passive attitude – the world-view implicit in 'traditional' theory, as he terms it – and the essentially Kantian conception behind 'Critical Theory', according to which:

The perceived fact is ... codetermined by human ideas and concepts, even before its conscious theoretical elaboration by the knowing individual.[74]

How this 'codetermination' takes place is, of course, the crucial point. It results, Horkheimer says, from the activity of society which is, he claims, in contrast to the passive individuals who comprise it, essentially an 'active subject'. Horkheimer makes a distinction between two ways in which this active subject operates: between constituting activity which is *subjective* and constituting activity which is *objective*:

The facts which our senses present to us are socially pre-formed in two ways: through the historical character of the object perceived and through the historical character of the perceiving organ.[75]

From the point of view of the Kantian theme, it is the latter that is important. In asserting that facts are preformed because of the 'historical character' of the perceiving organ, Horkheimer is committing himself to the instrumentalist view that the subject's encounter with reality is always informed by a prior conceptual framework: all perception is interpretation:

---

[72] Nietzsche was very much influenced by F. A. Lange, who held a not wholly dissimilar doctrine.
[73] I have discussed this in more detail in my paper 'Modernism and the Two Traditions in Philosophy'.
[74] 'Traditionelle und Kritische Theorie', p. 149 [Eng. trans., p. 214].
[75] Ibid., p. 149 [Eng. trans., p. 213].

The individual, however, receives sensible reality ... into his world of well-ordered concepts. The latter ... have developed along with the life process of society.[76]

Thus for Horkheimer it is the transcendental subject – society – which is the agent that determines the framework of concepts which, from the point of view of the individual, appear to be natural and objective. The objective of Critical Theory, as Horkheimer presents it, is to challenge this apparent naturalness in the name of 'the rational organization of society which it is its task to illumine and legitimate'.[77] Horkheimer does not, however, explain how it is that the individual should be able to climb out of his own received set of categories. He simply assumes that the system of categories contains the 'critical potential' for this to be possible. If 'we' (not, of course, the conscious, choosing individuals that we know ourselves to be, but ourselves as embodiments of transcendental agency) have 'codetermined' the world that encounters us as if it were mind-independent, then it should be possible by 'immanent critique' to recover that contribution: 'we' can know what 'we' have made.

Very much the same epistemological position is to be found in the major work published by Jürgen Habermas in the 1960s, *Knowledge and Human Interests*. Habermas endorses Horkheimer's anti-realist conception, according to which what we mean by 'reality' is always only 'reality as it is for us'. He identifies himself with the *pragmatist* doctrine that the framework of our encounter with reality is historically evolved: the product of the interests of a biological species rather than of a transcendental ego. Three important features separate Habermas's version of instrumentalism from traditional pragmatism, however.

1 First, Habermas, the reference to the species notwithstanding, rejects any suggestion that the nature of 'interests' can be interpreted from biology alone:

> The concept of 'interest' is not meant to imply a naturalistic reduction of transcendental-logical properties to empirical ones. Indeed it is meant to prevent just such a reduction.[78]

2 Secondly (and connected with this first point) Habermas claims that we must acknowledge the existence of what German Idealism called an 'interest of reason'; reason itself, that is to say, has independent force and does not require motivating by a non-rational 'passion' in order to be effective:

> In reason there is an inherent drive to realize reason.[79]

[76] Ibid., p. 151 [Eng. trans., p. 215].
[77] Ibid., p. 193 [Eng. trans., p. 223].
[78] *Knowledge and Human Interests*, p. 196.
[79] Ibid., p. 201.

3 Finally, although the 'synthesizing subject' is not, as in Kant, a transcendental dimension of the self, but a 'species-subject',[80] its accomplishments can be recuperated by 'reflection' that is guided by and serves the interests of cognitive emancipation:

> ... the pursuit of reflection knows itself as a movement of emancipation. Reason is at the same time subject to the interest in reason. We can say that it obeys an *emancipatory cognitive interest*, which aims at the pursuit of reflection.[81]

Habermas's epistemological anti-realism is open to an obvious objection in relation to the implications it has for notions such as truth and objectivity. If our encounter with reality is mediated by a matrix of concepts, and it is not possible to stand outside that matrix, what becomes of the idea of truth? Habermas accepts the challenge. We must give up, he says, the 'illusion of objectivism'. In the end, it is rational agreement (what he terms 'consensus') that is the goal, not the correspondence between thought and reality as it is in itself. Thus Habermas is untroubled by the criticism of *Knowledge and Human Interests* made by Michael Theunissen (from a standpoint extremely sympathetic to Hegel) that, on such an approach, the objectivity of knowledge becomes 'no more than' *intersubjectivity*. Habermas concedes the point – but sees no objection in it.[82]

But how can agreement be rational unless we can say that one particular set of concepts is better (more true – or, at least, less false) than another? Yet how can we tell if we are indeed moving in such a direction? It is one thing to argue that the ideal of objectivity requires that knowledge should not be distorted by interests, another to claim that it is actually possible to move our concepts in the direction of such an 'undistorted' communication. The latter requires both that it should be possible for reason to have sufficient independent motivating force to overcome the particularity of interests and that a 'critical potential' exists within perspectival conceptual schemes themselves. Although we cannot stand outside the conceptual apparatus altogether, we are able, Habermas claims, to draw on 'the experience of the emancipatory power of reflection, which the subject experiences in itself to the extent that it becomes transparent to itself in the history of its genesis'[83] in order to lead us away from distortion and towards neutrality and objectivity.

Yet Habermas offers no convincing argument to refute those who doubt that such an 'emancipatory power of reflection' exists, and, if it can be said to exist, that it enjoys the motivational and epistemic conditions that it requires for its realization (namely, (1) that it can assert itself effectively, and (2) that it can show that the 'immanent critique' of concepts is really

[80] Ibid., p. 31.
[81] Ibid., p. 197.
[82] Ibid., p. 380.
[83] Ibid., p. 197.

moving towards objectivity). Indeed, it is hard to imagine what, at this metaphysical level, an *argument* in its favour would have to look like. If we cannot step outside the framework of our own concepts (and Habermas explicitly argues with Kant and against Hegel on this point in the first chapter of his book) what is to say that reflection really has the potential to move us in the direction of truth (if there is nothing outside the categories to compare them with, how are we supposed to be able to tell when such a move has taken place)? And, since it is not a thesis in empirical psychology, what is to say that reason does have *motivating* force? In the end, these fundamental elements of Habermas's position are not so much matters of argument as the necessary presuppositions of a powerful and deeply held philosophical background belief.[84]

Even if these epistemological objections can be met, however, there are objections to anti-realism as a theory of ideology. Insofar as the categories through which we see the world are presented as ideological, anti-realist epistemology is an example of what I called in the previous chapter the 'interests' model of ideology, and it faces corresponding objections. By assumption, ideology, insofar as it plays the role of sustaining domination without coercion, goes against the interests *both* of the individual *and* of the subordinate class of which he is a member. The crucial explanatory

---

[84] For Horkheimer and Habermas the background belief that our encounter with reality is indirect leads to a version of the Kantian idea of the transcendental subject as a non-individual kind of agent. However, other authors are just as committed to the background belief without conceding the existence of a synthesizing subject.

Michel Foucault, for example, states his objective in *The Order of Things* in thoroughly Kantian terms: his aim, he says, is to establish 'the conditions of possibility' of knowledge (*The Order of Things*, p. xxii). This *episteme*, as he calls it, is governed, he asserts, by a 'historical *a priori*': a set of rules that 'come into play in the very existence of such discourse' and form a '*positive unconscious*' of knowledge. According to *The Archaeology of Knowledge*:

> ... this *a priori* does not elude historicity: it does not constitute, above events, and in an unmoving heaven, an atemporal structure; it is defined as the group of rules that characterize a discursive practice. (*The Archaeology of Knowledge*, p. 127.)

Now, since Foucault denies the existence of a transcendental subject, there is, of course, no question of a process of 'emancipatory reflection' of the kind that Habermas claims. Such evidence as there can be for the processes by which order is imposed on mind-independent reality is supposed to come, according to Foucault, at points of crisis, when order is breaking down, or in those marginal areas of social life that are, for the culture in question, somehow anomalous or deviant:

> It is here that a culture, imperceptibly deviating from the empirical orders prescribed for it by its primary codes, instituting an initial separation from them, causes them to lose their original transparency, relinquishes its immediate and invisible powers, frees itself sufficiently to discover that these orders are not the only possible ones or the best ones; this culture then finds itself faced with the stark fact that there exists, below the level of its spontaneous orders, things that are in themselves capable of being ordered, that belong to a certain unspoken order; the fact, in short, that order *exists*. (*The Order of Things*, p. xiv.)

Yet the objection to Foucault is the same as it is to Habermas: there is no explanation of how the individual subject relates to the superior order (the *episteme*) that dominates it – of why it should allow itself to be limited by the categories that are imposed upon it by a quasi-transcendental 'discursive practice'.

problem for the theory of ideology, therefore, is to explain how, *despite this*, ideological consciousness comes to be accepted.

Raising itself to the transcendental level, as an account of the formation of fundamental categories, it might seem that Critical Theory escapes the 'acceptance problem'. According to Horkheimer and Habermas, it is not the individual who voluntarily accepts a particular set of categories: they are not a matter of choice from the individual's point of view. But this is really only to solve the problem with an assertion: the claim that society as an 'active subject' (Horkheimer's phrase) has the power to impose its concepts on individuals, whether or not it is the latter's interests to accept them. There is no further explanation of why or how this should be so.

VI Conclusion

In this chapter, we have looked at three ways in which the members of the Frankfurt School have attempted to continue and extend the theory of ideology.

Of the three, it is Adorno's extension of Marxist-Hegelianism that remains closest to (one strand of) Marx's own thought. But, as Benjamin clearly saw, Adorno's theory carries a very heavy philosophical commitment: the idea that the labour-process, like Hegel's *Geist*, functions as the objective source of meaning in objects in general. Benjamin, on the other hand, requires us to accept a kind of intuitively accessible (but objectively uncheckable) 'tacit knowledge' to underpin the idea of correspondence between the various regions of social life. Finally, Habermas, following Horkheimer, restricts the idea of the transcendental subject to the framework through which individuals encounter the world. But not only is Habermas's epistemology open to objection philosophically, the model fails to explain the central feature of an interests-based explanation of ideology: namely, how is it that subordinated classes accept forms of thought that go against their interests?

In each case, the price of defending the theory of ideology is the acceptance of philosophical commitments that are, in the absence of independent support argument, highly dubious. Where, then, does that leave the theory of ideology?

8

The Theory of Ideology and Beyond

I Arguments against the Theory of Ideology

The previous chapters traced the emergence of the background beliefs sustaining the theory of ideology and looked critically at the forms taken by the theory itself in the writings of Marx and the Frankfurt School. It is now time to take a step back and put this history into perspective.

We have seen the crucial role that the background belief in society as a self-maintaining system plays for the theory of ideology. As Cohen puts it:

> The background against which consequence explanation is offered in biology or anthropology or economics is a conception of species or societies or economic units as self-maintaining and self-advancing . . .[1]

Yet Marxist theory contains no satisfactory elaborating explanation to support this conception equivalent to the account of natural selection to be found in evolutionary biology, so to endorse the conception of society as a self-maintaining system requires an ontological commitment that is not justified according to the explanatory standards of the natural sciences. Thus we are returned to the dilemma identified in Chapter 1. Which should be rejected – the methodological principles of the natural sciences or the ontological commitment? For positivists (I include the 'analytical Marxists' under this label) the answer is clear: if an ontological commitment goes beyond what can be justified according to commonly agreed scientific standards then, however painful it may be to have to do so, it must be given

[1] *Karl Marx's Theory of History*, p. 264.

up. Those on the other side will argue, however, that the principle that the only commitments we are entitled to make are those warranted according to the standards of the natural sciences is itself just as much of an unargued general assumption as the commitment to a collectivist ontology.

My own conclusion is on the side of the positivists – yet for reasons that are very different from those of the positivists themselves. I do not believe that the only methodological assumptions we are justified in making are those that are warranted according to the methodological standards of the natural sciences, so my argument against the collectivist ontology is not simply an inference drawn from this general principle. Indeed, I do not believe that it is possible to *prove* (or refute) the collectivist conception at all. Nevertheless, not all argument must amount to proof, and there are three considerations available against the collectivist ontology that should, in my view, persuade us against it: the fact that the background belief in society as a self-maintaining system required by the theory of ideology is historically specific; the fact that there are alternative answers available to Reich's question; and the fact that the theory of ideology itself can be understood as a form of consciousness that is appealing for non-rational reasons. I shall discuss these three claims in order.

The first claim is as follows:

The belief in society as a self-maintaining system is not part of that shared and unvarying stock of convictions which it would be more or less unthinkable to reject.

The observation that plants and animals are self-maintaining and self-reproducing is universal among human societies. In contrast, as we have seen, the idea that societies themselves are also self-maintaining systems became widespread only at a very late stage in the history of Western thought. This fact alone, of course, does not establish that the belief is not true (many of the modern world's most firmly held views about the nature of the universe made their appearance just as recently) but the absence of a historical consensus in favour of a belief is at least a reasonable ground for doubt.

Moreover, these doubts should be the stronger to the extent that we see the historical particularity of the belief in society as a self-maintaining system in conjunction with the two further claims.

Claim 2:

The belief in society as a self-maintaining system is not explanatorily mandatory – that is, it is not the case that it is something which has to be assumed in order to explain an unquestionable phenomenon that otherwise would remain unintelligible.

The second claim returns us to the issue from which this book started: Reich's question. If the question is a genuine one, and if the theory of ideology is the only plausible answer to it, then it would be reasonable to allow whatever the assumptions are on which that theory depends. But if there are alternatives to the theory of ideology, then, of course, the case for making those assumptions is undermined. We must return, then, to Reich's question and the possible answers to it. The theory of ideology gives an essentially two-fold explanation of why it is that the many accept the rule of the few; how it is that *prima facie* illegitimate societies – societies with which it would simply not be rational to comply – maintain themselves without depending solely on coercion:

1 they maintain themselves in virtue of false consciousness on the part of the citizens.

2 this false consciousness occurs in response to the needs of society.

The alternative answers to Reich's question that I shall now present challenge (1) and (2) respectively.

II Compliance without False Consciousness: The Coordination Problem

In outline, the argument for the theory of ideology was that, although the few may have control over the means of coercion, the disparity of numbers between rulers and ruled is such that, should the ruled choose to act against their oppressors, they could not but prevail. Hence, since it is in their interests so to act, the failure of those who are unjustly ruled to overthrow their rulers must be explained as a form of false consciousness on their part. But what this argument fails to take into account is the problem of collective action – the possible discrepancy that there may be between what is rational for the individual and what is rational for a group of individuals.

For an intuitive image of what is at stake, consider a gunman with a group of hostages. The hostages know that, if they were all to attack the gunman together, they would overpower him, although there would be some casualties. On the other hand, if any individual were to attempt such an attack, then they would be shot. What determines the individual's decision? Looking at it in narrowly prudential terms, we can say that the individual has a reason to act if the expected gain is greater than the expected loss. But both the gain and the loss will be dependent on what others will do: the expectation of gain will be the greater and the risk of loss will be the smaller the more that others participate.

Thus one can imagine a situation in which the individual would argue as follows: if I could be confident that others would follow suit then it would be prudentially rational to attack the gunman (the benefits outweigh the risks). But, if I were to be left on my own, then it would not. It follows that I have a good reason for acting myself if and only if others too have a good reason for acting. But let us assume that they are in exactly the same situation as me. Then they will argue in just the same way. In that case, they will realize that they have a good reason if I have a good reason – just as I have a good reason if they have a good reason. So it seems that our assessments of the situation will be mutually supportive and that it will be rational to take action.

Yet a very slight modification of this model in the direction of reality produces a quite different conclusion. Let us take it that the chances of successfully overpowering the gunman increase sharply with the number of hostages participating in the attack so that success becomes practically certain at some point well before unanimous participation. And let us take it, too, that the chances of becoming a casualty are greater for participants in an attack than for non-participants. In other words, treating the matter in purely prudential terms, there are three possible classes of outcome, in increasing order of desirability from the individual's point of view. (1) The first is that the gunman remains in charge. (2) The second is that a sufficient number of hostages, of which the individual is one, attack the gunman so that they overpower him at relatively small risk to themselves. (3) The third is that a group of hostages *other than the individual* overpower the gunman (thus the individual gets the benefit without assuming the risk).

The possibility of 'free riders' (those who benefit from collective action without contributing to its costs) changes the calculation facing each individual drastically. If the individuals are rational and motivated by narrow prudence then it will not be possible to assure themselves of the conditions required for it to be rational to act. For, although they would all prefer the second outcome to the first, the fact that they would prefer the third to the second means that each individual has a reason to doubt whether other individuals have a sufficient reason to participate in collective action – and hence they may not have such a sufficient reason themselves. In this way, mutually beneficial collective action may fail to take place, although not, it should be noted, because of 'false consciousness' or a failure of rationality on the part of the individuals. I am not *deluded* in thinking that you would prefer to have the benefits of an attack on the gunman without bearing the risks, and you – although you may not, perhaps, be heroically virtuous – are not at all unreasonable in so preferring.

Seen in this way, the rule of the many by the few becomes not so much a matter of false consciousness as a *coordination problem*. Simple though my presentation of it here has been, the model does seem to be very illuminating in helping to explain empirical processes. We can see, for example, how it is that dissent has a 'snowball' structure. By the assumptions of the model, individuals' willingness to participate in action against a regime will be extremely sensitive to their assessment of others' willingness. But the most obvious indicator of others' willingness to participate is participation itself. Thus once public actions against a regime reach a certain point they tend to expand rapidly. If it proves to be possible to *demonstrate* dissent successfully, then the willingness of non-participants to participate will rise exponentially. The history of the collapse of the communist regimes in Eastern Europe bears this out. A small group of dissidents became successful at the point at which others joined their demonstrations and the demonstrations became too large for the authorities to repress (or to be prepared to repress – it was not a purely technical matter) effectively.

The problem, then, is how the snowball gets moving. Again, the prudential model is illuminating – although this time negatively. It shows that, if individuals were to act purely from narrow self-interest, then the process of initiating dissent is very likely to be irrational. The hard core of dissidents in Eastern Europe in the 1970s and 1980s had a variety of motivations – not all of them particularly attractive – but what anyone who met them must concede is that these were people who were prepared to engage in political action *despite* a clear perception of the limited chances for success of what they were doing. (It is significant that many of the leading dissidents had strong religious convictions, and so were prepared to act publicly *simply because they believed that what they were doing was right*.) And here is the paradox: even instrumental political action may need to be initiated by non-instrumentally motivated agents if it is to be successful. Had there not been people willing to engage in political action in the expectation that it would not be successful in practice – action that would be 'irrational' from the standpoint of narrow prudence – then it seems certain that the practical success of the movement would not have been possible.

The few are able to dominate the many to the extent that they are able to prevent the latter from engaging in the initially crucial phases of organization and communication necessary to realize their potentially overwhelming strength in practice. In this way, it is possible to explain the survival of *prima facie* illegitimate societies without supposing that the oppressed are suffering from false consciousness.

III Non-Ideological False Consciousness

The second alternative to the theory of ideology as an explanation of uncoerced compliance is that societies *are* characterized by false consciousness (and that false consciousness is a central part of the explanation of how it is that they survive) without it being true that the false consciousness exists *because* it helps the society in question to survive; in other words, that false consciousness exists and is *functional for*, but not *functionally explained by*, the social system. On this view, the first of the background beliefs behind the theory of ideology would be true – illegitimate societies maintain themselves through false consciousness on the part of their citizens – but the second – that this is because societies are self-maintaining systems – would be false.

We have seen several historical examples of this view. In general it takes two forms. One is that a non-rational disposition on the part of the ruled to accept the authority of rulers is a part of all political systems. This is the idea to be found in Adam Smith – that human beings are inclined to sympathize with those whose situation they judge to be fortunate and so ordinary individuals take an interest in the welfare of the 'great' irrespective of the benefits that they receive from them. The second form is the claim that false consciousness is specific to certain forms of society which it helps to maintain, but that it is not functionally explained by that society. This is the view to be found in Rousseau, for instance, with his idea that modern society is dominated by *amour-propre*, and in Schiller's conception of the mechanical modern state grinding individuals remorselessly into fragments. In each case, false consciousness is a consequence of the essential nature of the social system, but it is not functionally explained by the social system. Are such views plausible?

One author who has pursued this line of argument is Jon Elster.[2] Elster shares the positivist view that the orthodox interpretation of the theory of ideology lacks 'micro-foundations'. Instead, he suggests, we can provide those foundations by a suitably adapted account based on social psychology. Elster describes what he is advocating as a reconstruction of the Marxist theory of ideology, but, in my view, it is better seen as an alternative to it. I am sympathetic to Elster's general line, but there are, I shall argue, serious weaknesses and omissions in the very unfocused account that he himself gives. Nevertheless, Elster has indicated the direction in which a theory of false consciousness should go in order to provide an alternative to the Marxist account of non-coerced compliance, so it is with his account that I shall start.

Elster divides forms of false consciousness along two axes. He distinguishes between cognitive and 'motivational' states of consciousness ('practical false consciousness' in the terminology of Chapter 2) on the one hand, and between cognitive and motivational mechanisms to explain those states, on the other. However, in identifying specific ways in which unequal societies receive voluntary but non-rational compliance, Elster concentrates on only three forms: (1) fallacies of inference (cognitive false consciousness that is cognitive in origin); (2) 'sour grapes' (a motivational state that has been altered by a motivational mechanism); and (3) wishful thinking (cognitive false consciousness that is motivational in origin). I shall take them in order.

1 *Fallacies of inference*

Elster describes feudalism and the Roman relationship of patronage between servants and masters as sustained by what he calls an 'optical

---

[2] See particularly *Sour Grapes* and *Making Sense of Marx*.

illusion'.[3] The servant in these societies characteristically believes that his relationship with his master is a mutually beneficial one, a conclusion he draws from the fact that his economic contribution to the welfare of the master is apparently matched by the protection that the master gives to him. The fallacy, as Elster sees it, is in the servant failing to recognize that the protection that he receives is from other masters: it is only a benefit to the servant so long as there are masters to be protected from.

The criticism to be made of Elster's account from the point of view of the theory of ideology is that he does not distinguish between cognitive failures that are the result of a general inadequacy of reasoning on the part of the individual, and those that result from specific features of the situation the individual faces. Yet this distinction is crucial for the explanation of political compliance. Even if it is true that individuals are prone to reason badly in certain ways, that is not sufficient to explain why they are more likely to accept a particular social order than they would be otherwise. Why, for instance, should it not make them prone to non-rational *dissatisfaction*, rather than tending to accept the existing order?[4]

Elster suggests that the illusion that servants and masters engage in mutually beneficial exchange results from the tendency individuals have to generalize illegitimately from particular cases. But this is not sufficient to explain why generalization (which, in the normal case, is a cognitively reasonable process) should here prove to be both misleading and conservative in its social consequences. Is it just a matter of good luck (from the point of view of the social system in question, that is) that human beings' cognitive limitations favour the existing social order, or is there something about the nature of that system that tends to encourage false beliefs about itself? In other words, is the system, to revert to my own terminology, a *deceptive object*? Marx himself, as we have seen, is strongly committed to this claim in relation to capitalism, but, as he presents it, the claim draws on a version of the distinction between essence and appearance that is, in the end, derived from a Hegelian ontology of social life. Nevertheless, the idea of a deceptive object does not have to be ontologically problematic (anyone, whatever their wider philosophical commitments, should agree that the tiger's stripes make the tiger a deceptive object).

The analytical Marxist such as Elster, I suggest, should be looking to develop and defend a non-Hegelian interpretation of the claim that capitalism is a deceptive object. In that case, it would be possible to present false consciousness as the result of the application of otherwise reasonable cognitive mechanisms in a situation which encouraged their failure. In fact, the outlines of such a defence are not hard to envisage. The best line of argument would seem to be the claim that societies that are individual-istically organized – societies in which economic life is a matter of market

---

[3] *Making Sense of Marx*, p. 488.
[4] The view that general human cognitive deficiencies lead to irrational non-compliance is, of course, Hobbes's. See the quotation at p. 127 above.

exchange and the social interactions of individuals are regulated principally by a system of enforceable individual rights – are prone to characteristic illusions regarding collective processes. For instance, it is plausible to think that it is the market itself that encourages the (false) belief that the returns an individual receives from market exchanges reflect the contribution he makes to the welfare of society. This claim has the advantage of explaining how a certain social system can encourage beliefs that are supportive of itself *without* committing itself to a view of those who hold such beliefs as doing so because they are some kind of passive victims of a manipulative agency.

Although it would be fair to call this account a reconstruction of the Marxist theory of ideology, it differs substantially from either the functionalist interpretation of the correspondence model or the Hegelian interpretation, both of which were examined in Chapter 6. What those approaches had in common was the commitment to the idea of societies as self-maintaining entities. On the view being canvassed here, however, the best explanation for the *deceptiveness* of capitalism is its *defectiveness*. Capitalism is defective in the individualistic way in which it organizes collective processes and deceptive in the way in which those processes present themselves at first sight to those who are engaged in them. Yet, although the deceptiveness of capitalism is *functional for* it, and although the deceptiveness is *explained by* the defectiveness, that explanation is not a functional one, derived from the nature of capitalism as a self-maintaining system.

2 Sour grapes

The name comes, of course, from the fable of the fox and the grapes, but the phenomenon it refers to represents, Elster believes, something of very general significance for social science: the ability of agents to affect their own immediate motivational states in response to underlying motivations. 'Sour grapes', as Elster presents it, is not so much an instance of false consciousness in the sense of a pathological phenomenon as a reasonable (although not rational) response to a situation in which a desired satisfaction is unobtainable – a response that advances the agent's interests in some degree but would not be the outcome achieved by the conscious application of *reasoning*. It seems to be in the interests of the fox to alter his attitude towards the grapes by altering his belief about them.[5]

The force of 'sour grapes' is less obvious than Elster assumes. The benefit for agents in believing that what they cannot attain is not worth having anyway may be thought to come in two ways: by increasing the

---

[5] Elster's own description of sour grapes as a 'motivational' change that is 'motivationally' explained is misleading, since the change in attitude towards the grapes is the result of a cognitive change. But it is true that that change is itself affectively motivated.

satisfaction they gain from what is in fact attainable and by reducing the frustration they feel in the face of what is not attainable. But why should what is available to us be more attractive or satisfying just because something else that is unattainable now seems worse? On the other hand, frustration, painful though it may be, is not in all cases against the agent's interests. It is motivating to the extent that it leads us to make efforts to achieve what we feel we could or should be able to attain (if only the fox had had one more try . . .). And anyway, if the reduction of frustration is really in our interests, would it not be better to adjust our desires by accepting the fact that the object is unattainable – rather than trying to persuade ourselves that it is not desirable at all?[6]

Even if these points can be dealt with, however, 'sour grapes' is insufficient to provide an alternative to the theory of ideology as an account of the voluntary acceptance of *prima facie* illegitimate social orders. As presented by Elster, sour grapes is an adaptation of one's desires to *force majeure* – that of the prisoner who adapts to the locked cell by failing to value his freedom. But Reich's problem, of course, was quite different – not: Why do prisoners locked in their cells abandon their appetite for freedom?, but: Why do they fail to notice that the cell door is open?

3 *Wishful thinking*

The third mechanism for false consciousness that Elster suggests is that of *wishful thinking* – the adaptation of our beliefs to our desires. Elster describes this phenomenon as being 'of overwhelming importance in human life'. Like other writers on the subject, Elster seems to regard the mechanism as unproblematic.[7] I want to argue, however, that wishful thinking is a good deal less obvious than Elster seems to think. I shall

---

[6] Incidentally – although it does not matter much to the substantive discussion – Elster's reading of La Fontaine's version of the fable (which he quotes at p. 109 of *Sour Grapes*) seems to me quite wrong.

The fox is, according to La Fontaine, '*mourant presque de faim*' (almost dying of hunger) when he sees the grapes. However, when he realizes that he cannot reach them, he says (note: '*dit-il*' – he *says* – not '*se dit-il*', says to himself) that they are 'too green' and that they are '*faits pour des goujats*' (my dictionary says 'boors' or 'churls' – I would suggest perhaps 'louts'). La Fontaine's next sentence – the conclusion – is to ask 'Did he not do better than to complain?'

La Fontaine does not suggest that the fox was less hungry at the end of the story than he would have been otherwise and so it seems clear that the fox himself did not believe that the grapes were really too green. From this I conclude that the proper reading is not as a fable about the fox's successful management of his own desires. The story is really about the aristocratic self-image – the *amour-propre* – that leads the fox to prefer to present a palpable falsehood to having to acknowledge in public the frustration that we, the readers, know that he still continues to feel. He dismisses the grapes *to others* as not being good enough for one such as himself, not as a way of managing his desires but as a kind of arrogant (or, if you follow La Fontaine, noble) gesture of dissimulation.

[7] *Making Sense of Marx*, p. 466. Elster's principal argument is directed towards distinguishing wishful thinking from *self-deception* – a phenomenon that he *does* think is paradoxical, since it seems to imply that the self is capable of selecting beliefs according to its perceived interests and that it is at the same time ignorant of those beliefs.

follow Elster's assumption that wishful thinking (like 'sour grapes') is something that is, very broadly speaking, reasonable (that is, that has benefits for the person who engages in it) rather than a perverse or pathological phenomenon.[8]

Certainly, we frequently have immensely strong reasons for wishing that a belief, p, is true. But this is not *wishful thinking*. Wishful thinking involves not just *wishing for* p, but being willing to believe p without good evidence, or, indeed, at the limit, in the face of good evidence to the contrary. Those, like Elster, who do not see a problem in explaining wishful thinking presumably make the following inference:

If it is true that we have strong reasons for wishing that a belief p *is true, then we have strong reasons for believing* p *whether it is true or not.*

But the inference is invalid. In general, the reason I have to wish that p is true is the benefit I would derive from the fact p, if it obtains. So there is a real problem in determining why, if p does not obtain, I should nevertheless benefit just from thinking that it does. If wishful thinking is to be understood in terms of the apparent benefits that it brings the believer, its benefits will be the *benefits of belief* (rather than the benefits of whatever would make the belief true).

Where should one expect to find those benefits? As a first hypothesis, let me suggest that wishful thinking will be the more likely the smaller the discrepancy there is between (1) a belief, p, being both believed to be true and actually being true, and (2) p being believed to be true, but in fact being false. It follows from this point that it is not true that the more important the *issue* (the content of the belief) is to the believer, the more likely beliefs about it are to be subject to wishful thinking. Although the 'pay-off' from a belief being true may be very high in such a case, it is also very likely to have strongly adverse practical consequences if it is, in fact, false and those practical consequences will be made even worse by the believer failing to recognize its falsehood – however good our reasons for wanting to become invisible, sticking our heads in the sand and believing that we *are* invisible is only likely to make matters worse.

A further suggestion that turns out to be less plausible than is commonly assumed is that the benefits of belief lie in giving the believer the opportunity to take satisfaction in an imagined state of affairs. However much stern moralists like Rousseau might regard it as perverse or reprehensible, it does indeed seem to be a fact that the imagination can

---

[8] Of course, it *could* be that wishful thinking is a pathological phenomenon: that the more important an issue is to us emotionally the less likely we are to reason clearly about it.

This is more or less Hume's view. For Hume, wishful thinking and fearful thinking go together – we are not more likely to err on the side of what we would like to be true than of what we fear. The emotions of hope and fear both increase credulity and lead us to move more easily from entertaining a proposition to believing it than we should do, whether that proposition is irrationally optimistic (the faith of the enthusiast) or fearful (the anxiety that leads to superstition).

give pleasures that are to some extent substitutes for the 'real thing'. Yet this does not explain wishful thinking. For wishful thinking goes beyond day-dream or fantasy: it is actually *believing* that a desired state of affairs exists, and it is not obvious why a desire for fantastic satisfaction requires us to take this extra step. Why should we delude ourselves for the sake of satisfaction when we might have that satisfaction *without* confusing imagination and reality?

Another apparently obvious benefit from wishful thinking is that of being able to avoid the effort of revising our beliefs, as we might have to should we accept a belief as true that we had not expected to be so. Yet it is important to see that the benefit here is generally one of being able to postpone a cost rather than being able to avoid it altogether: it may benefit us to carry on in the face of the facts in the short term, but, if the facts at issue really are salient ones for us, then, sooner or later, we will probably lose if we fail to face up to them. It is not difficult to appreciate why it should be that those faced with appalling news are not able to assimilate it initially, yet it is striking that this is a normal part of a process of shock, grief and mourning whose general outcome is the acceptance of even the most unpalatable reality: short-term avoidance is healthily associated with long-term acceptance.

Thus the kind of beliefs that will be particularly susceptible to wishful thinking will be beliefs whose falsehood does not have serious and immediate negative consequences for the subject's life. Obvious examples of such beliefs are beliefs about facts remote from ourselves, beliefs that are difficult to confirm or refute, and beliefs of the second order – religious, metaphysical or cosmological beliefs: in other words, just the kind of beliefs that we have, independently, found to be the typical subject-matter for the theory of ideology. The most important kind of benefit that holding such beliefs has for individuals is that they lead them to believe that their situation is *good, acceptable* or, at the least, *intelligible*.[9]

In this way we are returned to the Nietzschean perspective identified in Chapter 1. According to Nietzsche, it will be recalled, there are three basic strategies that (Western) human beings have used to make the world acceptable to themselves – three ways in which they have responded to the problem of suffering: through the intoxication of self-abandonment (Dionysianism); through the contemplation of a realm of beauty (Apollonianism); and through the attempt to make the world intelligible (Socratism). It is the latter two strategies that are particularly relevant here. Beliefs which

---

[9] Certainly, beliefs about ourselves as individuals will be also subject to wishful thinking. But the point made earlier will still apply: the potential for continuing to hold beliefs just because they are satisfying will be the greater the less harmful the immediate practical consequences of false beliefs are.

Thus someone at the end of a love affair may want to believe that their lover will return to them. But, rather than the strictly factual belief that the lover *will* return at some specific time, the belief that the break-up is not the individual's fault, that they are still lovable, and so on, are more likely to survive, since the benefits they offer in enhancing individuals' views of their situation are less obviously balanced by negative consequences.

show that the world is generally systematic, orderly and intelligible will be satisfying for the believer in ways that go beyond the empirical benefits of any true beliefs that might be contained in that view. In the first place, the idea of system is itself of aesthetic value (Apollonianism); secondly, finding a reason is of benefit to us not just in virtue of offering an explanation for a particular phenomenon but because it reassures us that things in general *are* explicable (Socratism).

That both providentialism and rationalism can be seen in this way does not require much argument. What could be more reassuring than to be able to see history and society as the result of action by a benevolent and overwhelmingly powerful creator? Nor is it difficult to fit rationalism into the Nietzschean schema. The important point here is the one made by Horkheimer and Adorno in the *Dialectic of Enlightenment*, namely, that the impulse behind rationalism is the desire for *control* – practical control over non-human reality, and, equally, control over a self that is potentially alien or threatening. While providentialism says that the world, overall, embodies a good order (apparent evil is a part of that order) rationalism offers the prospect that evil can to some extent be controlled or escaped by the subject's own discretionary power of choice. Where rationalism and providentialism appear together, as they do, for instance, in Plato and Hegel, the message is that the self has the power to adapt itself to the good order.

Yet, if we are to follow Nietzsche, it is not just the providentialist idea that the ultimate source of order is benevolent that is non-rationally appealing to the believer. The sheer promise that everything *can* be explained is itself consoling. A systematic scientific explanation shows that what happens is *necessary*, that it flows as a consequence from a timeless system of laws. It is significant from the Nietzschean point of view how often supposedly secular scientists and mathematicians characterize the value of their enquiries in aesthetic terms. In this way, the investigation of nature becomes an exercise in Apollonianism. The self can escape from its mundane cares and concerns to contemplate reality from the standpoint of a 'view from nowhere': necessity is aestheticized into the beauty of the eternal order. For Nietzsche, the cosmology of natural-scientific materialism is just as much of a myth as any other: an artificial matrix overlaid onto the anarchic diversity of the 'will-to-power'. But, even if we do not subscribe to Nietzsche's own purportedly anti-metaphysical metaphysics and to the general distrust of mechanical explanations to which this leads him, his account of the hidden appeal of the belief in order is worth taking seriously. At the least, it should lead us to be suspicious of the tendency to overextend explanations beyond what is warranted.[10]

To the extent that the characteristic form of such explanations is to

---

[10] I repeat here a point made in Chapter 1: it is wrong to assume that every phenomenon requires an explanation. The recognition that certain phenomena (phenomena under certain descriptions) are *not* susceptible to explanation can itself be an important form of intellectual progress.

represent the world as a natural order, its immediate implications are generally conservative: suffering, inequality, apparent injustice are presented as the inevitable results of natural laws and initial conditions. The point is expressed in the memorable quotation from Darwin used by Stephen Jay Gould as the epigraph to his study *The Mismeasure of Man*: 'If the misery of our poor be caused not by the laws of nature, but by our institutions, great is our sin.'[11] Gould's book, a brilliant exploration of the intrusion of bias into the study of intelligence testing, provides perhaps the best-documented specific account we have of the origins of false beliefs which have significant social consequences. Gould makes it clear that those whom he accuses of error (and, in one famous case, fraud) were sincere and regarded themselves as objective scientists. Although they had strong political views, there is no reason to suppose that their scientific research was simply a deliberate response to a political agenda (they were not Marx's 'hired prize-fighters' of the bourgeoisie). Nevertheless, it is plausible to suppose that the background beliefs on which the entire research programme to which they subscribed rested – that of finding an origin in biological nature for social distinctions and forms of behaviour – were ones that they found deeply (and, in my view, perniciously) intellectually satisfying. That these beliefs should have led to conclusions that they found congenial politically was no disadvantage.

IV Ideology as False Consciousness

I now come to my third claim:

The theory of ideology is a theory about false consciousness that is itself (in part at least) to be explained as a product of non-rational belief: part of its plausibility lies in the fact that it gives the world a particularly appealing kind of intelligibility.

The argument of this book has been that elements plainly incompatible with scientific materialism play a far more important role in Marx's mature thought than he or his defenders recognize or could accept. One way of looking at their presence is as a failure on Marx's part to carry through his own programme – to complete the purge of Hegelianism from his social thought and to replace its overarching collective subject with properly individualistic micro-foundations. On this view, Marx would remain basically a part of the great secularization: the deposition of providentialist and teleological world-views by the advance of impersonal, predictive scientific explanation. The theory of ideology might be an incautious

---

[11] The fallacy – as Hume noted in his essay *Of Suicide* – is to assume that institutions (or conscious human intervention) are any less 'natural' than the basic facts of biology.

overextension of progress – a 'bridge too far' – but still part of that enterprise.

In my opinion, however, these unscientific elements are too central to Marx's mature thought to be just imperfectly purged impurities in the social-scientific test-tube. Although it is not simply a piece of quackery, the theory of ideology runs far further in advance of the evidence than any natural scientist would find acceptable. Moreover, the fact that what makes a belief 'good for' a particular social order is left open (at least in the functionalist interpretation of the theory) means that the theory of ideology can operate as a kind of 'just-so' story: giving an apparently comprehensive explanation for phenomena of social life that would otherwise be explained only partially or not at all while protecting itself from the risks of refutation.

While Marx's own account of his theory is as a purely secular and scientific enterprise, both rationalism (explicitly) and providentialism (implicitly) are clearly present in it. Marx's conception of human beings as finding their true selves through the conscious (and collective) exercise of control over the natural world is plainly rationalist, while his depiction of history as a series of stages in which oppression and exploitation are finally redeemed by the realization of a new, emancipated form of human community shares the providentialist structure that depicts evil as part of the price to be paid for the achievement of what is good.[12] The ontological doctrine of society as self-maintaining was itself an inheritance from providentialist thinkers – Smith, Herder and Hegel, in particular. So far from being a mere survival of pre-modern views, these providentialist attempts to trace progress in history were products of a period that saw the rise of the secular natural sciences at its most rapid. They represent the transfer of the search for meaning from the disenchanted world of the physical sciences to human history, and it is surely plausible to suppose that the continuation of this motivation explains part of the appeal of Marx's own theory in general and of the theory of ideology in particular.

What is most pernicious, however, is the way that the theory of ideology enables those who hold it to divide the world between those who are (presumed to be) and those who are not in ideology's grip. The theory of ideology offers its holders the psychic benefits that come to those who believe that they are part of an elite or vanguard. It licenses that vanguard to ignore the actions, attitudes and even votes of those in whose names they claim to act. The Leninist party, the presumed repository of correct consciousness, acts in pursuit of the interests of the working class, as it understands them; but it acts *on behalf of* the working-class, rather than as its representative, for it follows from the theory of ideology that the working class's own perception of what would further its interests is

---

[12] There is, of course, no conflict between rationalism and scientific materialism: on one (in my opinion, mistaken) view, the former is the necessary consequence of the latter. On the other hand, the *appeal* of rationalism goes beyond the merely factual.

distorted and inadequate.[13] In allowing those who hold it to distinguish between what people actually believe and what they *ought* to believe – their *imputed* class-consciousness, in Lukács's phrase – the theory of ideology immunizes those who hold it against unpleasant reality. The history of the Marxist left shows all too clearly how such short-run benefits of belief can lead to catastrophe in the long term.

V Beyond Rationalism and Providentialism

Thus the theory of ideology – a theory that was presented as an objective attempt to understand the nature of beliefs held for non-rational reasons – can be seen as a part of the phenomenon that it purports to explain. But the problems that the theory of ideology addresses remain real, even if we are sceptical about the solutions it offers. In conclusion, I want to identify three issues that remain of central importance for social theory, even if we no longer look to the theory of ideology to resolve them.

I *Non-rational belief*

There is little difficulty in explaining why rich people tend to argue (and, indeed, argue sincerely) that social inequalities are a good thing; the important question is why poor people believe them. I have indicated in the previous two sections where I think we should start in our attempts to construct accounts of non-rational beliefs that go against the interests of those who hold them.

Non-rational beliefs should be approached, in my view, not as something wholly *pathological* – a deviation from reasonable processes for the formation of consciousness – but as attempts to make the world acceptable by making it intelligible. Both *The Birth of Tragedy* and *The Dialectic of Enlightenment* remain fertile accounts of the ways in which Western culture has tried to satisfy this need. But they are formulated, it must be admitted, at the level of heroic generality, with very little detailed historical scrutiny. The task would be to apply these general perspectives in ways that are historically and socially specific: to explain how certain paradigms of intelligibility and models of the nature of reality come to exercise a hold over particular societies (or of certain groups within societies) at particular times by meeting the need for explanation in different ways.

Such explanations will be less clear-cut and deterministic than either the theory of ideology or its Hegelian predecessor, for there is no suggestion that the search for meaning is inescapably determined to take

---

[13] This point has been pressed both by the anti-communist right and the libertarian left. See, for example, Kolakowski, *Main Currents of Marxism*, and the writings of Cornelius Castoriadis (particularly those published under the name of P. Cardan).

only particular forms at particular times (or, indeed, that it is itself the sole determinant of ideas). Thus, even at its most dominant, the providentialism of the seventeenth and eighteenth centuries remained contestable in principle – it was never some inescapable categorial framework limiting human beings' access to the world.

What providentialism offered was a ready model that satisfied a series of (broadly speaking) explanatory needs in ways that were thought to be consonant with the developing science of the time. Once established, providentialism, like all such models, became part of the intellectual division of labour: it offered the benefits of quick and easy explanation and attention was focused less on whether the underlying model was true than on how it was to be applied. Just as contemporary zoologists start from the assumption that salient, genetically heritable characteristics of species are capable of being given an evolutionary explanation and concern themselves solely with *what* that evolutionary explanation might be, so a very high proportion of eighteenth-century thinkers were prepared to apply the model of providentialism ubiquitously.

The providentialist literature of the time includes works on the origin of social inequality, such as Swift's *Sermon on the Poor Man's Contentment* and Sterne's *The Ways of Providence Justified to Man*.[14] These works contain attempts – some ingenious, some ingenuous – to square inequalities of wealth with divine benevolence, and there can be no doubt whatsoever that they served the existing social order. Moreover, clergymen such as Swift and Sterne were, if not exactly 'prize-fighters', certainly hired by that order. Nevertheless, the providentialist defence of social inequality is not to be explained simply as the inevitable result of the social position and the class-interest of those who held it. No conceptual barriers prevented Samuel Johnson (no less of a religious man, and no less of an adherent of the established order than Swift or Sterne) from ridiculing such efforts to Boswell:

> Sir, the great deal of arguing that we hear to represent poverty as no evil shows it to be evidently a great one. You never knew people labouring to convince you that you might live very happily upon a plentiful fortune.[15]

With the decline of providentialism, the character of non-rational belief about society changed significantly. The nineteenth century saw the displacement of providentialist justifications of social inequality by biologistic ones. Such doctrines as Social Darwinism were presented as the natural extension of a prestigious form of scientific theory (one which was, after all, unimpeachable in its own sphere) yet they went far beyond what could be justified scientifically. An analysis of the contemporary role of non-rational belief should explore the ways in which *scientism* – the

---

[14] Discussed by Viner, *The Role of Providence in the Social Order*, pp. 86–113.
[15] Boswell's *Journal*, quoted by Viner, p. 105.

extension of elements of either the form or the content of science beyond their proper sphere – has displaced providentialism in giving a consoling apparent intelligibility to the social order.[16]

2 *The unity of culture*

One of the themes that Marx took up from his predecessors was the idea that the different parts of social life are held together in such a way that one area can be seen to correspond in some sense to another. As it appears in Hegel, this idea depicts society as a set of diverse forms of life through which a single common principle runs; a principle that is derived, in the end, from the structure of *Geist*. Yet, while this notion is derived from Hegel's metaphysics of an overarching subject realizing itself in and through material reality, those metaphysics themselves can no longer command acceptance. Is it possible to defend a form of what Gombrich calls 'Hegelianism without metaphysics'?

Marx's own answer, as we have seen, lies in postulating a correspondence between economic and non-economic life such that the latter are 'reflections' of the former. Yet Marx himself gives no adequate suggestion regarding the mechanism by which the two might be connected. The best suggestion is that to be found in Benjamin and Lévi-Strauss: that there exists some form of tacit knowledge by which particular structures and kinds of content are brought to expression in a diversity of human cultural products. If so, then the identification of such affinities will be of central importance to the history of art and to cultural studies in general.

3 *False consciousness*

I have criticized the Western tradition for having a rationalist conception of the good for human beings. The Marxist critique of false consciousness is itself part of that rationalist tradition. Thus the Marxist ideal is of a reintegrated collective subject in which each individual will engage in fully transparent productive activity. Although a critique of rationalism is to be found in different forms in the writings of Rousseau, Stendhal, Nietzsche, Proust and Benjamin, that critique is often questionable and lacks the foundations that would be needed to constitute a truly effective alternative to the dominance of rationalism. Freudianism has represented a challenge to rationalism, in some respects, but in others it has obscured the issue, for the Freudian tradition itself has remained equivocal between *pessimism* (endorsing rationalist ends, while disputing the effectiveness of reason as a means for achieving them) and rationalism (believing that it had discovered

---

[16] On this point I agree with Jürgen Habermas, who has explored this theme in much of his most interesting writing.

a peculiarly rational means for effective intervention to alter the determinants of human beings' actions). The challenge, I suggest, is to pursue the construction of a genuinely anti-rationalist understanding of the self that will not simply capitulate to unreason. The task will be both conceptual (in developing a plausible alternative to the ideals of control and discretionary power) and, of course, empirical.

These, then, are three large, complex and difficult projects. Nor can their success be guaranteed, short of assuming the *a priori* truth of another overarching grand theory. But the questions that are involved are of exceptional importance, both theoretically and practically. If the argument of this book has persuaded any of its readers to turn their energies to addressing them, then writing it will have been worth while.

Bibliography

Adorno, T. W., *Ästhetische Theorie* (Frankfurt am Main: Suhrkamp, 1974).

Adorno, T. W., *Drei Studien zu Hegel* (Frankfurt am Main: Suhrkamp, 1970).

Adorno, T. W., *Introduction to the Sociology of Music*, trans. E. B. Ashton (New York: Continuum, 1988).

Adorno, T. W., *Minima Moralia* (Frankfurt am Main: Suhrkamp, 1951).

Adorno, T. W., *Negative Dialektik* (Frankfurt am Main: Suhrkamp, 1975).

Adorno, T. W., 'Ideologie', in *Soziologische Exkurse* (Frankfurt am Main: Europäische Verlagsanstalt, 1974).

Adorno, T. W., *Über Walter Benjamin* (Frankfurt am Main: Suhrkamp, 1970).

Adorno, T. W., and Horkheimer, M., *The Dialectic of Enlightenment* (London: Allen Lane, 1973).

Althusser, L., 'Ideology and Ideological State Apparatuses', in *Essays on Ideology* (London: Verso, 1984).

Aristotle, *Nichomachean Ethics* (Harmondsworth: Penguin, 1963).

Aristotle, *The Politics*, trans. T. Sinclair (Harmondsworth: Penguin, 1962).

Augustine, St, *City of God* (Harmondsworth: Penguin, 1972).

Augustine, St, *Confessions* (Oxford: OUP, 1991).

Avineri, S., 'Consciousness and History: *List der Vernunft* in Hegel and Marx', in W. Steinkraus (ed.), *New Studies in Hegel's Philosophy* (New York: Holt, Rinehart and Winston, 1971), pp. 108–18.

Bacon, F., *Novum Organon* (Indianapolis: Bobbs-Merrill, 1960).

Barnard, F. M., *Herder's Social and Political Thought* (Cambridge: CUP, 1969).

Barthes, R., *Critical Essays* (Evanston, IL: Northwestern University Press, 1972).

Bayle, P., *Historical and Critical Dictionary*, trans. R. Popkin (Indianapolis: Bobbs-Merrill, 1965).

Becker, C., *The Heavenly City of the Eighteenth-Century Philosophers* (New Haven: Yale University Press, 1932).

Becker, H. and Barnes, H., *Social Thought from Lore to Science* (Boston: Heath, 1938).

Beiser, F., *Enlightenment, Revolution and Romanticism* (Cambridge, MA: Harvard University Press, 1992).

Beiser, F., *The Fate of Reason* (Cambridge, MA: Harvard University Press, 1987).

Benjamin, W., *Briefe* (Frankfurt am Main: Suhrkamp, 1978).

Benjamin, W., 'Das Kunstwerk im Zeitalter seiner technischen Reproduzierbarkeit', in *Gesammelte Schriften* (Frankfurt am Main: Suhrkamp, 1974), vol. I.2, pp. 471–508.

Benjamin, W., *Einbahnstrasse*, in *Gesammelte Schriften* (Frankfurt am Main: Suhrkamp, 1974), vol. IV.1, pp. 84–148.

Benjamin, W., *Das Passagen-Werk*, in *Gesammelte Schriften* (Frankfurt am Main: Suhrkamp, 1974), vol. V.

Benjamin, W., 'Über das Programm der kommenden Philosophie', in *Gesammelte Schriften* (Frankfurt am Main: Suhrkamp, 1974), vol. II.1, pp. 157–71.

Benjamin, W., 'Über den Begriff der Geschichte', in *Gesammelte Schriften* (Frankfurt am Main: Suhrkamp, 1974), vol. I.2, pp. 691–704.

Benjamin, W., 'Über einige Motive bei Baudelaire', in *Gesammelte Schriften* (Frankfurt am Main: Suhrkamp, 1974), vol. I.2, 607–53.

Benjamin, W., *Der Ursprung des deutschen Trauerspiels*, in *Gesammelte Schriften* (Frankfurt am Main: Suhrkamp, 1974), vol. I.1, pp. 202–430.

Berlin, I., *Vico and Herder* (London: Chatto & Windus, 1975).

Berger, P., *Invitation to Sociology* (New York: Anchor, 1963).

Berlin, I., *The Magus of the North: J. G. Hamann and the Origins of Modern Irrationalism* (London: John Murray, 1993).

Berman, M., *The Politics of Authenticity* (New York: Atheneum, 1970).

Blumenberg, H., *Die Legitimität der Neuzeit* (Frankfurt am Main: Suhrkamp, 1966).

Blumenberg, H., *Die Lesbarkeit der Welt* (Frankfurt am Main: Surhkamp, 1981).

Blumenberg, H., 'Paradigmen zu einer Metaphorologie', in *Archiv für Begriffsgeschichte*, 6 (1960), pp. 7–142.

Bock, K., 'Theories of Progress, Development, Evolution', in T. Bottomore and R. Nisbet (eds), *A History of Sociological Analysis* (London: Heinemann, 1978), pp. 39–79.

de la Boetie, E., *De la servitude volontaire*, trans. as *The Politics of Obedience* (New York: Free Life Editions, 1975).

Bossuet, J.-B., *Discourse on Universal History*, trans. E. Forster (Chicago: University of Chicago Press, 1976).

Boyle, Robert, 'About the Excellency and Grounds of the Mechanical Hypothesis', in *Selected Philosophical Papers of Robert Boyle* (Manchester: Manchester University Press, 1979), pp. 138–54.

de Brosses, C., *Du culte des dieux fétiches, ou parallèle de l'ancienne réligion de l'Egypte avec la réligion actuelle de Nigritie* (1760).

Brown, R., *The Nature of Social Laws* (Cambridge: CUP, 1973).

Burton, R., *The Anatomy of Melancholy* (London: Dent, 1977).

Castro, Fidel, *History Will Absolve Me* (London: Cape, 1969).

Clark, R. T., *Herder: His Life and Thought* (Berkeley: University of California Press, 1955).

Cohen, G. A., *Karl Marx's Theory of History: a Defence* (Oxford: OUP, 1978).

Coleridge, S. T., *The Statesman's Manual*, in *Collected Works*, ed. R. J. White (London: Routledge & Kegan Paul, 1972), VI.

Coward, R. and Ellis, J., *Language and Materialism* (London: Routledge & Kegan Paul, 1977).
Craig, E., *The Mind of God and the Works of Man* (Oxford: OUP, 1987).
Debord, G., *The Society of the Spectacle* (Detroit: Black & Red, 1970).
Deleuze, G. and Guattari, F., *L'Anti-Oedipe: capitalisme et schizophrénie* (Paris: Minuit, 1972).
Dent, N., *Rousseau* (Oxford: Blackwell, 1988).
Diderot, D., *Rameau's Nephew and D'Alembert's Dream*, trans. L. Tancock (Harmondsworth: Penguin, 1966),.
Dodds, E. R., *The Greeks and the Irrational* (Berkeley: University of California Press, 1973).
Douglas, M., *Purity and Danger* (London: Routledge, 1978).
Durkheim, E., *The Elementary Forms of Religious Life* (London: Allen & Unwin, 1976).
Eckermann, J. P., *Gespräche mit Goethe* (Frankfurt am Main: Insel, 1980).
Elster, J., *Making Sense of Marx* (Cambridge: CUP, 1985).
Elster, J., *Sour Grapes* (Cambridge: CUP, 1983).
Erikson, K., *Wayward Puritans* (New York: Wiley, 1966).
Ferguson, A., *An Essay on the History of Civil Society* (1767) (Edinburgh: Edinburgh University Press, 1966).
Fichte, J. G., *Grundlage des Naturrechts nach Prinzipien der Wissenschaftlehre* (Hamburg: Felix Meiner, 1960).
Forbes, D., *Hume's Philosophical Politics* (Cambridge: CUP, 1975).
Foucault, M., *The Archaeology of Knowledge* (London: Tavistock, 1972).
Foucault, M., *The Order of Things* (1966) (London: Tavistock, 1970).
Freud, S., 'Thoughts for the Times on War and Death', in *The Pelican Freud Library*, Vol. 12 (Harmondsworth: Penguin, n.d.).
Geschichtliche Grundbegriffe, ed. O. Brunner, W. Konze and R. Koselleck (Stuttgart: Klett, 1972–92).
Geuss, R., *The Idea of a Critical Theory* (Cambridge: CUP, 1981).
Goethe, J. W., *Gespräche* (Leipzig: Biedermann, 1910).
Goethe, J. W., *Maximen und Reflexionen*, in *Werke* (Munich: DTV, 1982), XII.
Goethe, J. W., 'Über die Gegenstände der bildenden Kunst', in *Werke* (Stuttgart: Cotta, n.d.), XVI, pp. 459–62.
Gombrich, E. H., *In Search of Cultural History* (Oxford: OUP, 1969).
Gould, S. J., *Ever Since Darwin* (Harmondsworth: Penguin, 1978).
Gould, S. J., *Hen's Teeth and Horses' Toes* (Harmondsworth: Penguin, 1984).
Gould, S. J., *The Mismeasure of Man* (Harmondsworth: Penguin, 1984).
Habermas, J., *Knowledge and Human Interests* (1968) (London: Heinemann, 1978).
Hacking, I., *Why Does Language Matter to Philosophy?* (Cambridge: CUP, 1975).
Hale, D. G., 'Analogy of the Body Politic', in *Dictionary of the History of Ideas*, ed. P. Wiener (New York: Scribner, 1973), I, pp. 67–70.
Hamann, J. G., *Aesthetica in nuce*, in *Schriften zur Sprache*, ed. J. Simon (Frankfurt am Main: Suhrkamp, 1967).
Harré, R., *The Philosophies of Science* (Oxford: OUP, 1972).
Heer, F., *The Intellectual History of Europe* (New York: Anchor, 1968).
Hegel, G. W. F., *Werke*, ed. K.-M. Michel and E. Moldenhauer (Frankfurt am Main: Suhrkamp, 1971).
Hegel, G. W. F., *Phänomenologie des Geistes*, ed. J. Hoffmeister (Hamburg: Meiner, 1952).

Hegel, G. W. F., *The Philosophy of History*, ed. J. Sibree (New York: Dover, 1956).

Hegel, G. W. F., *Wissenschaft der Logik*, ed. G. Lasson (Hamburg: Meiner, 1971).

Heidegger, M., *Being and Time*, trans. J. Macqarrie and E. Robinson (Oxford: Blackwell, 1967).

Heine, H., *Englische Fragmente*, in *Sämtliche Werke* (Hamburg: Hoffman & Campe, 1986), VII/1.

Herder, J. G., *Plastik*, in *Sämtliche Werke*, ed. B. Suphan (Berlin, 1877–1913), VIII.

Herder, J. G., *Reflections on the Philosophy of the History of Mankind* (1784–91), trans. W. Churchill (Chicago: University of Chicago Press, 1968).

Herder, J. G., *Herder on Social and Political Culture*, ed. F.M. Barnard (Cambridge: CUP, 1969).

Hirschman, A. O., *Exit, Voice and Loyalty* (Cambridge, MA: Harvard University Press, 1970).

Hirschman, A. O., *The Passions and the Interests* (Princeton: Princeton University Press, 1977).

Historisches Wörterbuch der Philosophie, ed. by J. Ritter et al. (Stuttgart: Schwabe, 1971).

Hobbes, T., *Leviathan*, ed. C. B. MacPherson (Harmondsworth: Penguin, 1968).

Horkheimer, M., 'Traditionelle und Kritische Theorie', in *Kritische Theorie*, 2 (1968) trans. in P. Connerton (ed.), *Critical Sociology* (Harmondsworth: Penguin, 1976).

Hume, D., *Dialogues Concerning Natural Religion* (Indianapolis: Hackett, 1983).

Hume, D., *Enquiry Concerning Human Understanding*, in *Enquiries* (Oxford: OUP, 1986).

Hume, D., *The Natural History of Religion*, ed. H. E. Root (Stanford: Stanford University Press, 1985).

Hume, D., *Treatise of Human Nature*, ed. L. A. Selbey-Bigge (Oxford: OUP, 1968).

Jamme, C. and Schneider, H. (eds), *Mythologie der Vernunft: Hegel's 'ältestes Systemprogramm des deutschen Idealismus'* (Frankfurt am Main: Suhrkamp, 1984).

Jay, M., *Downcast Eyes: the Denigration of Vision in Twentieth-Century French Thought* (Berkeley: University of California Press, 1993).

Jay, M., *Force Fields* (New York: Routledge, 1993).

Kant, I., *Critique of Judgment* (1790), trans. J. H. Bernard (New York: Hafner, 1968).

Kant, I., *Critique of Pure Reason* (1781/1787), trans. N. Kemp Smith (London: Macmillan, 1970).

Kant, I., 'Idea for a Universal Natural History with a Cosmopolitan Purpose' (1784), in H. Reiss (ed.), *Kant's Political Writings* (Cambridge: CUP, 1970).

Kant, I., 'Perpetual Peace' (1796), in H. Reiss (ed.), *Kant's Political Writings* (Cambridge: CUP, 1970), pp 93–130.

Kemp Smith, N., *The Philosophy of David Hume* (London: Macmillan, 1941).

Kennedy, E., *A Philosophe in the Age of Revolution: Destutt de Tracy and the Origins of 'Ideology'* (Philadelphia: American Historical Society, 1978).

Kolakowski, L., *Main Currents of Marxism* (Oxford: OUP, 1975).

La Rochefoucauld, *Maxims*, trans. L. Tancock (Harmondsworth: Penguin, 1959).

Larrain, J., *The Concept of Ideology* (London: Hutchinson, 1979).

Leach, E., *Political Systems of Highland Burma* (London: Athlone, 1964).

Lévi-Strauss, C., *The Savage Mind* (London: Weidenfeld & Nicolson, 1966).

Lévi-Strauss, C., *Structural Anthropology* (Harmondsworth: Penguin, 1972).

Locke, J., *Second Treatise of Government*, in P. Laslett (ed.), *Two Treatises of Government* (Cambridge: CUP, 1967).

Löwith, K., *Meaning in History* (Chicago: University of Chicago Press, 1949).

Lovejoy, A. O., *The Great Chain of Being* (Cambridge, MA: Harvard University Press, 1936).

Lovejoy, A. O., *Reflections on Human Nature* (Baltimore: Johns Hopkins University Press, 1961).

Lypp, B., *Ästhetischer Absolutismus und politische Vernunft* (Frankfurt am Main: Suhrkamp, 1972).

Machiavelli, N., *Discourses* (Harmondsworth: Penguin, 1970).

MacIntyre, A., *After Virtue* (London: Duckworth, 1984).

Manuel, F., *The Eighteenth Century Confronts the Gods* (Cambridge, MA: Harvard University Press, 1959).

Manuel, F., *Shapes of Philosophical History* (Stanford: Stanford University Press, 1965).

Martindale, D., *The Nature and Types of Sociological Theory* (London: Routledge, 1960).

Marx, K., 'Towards a Critique of the Hegelian Philosophy of Right. Introduction' in *Critique of Hegel's "Philosophy of Right"*, ed. J. O'Malley (Cambridge: CUP, 1970), pp. 131–42.

Marx, K., *Critique of Hegel's "Philosophy of Right"*, ed. J. O'Malley (Cambridge: CUP, 1970).

Marx, K., *Economic and Philosophical Manuscripts* (1844) in *Early Writings*, ed. Q. Hoare (New York: Vintage, 1975).

Marx, K., *The Holy Family*, in *Collected Works*, Vol. IV (London: Lawrence & Wishart, 1975).

Marx, K., 'Theses on Feuerbach', in K. Marx and F. Engels, *The German Ideology*, ed. C. J. Arthur (London: Lawrence & Wishart, 1970), pp. 121–3.

Marx, K., *Grundrisse der Kritik der politischen Ökonomie* (Berlin: Dietz, 1980); trans. M. Nicolaus (Harmondsworth: Penguin, 1973).

Marx, K., *A Contribution to the Critique of Political Economy* (London: Lawrence & Wishart, 1971).

Marx, K., *Das Kapital*, 3 vols. (Berlin: Dietz, 1980): Vol. 1, trans. E. Aveling and S. Moore (New York: Modern Library, 1906); Vols. 2 & 3 (London: Lawrence & Wishart, 1972).

Marx, K., *Critique of the Gotha Programme*, in, D. McLellan (ed.) *Karl Marx: Selected Writings* (Oxford: OUP, 1977), pp. 564–70.

Marx, K. and Engels, F., *The German Ideology*, ed. C. J. Arthur (London: Lawrence & Wishart, 1970).

Marx, K. and Engels, F., *Selected Correspondence* (Moscow: Progress Publishers, 1955).

Meek, R., 'The Scottish Contribution to Marxist Sociology', in *Economics and Ideology and Other Essays* (London: Chapman & Hall, 1967), pp. 34–50.

Meek, R., 'The Rise and Fall of the Concept of the Economic Machine', in *Smith, Marx and After* (London: Chapman & Hall, 1977), pp. 176–88.

Meek, R., *Social Science and the Ignoble Savage* (Cambridge: CUP, 1975).

Merquior, J. G., *The Veil and the Mask* (London: Routledge & Kegan Paul, 1979).

Moeller-Gambaroff, M., 'Emanzipation macht Angst', in *Kursbuch*, 47 (1977).

Montesquieu, Baron, *The Spirit of the Laws* (1748), trans. T. Nugent (New York: Hafner, 1949).

More, H., *Enthusiasmus Triumphatus*, in *A Collection of Several Philosophical Writings of Dr Henry More* (London, 1712).

Nagel, T., 'Panpsychism', in *Mortal Questions* (Cambridge: CUP, 1979), pp. 181–95.

Nietzsche, F., *On the Genealogy of Morals*, trans. W. Kaufmann and R. J. Hollingdale (New York: Vintage, 1969).

Nietzsche, F., *The Birth of Tragedy* (1872), in *The Birth of Tragedy and The Case of Wagner*, trans. W. Kaufmann (New York: Vintage, 1967).

Nisbet, H. B., *Herder and the Philosophy and History of Science* (Cambridge: MHRA, 1970).

Norton, D. F., *David Hume: Common-Sense Moralist, Sceptical Metaphysician* (Princeton: Princeton University Press, 1982).

Nove, A., *The Economics of Feasible Socialism* (London: Allen & Unwin, 1983).

Oertel, H., 'Zur Genesis des Ideologiebegriffs', *Deutsche Zeitschrift für Philosophie*, 18 (1970), pp. 206–11.

Pascal, B., *Pensées*, trans. A. J. Krailsheimer (Harmondsworth: Penguin, 1966).

Pascal, R., *The German Sturm und Drang* (Manchester: Manchester University Press, 1953).

Pascal, R., 'Herder and the Scottish Historical School', *Publications of the English Goethe Society*, New Series, XIV (1939), pp. 23–42..

Pickering, F. P., *Augustinus oder Boethius?* (Berlin: Erich Schmidt, 1967).

Plant, R., *Hegel* (London: George Allen & Unwin, 1973).

Plato, *The Republic*, trans. H. D. P. Lee (Harmondsworth: Penguin, 1955).

Plato, *Symposium* (Harmondsworth: Penguin, 1974).

Prawer, S., *Karl Marx and World Literature* (Oxford: OUP, 1976).

Rauh, H.-C., 'Zur Herkunft, Vorgeschichte und erste Verwendungsweise des Ideologiebegriffs bei Marx und Engels bis 1844', *Deutsche Zeitschrift für Philosophie*, 18 (1970), pp. 689–715.

Reich, W., *The Mass Psychology of Fascism*, trans. V. R. Carpagno (Harmondsworth: Penguin, 1975).

Reisman, D., *Adam Smith's Sociological Economics* (London: Croom Helm, 1976).

Rieff, P., *Freud: the Mind of a Moralist* (Chicago: University of Chicago Press, 1979).

Rorty, R., *Philosophy and the Mirror of Nature* (Princeton: Princeton University Press, 1979).

Rosen, M., *Hegel's Dialectic and its Criticism* (Cambridge: CUP, 1982).

Rosen, M., 'Modernism and the Two Traditions in Philosophy', in D. Bell and W. Vossenkuhl (eds), *Science and Subjectivity* (Berlin: Akademie Verlag, 1992).

Rosenblum, N., *Another Liberalism* (Cambridge, MA: Harvard University Press, 1987).

Rousseau, J.-J., *Confessions*, trans. J. M. Cohen (Harmondsworth: Penguin, 1953).

Rousseau, J.-J., *Discours sur l'origine de l'inégalité* (Paris: Garnier-Flammarion, 1971).

Rousseau, J.-J., *Du contrat social*, Bk I, Ch. 3 (Paris: Garnier-Flammarion, 1966).

Rousseau, J.-J., 'Économie Politique', in *The Political Writings of Rousseau*, ed. C.E. Vaughan (Oxford: Blackwell, 1962).

Rousseau, J.-J., *Émile*, trans. B. Foxley (London: Dent, 1984).

Rousseau, J.-J., *The Indispensable Rousseau*, ed. J. H. Mason (London: Quartet, 1979).

Rousseau, J.-J., *Lettre à M. D'Alembert* (Paris: Garnier-Flammarion, 1967).

Schiller, F., *Letters on the Aesthetic Education of Man* (1795), trans. E. Wilkinson and L. Willoughby (Oxford: OUP, 1967).

Schlanger, J., *Les métaphores de l'organisme* (Paris: Vrin, 1971).

Schlegel, F., *Philosophie des Lebens* (Vienna: Carl Schaumburg, 1828).

Scholem, G., *Walter Benjamin: die Geschichte einer Freundschaft* (Frankfurt am Main: Suhrkamp, 1975).

Smith, A., *The Theory of Moral Sentiments* (1759) (Oxford: OUP, 1976).

Smith, A., *Lectures on Jurisprudence* (Oxford: OUP, 1978).

Smith, A., *The Wealth of Nations*, ed. E. Cannan (Chicago: University of Chicago Press, 1976).

Sperber, D., *On Anthropological Knowledge* (Cambridge: CUP, 1985).

Sperber, D., *Rethinking Symbolism* (Cambridge: CUP, 1975).

Stendhal, *Love*, trans. G. and S. Sale (Harmondsworth: Penguin, 1975).

Stepelevich, L. (ed.), *The Young Hegelians* (Cambridge: CUP, 1983).

Tanner, T., 'In Two Voices', *Times Literary Supplement* (2 July 1993).

Taylor, C., *Hegel* (Cambridge: CUP, 1975).

Taylor, C., *Sources of the Self* (Cambridge: CUP, 1989).

Thompson, J. B., *Ideology and Modern Culture* (Cambridge: Polity, 1990).

Tiedemann, R., 'Aura', in J. W. Ritter (ed.), *Historisches Wörterbuch der Philosophie* (Basel: Schwabe, 1971)..

Tillich, P., *The Socialist Decision*, trans. Franklin Sherman (Lanham, MD: University Press of America, 1977).

Trenchard, F., 'The Natural History of Superstition', in *A Collection of Scarce and Valuable Tracts on the most Interesting and Entertaining Subjects*, Vol. III (London, 1748).

Tugendhat, E., *Vorlesungen zur Einführung in die sprachanalytische Philosophie* (Frankfurt am Main: Suhrkamp, 1976).

Turgot, A., 'A Philosophical Review of the Successive Advances of the Human Mind' (1750), in *Turgot on Progress, Sociology and Economics*, ed. and trans. R. Meek (Cambridge: CUP, 1973), pp. 41–59.

Turgot, A., 'On Universal History' (1751 [?]), in R. L. Meek (ed.), *Turgot on Progress, Sociology and Economics* (Cambridge: CUP, 1973).

Vico, G. B., *The New Science*, trans. T. Bergin and M. Fisch (Ithaca: Cornell University Press, 1970).

Viner, J., *The Role of Providence in the Social Order* (Princeton: Princeton University Press, 1972).

Voltaire, F. M. A. de, *Dictionnaire Philosophique*, in *Oeuvres Complètes* (Paris: Garnier, 1879).

Voltaire, F. M. A. de, *Traité de métaphysique*, ed. H. Temple Patterson (Manchester: Manchester University Press, 1957).

Whitehead, A. N., *Science and the Modern World* (Glasgow: Fontana, 1975).

Wind, E., *Pagan Mysteries in the Renaissance* (London: Faber & Faber, 1968).

Wood, A., *Karl Marx* (London: Routledge & Kegan Paul, 1981).

Wright, J. P., *The Sceptical Realism of David Hume* (Manchester: Manchester University Press, 1983).

Index